Fasting and Feasting
Then & Now

Mohini Sethi
Ph.D., MHCIMA (U.K.)
Former Reader
Department of Foods & Nutrition
Institute of Home Economics
Delhi University

Barkha Jain
M.Sc.
Lecturer
Department of Foods & Nutrition
Delhi University

PUBLISHING FOR ONE WORLD

NEW AGE INTERNATIONAL (P) LIMITED, PUBLISHERS

New Delhi • Bangalore • Chennai • Cochin • Guwahati • Hyderabad
Jalandhar • Kolkata • Lucknow • Mumbai • Ranchi
Visit us at **www.newagepublishers.com**

Copyright © 2008, New Age International (P) Ltd., Publishers
Published by New Age International (P) Ltd., Publishers
First Edition: 2008

All rights reserved.
No part of this book may be reproduced in any form, by photostat, microfilm, xerography, or any other means, or incorporated into any information retrieval system, electronic or mechanical, without the written permission of the copyright owner.

ISBN 13: 978-81-224-2229-0

ISBN 10: 81-224-2229-2

Rs. 295.00

C-07-11-2087

Printed in India at Nisha Enterprises, Delhi.
Typeset in-house.

PUBLISHING FOR ONE WORLD

NEW AGE INTERNATIONAL (P) LIMITED, PUBLISHERS
4835/24, Ansari Road, Daryaganj, New Delhi - 110002
Visit us at **www.newagepublishers.com**

Dedicated to the Cause of
Truth and Value Education
with Reverence to the Lord
for His Inspiration and Constant Guidance.

ABOUT THE AUTHORS

Dr. Mohini Sethi is an alumnus of Lady Irwin College, having graduated and postgraduated from there. She was among the first batch of students to do her M.Sc. (Nutrition) from Delhi University in 1960, and also the first to teach Nutrition to Nursing students in the same year. A Ph.D. from Delhi University, she also holds a degree in Food Management from London, and was awarded the degree by the Council of National Academic Awards, U.K.

Dr. Sethi has been a reader in the Department of Foods and Nutrition at the Institute of Home Economics, University of Delhi since 1972. For over 32 years she taught the subject to under and postgraduate students as well as guided Ph.D. research till she retired in 2004. She has also taught in other universities of the country, and served as Nutrition Advisor to South India Shipping Corporation, Madras (now Chennai), Consultant to US Wheat Associates, India, Scindia School Gwalior, Gulmarg Skiing Association, Voluntary Health Association of India, VOICE and Resident Welfare Associations.

She has authored six books of academic and general interest and contributed by way of publishing research papers in professional journals and chapters in government sponsored publications. She has written a number of lesson books for courses of Open School and University. Her students have won several *young scientist* awards and best poster presentation awards at national and international conferences.

At present, Dr. Sethi is a Visiting Professor to Jamia and Allahabad Universities and a subject expert on various panels of the UGC, NIOS, IGNOU and Delhi University. She is also involved with voluntary work in the field of health and wellness.

Dr. Mohini Sethi is a Life Member of a number of professional Associations in her field and continues to share her knowledge through her writings, lectures as well as voluntary work for the benefit of promoting value education.

Ms. Barkha Jain has done her Masters in Foods & Nutrition with specialization in Dietetics and Institutional Food Administration from Institute of Home Economics, Delhi University in 2002.

She has been teaching Nutrition & Dietetics, Therapeutic Nutrition, Community Nutrition, and Food Science to undergraduate and postgraduate students of Home Science and Nursing colleges of Delhi University and IGNOU for more than three years.

Ms. Jain is the paper setter and examiner of B.Sc. (Nursing) course of Delhi University, Jamia Hamdard and Kurukshetra Universities.

Ms. Jain has contributed chapters for Health & Nutrition Education publications and has also edited books on the subject for the School of Correspondence Studies, Delhi University.

Her master's dissertation included research on fasts and development and standardization of recipes specially prepared for fast days.

This is her first book.

FOREWORD

Fasting has been considered to be one of the essential ingredients of religious observances. It is conducive to the transference of the consciousness from one's physical body to one's own astral body in that, the physical sufferings like extreme hunger or thirst consequent to going without food or water, enhances the intellectual and mental strength, adducing to the fact that the intellect controls the mind and the latter controls the cognitive senses and those of action. Since the physical body depends for its life on the coincidence with the astral body, the latter is stronger than it and, lasts so long as it is permeated by the causal body, with the Self residing in it, but ultimately it is the Self which provides life and power to one's causal, astral and the physical bodies. Thus, shifting the consciousness from the physical to the astral is a step towards the realization of the Self.

In this connection, while replying to the query of a disciple as to how one can subdue the sense of taste, Bhagavan Swaminarayan says that it can be done by controlling one's diet and by avoiding one's favorite food, that overcoming the sense of taste will automatically subdue the other senses of cognition and those of action. Further, while showing correct way of dieting, He observes that one's diet cannot be controlled by merely observing several fasts consecutively. That only increases one's desires and diet, because when one breaks a fast, one tends to eat twice as much. But, if a person begins to reduce his diet gradually, it can be controlled. For example, even though clouds cause rain to fall in tiny drops, water still collects in a large quantity. Similarly, one should control one's diet gradually as a result of which the senses (*indriyas*) will also be controlled. Then, if one lovingly engages in devotion (*bhakti*), one can remain in *Satsang,* till the end. This is a fact (*Gadhada III-32*).

In this connection, I may be allowed to cite my own technique and experience. If you can join the name of one's favorite deity with one's own heart-beats, one gradually feels them whenever one's mind in not engaged in any mental work, and it goes on for twenty-four hours of a day till the end of one's life. This helps much in controlling not only the senses, but also the mind, because whenever it tries to waver or go astray, the ever felt memory of God's name checks and stops it. This helps in observing the fast which is in fact undertaken for pleasing God, and God is pleased with penance which ultimately helps in the observance of the Five Vows (*panch vartaman*) for the *sadhus,* viz. *nishkam* – eightfold celibacy (*brahmacharya*), *nissneha* – non-attachment, *nirman* – non-ego, *niswad*–non-taste, and *nirlobha* – non-avariciousness. Along with these Five Vows, one needs full and unwavering faith (*nishhtha*) and invariable resorting (*asharay*) to God in all walks of life, and one-pointed devotion (*ekantiki bhakti*). All these combined constitute the path to liberation from the cycle of rebirths, and qualifies for entry into the *Akshardham,* the residence of God.

I congratulate Mohini Sethi and Barkha Jain for undertaking an unprecedented task of revealing the scientific base of the various vows of fasting and feasting in all the major and minor religious faiths of the world. The authors deserve the encomiums from all of us, and from all the religious heads of the world, as it provides a scientific backing to enhance the inspiration of those interested in undertaking and observing various vows, irrespective of their particular religious faith.

N. M. Kansara
Director, AARSH, Akshardham,
Gandhinagar.

PREFACE

Festivals have always been an integral part of Indian culture, but their perceptions have changed over time to keep in line with changes in living styles and the resulting environment.

Fasting and *Feasting* is the result of research conducted to understand why people resorted to these practices the way they did in ancient times, and analyze the changes that have affected the manner in which these are observed today. Several customs of the past persist, some without any logical reason, among families and communities in different regions of our country. The customs of fasting and feasting have changed over the decades, although habits of observing them as rituals on special days have been passed down through generations.

Research conducted revealed that several trends in fasting and feasting are followed among households covering all age groups. The majority of women showed ignorance regarding the purpose for which they resorted to these practices. Generally, they reported it as a traditional household practice which they were carrying on just as any household profession which was passed down in joint or undivided families.

In nuclear households with working women however, these traditional practices were modified to suit their working routines. Other findings indicated that many of the traditional practices were dropped for various reasons in the garb of modernization. Further, a trend was evident through which fasting was practiced for social reasons, an occasion for women to move out of their homes in groups to meet, even though only to temples or for community celebrations and festivities.

Today too, parental and peer group pressure exists, but the meaning and purpose of fasting and socializing have changed, the youth even being ignorant of the origins of fasting and feasting, following these practices more for social reasons rather than moral, spiritual or for self development. But, everything in life being cyclic, one sees a reincarnation of the traditional fanfare that went with fasting usually followed by feasting, that follows the successful completion of the events.

The book is unique in its approach towards traditional practices of fasting and feasting in that, it attempts to trace the origins of the observances as carried out *then* and *now.* The idea was to familiarize people especially the youth, with traditional concepts associated with some observances which they may have been involved with against their logical sense. It attempts to clarify concepts of which people are generally ignorant, following traditions blindly even though they may not apply to today's knowledge society.

The work is based on years of social interaction and documentary research, but written in simple language and presents a clear classification of fasts that appeals to logic and common sense. Celebrations too, have been classified and discussed in the global cultural context as well. The effort is expected to add meaning and value to observances that have been blindly practiced for generations. It also discusses the usefulness of fasting for health and wellness and describes briefly the adaptive changes that the body makes to cope with the changes required in eating routines on fast and feast days.

Since there are wide variations in the observances from one part of the country to another and within religious and other community groups, only a few commonly practiced fasts and celebrations have been covered. Available information about rituals followed is scanty and this work is an attempt to bridge the gap between blind and meaningful observance of fasts and festivities.

This publication is divided into four parts. Part I is an introduction to fasting and feasting introducing the concepts of the book. Part II discusses the origins of fasting and some of the rituals that go with it, and the methods followed for breaking the fasts. It also discusses advantages in terms of general health benefits, value inculcation, social interaction and spiritual development as perceived, highlighting the metamorphosis from ancient to modern practices.

Part III describes feasting practices that usually followed fasting and their evolution over time, including celebrations of festivals as was intended *then* and practiced *now*. The impact of feasting on health and wellness has also been discussed.

Part IV presents some selected recipes suitable for certain fast and feast days commonly prepared and suggested, keeping in mind the changing mindsets of people over time. The nutritional values of these recipes have been calculated and presented to keep in line with present day eating habits and the increased awareness of health and wellness in today's fast changing living environment. Illustrations through figures, tables and plates have been included for clarity, with which the reader can identify.

Some readers may however find, that they observe certain fasts and festivities that are not covered. This is because only a few generally observed fasts and practices have been included. Besides, it is not possible to know about all of them in such a vast country and around the globe. Readers are therefore requested to interact with the authors to enable them to include their traditions and present day observances in the next edition, and improve the available literature, experience and practices followed, on the subject.

So relax, read, enjoy and interact!

mohinisethi@hotmail.com
birks_7@yahoo.com

ACKNOWLEDGMENT

It took four long years to conduct the research which involved interviews, social interactions for this work to see the light of day. Understandably there are many institutions and persons to thank.

Firstly, a visit to Akshardham in Delhi gave an insight into the blending of the ancient with modernity and generated the ideas for the book. Further a visit to their bookshop provided the opportunity to purchase Sadhu Mukundcharandas's book on Hindu Festivals and rituals that was very informative, motivating and inspiring. My request to the author to permit me the use of some material was later granted, which has been methodically referenced pagewise where used. We appreciate his generosity and blessings for this work and also thank Akshardham, Amdavad, for the prompt e-mail responses to our requests and queries.

Our thanks also go to the Ashram for introducing to us Prof. N.M. Kansara, Director Akshardham Academy for Research on Social Harmony (AARSH), who so graciously accepted to write the foreword for this book. Our namaskar, thanks and regards to him for his patience in reading the entire manuscript and sending us the foreword.

We are also grateful to Dr. Nand Kumar Acharyaji who conducted 7-day discourses on the Bhagavad Gita, during which time we could confirm a lot of ritualistic facts about the leelas of Lord Krishna and their intended meaning. On the last day he was kind enough to grant an appointment and spend an hour and more of his precious time to satisfy our doubts, and answer all our queries in person.

Our gratitude goes to the Sri Satya Sai Publications Trust who has been regularly publishing Baba's Avatar Vani in the Sanathana Sarathi, through which we could quote Baba's words and teachings on every important festival or occasion.

In addition, we thank the Gymkhana Club Library and the Purushotamdas Tandon Library at Lajpat Bhawan, for enabling us to access some valuable ancient texts. Not to forget the priests in temples who helped with explanations to certain rituals.

We are grateful for all the website material we could search for the different religious fasts and feasts. These have been referenced in footnotes as well as at the end of the book along with other documented material available.

The Hindustan Times for their column entitled *Inner Voice* which provided some important reference articles by known personalities. The Times of India whose regular feature *The Speaking Tree* did the same, along with regular coverage on Health and Wellness, for which we thank the editors of both dailies.

A special thanks to all the housewives from different social and religious backgrounds and regions, who took out time for interviews and completing structured questionnaires, to help us understand why and how they fast and their ideas on fasting and feasting.

To add to this are the numerous friends who cannot be mentioned individually, but who helped through lending us ancient texts, temple puja booklets, lunar calendars for reference and answered questions about how they observe various festivals and fasts. A special mention goes to a few of them —Raj Verma, Kanta Kapur, Krishna Bhatt, Palka Rana, Urmil Rawal, Shiela Vasudeva and Girija Eswaran. To them we add our families who have patiently stood by us when computers failed and printers stopped midway. They absorbed our frustrations with love, care and encouragement.

Last but not least, Mr. Saumya Gupta (Managing Director) and Mr. Damodaran (Chief Editor) of New Age International (Pvt. Ltd.) Publishers, who have patiently stood behind and egged us on to complete the project. What is worth admiration is the way they steered the book in the direction which it has taken through a meticulously structured questionnaire that took us a week to fill up and return to them. Their responses to our queries have been extremely prompt and hard work on their part has placed the publication in the hands of the reader to react to and enjoy.

Thank you all.

Authors

CONTENTS

— SECTION III —

— SECTION IV —

1

INTRODUCTION

This section is an introduction to fasting and feasting discussing the origins and methods of observance related to certain rituals and their perceived advantages in terms of health benefits, value inculcation, social interaction and spiritual development, highlighting the metamorphosis from ancient to modern practices.

INTRODUCTION

Fasting has been practiced over centuries in its many forms, associated with purity, religious fervour, sacrifice and a sense of achievement leading to control over a natural desire for food within the family, society and the living environment.

Fasting in India is linked to the cultural and social fabric of society in the country. The observance of fasts spans religious boundaries, social classes, castes, creeds and even sectarian affiliations. Fasts have been observed by all age groups for a variety of reasons from time to time, varying from those associated with religious rituals, beliefs, celebrations or festivities as the focus, to others as in bereavement, prayer, thanksgiving, social and health maintenance reasons.

India is a secular country with physical and cultural diversity, there being hardly any religion that does not flourish on her soil. Its culture has been preserved and handed down through spiritual masters, seers, recorded ancient texts and oral preaching. The main aim was to inculcate in people values like chastity, truthfulness, respect for elders who nurtured good family relations. Households held women in high esteem as they preserved nature and environment, spread love and kindness towards all creatures and accepted nature's gifts as boons from the

Almighty. Women thus spread devotion or *bhakti* among families and communities which helped to uphold the human values of truth, love and peace, thereby shedding hatred, pride, jealousy and anger among people. The latter negative qualities have been decried repeatedly in religious texts especially in the *Bhagavad Gita* as *Kama, Krodha, Lobha, Moha.* Value-based qualities were followed in practice through discipline, self-control and living of austere lives.

Observance of fasts was a powerful tool used to curb desires, control the mind and steer the senses away from material possessions. Thus, fasting helped to divert attention from food and eating to prayer and divinity, at the same time providing rest to the natural systems of the body, simultaneously establishing patterns of eating that formed the basis of physical and mental development and rejuvenation. Removing the thought of food, eating and related activities from the mind also led to inner spiritual development associated with family peace, unity and understanding.

PATTERNS OF FASTING AND FEASTING

India being heterogenous in its composition, each community performed its rituals related to *fasting* and the breaking of the fasts or *feasting* together, in different ways. These differences led to many varied patterns of abstinence and eating in every region, where they emerged in their own characteristic ways. It is believed that fasting increases spiritual consciousness whereas feasting stimulates the palate and diverts and drains vital energy. True vedic traditions never advocated feasting in the way it is practiced today, but only controlled breaking of fast. This is also done with foods that gradually stimulate the production of gastric secretions and activity of the digestive system.

Offerings During Observances

Many occasions have their own traditional offerings each conducive to the season, climate and geographical location. Sages and seers have laid down requirements with respect to certain foods permitted and those not permitted because they are likely to disturb the equilibrium of the body when the offered food is consumed as *prasaad.*

Besides the patterns of fasting and feasting, human nature required to celebrate and share many happy occasions together. In contrast, occasions of grief also demanded community help and people gathered together to offer condolences and share grief to lessen its impact on the affected households. This was accompanied by people pooling in money and food to feed the community gathered for the purpose. Though on such occasions eating together could not strictly be called *feasting*, but the fact remains, that foods were prepared by friends and neighbours and brought together in an act of sharing to indicate support, care, love and harmony, which created an atmosphere of peace, goodwill and wellbeing with time.

Celebrations

India is also known for its celebration of festivals representing the birthdays of Gods and Goddesses, rituals to propitiate God's grace by worshipping Gods with form, of which there are many, often referred to as deities in temples, installed at home or outside. Also, celebrations of National Days are intended to make a country proud by inculcating patriotic fervour. Although the basic reasons for fasting and feasting remain the same today, the methods followed have changed to suit present day lifestyles and eating patterns. Present day patterns are more flexible since women have to balance their time and energies between work and home duties. A lot more celebrations are being added to the list such as each individual's anniversaries, birthdays, successes and so on, although the fervour has shifted from their strictly religious roots and associations, to a display of greater pomp and show as seen in social functions, marriages and the like. The pressures so placed on households have made them split into nuclear families, resorting to outside catering, increased materialism, and a noticeable loss of values in society.

Need of the Hour

The role of fasting in restoring value systems and internal peace, unity, strength, including charity to further equitable distribution of wealth and resources, is the need of the hour. Exposure to positive media messages not on exclusive channels but on all channels, through serials depicting traditional values rather than only disturbing news, will help to revive the mental environment to combat terror. While arms and ammunition are important symbols of security, the positive values such as honesty, integrity, truth, justice, love and peace need to be revived to build the internal strength of the youth and through them, the strength and unity of the country.

Our children are very intelligent and curious for knowledge in different fields, and if they know the meaning of rituals, prayer and fasting they are more likely to follow them if it satisfies their logical minds. However, the days of strict observances are over and adaptation in every field including rituals is the key to a healthy, vibrant nation where young people find the right balance between tradition and modernity in a global context, as long as they do not see them as hindrances to their material, physical, mental growth and progress.

Swami Vivekananda once said to his overseas devotees:

> *This is the old India that you have seen, the India of prayers and tears, of vigils and fasts, that is passing away*

Young parents and children who shy away from *satsangs*, gatherings and festivals should reconsider the timeless messages of our seers and motivate themselves and their children to celebrate important days in temples and churches or other congregational places. In celebrating under the guidance of a guru, devotees consolidate their faith and devotion in God with form.

The goal of the future is happiness and people will strive to achieve it by any means according to their capabilities, personalities and visions of their future. But is worldly or material happiness lasting? The answer is given by Leo Tolstoy, a Russian novelist and social reformer who aptly said:

> *Just imagine that the purpose of life is your happiness only, then life becomes a cruel and senseless thing. You have to embrace the wisdom of humanity. Your intellect and your heart tell you that the meaning of life is to serve the force that sent you into the world. Then life becomes a joy.*

According to traditional Hinduism, the only way to approach God or divinity is by practicing any one or more of the five attitudes or moods, that are manifested in the relationship between a devotee and God. These are presented below:

- Shanta Bhava — peace of stillness felt in the presence of God.
- Dasya Bhava — attitude of a servant to his master.
- Sakhya Bhava — attitude of a friend towards a friend
- Vatsalya Bhava — attitude of a parent towards a child.
- Madhur Bhava — attitude of a lover towards the beloved.

The idea behind this classification is to help the aspirants to intensify their relationship with God according to their own inner nature. The more spiritual life remains hidden, the stronger and more fruitful it becomes, quite unlike stage shows which depend upon exaggerated expressions and applause from audiences.

All these attitudes have been exemplified in the lives of saints, sages and avatars through their *leelas,* which have everlasting effects that have stood the test of time.

When man emulates even one of these attitudes in dealing with others, one feels a sense of attraction towards the concerned people. This effect is experienced in everyday life when one sometimes meets a stranger, but feels attracted to him or her with a wish to meet again. The feeling expresses itself in remarks like... ***We've just met but it seems we know each other from ages,*** and out of nowhere love and concern pulls them together.

Scientific Proof

People today, are inclined to be logical, scientific and skeptical and therefore, find it difficult to accept people's experiences of visions and divine manifestations. However, even scientists and thinkers agree, that there are much finer states of consciousness than the one we experience in the sense world.

Social scientists have shown the effects of congregational living styles and regular church attendance on improved health and longevity. Further the neurobiological effects of rituals and of repetitive behaviors such as rhythmic chanting, collective clapping, blowing of conches, ringing of bells, singing and dancing in ceremonies have been established. It has been reported that when combined with other rituals such as fasting, deep breathing, burning of lamps and inhalation of fragrances of flowers, incense and so on, all lead to experiences of religious awe, and it is the synthesis of rhythm and meaning that makes a ritual powerful and leads to soulful experiences. It also provides solace to the disturbed mind that is lasting. Congregational devotional music and readings from sacred texts *(satsang)* does precisely that. The soothing effect of Indian music has been also noted by biologists on plants which have been seen to flourish in an environment of devotional and instrumental music. The *darshan* of the divine through deities and pictures of *avatars* itself gives spiritual benefit or *punya.*

Experiential Proof

Experiences of *saints* and *seers* have been repeatedly substantiated and recorded in the lives of avatars by their direct devotees.

Many such experiences are recorded in which a devotee meditated on Sri Krishna so much that her mind became very pure[1]. As a result, she entered the realm of super consciousness and wherever her eyes fell she saw *Gopala*. In this realm of mystical experience the only consciousness is the direct consciousness of God. Verbal expression, mental cognition and intellectual reasoning do not function in that domain.

One has to find a balance between the levels of consciousness and living happily and blissfully in this world which was created for us to enjoy and learn from. The surest way is to live as close to nature as possible and revere and respect our traditions as far as they apply to the modern world.

Health Implications

Present day lifestyles bend towards solitude and privacy in personal life. This is evident from the increase in cases of depression, diabetes, heart and other chronic diseases in both children and adults. In the West the cases of mental disorders are far greater but countries imitating their living and working styles are not too far behind. This is seen in the

1 Swami Chetanananda. 1991. p. 335 - 351

progressive rise in cases of suicide, road rage, lack of self-confidence, assaults and so on. All this is the result of lack of the natural social interactions that was the norm in traditional India. The world is now recognizing and looking up to our country for help through meditation and techniques like fasting, prayer, chanting, music, and other natural cures. The establishment of spiritual and religious centres worldwide is evidence of this trend.

THE FUTURE

According to Swami Chinmayananda, the past can be reversed only by intelligent, well planned continuous efforts put into the present. For this many sacrifices will have to be made. But, if the youth has no ability to think, plan and bring about the necessary changes or has not the consistency of effort, a better future cannot be built. Only a future sadder than the present may be expected.

Osher offers another simple way of acceptance. He says relax into yourself, close your eyes and listen to all that is happening around. Do not deny or reject but only accept because denials create tension. Let the happenings unite into an organic whole because everything is interrelated — the birds, sky, sun, earth, you and me. If the sun disappears so will the birds, trees, you and me. The moment you deny you are denying something in you. Echhart Tolle too, asks us to be aware of life in the form, the sacred mystery, and perceive its all encompassing consciousness.

Let us all therefore, teach ourselves techniques by which we can find connectivity within ourselves and live our lives as close to nature as possible so that we can be guided by it in our decisions and at the same time enjoy the messages built into our natural surroundings, for us to follow and hold dear.

2

FASTING

Fasting has been practiced over centuries in its many forms, generally associated with feelings of purity, religious fervour, sacrifice and a sense of achievement leading to control over the mind and the natural desire for food within the family, society and the living environment. It is a time to experience silence, stillness, relaxation and freedom. The time and energy thus conserved is diverted to prayer, a time to be with oneself in complete harmony and peace and experience the oneness in life. This section has 5 chapters:

- ❒ Fasting
- ❒ Religious Fasts
- ❒ Social Fasts
- ❒ Circumstantial Fasts
- ❒ Fasting and Health

[illegible] were observed by women [illegible] men who went [illegible] work, and [illegible]

[illegible]

[illegible] traditional ways of [illegible] in the community. They also have lesser time and energy [illegible] household chores related to cooking special foods which are religious[illegible]

FASTING

Chapter 2

Traditionally fasts were observed by women of households since the men who were the sole breadwinners ventured out of the home for work, and therefore did all the jobs outside including purchases for the house, on their way to and from work. The women were mostly uneducated and were required to stay at home, catering to household chores, and upbringing and care of the family, which they learnt from elders around them and in the community.

Since *fasting* was related to religious rituals, it provided women and children a means of going out of their homes to temples where they collectively offered prayers and *prasaad* to their chosen deities and rejoiced in the form of feasting after fasting the whole day. This also provided occasions for preparing special foods which were not made on other days and added variety to routine menus.

Gradually with children moving out to schools, and women to colleges, offices, markets and social functions, today they do not feel the need to depend strictly on traditional ways of conducting themselves at home or in the community. They also have lesser time and energy for household chores related to cooking special foods which are religiously eaten during fast days.

WHAT ARE FASTS ?

Fasts are votive rights practiced throughout India, usually undertaken for the purpose of purification, to propitiate the Gods and unleash the power within for a socio-religious event, or for the simple joy of partaking special fasting foods on occasions, to prevent menu fatigue of daily household meals.

The terms *upwaas* or *vrat* are used synonymously with fasting which is basically a means of diverting attention from food with the aim of achieving better concentration through sense control leading to mental and spiritual development, through connectivity with one's higher consciousness. Furthermore, abstinence from food, restrictive and disciplined eating helps to rest the body physiologically leading to the rejuvenation of the systems necessary for maintaining health.

OBSERVANCE OF FASTS

Fasts may be observed without food or water or by partaking of certain prescribed foods. Thus they may be partial or complete according to the faiths, beliefs, traditions and regional culture. The complete fast is called *nirjal vrat* or *upvaas. Kalpavasa* is a spiritual vow in which a householder gives up drinking water for as long as six months and taking milk instead.

Seasonal Fasts

There are a number of fasts observed throughout the year, some according to seasons which influence the type of offerings made to deities during particular fast days. Others go by the waxing and waning of the moon and are known as *Ekadashi* fasts.

There are a number of fasts during the monsoon season when outdoor activities get restricted and people have more time on their hands. People had a tendency to use this extra time in sensual pursuits like drinking, gambling, sex and other addictions. To curb this degradation of values in society, the *shastras* or holy texts, sages and seers laid down norms advocated for keeping people healthy physically, mentally and spiritually, by introducing rituals.

The shastras advocated different offerings for different occasions according to the type of weather prevailing and effects that were produced in disturbing the equilibrium of the body.

One-Off Fasts

These occur once in a while in the form of days on which there are solar or lunar eclipses or during the *Kumbh,* which occurs once in 12 years and is celebrated at Prayag (Allahabad), Haridwar, Ujjain and Nasik. It involves bathing in holy rivers in each region, for spiritual purity. In the *dharma-parva,* people fast for many days having food every alternate day. In *Chandrayan*-fasting, people have a certain number of small balls of food a day sequential to the lunar cycle. Again in bereavement or a natural disaster when food availability is severely cut, fasting is enforced by circumstances beyond immediate human control.

There are strict routines for fasting during eclipses also. On days of the eclipses, all activities are suspended and fasting is advocated in the scriptures and by rishis many hours before and during the eclipse. The exact period of fasting is calculated by astronomic guidelines. People fast, pray and chant the Lord's name in an attempt to ward off evil, because the period is considered inauspicious. After an eclipse, devotees have a ritual of purification by bathing in holy rivers and then distributing alms to the poor.

Today, science has given meaning to these rituals by establishing that harmful radiations are transmitted to the earth during eclipses which affect all lives. The sages exhorted that the effect harms the mind and digestive system and therefore, advocated strict fasting and religious observances.

Fast days were spent in *pradakshana* of deities, chanting and singing devotional music listening to sacred texts and so on. This not only provided a change in daily household routines but also exposed people to their own divinity instead of increasing body consciousness. This brought about a change in the mental, intellectual and emotional sphere. Thus places of worship served important functions.

Role of Temples

Temples, shrines and ashrams have played an important role in perpetuating cultural and spiritual traditions. They have helped to effectively maintain unity, traditions and spiritual upliftment of people not only in India but around the world. Temples make available learned priests who can guide people in the correct ways of performing rituals for each occasion to reap the maximum benefit from fasts and *yagnas* or *havans*. Other functions of temples are:

- Learning through discourses
- Preserving architectural heritage
- Social interaction
- Developing brotherhood and social cohesiveness
- Facilitating worship
- Connectivity with self
- Resting place for travelers
- Perpetuating cultural traditions
- Promoting art through devotional music and dance forms
- Inculcating discipline through observances
- Inculcating spirituality in people
- Helping transmit cultural identity to next generations

The fact that today any damage to a place of worship brings about riotous situations that are difficult to control without stern action, indicates the type of sanctity and fervor traditions hold in their perpetuation. Religious fervor in any community is the binding force in any country and if handled with care can lead to the highest achievement, respect and unity, unifying globally for peace in the world.

CLASSIFICATION OF FASTS

Fasts can be classified as complete or partial. Complete fasts are those in which no food or drink is consumed throughout the day, whereas in partial fasts traditional custom and practice dictate that only fruits, roots, tubers or nuts may be consumed, in others there may be restrictions with respect to consumption of acidic or sour foods and grains such as cereals and pulses.

Irrespective of the type of fasts observed by various families, communities, countries or regions and their purposes, fasts have been the norm for religious, social and health reasons. A classification has been presented in Fig. 2.1.

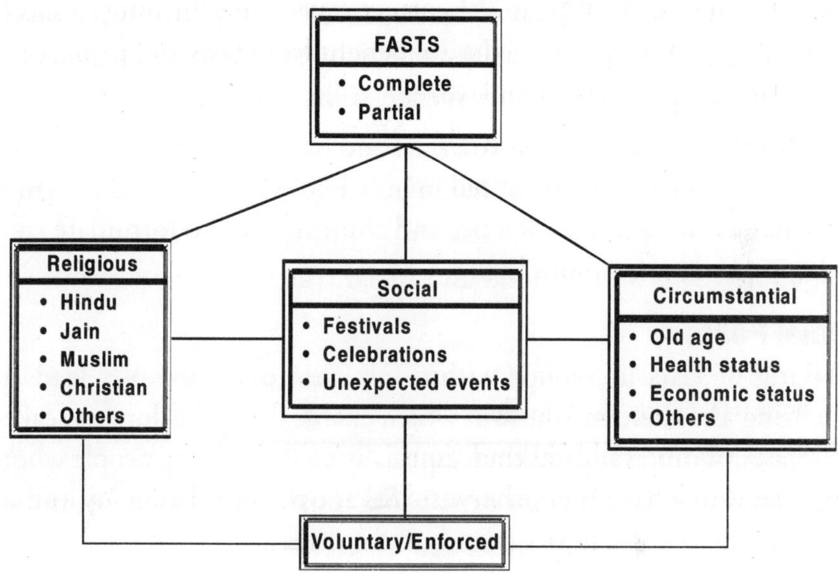

Fig. 2.1 Classification of Fasts

As seen from Fig. 2.1 fasts are basically complete or partial in that people may not eat or drink anything on the day or may simply abstain from consuming certain foods or opt for only one meal in the day. Whatever the nature of the fasts, they may be observed on a voluntary basis or enforced by virtue of environmental, economic or other circumstances such as poverty, ill-health or pressure from elders and peers. Fasts are basically divided into three types namely religious, social and circumstantial depending on their origins. Each category is being briefly discussed for clarity.

Religious Fasts

Religious fasts vary in every community according to their ancestral traditions which have been built up over centuries. In India, the *Hindus, Muslims, Jains, Buddhists, Christians* and other religious communities follow a number of different fasts as a means of penance, thanksgiving, prayer for fulfillment of desires or boons which may vary from the birth of a son to successes in life.

Fasting for religious purposes is a matter of individual experience meant to detach oneself temporarily from routine activities and focus more closely on the internal values which one holds dear. Fasts when used as a means of penance, help to drive away evil or negative thoughts, words and deeds, and inculcate a habit of renunciation, leading to charitable thoughts and actions. It is a time to experience silence, stillness and solitude.

Indian culture has been preserved and handed over to generations through oral preachings recorded in holy books by sages in the form of the Vedas, which guided societies and communities to formulate rules for happy and harmonious living.

Social Fasts

Breaking of fasts in groups within families or in temples leads to socializing and therefore the fasts which enable this to be done are called social fasts. Women and children especially enjoy meeting people whom they would not have met otherwise. Such occasions bring joy and an opportunity to make newer friends and contacts.

Circumstantial Fasts

These fasts are imposed by virtue of the circumstances on people and may take the form of penance, protest or retaliation against injustices. In such cases fasting is used as a tool to pressurize authorities for achieving goals or at least express strong feelings about an issue. Sometimes disasters or actions causing displacement of communities, who then do not get relief, may resort to prolonged fasting to press their demands. Trade union members may go on indefinite fast for increase in wages, better living conditions, compensations and so on. Sometimes emotional disturbances caused by bereavement may cause people to stop eating for long periods, a situation produced unexpectedly by circumstances, leading to enforced or involuntary fasting.

Thus, fasting and *ahimsa* or *non-violence* are more potent tools of protest than arms and ammunition to achieve goals. There are ample examples in India in which these have been used to gain our independence by leaders of eminence.

RELIGIOUS FASTS

Religious fasts were meant to draw attention of people from the external to their internal world using deities or images of God with forms suited to the mindset, beliefs and traditional suitability of each family or community. The idea was to make people focus on some image or point, in order to withdraw oneself temporarily from the physical, material, mental, and intellectual, to the level of the superconscious to experience the quietness, calm, peace and unity within. These practices helped in adhering to certain rules for disciplined living and inculcated the values of chastity, truthfulness, charity and service to elders and the needy, thereby spreading the message of love and peace throughout their environment. In addition, people developed control over eating and food preparation activities from time to time, giving a break to the routine physical, physiological and mental functions of the body to rejuvenate them in the process.

A study of the manner of fasting resorted to by different religious and social groups or communities shows that different values were inculcated in people by focusing on different deities for prayers, which began to be associated with love, wealth, strength and so on. Prayers were the means for propitiating their particular God with form, to grant their favors or boons for family or community. This sentiment is apparent from the traditional practice of naming children in the family after the chosen deity, in the hope that the child will develop the qualities associated with that form.

HINDU FASTS

The word Hindu has been explained variously by our ancient saints, sages and gurus who taught the meaning through the scriptural texts. However Sathya Sai explains the meaning of the term very simply, by breaking up the word and equating it with five human values that it represents, namely: **H**umility, **I**ndividuality, **N**ationality, **D**evotion and **U**nity[2]. Hindu fasts are numerous and followed in different ways by the various religious groups and communities as learnt through family traditions and institutional affiliations in every region. A glimpse of a few well known, widely practiced although sparsely documented ones, which are observed in the country are presented in this chapter. Hindus visit some temple or place of worship according to their faiths and beliefs, following the rules of fasting laid down by the sacred texts or the priests who perform and guide the rituals in traditional families.

Hindu fasts are numerous but a few important ones are discussed in the following order :

1. Ekadashi
2. Mahashivaratri
3. Navaratri
4. Ramnaumi
5. Janamashtami
6. Ganesh Chaturthi

All fasting and other practices are only symbolic of the journey of life. Thus, people undertake many kinds of spiritual practices little realizing that they all lead to the same goal, just as the rivers ultimately merge in the ocean, prayers will all reach God.

---

[2] *Sanathana Sarathi,* Vol. 49 No. 10, October, 2006, p. 298

There are certain days of the year considered particularly sacred, on which people fast calculated according to the lunar calendar that basically divides the month into two fortnights according to the position, size, movement and brightness of the moon. These are being discussed under each fast, as they occur according to the Indian calendar.

THE INDIAN CALENDAR

The Indian calendars used for the purposes of fixing religious days for fasting and celebrations are the Solar and Lunar calendars, each used in different regions of the country. These are being briefly discussed.

The Solar Calendar

The Western or Gregorian calendar as it is called, after its inventor, is sun-based and is therefore called the solar calendar. This is based on the rotation of the earth around the sun, which takes approximately 365 days with one extra day added to the month of February every four years, called the *leap year*, which then has 366 days. The basis for this calculation is that the rotation of the Earth around the Sun takes approximately 365¼ days to complete. It is this calendar that we in India use in our daily lives for planning the day, week, month and year. This is still referred to as the English calendar because of their long colonial reign although, it is used universally and it is virtually the calendar of every country today.

The 365 days of the solar calendar are divided into 12 months having unequal number of days in some months than in others. The thumb rule is expressed poetically through the lines taught to children in nursery classes as follows:

Thirty days of September, April, June and November
All the rest have 31 excepting February with 28.

Each day of the solar calendar has a fixed length of 24 hours, being calculated from midnight to midnight, thus the date changes at midnight of each day as per local or standard time for a particular location. There is therefore a definite correlation between the date and the corresponding day of the week.

Lunar Vs Solar Calendar

Our sages and seers preferred to use the Lunar Calendar in preference to the solar calendar for three important reasons:

(i) ***Was practical and easy to use***— This is because when a person looked at the sun, he could not distinguish one day from another, because the differences were too slight to be noticeable. Whereas with the moon, waxing and waning was clearly observable in terms of the size and shape of the crescents formed, and so the days could be counted with full moon and new moon as the starting and ending points of a fortnight. This was convenient as there were no clocks or printing at the time.

(ii) ***Served as a good navigational tool*** — The Lunar system was a useful navigational tool for ancient Indian seafarers. Minor difficulties did occur during the monsoons when the moon got covered, but this was made up by counting the days from the last moon sighted.

(iii) ***Had health benefits*** — The sages were aware of the beneficial effects of the moon on the oceans, creatures and vegetation. The full moon had special significant effects on life.

It was believed that since the human body is made up of 80% water, on full moon day, man's instincts become unstable and he gets prone to impulsive behaviour. Bearing this in mind many religious observances such as fasting and devotional pursuits were planned and propagated in the form of *nirjal* fasting. It was an attempt to reduce the fluid in the body and thereby minimize the moon's detrimental effects on the mind of man. In addition the *bhakti* keeps the mind focused and curbs the pursuit of mundane activities including eating.[3]

The Lunar Calendar

The lunar calendar is believed to have originated in India and has been around for a very long time, even before the solar calendar came into existence. It is also popular and widely used in the Asian countries like

3 Sadhu Mukundcharandas (2005), p. xliii

China, countries bordering the Pacific, Middle East and India, where it is largely used to fix the dates and timings for festivals and important days during the year.

The lunar calendar is based on the moon's synodic revolution, that is, rotation around the earth as well as the earth's revolution around the Sun, with every complete rotation corresponding to one lunar month. The length of a lunar month thus varies, with the variation in the period of rotation of the moon, therefore some months are shorter than others and *vice versa.* On average, the lunar month has about 29½ days. In general, the lunar year has 12 lunar months of approximately 354 days, thus making it shorter by about 11 days as compared to the solar year. However, this difference is accounted for by adding an extra lunar month once every 2½ years. The extra lunar month is commonly known as *Adhik Mas*[4] in India, *Adhik* meaning extra or more and *Mas* meaning month. The concept of this extra month is similar to the *Blue Moon* concept in the West, which occurs almost with the same frequency of 2½ years.

For the purpose of understanding the fixation of dates and timings of festivals, rituals, fasting, prayers and auspiciousness of celebrations, it is important to understand the structure of the calendars on which the dates and timings of the various observances are fixed on an annual basis.

For fixing of fast and festival days and dates therefore, the solar and lunar calendars are used in different regions of the country depending on the appearance and position of the moon or sun as it appears in a particular geographical region. In general the solar calendar is followed in the South and the lunar in the Northern regions of the country.

For the purpose of fixing the days for certain religious rituals and fasts or breaking of fasts, each lunar month is divided into two fortnights, the bright fortnight or *Shukla paksha* starts with the crescent moon which waxes and culminates into the full moon, that is at its fullest in

---

4 *Adhik Mas* occurs only when two *amavasyas* (no moon day) occur while Sun remains in the same zodiac sign. For more information on zodiac system refer to Maheshri 1997.

size and brightness on the 15th day known as *Purnima*. The next day the moon starts to shrink in size as far as the lighted side is concerned and gradually wanes in brightness and size, till it reaches a stage of complete darkness. This waning fortnight is known as the dark fortnight or *Krishna paksha* and the night when the moon is not visible at all and is pitch dark, that day is known as the *Amavasya,* new moon or no moon day.

A lunar day usually begins at sunrise, and the length of lunar day is determined by the time that elapses between two successive sunrises. As per Jewish calendar, their lunar day begins at sunset, and lasts through the next sunset. A lunar day is essentially the same as a weekday, in the English calendar. The corresponding Indian names for the days of the week, the deities worshipped and the color considered auspicious for each are presented in Table 3.1.

Table 3.1: Weekdays, deities and auspicious colours

Indian calendar (lunar)	Western calendar (solar)	Deities worshipped	Auspicious colour
Sunday	*Raviwar*	Lord Surya	Red
Monday	*Somwar (Chandrawar)*	Lord Shiva	White
Tuesday	*Mangalwar*	Lord Hanuman	Red
Wednesday	*Budhwar*	Lord Shankar	Green
Thursday	*Guruwar*	Lord Vishnu	Yellow
Friday	*Shukrawar*	Goddess Lakshmi	White
Saturday	*Shaniwar*	Lord Shani	Black

Any fasts observed on particular days too, have different norms for observance laid down in the texts, or have folk tales or stories built around them to follow. Perhaps because illiteracy and strict obedience to elders, Brahmins or priests was the norm, who would tell the householder what to do by word of mouth and experience, guiding them to understand their own divinity through the observances, and spiritual discourses, *kathas* and congregational singing of *bhajans.*

Similarly each day of the week is associated with a particular colour, and people who believe that it affects their inner vibrations wear clothes accordingly on those days. Astrologers too, have predictions for certain lucky colours, numbers and so on, which are supposed to enhance health, bring happiness, peace and so on, for people born under a certain sun sign. This may have an influence as astrology is a well-developed natural science, but for non-believers, it is considered a myth.

Scientifically though, light which is colourless, when viewed through the rainbow or seen through a prism splits into 7 colours. These are allotted to each day of the week depending on their intensity, band width and according to the important deities, that are dominant and specially worshipped on particular days.

The colours given in Table 3.1 are only primary, all or no colours, but perhaps mixtures producing their numerous shades or hues are also acceptable and worn today by men, women, children and even the elderly who are outnumbering all. There is of course no doubt that there is a relationship between a season of the year and colour used. In bright hot summers no one would like to wear red colours even if the day for it is auspicious and *vice versa*. However, the temple or ritual colour considered auspicious is red whether it is worn for weddings, or used for dressing up deities in temples for festivals or the red vermillion dot on the foreheads of married women, irrespective of the day.

No documented evidence has been found on the auspiciousness of different colours on different weekdays, the above information has been collected through interviews with people and confirmed from priests. It is possible that these views may have been passed down by women who traditionally lived their lives closest to nature, and the rainbow is a natural phenomenon that makes everyone happy. So do the wearing of certain colors which become favorites of designers, actresses and the people during certain seasons. Also certain colors seem to suit some people, whether this has any astrological or personality connections is not known, and is in any case beyond the scope of this work.

The different seasons and the lunar months in which they fall are presented in Table 3.2.

Table 3.2: Months in lunar and solar calendar

Lunar Month	Days	Seasons	Solar Months
Chaitra	30 days	Vasant (Spring)	March – April
Vaishak	31 days	Vasant (Spring) – Grishm (Summer)	April – May
Jyaistha	31 days	Grishm (Summer)	May – June
Asadha	31 days	Grishm (Summer) – Varsha (Monsoon)	June – July
Srawana	31 days	Varsha (Monsoon)	July – August
Bhadrapada	31 days	Varsha (Monsoon) – Sharad (Autumn)	August – September
Asvina	30 days	Sharad (Autumn)	September – October
Kartika	30 days	Sharad (Autumn) – Hemant (Winter)	October – November
Magasirsa	30 days	Hemant (Winter)	November – December
Pousha	30 days	Hemant (Winter – Shishir (Dewy)	December – January
Magha	30 days	Shishir (Dewy)	January – February
Phalguna	30 days	Shishir (Dewy) – Vasant (Spring)	February – March

It is evident from the Table 3.2, that there are six seasons in the lunar calendar. In comparison, the solar calendar only has four seasons – spring, summer, autumn and winter. India being a tropical country, additional monsoon and dewy seasons are a regular annual feature. This is extremely significant for all agro-based societies and economies. It is for this reason that farmers pray for rain coming at the right time, for sowing in different geographic areas of the country which is prone to both floods and drought and thereby destruction of farm produce.

The length of the lunar months also varies since there are only 354 days as against 365 in the average solar year. The dates for events therefore shift every year for the fixation of which the lunar calendar is used. Further, each day is believed to be strongly influenced by certain deities who are given preference in terms of worship.

FIXATION OF NEW YEAR'S DAY

This is done in the different regions using both solar and lunar calendars depending on what is followed traditionally. In the states of Assam,

Bengal, Kerala, Punjab and Tamil Nadu, the solar calendar is used, as the New Year falls on the same day each year. In other states, the lunar calendar is used and the year begins on different dates every year. The first day of *Chaitra* is the Tamil New Year and falls on 12 April every year. Whereas in Kerala, the New Year's day is celebrated as *Onam* in the month of *Bhadrapada* (August –Sept), same as *Baisakha* in Punjab. In Gujarat and Rajasthan, the New Year falls in the month of *Kartik* in *Shukla paksh* or the bright fortnight.

According to the Muslim calendar which is widely followed in Middle East and in other Muslim countries the lunar year is strictly based on 12 lunar months of 354 days per year. That is why their holy month of *Ramadan* occurs approximately 11 to 12 days earlier than the date on which it occurred in the preceding year. Very often the timings of the festivals or beginning of fasts follow through to the next day getting out of line with the dates of the solar calendar and overlapping with the succeeding day.

The lunar date however, varies approximately between 22 and 26 hours based on the angular rotation of moon around the earth in its elliptical orbit and is referred to as *tithi.* Most of the Indian social and religious festivals are celebrated based on the *tithi.* The basis for the length of a lunar date is the angular distance between the sun and the moon as seen from the earth. As the moon rotates around the earth, the angular distance between the sun and the moon increases from 0 degrees to 360 degrees. It takes one lunar month or about 29 ½ solar days for the angular distance between the sun and the moon to be covered from 0 to 360 degrees. When the angular distance reaches zero, the next lunar month begins.

Thus, at the new moon a lunar month begins, while at full moon the angular distance between the sun and the moon as seen from the earth becomes exactly 180 degrees. The interval between 2 new moons is 29 days 12 hours and 44 minutes and the rotational period is 27.3 earth days. The same side of the moon always faces the earth. We can see more than the face of the moon, because the moon's orbit is not circular and it travels at different speeds. The phenomena called *libration* means 59 % of the moon's surface is visible from the earth. Fig. 3.1 shows the various faces of the moon as we see it.

Fig. 3.1: Visible faces of the moon
(*Courtesy: Artist J. P. Sharma*)

VISIBLE FACES OF THE MOON

As seen from Fig. 3.1, the waxing crescent is seen at 4 days, the full moon at 14 days, after which it starts waning gradually to reach the 4-day crescent at 24 days before it reaches the dark new moon, also referred to as the *no moon* day. According to Indian lunar month, the crescent lunar phase fortnight is called as *Shudha or Shukla paksha* and the waning phase of the lunar cycle fortnight as *Wadya or Krishna paksha.*

During *Shudha or Shukla paksha,* the angular distance between the moon and the sun changes from 0 degrees to 180 degrees while during the *Wadya or Krishna paksha,* it returns from 180 to 0 degrees. If this angular distance of 180 degrees is divided into 15 equal parts, then each part will have an angular distance of 12 degrees.

The lunar cycle thus, begins with the crescent moon and the crescent phase lasts till that phase culminates in the full moon, typically lasting for about 15 days. Then the moon enters into the waning phase until it disappears from the sky by lining up with the Sun. The waning phase also lasts for about 15 days.

To understand what degrees in length signify it is important to remember Kepler's rule which states that the angular velocity of the moon in its elliptical orbit around the earth continuously varies as it is affected by the relative distance between the earth and the moon, and also by the earth's relative distance from the sun. As a result, the daily angular speed (the speed of the angle between the moon and the sun as seen from the earth) varies somewhere between 10 and 14 degrees. Since the length of a *tithi* corresponds to 12 such degrees, the length of a *tithi* also varies accordingly. Therefore, a *tithi* can extend over one day (24-hour period) or it can get skipped if two *tithis* fall together on the same day. *Adhik Mass* occurs only when two *Amavasyas* or no moon days occur while the sun remains in the same zodiac sign[5].

Since the angular distance between the moon and the sun as referred here is always relative to the entire earth, a lunar day or *tithi* starts the same time everywhere in the world but not necessarily on the same day. Thus, when a certain *tithi* starts at 10:30 pm in India it also begins in New York at the same time, which is 12 pm (EST) on the same day. Since the length of a *tithi* can vary between 20 and 28 hours, its correspondence to a week day becomes little confusing.

Thus, in each twelve-degree portion of angular distance between the moon and the sun as it appears from the earth, lies the lunar date or *Tithi*. The first *Tithi* or lunar date in *Shukla paksha is* called *Prathama* , second *Dwitiya,* third *Tritya* and so on till we reach the *Poornima*, the lunar date for full moon day. Similarly for the waning fortnight of the lunar cycle or *Krishna paksha, tithis* begin again with *Prathama, Dwitiya* and so on till we arrive at *Amavasya* or a day before the new moon. So, when we refer to *Ramnavami* (the birthday of Lord *Rama*), it's *the Navami* (ninth lunar day) of *Shukla paksha* of the lunar month *Chaitra,* also called *Chaitra Shukla Navami*. Similarly, the *Gokulashtami* (also called *Janmashtami*, the birthday of Krishna) occurs on *Shrawan Krishna Ashtami* (eighth lunar day of *Krishna paksha* of the lunar month

---

5 For more information on zodiac system, refer to Maheshwari (1997).

Shrawan). In this manner, the dates and month are indicated for each special fast day or event in the year.

As per Indian calendar, the *tithi* for a given location on the earth depends on the angular distance between the moon and the sun relative to the earth at the time of sunrise at that location. Thus, for instance, assume on a November Monday, sunrise in New York city occurs at 8:30 am (EST). Further assume that at 9 am (EST) on Monday the angular distance between the sun and moon is exactly 12 degrees just following the new moon of the Indian lunar month *Kartik.* Since the length of a *tithi* is 12 degrees, the *tithi, Kartik Shukla Dwitiya* (second day) begins exactly at 9 am on Monday of that November in New York. However, at the time of sunrise on that Monday the *tithi Dwitiya* has not begun. Therefore, the *tithi* for that Monday for city of New York is *Kartik Shukla Prathama* (first day).

On the same Monday morning, the sunrise in Los Angeles occurs well past 9 am (EST). Since the *tithi Dwitiya* occurs everywhere in the world at the same instant, therefore, for Los Angeles, the *tithi* for that Monday would be *Kartik Shukla Dwitiya.*

For the same Monday at 9 am (EST), it would be 7:30 pm in Mumbai or New Delhi. Thus, *tithi* for that Monday for city of New York, Mumbai, and New Delhi is *Kartik Shukla Prathama* (the first day of Indian lunar month *Kartik*) while for most of the regions, west of Chicago or St. Louis the *tithi* for that Monday is *Dwitiya.* In other words, the *tithi Kartik Shukla Prathama* for regions west of Chicago or St. Louis should occur on the preceding day, the Sunday.

Kartik Shukla Prathama (the first day of Indian lunar month *Kartik*) also happens to be the first day after *Diwali.* Most of the Indians celebrate this as their New Year's day. Indians living in India, Europe, and eastern part of the United States thus should celebrate their New Year on that Monday while regions west of Chicago would do so on the preceding day, the Sunday.

ECLIPSES

The word *eclipse* comes from the Greek word meaning *abandonment.* Ancient Chinese believed a solar eclipse to be a demon's dragon that devours the sun. There are two types of eclipses that affect religious days and the performance of rituals as also health. These also occur because of rotational activities of the moon and earth.

Solar Eclipse

A solar eclipse occurs when the moon passes directly between the sun and the earth in its Amavasya or new moon phase, at such an angle that its shadow falls on the earth. This phenomena occurred in 2005 and is depicted in Fig. 3.2, when it appeared that the moon had blocked out the light of the sun. Total eclipses of the sun are very rare in any given location, occurring once in 360 years in the same place. However, several solar eclipses may occur each year.

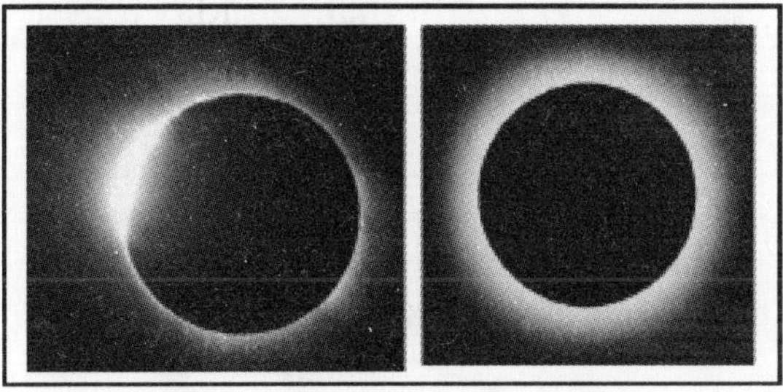

Fig. 3.2: Total solar eclipse

Astrologically, solar eclipses have always inspired awe or dread. In China, people beat drums to frighten the so called *demon* away. In India, people bathe in the holy rivers as a ritual during an eclipse. It is considered an act of solidarity with the sun to help it to fight the darkness that has blocked its energies. Since the sun is the source of all energies, a solar eclipse is considered inauspicious and therefore, pundits and priests advise that the time should be spent in meditation, prayer and chanting at home.

A total solar eclipse looks like a huge eye in the sky, and is said to represent the eye of God and therefore prayers offered when the eye is watching are said to be really heard by God. Fig.3.2 shows such an eclipse. It is customary to bathe once the eclipse is over and give away the clothes worn at the time in charity. It is said that one should refrain from eating and sleeping during an eclipse too, and pregnant women are advised not to venture outdoors to protect the unborn child from the harmful rays emitted at the time. Those at work should stay indoors, say prayers for at least five minutes, and avoid looking at the eclipsed sun directly with the naked eye.

It is recommended that after an eclipse charity in the form of wheat or any staple cereal, jaggery, gold, whole red chillies or red coloured clothes according to whatever one can afford to the under-privileged.

Lunar Eclipse

A lunar eclipse takes place when the earth passes directly between the sun and the full moon, so that the earth's shadow falls on the surface of the moon. This covers the moon for the duration of the eclipse. Fig. 3.3 represents the eclipses as they occur. The same restrictions and rituals apply as in the case of solar eclipse.

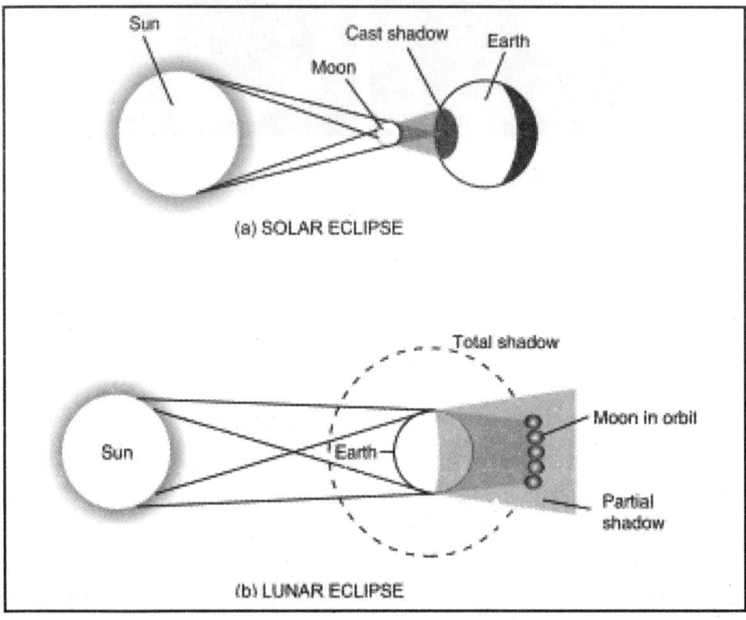

Fig. 3.3: Solar and lunar eclipse formation

Impact of Seasons

Festivals and rituals are fixed according to the solar and lunar calendars but the dates are also dependent on the seasons in which they are celebrated, the monsoon season having more religious and ritualistic connotations than the other seasons. Similarly more festivals come during spring and autumn than in summer and winter. Except for days like birthdays, anniversaries and marriages which go by actual dates of the solar calendar, those who follow the lunar *tithis* celebrate these days too by the lunar dates that keep shifting every year.

Thus, every Indian buys a solar or lunar calendar according to their personal requirements for dates for the various fasts, feasts and celebrations to plan for, through the year. The calendar is available from priests in temples or bookstores at the beginning of the year.

EKADASHI

According to the Lunar calendar which is followed for all religious and festive purposes in the North and Central parts of India, *ekadashi* is considered a sacred day. It falls on the 11th day of every fortnight after a new moon or full moon day. The 15th full moon day is called *Purnima* whereas the 15th moonless night is called *Amas* or *Amavasya,* the dark night. The *ekadashi* fast is considered superior to all other fasts and has the power to obliterate all sins and evils, provided it is observed in good faith.

The bright fortnight is known as the *Shukla paksh* and the dark one as the *Krishna paksh*. Thus, there are normally 24 *ekadashis,* but when some months get extended, 2 additional *ekadashis* are added in certain lunar years taking the total to 26 *ekadashis* in that calendar year. This happens after every 32 months. A number of them have greater significance and sanctity from the point of view of religious rituals and observance of fasts than others. The fast may be observed as a complete one without food or water or as a partial fast in which certain prescribed foods are taken at meal times.

Each *ekadashi* has a special name, and according to the month, season and *paksh* in which it occurs instructions are available with respect to their observances. Some salient features are indicated in Table 3.3:

Table 3.3: Ekadashis and their significance

S. No.	Ekadashi	Month/paksh	Observance and significance
1	*Utpana*	*Maghshirsh/Krishna*	This *nirjal* fast is observed in the *Hemant* season and starts in the evening of the 10th day and follows through the 11th or *ekadashi* day. After prayers in the evening and offering of *prasaad*, the fast is broken. It should be accompanied by offering charity to the deprived.
2	*Mokshda*	*Magh/Shukla*	This fast is believed to bring prosperity, manifold. Prayers are offered to Lord Damodar. Its observance is believed to pardon all sins committed present and past, and lead to liberation. The fast is considered more effective than going to all the places of pilgrimage.
3	*Saphala*	*Paush/Krishna*	Whole night *jagran*, with fasting

(Contd...)

			and prayers to *Narayana* and offering of fruits according to season.
4	*Putrada*	*Paush/Shukla*	Fasting enhances devotion to *Narayana* who endows wisdom and prosperity. People keep this fast in the hope of being blessed with a son.
5	*Shattila*	*Magh/Krishna*	Fasting, charity and prayer for health and prosperity.
6	*Jaya*	*Magh/Shukla*	Fasting and prayer leads to liberation.
7	*Vijaya*	*Phagun/Krishna*	Fast and prayer for victory.
8	*Amal*	*Phagun/Shukla*	Fast and prayer for success.
9	*Papmochani*	*Chaitra/Krishna*	By observing fast all sins are forgiven.
10	*Kamda*	*Chaitramash/Shukla*	Believed that those who observe this fast go to heaven.
*11	*Varuthani*	*Baisakh/Krishna*	Fast of silence or *Maun*, especially for those who fear death. They are required to abstain from using copper utensils, non-vegetarian food, *chana, masoor dal*, honey and gourds. Also no to addictions and sex. If a woman is

(Contd...)

			in grief she gets good tidings with this *vrat.*
12	*Mohini*	*Baisakh/Shukla*	Fasting and prayer leads to detachment and blessings.
13	*Apra*	*Jaisth/Krishna*	Fast with prayers to Lord Vishnu for forgiveness of sins and liberation. Equivalent to visiting all places of pilgrimage.
*14	*Nirjala*	*Jaisth/Shukla*	Fast and prayer to Lord Vishnu for liberation. Charity to the disabled is an important component. This is equivalent to fruits of all the *ekadashis.* Also called *Bhim ekadashi.*
*15	*Devshayani*	*Ashad/Shukla*	Also known as *Padma, Ashadi* or *Maha ekadashi*. In South India it is called *Toli ekadashi.*
16	*Yogini*	*Ashad/Krishna*	Fast and devotion to Lord Shiva ensures freedom from sin.
17	*Kamika*	*Shravan/Krishna*	Fast with Vishnu *tulsi puja* using *shankh*, *charka*, etc., considered greater than the

(Contd...)

			fruits of *Ganga snan.*
18	*Pavitra*	*Shravan/Shukla*	Important for self-purification.
19	*Aja*	*Bhado/Krishna*	Fast, *jagran* and *yagna* are its features.
*20	*Parivartini*	*Bhado/Shukla*	Also called *Jal Zalini* or *Parshva Parivartini Ekadashi.* Observing fast on this day is believed to be more fruitful thanperforming *yagya.* Charity to the poor and prayers to *Vaman devta* is equivalent to praying to the Trinit of *Brahma, Vishnu, Maheshwara.* This *ekadashi* gets its name because while resting, Lord Vishnu supposedly turns a side, changing his position. Fasts are kept with *jagrans* and *satsang.*
21	*Indira*	*Ashwin/Krishna*	This is a fast observed for the liberation of souls of ancestors with prayer, offerings and charity.
22	*Pashankusha*	*Ashwin/Shukla*	Fast, prayer and offering.

(Contd...)

23	*Rama*	*Kartik/Krishna*	Fasts, prayers, charity. Imparts prosperity and liberation.
*24	*Prabodhini*	*Kartik/Shukla*	Also called *Kartik ekadashi*, *Dev Prabodhini* or *Devothyani*. Offerings of winter's first harvest of fresh vegetables. Fast destroys past sins and is equivalent to fruits of hundred *yagnas*. All night *jagran* and breaking fast next evening as it is a *nirahar* fast.
*25	*Padmini*	*Laundh/Shukla*	This is the *ekadashi* of the extra month, which comes once in 3 lunar years.
*26	*Parma*	*Laundh/Krishna*	Same as *Padmini*. Fast, prayers and offerings to *Krishna Radha*.

* *Ekadashis* are specially significant.

Thus, *ekadashi* fasts were a way of inculcating in people the habit of fasting regularly once or twice a week, fortnightly or monthly. Although there are astrological implications affecting health on those days, religious guidance was better understood and practiced, since women lived more with their hearts than their heads. Even today people consult astronomers for good and inauspicious days and do not perform rituals on those days. *Adhik mas* refers to the extra or residual month in the lunar calendar also called *Laundh* which occurs once every 32 months. In this month, the sun does not transmigrate clearly.

Sages declare that when the moon is in the sun's aura, and the sun transmigrates from one zodiac sign to another, it destroys the merits of rituals and *yagnas*. Therefore, rituals are not performed during this period when only holy acts were recommended such as offering charities, bathing in sacred rivers, listening to *kathas* and so on. The merits of *adhik mas* falling in the different months have been detailed[6].

Literature has it that King Ambarisa observed the *ekadashi* fast very strictly to achieve the status of *Indra*. The fast is believed to fetch food for the hungry and salvation for those in search of it (*Agni Purana*). Anecdotes have been built around all the *ekadashis* and the norms for each fast have been outlined for practice[7].

Thus, there are certain days of the year which are considered particularly sacred on which people fast according to their different beliefs and faiths. For devotees of Lord *Ganesha*, the 4th of both *paksh* (fortnights) dark or bright, are important, while devotees of Mother, the female forms of *Shakti* revere the 8th known as *ashtami*, and the 9th of the bright fortnight marks *Bhagwan Swaminarayan's* incarnation and *Purnima* the appearance of his 1st spiritual successor.

Thus, *ekadashi* fasts are believed to absolve people of their sins and lead to prosperity, success, victory and therefore happiness and liberation.

The other important *tithis* are *purnima* i.e., 15th full moon day, which then wanes into the 15th moonless night called *amavasya*. The moon then waxes till it reaches the brightest or full moon.

PURNIMA

As already mentioned, the Purnima day falls on the 15th full moon day. There are thus a number of Purnimas throughout the year. These too are known by various names that are significant in terms of fasting and feasting. These are indicated in Table 3.4.

6 Sadhu Mukundcharandas (2005), p. 206.

7 Vishwanath Shastri, 1985

Table 3.4: Significant purnima days

Purnima	Month	Significance
Guru	*Ashad*	Also known as *Vyas purnima* since he was the first guru to classify the Vedas, write 18 *Puranas* and the *Mahabharata*. On this day, worship is offered to the Guru[8].
Shravan purnima	*Shravan*	*Raksha Bandhan* is celebrated on this day. A ritual to strengthen the *guru-shishya* and brother-sister bond. Also known as *Shravani.*
Sharad purnima	*Aso*	On this night, the moon imparts its best resplendence. Believed that Goddess Lakshmi gifts wealth to those who are awake this night.
Ras purnima	*Sharad*	The full moon night of Autumn when Krishna played with the *gopis.*
Buddha purnima	*Vaishakh*	The underlying message of this is that the mind should shine with total purity like the full moon
Amavasya	*New moon every month*	On this day, people put down their tools as offering to Lord Vishwakarma. Artisans fast and pray for prosperity in their respective professions.

The period which combines *Ekadashi* with *dwadashi* (12th day) is called *harivasara* because of the presence of Vishnu at that time, it is considered a good time for fasting, prayer and feasting.

If *ekadashi* combines with *dasami*, however, it is not considered a good omen, and a fast should not be observed. However, if an *ekadashi* falls on a *puyam* day in the bright half of the month, the *vrat* should be

[8] Guru means the remover of ignorance, a person who guides and inspires students to realize their divinity. Today teachers may be called gurus by their students but they only impart worldly knowledge and therefore do not actually qualify as gurus in the ancient sense of the term.

observed, as the effect is believed to be good and destructive of evils. The *ekadashi* falling in the month of *Phalgun* or March is supposed to have good effects and fasting with Vishnu *puja* brings universal happiness.

The four monsoon months referred to as *chaturmas*, have the largest number of sacred days because Vishnu sleeps during this period and people need to be vigilant for themselves through fasting and prayer.

In Maharashtra, after every *purnima* some women observe a fast on every 4th day, called the *Chauth Vrat* which is similar to the *Karva chauth* observed in the Northern states of the country.

Mode of Fasting

The fast observed on this day is called *ekadashi vrat* and may be observed as a complete one without food and water or a partial fast in which certain prescribed foods are taken at meal times. Those who observe the fast are expected to be on a regulated diet excluding meat. Sex too, is to be avoided on the day preceding the *ekadashi* fast. On both days of the month (Ekadashis), no food should be taken. All strong smelling vegetables are avoided as offerings for fast days and therefore not consumed.

Breaking of Fast

Culmination of fast had to be done in a particular way on certain days and at auspicious times. The day which merges *dwadashi* into *trayodashi* or 13th day is best for breaking the fast but if a complete fast is observed it can be broken on the 12th day. All fasts are broken with prayers and *satvik* foods. Women too had a lot of time on their hands and were more gullible to be taught through folk tales and stories. It is for this reason that every *ekadashi* was given a name and a ritual to be followed.

Present Practices

In ancient times, people looked up to priests to guide them in their lives as householders, who set regular routines of fasting and feeding, charity and certain disciples to be observed for each fast as well as for the preparation of offerings. Further these occasions not only provided a means of leaving home for temples with friends and neighbours but also provided a sustained profession for temple priests while giving them a status because of their knowledge of the *shastras* and the celestial movements.

Stories built around each fast were the only way to transmit spiritual and value-based knowledge to people especially women who in those days were not literate or educated in matters external to their homes.

Today people do not observe all the *ekadashis* as fast days. In fact there are more non-believers today than ever before, because who cares for liberation in an unknown future? Yet, when one feels aggrieved or sorrowful, prayer is the only one thing that people turn to, praying for peace, love and harmony by lighting candles or incense sticks and so on. The fact that these acts provide solace, the link with their inherent divinity is undisputed. Doubtless, fasting routinely also has a positive effect on health and people observe the same according to their routines, working hours, professions and faiths. Fasting has been modified to suit lifestyles and convenience although people do enjoy visiting temples for the special *prasaad*.

MAHASHIVRATRI

Shivaratri is considered the spring festival of Lord Shiva. As the name suggests, this is a night devoted to Lord Shiva, and is a holy day observed on the eve of the new moon day or *Chaturdasi* falling in the middle of the months of *Magh* and *Phalgun* (Feb.-March). The moon is the presiding deity of the mind since its 16 phases coincide with the 16 aspects of the mind. Of the 16 phases of the moon, the 14th day of *magh* is special because rest of the 15 phases are absent on this day. It is therefore possible to get full control of one's mental faculties making it auspicious. This night is characterized by penance, fasting and worshipping of Lord Shiva, without food or sleep.

Significance of Shivratri

This is a festival observed in honor of Lord Shiva as it represents the marriage of Lord Shiva to Parvati on this day. The day is considered especially auspicious for women. Married women pray for the well being of their husbands and sons, while unmarried women pray for a husband like Shiva, who is considered the ideal husband.

The onset of *dwapar yug* was characterized with manifestations of 12 self-formed *jyotirlings* of India and this occurred on *Mahashivaratri* day.

We experience a night every day of our lives, why then is *Shivratri* more important and treated as an auspicious night? According to Sri Sathya Sai, the entire cosmos is governed by three states namely creation, sustenance and dissolution (*srishti*, *stithi* and *layam*) which are also identified in the Vedas as *Sathya*, *Rajas* and *Tamas*. Man is thus an embodiment of these three *gunas* representing the Trinity worshipped as *Brahma, Vishnu* and Shiva or *Maheshwara,* who are regarded as components of Divinity, and present together in every being. They are therefore regarded as one and worshipped as *Shivam*—the embodiment of auspiciousness. The divinity which fills the cosmos is a representation of the Trinity consisting of *Brahma-Vishnu-Maheshwara* (Shiva) existing in man as heart, soul and mind. When man recognizes the unified form of the Trinity, his humanness acquires auspiciousness.

Auspiciousness consists of diverting the mind towards God and therefore calls for getting rid of the inherited sensuous tendencies in man. It follows that whomsoever you adore or condemn, you are adoring or condemning Him. The message therefore is *Help ever, Hurt never*.

Creation is thus, an expression of the will of God and is called *Nature*. Thus man exists to manifest the powers of nature which are not found equally in all beings, thus the cosmic process goes on. Sai explains, that spirituality does not mean living a lonely ascetic life, but getting rid of the enemies of attachment, hatred, lust, anger and greed, and seeing all people as one humanity with its greatest quality being Love.

What does the Trinity Represent?

The answer to this question was given by Baba in his *Gurudev vani*[9] in which he explains that unlike avatars, *Brahma-Vishnu-Maheshwara* are not embodied beings, but symbolize the attributes or *gunas* that

9 *Sanathana Sarathi,* Vol. 43, No. 8 August 2000, p. 249

exist in the human body and make it perform various functions. Vishnu is omnipresent as seen through man's mind which wanders everywhere at any time and is not bound by time, space and circumstances.

Brahma signifies vastness or oneness with the cosmic forms as represented by the primordial sound. Thus, the Trinity permeates the entire *cosmos* and is present in its microscopic forms in the human body. Since man is unable to understand his own humanness, he is therefore incapable of recognizing the divinity within.

Ancient sages laid down the *sadhna* or practice of *maunam* i.e., silence to maintain purity of speech believing that excessive talk could lead to sins and abuses that hurt others through speaking of untruths or creating emotional excitement. *Maun* does not mean absence of speech alone but also absence of thoughts. If thoughts are removed, the mind gets dissolved and one recognizes the divinity within and experiences Him.

A *satvik* individual is one who is free from the shackles of *Irsha, Dvesh, Kama, Krodha* or *Lobha* whose goal is attainment of enlightenment and spiritual bliss. A *rajasik* person is attached to worldly pleasures and comforts of life and is a *karma yogi,* whereas a *tamasic* person is one who is involved with a mixed disposition and is usually seen as lethargic or idle. All these behavioral qualities are found in all persons to different extents. By controlling the negative qualities a *tamasik* person can become *rajasic* and then *satvik.*

We are all embodiments of trinity or three attributes and therefore, Lord Shiva is propitiated by offerings and prayers to enable us to achieve purity of heart, mind and speech and thus gain the divine experiences.

Shivratri Observances

This is an important day for the devotees of Shiva, who stay awake throughout the night, praying to Him. From the very early morning, Shiva temples are flocked by devotees, who come to perform the traditional worship of the *Shivling.* Lord Shiva is worshipped in the form of the *Shivling* which is a symbol of *jyoti* or light and *shakti* or strength. In the *Shiv Puran,* it is stated *one who offers puja to me on this day will attain divine power (4th chapter).* The linga is bathed with milk, water, and honey. It is then anointed with sandalwood paste. People offer wood apple or bael leaves and fruit, milk, sandalwood and jujube fruit (*bér*) to the linga. Shiva is believed to be very hot tempered, and hence things that have a cooling effect are offered to him. The trifoliate *bael* leaves is symbolic of the body with three attributes to the three-eyed Shiva who carries the trident and has the potency to destroy the sins accumulated over three births and are therefore considered specially holy as offerings. People decorate the linga with flowers and garlands and offer incense sticks and fruit. In bigger temples, there is almost a stampede as devotees seek favours from their beloved god. Many also employ the services of a priest to perform special prayers. *Thandai,* a drink made with cannabis, almonds, and milk, is essentially drunk by the devout. This is so because cannabis is said to have been very dear to Shiva. It is believed that Lord Shiva reveals himself to devotees on *Shivratri.*

In ancient Kashmir, which was considered the seat of saints and renunciation, *Shivratri* was observed for 12 days during which fasting, prayer, *grahasthya* and *vanaprasth* representing the stages of a man's life were observed. Householders or *grahasthyas* used to pray to their chosen deities on *Amavasya* day and return to their homes while saints sat in meditation for the entire period. Even today Hindu *Kashmiris* fast and pray from the start of *Phalgun Krishna paksh* to *Amavasya* night. Till *ekadashi* they clean their homes and pray. On *Dvadashi* they fill two large vessels with walnuts representing Shiv and Parvathi and pray the whole night, as this day represents the wedding day of the Lord. The *Kashmiris* worship the *akhrot* or walnut because:

- It is a time when the mountainous regions are covered in snow, and no fruits or vegetables can grow.
- Walnuts are dry and preserved to be offered and eaten when nothing else is available.
- They provide a lot of protein as well as energy through the oil present in it to keep people warm.
- The structure of the walnut symbolically represents the four Vedas as the internal segments are joined together from *amavasya* to *dvadasi.*

During prayers, devotees offer *misri*, milk, red sandalwood, *dhatura, jau,* black sesame and flowers to the symbolic vessels. Walnuts are kept in smaller vessels also. Salt and *tamasic* food is also placed in containers. These smaller vessels symbolize the *baraatis* or wedding guests since *Shivratri* is a day celebrated as the wedding day of the Lord with Parvati and all kinds of people can be expected in a marriage party.

On *dvadasi* day, the walnuts are soaked in water and right till *amavasya* the water is changed every day, and the walnuts are offered with prayers and *aarti* every day. The offering is then distributed as *prasaad.*

Mode of Fasting

A strict day-and-night fast is kept on this day and the fast is believed as being equivalent to the fruits of all the fasts in the year. Some devotees observe a complete *nirjal* fast and do not take even a drop of water whereas *phalahar* preparations made of *makhane, sabutdana, chaulai ladoos* and fruits are consumed by some. Some take one meal a day consisting of dishes made of *kootu* (buckwheat), *singhara atta* (water chestnut flour) or *samak ke chawal.*

There is mention of a devotee of Sri Ramakrishna who used to fast during *Shivratri* even at a ripe old age. When asked why he continued when he was old and not well, he replied:

I get something — a vision of the Master. So, someone asked ***Does he talk to you?*** The answer was ***No. That is my last wish***[10].

Breaking of Fast

All through the day, devotees abstain from eating food and break their fast only the next morning, after the night-long worship.

Present Scenario

Generally *Shivaratri* occurs every month of the Hindu calendar but is celebrated only twice a year namely *Kawad* (falls in rainy season) and *Shiva Vivaha* (falls in Spring). Today, however, people who are too involved in the material and sensuous world celebrate only one day as *Shivratri.* As a result they do not have the inclination towards austerity

10 Swami Chetananada, 1991, p. 289

and always seem to have time constraints and no patience or energy, even though the wise have established that *the busy man has time for everything whereas an idle man has time for nothing.* So, it amounts to willpower, determination and requires only management of precious time for activities that one wants to indulge in and complete successfully.

NAVRATRA

The term *Navratra* means nine nights, indicating that the fasting lasts for that period. It commences on the first day of *Amavasya* and ends on the ninth day of *Aswayuja* (September-October). *Navratri* comes twice in the year once in spring and again in autumn when it overlaps with *Durga Puja.* The dates are fixed according to the lunar calendar and therefore change every year.

Significance

The first three nights are devoted to Goddess Durga, the goddess of valour, the next three to *Lakshmi,* the goddess of wealth and the last three to *Saraswati,* the fountainhead of knowledge, speech, art and music. Indian culture and tradition considers mother as the most sacred. In times of difficulties, one always thinks and calls on one's mother and not father, the word mother or *maa* being a source of mental strength and physical comfort. The first word a child utters is *maa* and in nature too, the earth is referred to as mother Earth and it is for this reason that in India, mother is accorded the highest place ahead of father, teacher and God.

Observance

Navratri celebrations begin with a period of fasting in which beautifully sculptured and dressed images of the goddesses are installed in temples, on specially built and decorated covered podiums for the deities in open spaces and homes. This 10-day long period offers shopping bonanza, fun for children and opportunity for all devotees to offer prayers and partake of the blessings with sanctified sweets and fruit after the day's fast. It is also a period of socializing with friends, neighbours and extended families. The observance of fasts during *Navratra* varies in different regions depending on their traditional customs and practices.

In northern India, *Navratri* is a period of fasting for seven days. On the eight day of *ashtami,* devotees break their fasts by offering prayers to the goddess and symbolically inviting young girls to their homes as they are considered as living images of the Goddess. People ceremonially wash the children's feet, worship them and then offer them food which has been offered to the deity and considered *satvik,* which includes *puri, halwa*, and *channa* distributed as *prasaad.* They are also offered gifts of bangles and red scarves with token money as charity.

During the nine days of *Navratri,* fasting and feasting take precedence over all normal routine activities amongst the Hindus. Evenings witness group dances performed in ecstatic worship of Goddess *Durga Maa*.

In Assam, Bengal and Orissa, it is celebrated as *Kali Puja,* highlighting woman power as symbolized by the victory of Durga over Mahishasur, the buffalo-headed demon. The climax of the celebrations is followed by immersion of the deities. With a heavy heart, the devotees immerse the clay idol of Durga in the sacred Ganges or other rivers bidding her good bye as she departs to unite with Lord Shiva. The tenth day of *Navratri* is called *Vijay Dashmi* day which is the fourth day of *Durga Puja.*

In many northern states and some parts of Maharashtra, the festival is known as *Dusshera*, celebrating the victory of Rama over Ravana. The day is characterized by burning effigies of Ravana on this day to signify victory of good over evil.

Mode of Fasting

The fast is a partial fast in which only one main meal is eaten by the devout. It is believed that if a couple or any two members of the family keep the fast together, a single day of fasting is considered equivalent to two fasting days. This is a useful concept for those who fast under compulsion, because the rest in the family do so. In some households, the fast days observed are the last two prior to the breaking of the fast.

The fast is characterized by replacing cereals from the diet with roots, tubers, seeds, stems, buckwheat and lotus stem flours and other non-cereal substitutes. Fruits and special foods made from potatoes, *kootu* flour (buckwheat), milk and milk products are allowed on fast days. Usually the number of meals is restricted to one per day and liquids can be taken freely. On the whole *Navratra phal- ahaari- khana* is of very high calories, protein dense and carbohydrate rich. Since the devotees have only one meal, it provides them with enough energy and satiety value to take them through to the next fast day.

Over time the strict nine-day fasts have been modified and different versions exist today. Some observe the fast only on the first and last day, some fast for any two consecutive or preferably last two days, some observe it for full seven or eight days while others do not fast at all. Very often, couples keeps a fast together, since it is considered equivalent to two fasting days. This is a useful concept today, as many people observe fast under compulsion of family or peers and if they are working on those days at jobs, fasting becomes difficult to maintain for the whole period. People who do not fast however, generally abstain from eating eggs, meat and other non-vegetarian foods and alcohol consumption during these nine days as a mark of respect to the goddess. In very strict households, refrigerators and cabinets are thoroughly cleaned of all non-vegetarian foods and alcoholic drinks and replaced with fresh vegetables, fruits and milk products before the first fast day.

Breaking of Fasts

Since *Navratri* fasts are partial fasts, they are broken by a meal which only replaces cereals with *farari* foods consisting of *kootu* (buckwheat), *singhara* flour (water chestnut), s*amak ke chawal*, roots, tubers, fruits, seeds, milk and milk products and so on with regional variations in their preparations. However, strongly flavored foods like onions, garlic and turnips are avoided. The one meal taken may be an afternoon or evening meal. These days special *Navratri* snacks are also available in the market which are made use of.

The final fast is broken on the eighth or ninth day depending on regional beliefs. Early morning after bath, prayers are offered to the Goddess, symbolically the *prasaad* offered is then distributed to young girls after performing *aarti*. Only then do women partake of the offerings and break their fasts. The same offerings are then distributed among the family members.

Present Scenario

To suit the changed lifestyles and taste buds of the modern world in which people are eating out more often and have less time to observe traditional fasting procedures, there are various forms of quick navratra meals and snacks offered by restaurants and other eating places as presented in Table 3.5.

Table 3.5: Some navratra offerings of restaurants

Nirulas	– offers a varied navratra menu everyday. The items are changed daily to include *kashiphal masala, aloo dahi* curry, *paneer* with butter gravy, *lauki kofta* curry, *arbi* curry, *navratra chawal, sabudana papad*, cucumber or *aloo raita*, green salad and *makhana* or *sabudana kheer.*
Banana Leaf	– special navratra thali comes with a *paneer* dish, rice, *puri, rasam, sambhar*, sautéed vegetable and curd often served on banana leaf.
Iskcon's Govinda	– the navratra buffet is a huge spread with *samak ki khichri, paneer* dishes, *sitaphal masala, amrud* vegetable, *methi*, curd, tomato *jhol, samak kheer* and salads.
Indi Spice	– special navaratra thali comprising of *paneer* and *makhana subji*, potato dish, *ghia* or *sitaphal raita, swang ki kheer, singhara atta puri*, rice.

People's inclination towards traditional fasting today is seen through the popularity of these meals, while many look at the changing trends with skepticism. Others feel that such transformation does not matter a lot as long as people have faith in Durga *Maa*.

As the countdown begins for Navratra, people are specially drawn to the *Garba*, the longest dance festival in the world. It is a nine-day dance festival held during Navratris characterized by colourful dresses and gaeity. In recent years, many foreigners are coming from different corners of the world to participate in garba dances. It is a boom time for garba classes as well, who along with locals have had many foreigners turning up to learn the intricate steps.

RAMNAUMI

Ramnaumi falls on the 9th day in the bright fortnight or *Shukla paksh* of the lunar month of *Chaitra* in March-April. It marks the day of the birth of Sri Rama who is considered the seventh avatar or incarnation of Lord Vishnu. Many sages and seers undertook penance and strict vows to spread the glory of *Rama naam*, propagating the *Rama Tattwa*, the principle of Rama since ancient times. The Ramayana belongs to the *Treta Yug*, but even after thousands of years it is still being read with reverence in every town, village and hamlet of the country. The Indians have also taken it all over the world, where Rama's name is chanted with great devotion. In fact, Rama never wished or told anyone to chant his name, he only declared that all are the embodiments of divinity.

Ramnaumi is an important religious day for Hindus. Even those who adore Lord Shiva celebrate this occasion.

Mode of Fasting

Some observe a fast the whole day before *Ramnaumi* which may be a fruit and milk one or a non-cereal fast, others may take only one meal or keep a strictly *nirjal* fast. The temples are decorated and the richly adorned image of lord Rama is installed for *darshan* or worship. Readings from the Holy Ramayana are heard in homes and temples. In Ayodhya, the birthplace of Sri Rama, a huge fair is held on that day as part of the festivities.

Breaking the Fast

Since Sri Rama was born at 12 noon on the next day the fast ends then, and rejoicing and celebrations begin.

In South India, the *Ramnaumi Utsavam* is celebrated for 9 days with great fervour and devotion. Those who are talented in the art of story telling narrate the thrilling episodes from the Ramayana. The *kirtanists*, singers of devotional music, celebrate the wedding of Sri Rama with Sita on this great day. It is an extremely colourful ceremony, which is highly inspiring, instructive and enjoyable for all.

Message of Lord Rama

Sri Sathya Sai Baba has beautifully summarized the message of Lord Rama to mankind, through interesting anecdotes relating to everyday life, in his *Avtar vani* as follows[11]:

---

11 *Sanathan Sarathi* of May 2006 for Baba's Ramnaumi discourse, p. 139

- Follow *Sathya* or Truth to *promote Dharma* or Righteousness.
- Spread goodness
- Sense control
- Care and Share
- Serve and respect parents (elders).
- Be an example to others

There is an episode in the Ramayana which reveals the truth about Sri Rama and his mission. When he was in Chitrakoot, his brother, Bharata and Shatrughna, appealed to him to return to Ayodhya to rule His kingdom. Rama then said:

> ***My pledged word is sacred and I will not go back on it. I will give up my life rather than go back on my word.***

When Jabali the sage reminded him that his father Dashratha was no longer alive, and there was no need to adhere to the word any longer. Rama replied:

> ***The body is perishable but the promised word remains. Truth has no form it is eternal and omnipresent unchanged in the past, present and future.***

Thus, the life of Sri Rama established *Dharma* and the ideals of character worth emulating in our lives especially today, when we are surrounded by *adharma*, selfishness, neglect of parents and elders and running after material gains earning only fatigue, but no satisfaction, peace or happiness.

JANAMASHTAMI

Janamashtami commemorates the birth of Lord Krishna who was born in the *Yadava* dynasty as the son of Vasudeva and Devaki, and was the 9th of the 10 incarnations of *Mahavishnu*[12]. He was born in the month of *Simha (*Leo) which falls on the 8th day of the dark half of the month of *Bhadrapada* usually in August-September every year. His birthday is celebrated over two days, the first known as *Krishna* or *Gokulashtami,* and the second day as *Kalashtami* or more popularly *Janamashtami.*

12 Sri Krishna incarnated more than 5000 yrs ago at the end of the 3rd cosmic phase – the Dwapur Yug.

His name too, is not understood clearly by many, the word *Krish* means one who cultivates the heart or one who attracts almost like a magnet. The subtle truths relating to an *avatar* or incarnation cannot be easily understood, because their ways are infinite and inscrutable.

Significance

The true spirit and message of *Janamashtmi* is for devotees to implicitly surrender at the Lord's lotus feet, and strictly observe truth and Dharma. In the *Bhagawad Gita* (Ch.4, verse 7) Krishna proclaims:

> ***I incarnate wherever dharma declines and evil predominates, to establish dharma and vanquish evil.***

Although centuries have passed since Sri Krishna's advent. His life and messages guide people afresh every year.

Messages of Lord Krishna to the World

The message of Lord Krishna to the world is enunciated in two chapters of the Gita. The principles he followed in his life for happiness will help humanity to overcome the misery that surrounds us, and move on happily in the cycle of life. These are:

- *Matru Bhakti* – reverence of parents.
- *Go-pal* – Love of cows and their caregivers.
- *Nishkam Karm* – Work sincerely and without expectations
- *Dharma* – righteousness, to uproot evil[13]
- *Ahimsa* – peace through diplomatic means for peaceful coexistence.
- *Detachment* – by focusing on the ideals of *Dharma*, and treating others as oneself, yet not too attached to move on to your individual goals of peace and happiness after attending to your duties.

These messages if followed dutifully and noble heartedly, in spite of provocations in life will lead to world peace, and therefore the

[13] Krishna holds the *Sudarshan Chakra* (disc) in one hand to vanquish *adharma* and the flute in the other symbolizing *bhakti*.

importance of incarnations or *avatars* in human form, appearing from time to time leading the way to unity and peace through love and prayer.

Mode of Fasting

The first day is marked strictly by a *nirjal* fast in which even water is not consumed, as the parents of Lord Krishna were tortured on this day and imprisoned by Kans, brother of Devaki. Some may observe a partial fast by only eating *farari* foods such as fruits, vegetables, nuts and seeds to suit their individual routines.

The day is spent tastefully decorating the deity with flowers, new clothes, flute and so on, in prayers, devotional songs, meditation and in preparation of special foods to be offered, for the birth of Lord Krishna, who was born at midnight of that day. His birth, signals the end of the fast and beginning of celebrations, marked by breaking of the fast, singing devotional songs and visiting temples for *prasaad.*

Breaking the Fast

Those who observe the fast break it at home by offering dishes like *panjiri, dhania burfee*, coconut *burfee,* fruits, *kheer* and so on after offering it to the deity or alternately, they may visit the temples with their offerings for partaking of *prasaad*, and enjoy the congregational ambience of the occasion with family and friends.

Ancient *ayurvedic* claims that, *panjiri* is beneficial since it has carminative properties and stimulates the digestive system afresh after the long complete fast. True Vedic traditions advised followers to offer *pucca* food *that is*, food cooked in ghee or milk which was offered to the deities in the form of *bhakti* before partaking of it as *prasaad.* The texts never advocate feasting after a fast, but only controlled breaking of fasts.

According to the International Society of Krishna Consciousness (ISKCON), the typical festive activities are:

- Cooking 108 different delicacies for offering to the Lord at midnight, and distribution to all guests and devotees as *prasaad.*
- *Abhisheka*, that is, public bathing of the form of the Lord with fruit juices and milk products.
- *Darshan* of the Lord in all the finery, the *murti* or statue placed

on a flower-laden alter. Depictions of the infant Krishna in a *Jhula* at every temple are an added attraction.

- Singing of devotional songs or *bhajans* accompanied by traditional instruments.
- Plays enacted in dance and music recreating the pastimes of *Bal Krishna* and other facets of his life and teaching.
- Readings from the scriptures describing the Lord's unique birth and the events leading to his arrival.
- Congregational chanting of the Krishna *mantra* and offering of *aarti.*

Krishna periodically appears in other forms but this festival celebrates his arrival as a beautiful cowherd boy with bluish hued skin, who plays the flute and enjoys family and village pastimes with his most intimate and loving devotees, who aspire to join Him at home in *Vrindavan.*

The second day of *Janamashtmi* is therefore, one of gaiety and celebration recounting the joy of Krishna's birth and life of meaningful play called *leelas.* Children especially enjoy the theatres, the pulling of the infant Krishna's *Jhula* and the popular ceremony of the *Dahi-handi* so named because *dahi* or curds used to be suspended in a *handi* to prevent spoilage in earlier days. This involves an earthenware pot suspended from a height of 20 to 40 feet filled with milk, *dahi* (curds), butter, honey and fruits. Sporting young children climb on each other and try to claim the prize by breaking the pot and collecting the contents as Bal Krishna used to do. Furthermore, the *Dhol yatra* known as the spring festival is also associated with Lord Krishna, as is *Ras Purnima* which falls on the full moon night when Sri Krishna played with the *gopis.* Sri Krishna thus enamoured most people especially children, who thereby identify easily with the child Krishna and his mischievous ways with his mother.

By associations with such divine pastimes, followers experience tranquility and contentment, performing or witnessing *leelas* of Krishna in large gatherings in temples, complexes or open spaces close to the natural environments of Lord Krishna where the call of his flute summons the *gopis* of *Vrindavan.*

Present Scenario

It is interesting to note that *Vrindavan* where Lord Krishna spent his childhood, is the centre for making dresses for him and his consort *Radha*, and most of them are embroidered and made by Muslims. Even today, making clothes for the idols of Lord Krishna, Radha and the Gopis, is not only a lucrative profession but is an emotional offering for the Muslim artisans. Not only that, there are strict instructions given to them to wash their hands and feet well before they touch any item of work. The workers respect the Hindu deities as much as they revere their own God. This is an outstanding example of communal harmony especially in the troubled times of today.

Today there is a visible change in the psyche of young people who hate crowds as they live in nuclear families and believe in solitude and privacy. Yet, the very same people are in the crowds for a sports event or a rock concert when they can watch the same on their own TVs at home.

Perhaps we need a Krishna avatar[14] today, when people are surrounded by noise, pollution, hatred, terror and complete disregard for moral and ethical values in society. All we need to do is to look inward instead of imitating materialistic tendencies of the western world, which having become degraded are already looking to India and Asia for *gurus* to guide them towards unity and peace. How else can one explain the concentration of foreign devotees at Puttaparthi, Varanasi, Haridwar and other religious destinations in the country?

GANESH CHATURTHI

Ganesh is often known as *Vinayaka* or *Lambodara,* which means guardian of wealth. There is historic evidence that *Vinayaka* worship has been in vogue even in other countries such as Thailand, Japan, Germany and UK[15]. Adoration for Lord Ganesha as a principal deity

[14] The avatar of the 21st century is Sri Sathya Sai Baba, who advocates *Sathya*, *Dharma*, *Shanti*, *Prema* and *Ahimsa* for the spiritual upliftment of humanity. (*Sanathana Sarathi*, Vol. 39, No.6, June 1996, p.148).

[15] He is known by many names according to the different regions and languages in which He is worshipped.

has been mentioned in the Vedas. He is remembered on *chauth* or *chaturthi*, the 4th day of every month of the Hindu calendar, but most of all on *Ganesh Chaturthi* which is celebrated as His birthday which falls in the month of *Bhadrapada.*

Significance

Ganapathi is one who gives us spiritual potency and supreme intelligence, the two together termed as *Siddhi* and *Buddhi* respectively, which are referred to as His two consorts. *Ga* stands for *buddhi, na* for wisdom and *pathi* for master. Therefore, He is considered as the master of all knowledge, intelligence and wisdom and therefore, the Master of all *Ganas* — celestial beings. Knowledge of the seen and the unseen is the message of *Ganapati* whose advent is celebrated on *Ganesh Chaturthi.*

The main significance of the deity is symbolic and represented by His body parts. The symbolic significance of Ganesha's head is that He is equipped with elephantine intelligence. The large ears are equipped to hear even the minutest sounds, which emanate from the prayers and hymns of His devotees. His speech represents upholding of truth. Importance to His tusk has been highlighted as given in the *Gayatri Mantra* as He is one who instills purity in body and fearlessness in the mind. Charities are the ornaments of His hands. The elephant takes the praise and blame equally and is therefore, not only symbolic of strength but remover of obstacles and retainer of good things in an atmosphere of equal mindedness. He is therefore loved and celebrated[16].

The *Mooshika* (mouse) is His vehicle since it represents darkness and He rides it indicating that *Ganesha* dispels darkness and sheds light on the world and also reflects how much importance a wise man gives to the smallest of life forms.

One of the most popular Gods in India, Lord Ganesha is considered a symbol of auspiciousness and therefore important occasions, gatherings, weddings, functions and celebrations begin with a prayer to Him. No new venture – be it a new company, a new house, a new shop – is

---

16 *Avatar Vaani : Ganesh Chaturthi Sandesh, Sanathana Sarathi,* Vol 37, No. 10, Oct. 1994, p. 263.

inaugurated without praying to Ganapati. He is displayed at entrances, either by visuals or symbols, generally facing the rising sun in the east.

Mode of Fasting

Only a few people observe a fast on this festival as, for the most part, the general feeling is that Ganesha's birthday should be an occasion for feasting and not for fasting. The few who do keep a fast are allowed to eat various sweets like *til ladoo* (a round sweetmeat made of sesame, flour and sugar), *gajak, rewari* (sweets made of jaggery and nuts), along with tea and coffee.

It is a practice among Hindus when they visit the city of Gaya in Bihar, to give up what they relish most among fruits and vegetables. Today, unfortunately, this has become a way of giving up what we do not like.

In this connection, there is a mythological story, which reveals how the offering of fresh green grass to *Ganapati* during the festival, came about. The story goes that Parvati and Shiva were playing a game of dice with *Nandi,* the bull as the umpire. Because he declared Shiva the winner, although He had lost, Parvati cursed him. He sought forgiveness, as his verdict was given because he was doing his duty as a servant to his master. So Parvati withdrew the curse and asked him to offer to her son, Ganesha, what he most relished. *Nandi* declared that he loved fresh green grass and thus the practice of offering it to *Ganapati* was started.

Observance

Fasting, feasting and distribution of sweets offered to Lord Ganesha are important aspects of *Ganesha Chaturthi* rituals in India. Hindus pray to images of Lord Ganesha made especially for the occasion by craftsmen and street artisans.

On the day of the festival, idols of Lord Ganesha are placed on raised platforms in homes or in elaborately decorated outdoor *mandaps* for people to view and offer their reverence. A life-size clay model of Lord Ganesha is made 2-3 months prior to the day of *Ganesh Chaturthi.* The size of this idol may vary from 3/4th of an inch to over 25 feet. During installation in a temple, the priest, usually clad in red silk dhoti and shawl, invokes life into the idol amidst the chanting of mantras. This ritual is the *pranapratishhtha.* After this the *shhodashopachara,* that is, 16 ways of paying tribute follows. Coconut, jaggery, 21 *modakas* (rice flour and jaggery balls), 21 *durva* (trefoil) blades and red flowers are offered. The idol is anointed with red sandalwood powder (*rakta chandan*). Throughout the ceremony, Vedic hymns from the Rig Veda, *Ganapati Atharva Shirsha* Upanishad, and *Ganesha stotra* from the *Narada Purana* are chanted.

The whole community comes to worship *Ganesha* in beautifully decorated *mandaps.* These also serve as the venues for free medical checkup, blood donation camps, charity for the poor, theatrical performances, films and devotional songs, etc. during the days of the festival.

The entire family wears fresh clothes and assembles in the sacrosanct area. As they sing hymns, everyone is given some flowers and rice in their hands. These are later showered on Ganesha. *Ladoos* are placed in different corners of some households and eaten before the meal. Milk is offered to idols of Lord Ganesha at home and at temples, and *Ganesha puja* is performed at all temples. Sometimes a few families get together in one place for the *aarti.* Each ceremony is rounded off with people eating *modaks*, in keeping with Ganesha's style.

Hindu mythology has a story that Ganesha loved *modaks* and simply could not stop himself from eating them. In fact he devoured them by the hundreds. Amused by Ganesha's obsession with *modaks,* once the beautiful moon made fun of the chubby God. Ganesha was so furious with the moon that he cursed him, saying that his beauty would never remain constant. Since that day, the moon reveals itself in all its magnificence only once in 28 days. It is not considered auspicious to look at the moon on *Ganesha Chaturthi* as it is unbecoming towards the Lord. The message being to avoid anything associated with darkness or evil.

According to Swami Sivananda, one must read the stories connected with Lord Ganesha early in the morning on *Ganesh Chaturthi* day during the *Brahmamuhurta* period. If one prays with faith and devotion, He may remove all the obstacles that may be experienced on the spiritual path.

The sages believed that the hours of the very early part of the morning have an almost mystical quality that offers an excellent space for learning and deepening.[17]

In Rajasthan, people place a garlanded idol of Ganesha smeared with vermilion, right outside their homes. In front of the image, they keep a plate with some vermilion and turmeric powder so each passerby can put a pinch of the sacred powder on his forehead and feel blessed by Ganesha.

For 10 days, from *Bhadrapad Shukla Chaturthi* to the *Ananta Chaturdashi*, Ganesha is worshipped. The festival comes to an end on the day of Anant Chaudash. The image is taken from various *pandals,* doorsteps, localities and *puja* rooms through the streets in a procession accompanied by dancing and singing. After the final offering of coconuts, flowers and camphor is made, people carry the idol to the river or sea for immersion, symbolizing a ritual see-off to the Lord in his journey towards his abode in *Kailash* while taking away with him the misfortunes of mankind. The streets of Mumbai are packed with multitudes as each locality comes out on the streets with its Ganesha idols.

Firecrackers announce the arrival of the procession that halts every now and then for people to get a last glimpse of their favourite God and seek his blessings, for He is the remover of all obstacles. All join in this final procession shouting *Ganapathi Bappa Morya, Purchya Varshi Laukariya* calling Him to come again early next year. At dusk people return to their homes, awaiting Ganesha's return the following year.

Artists and sculptors start imagining how they will make an even nicer Ganesha next year. Housewives fret about making better *modaks* and *pedas* than others. The community at large thinks of superior and more elaborate *pandals* and processions, on there way back home and to work. In this country of more than a billion people, Ganesha plays his part. He generates work, adds meaning to their life and gives them hope.

---

17 Robin Sharma: *Discover Your Destiny*, p. 59.

Lokmanya Tilak's[18] strongest act to evoke nationalism through religious passions was the organization of festivals like *Ganesh Chaturthi* in Maharasthra, which not only inspired feelings of Hindu unity in Maharashtra, but gave freedom fighters an opportunity to meet when the British government illegalized gatherings, writings and slogans that could incite violence. Thanks to Tilak, *Ganesh Chaturthi* became a major festival of Maharashtra, where thousands of gigantic idols of Lord Ganesha are immersed by huge processions of worshipers shouting, Ganapathi *Bappa Morya,* in the Arabian sea and rivers of the state. The festival has now gained popularity all over India, with celebrations in South India and Gujarat being no less spectacular than those of Maharashtra.

Offerings

Every festival is celebrated by offering various culinary preparations. For *Vinayaka Chaturthi,* these preparations are of a very special kind without onion and garlic. In most parts of the country people offer *prasaad* to the image. The edible offerings are usually oil free and cooked by steaming. According to *Ayurveda,* food cooked through steam is easily digested. In addition, the festival is celebrated in month of *Bhadrapada,* when sesame and jaggery are newly harvested and easily available. The sesame seeds are powdered and mixed with rice flour and jaggery, made into balls and steamed, called *modaks* for the offering. This is seen in the hands of Lord Ganesha in every idol. Also, jaggery or *gur* is a cure for several ailments related to phlegm and bile, and therefore used during the monsoon season. Sesame seeds have the power to cleanse the lungs and improve vision. These offerings therefore, are made for their medicinal properties with the aim of curing both external and internal ailments.

Present Scenario

Each locality makes its own special *pandal.* People attribute considerable social significance to the festival, and communities compete with each other to put up the most outstanding *pandal,* choosing the best priest for each.

---

[18] Freedom fighter and statesman

Amidst much fanfare and revelry, the priest installs the idol of Ganesha in the locality to the chanting of *shlokas. Aarti* is performed twice a day — in the morning and in the evening. Most people of the community attend the evening *aarti.* They actually rush home from work to take part in the festivities and gather around the brightly-lit Ganesha.

Today, *Ganapati,* the elephant headed deity who is the most lovable God has everyone reacting with an instant smile, regardless of their religious beliefs. The scenario on the roads during this festival strikes one with awe, where trucks carry jumbo-sized images with carts tugging along carrying brightly painted idols of all sizes, all over the country.

However, *Ganesha Chaturthi* celebrations in post-blast Mumbai were heavily guarded with fewer visitors to the *pandals.* Those who came were cautious but who would want to harm beloved *Ganeshji*? A celebration that once symbolized solidarity and community-feeling has gradually become a self-conscious ritual. The state of affairs has hit the sentiments of even beggars who used to accompany processions for the celebrations and immersions and feel rich with *Ganapati's* benevolence.

Standing in the presence of Ganesha whether at home or in temples is a deeply moving and humbling experience. Hopefully with time He will uphold the safety of the country by His grace and love for mankind.

CHRISTIAN FASTS

Christianity has its roots in two ancient faiths, *Semitic* and *Persian.* The disciples of Jesus in Palestine in the year AD 30, believed in the coming of God's kingdom to mankind. This was because of the extraordinary wisdom of His teachings, the simplicity in His own life and the power He possessed to touch people's hearts, leading them towards goodness. Jesus was thus the Jewish Prophet whose teachings are the foundations of the Faith.

Christianity took root in India in AD 56, centuries before it reached Europe. It was St. Thomas an apostle of Christ, who founded the first Christian settlement in South India. Today there are more than 25 million Christians spread all over the country and form an inseparable part of society.

During colonial power, churches came up all over and represented the institutional form of shared faith and brotherhood. It is with Jesus of Nazareth that Christianity began, with immediate followers being Jews and therefore the affinity with Judaism and Israel remains till today. It was St. Paul who reinterpreted the memories and message of Jesus and transformed Christianity from a Jewish sect to a Gentile movement by the end of the first century. The Hebrew scriptures were sacred for early Christians who celebrated an ancient festival called *Epiphany* that focuses on God's revelation of Himself to the world, through the incarnation of Christ.

History

Christianity began with the belief in *One God* the god of Judaism, Christianity and Islam, and grew in opposition to the *Many Gods View*, rather than evolving from it. This unitarian view was gradually corrupted and the doctrine of the Trinity came to be accepted. The followers of Jesus however, continued to affirm the Divine Unity, as illustrated by the first commandment as quoted in the *Shephard of Hermas*[19] which is regarded as a book of revelation by the church. The commandment states:

> ***First of all believe that God is one and that He created all things and organized them and out of what did not exist, made all things to be, and He contains all things but alone is He uncontained.***

By the 4th century, the living Gospel had been masked in Greek philosophy. The gospel of Barnabas is the only surviving gospel written by a disciple of Jesus who was with him for 3 years, when he delivered His message.

There was a lot of rift between Christianity and the Roman Empire seen through the persecution and martyrdom of Jesus. It was only in the 4th century that Emperor Constantine accepted the faith and made it the official religion of his empire, and stabilized the internal structure of the Christian movement. This became a continuation of ancient

---

19 In: Ataur-Rahim (1991), p.9.

Greece and Rome, thus infusing spiritual power of Christ as Lord, and this spread gradually to Eastern Europe.

In 1483-1546, Martin Luther's reform movement divided the Christian community into Roman Catholics and Protestants. Separation of Church and State as developed in the US, led to religious toleration and freedom, which have since been the social and political expressions of Christianity since the 19th century. Today, it has emerged as a religion of faith, hope, love and a way of life seen in all communities.

The good that is being done through the communities in the field of education, empowerment and upliftment of the society in every country and globally, is proof of the practice of faith and devotion to the messages of Christ who exemplified patience, forbearance, love, sympathy and unity in His life. Outstanding examples are those of the Missionaries of Charity and Mother Teresa's contributions, the impact of the work of Deepalaya, World Vision—all organizations working untiringly for the upliftment of society in every country.

Those working with missionary zeal in India and globally are, Institutions of the Ramakrishna Order, Institutions of Sri Aurobindo, Sri Sathya Sai, Sri Chinmayananda and many more. Of course there are Indian organizations established by visionaries on the faith and hope of their founders, like Child Relief and You (CRY), Lok Kalyan Samiti and others, some are not even government aided who are doing excellent work in the area of education, healthcare and so on.

The Christian Year

This is also called the *church year* and is divided up by various festivals and seasons. Some like Christmas day fall on the same date every year, while others like Easter change, as do Indian fasts and festivals. Since many other festivals have their dates fixed in relation to the Easter date, they change every year with it. The list of festivals and fast days is presented in Table 3.6 in alphabetical order with short descriptions.

Table 3.6: Alphabetic list of festivals and holy days

No.	Day	Description
1.	All Saints' and all Souls' Day	Roman Catholics and Anglicans commemorate their saints and martyrs.
2.	Annunciation	Marking the visit of angel Gabriel to Virgin Mary, informing that she would be the mother of Jesus.
3.	Ascension	Commemorating the ascension of Christ, falls on 40th day after Easter Sunday.
4.	Ash Wednesday	Marks the beginning of Lent, and is a day of penitence.
5.	Assumption	Roman Catholics believe that Mary *assumed* body and soul into heaven.
6.	Candlemas	Commemorated the ritual purification of Mary 40 days after Jesus was born.
7.	Christmas	Holy day marking the birth of Jesus. Not only a Christian festival.
8.	Easter	The day of resurrection of Christ, and the most important Christian festival of Joy.
9.	Epiphany	Ancient festival focusing on revelation of God to the world through the incarnation of Christ.
10.	Eucharist	Ceremony when Jesus washed the feet of His disciples before the Last Supper.
11.	Good Friday	Celebrating the death and resurrection of Christ.
12.	Immaculate Conception	Roman Catholics celebrate Mary's conception without sin.
13.	Lent	Forty day's fast before Easter.
14.	Maundy Thursday	The Thursday before Easter, the day of the Last Supper.

(Contd...)

15.	Palm Sunday	Holy week leading up to Easter begins on Palm Sunday. Christians remember the last week of Jesus' life.
16.	Passion Sunday	Fifth Sunday in Lent and 2nd before Easter. Roman Catholic churches refer to the 6th Sunday in Lent since 1969 when the Liturgical calendar was revised.
17.	Pasch of the Crucifixion	Remembering the sacrifices Jesus made for mankind. A day of mourning.
18.	Pentecost	Celebrating gift of the Holy Spirit on a Sunday 50 days after Easter.
19.	Shrove Tuesday	Tuesday before Ash Wednesday, day of penitence and celebration being the last day before the fasts of Lent begin.
20.	White Saturday	The last day of the fast of Lent.

There are only a few recorded Christian fasts that are mentioned in the sacred text and other literature. These are:

- Lent
- Fast before Christmas

While people may choose to fast on certain holy days otherwise according to their individual sentiments, there is no religious rule that makes it compulsory.

LENT

Lent is an old English word meaning *spring,* the season of the year during which it falls. It recalls the events leading up to and including Jesus' crucifixion which is believed to have taken place in Roman occupied Jerusalem. This is the time leading up to the commemoration of Jesus' death and His resurrection, since He died for our sins and resurrected for our salvation. It is therefore a time to repent for the sins, by fasting.

Lent is the period of 40 days, when Christians replicate Jesus Christ's fast, sacrifice and withdrawal into the desert for that period. It is believed that by denying ourselves something we enjoy, we discipline our mind so that we are not slaves to our pleasures. Lent comes before Easter in the Christian calendar, and is a season of reflection and preparation before the celebrations of Easter that fall in the spring, when the days begin to get longer.

The date of the fast depends on the date of Easter and always begins on a Wednesday, no earlier than the 8th of February and no later than the 14th of March. This Wednesday is called *Ash Wednesday*, and the fast ends on the night after *White Saturday,* on the Holy Feast of Easter, or Easter Sunday.

Both the eastern and western churches observe Lent but they count the 40 days differently. The western church excludes Sundays (which is celebrated as the day of Christ's resurrection) whereas the Eastern Church includes them. The churches also start Lent on different days. Western churches start Lent on the 7th Wednesday before Easter (Ash Wednesday). Eastern churches start Lent on the Monday of the 7th week before Easter and end it on the Friday, 9 days before Easter. Eastern churches call this period the *Great Lent.* All days in Lent are appropriate for fasting or abstaining, but such fasting or abstinence is voluntary, and not required by cannon law.

Observance

All churches do not observe Lent, those that do observe it do so as a time for prayer and penance. Only a small number of people today, fast for the whole period of Lent, although some observe fast on *Ash Wednesday* and *Good Friday*. It is more common these days for believers to surrender particular favorite foods or a habit such as smoking. Some sacrifice non-vegetarian foods and some fast on Fridays, while others eat after 12 noon for the period of 40 days. Whatever the sacrifice, it is a reflection of Jesus' deprivation in the wilderness.

The symbolic colour used in some churches throughout the Lent period is purple, for drapes and alter frontals. This colour is chosen because, it is associated with mourning and therefore pain and suffering caused by the crucifixion, and also because it is associated with royalty, that celebrates Christ's resurrection and sovereignty.

Other observances followed during Lent are, giving up something we enjoy, doing of physical or spiritual acts of mercy for others, prayer, fasting, abstinence, going to confession and indulging in other acts that express repentance in general.

Mode of Fasting

Lent is marked by fasting and abstaining both from food and festivities. Under current Canon law in the Western Church, a day of fast is one on which Catholics who are between 18 to 60 years of age are required to keep only a limited fast. One may eat a single, normal meal and have two snacks, so long as these snacks do not add up to a second meal. Children are not required to fast, but their parents must ensure they are properly educated in the spiritual practice of fasting. Those with medical conditions requiring a greater or more regular food intake can easily be excused from the requirement of fasting by their pastor.

A day of abstinence is a day on which Catholics, 14 years or older are required to abstain from eating meat. Under the current discipline in America, fish, eggs, milk products, and condiments or foods made using animal fat are permitted in the Western Church, though not in the Eastern. Again, persons with special dietary needs can easily be excused from fasting by their pastor. Ash Wednesday and all Fridays during Lent are days of abstinence. Also, Good Friday, the day on which Christ was crucified, is another day of fasting and a test of self-discipline.

Ash Wednesday

Ash Wednesday is the beginning of Lent for Western Christian churches and was also popularly known as *Spy, Black* or *Mad Wednesday.* Traditionally, though Easter Sunday, the day of Resurrection, is the main festival , the Easter season starts from Ash Wednesday, the first day of Lent.

Significance

It is a day of penitence aimed at cleansing the soul before the Lent fast. *Palm Sunday* celebrates Jesus' triumphant entry into Jerusalem, so when the crosses used in the Palm Sunday service are converted to ashes, the worshippers are reminded that defeat and crucifixion swiftly followed triumph. Using the ashes to mark the cross on the believer's forehead symbolizes that through Christ's death and resurrection, all Christians can be free from sin.

Observance

On Ash Wednesday, believers in Catholic churches are given sanctified ash, which is made by burning palm crosses from the previous year's Palm Sunday. With the ashes, which are a symbol of penance and humility as mentioned in the Old Testament, the priest makes the sign of the cross on the forehead of the believer as a sign of penitence and mortality. The ash is sometimes mixed with anointing oil, which makes sure that the ashes make a good mark. The use of anointing oil also reminds the church goer of God's blessings and of the anointing that took place at their baptism. At some churches the worshippers leave with the mark still on their forehead so that they carry the sign of the cross out into the world. At other churches the service ends with the ashes being washed off as a sign that the participants have been cleansed of their sins. The marking of their forehead with a cross made of ashes reminds each churchgoer that:

- Death comes to everyone
- They should repent for their sins
- They must change themselves for the better
- God made the first human being by breathing life into dust, and without God, human beings are nothing more than dust and ashes

The shape of the mark and the words used are symbolic in other ways:

- The cross is a reminder of the mark made at baptism
- The phrase often used when the ashes are applied reminds Christians of the doctrine of original sin
- The cross of ashes may symbolize Christ's sacrifice on the cross as atonement for sins, which replaces the Old Testament tradition of making burnt offerings to atone for sin.

Mode of Fasting

Today, only a small number of people fast for all the days of Lent, although some observe fast on Ash Wednesday. Believers surrender favorite foods or smoking or other habits while others sacrifice non-vegetarian foods. Some churches focus less on fasting and encourage the performance of charitable deeds.

GOOD FRIDAY

Good Friday occurs between March 20 and April 23 on the Friday before Easter and is the day in the Holy Week on which the yearly commemoration of the Crucifixion of Jesus Christ is observed. It is observed every year on the Friday before Easter. There are few explanations as to why the holiday is known as *Good Friday* since it commemorates a sorrowful time in Christianity. Some scholars believe that *good* is a corruption of the word *God's* while others speculate that good was used to denote *holy*. In Portugal, the day is called the *Holy Friday* and in Denmark, Norway, Sweden, Finland and Iceland the day is called *The Long Friday*. On Good Friday, the entire Church fixes its gaze on the Cross at Calvary. Each member of the Church tries to understand at what cost Christ has won our redemption. In the 4th century the Apostolic Constitutions described this day as a day of mourning, not a day of festivity or joy, so this day was called the *Pasch (passage) of the Crucifixion*.

Significance

The day marked the crucifixion of Lord Jesus and is therefore a very important day for Christians as they try to seek forgiveness from Christ for His sacrifice. Since Christ was crucified for the welfare of people, some feel that this day is even more important for Christianity than Christmas. Good Friday brings together the religious sentiments of Christians all over the world.

Observance

A commonly observed scene at cathedrals and churches is pin-drop silence, hushed prayers and devotees silently chanting hymns as the

Christian community set aside their daily tasks to revere the sacrifice of Jesus on Good Friday. They offer prayers to God all day to relieve them of their sins and to enable them to be at peace with themselves.

The liturgy consists of three distinct parts, readings and prayers, the veneration of the cross, and the communion. Special prayer services are often held on this day with readings from the Gospel elaborating accounts of the events leading up to the crucifixion. The service is a three-hour-long one taking place from 12 noon to 3 p.m., consisting of sermons, hymns, and prayers centered around Christ's seven last words on the Cross.

The liturgical observance of this day of Christ's suffering, crucifixion and death evidently has been in existence from the earliest days of the Church. No Mass is held on this day, but the service of Good Friday is called the *Mass of the Presanctified* because Communion (in the species of bread), which had already been consecrated on Holy Thursday, is given to the people. Traditionally, the organ is silent from Holy Thursday until the *Alleluia* at the Easter Vigil, as are all bells or other instruments, the only music during this period being unaccompanied chanting.

The omission of the prayer of consecration deepens the sense of loss, since Mass throughout the year reminds us of the Lord's triumph over death, the source of our joy and blessing. The silent quality of the rites of this day reminds us of Christ's humiliation and suffering. Some congregations also re-enact Jesus' procession to the cross in a ritual known as *Stations of the Cross*, a Catholic tradition at the Good Friday service, where paintings and banners are used to represent scenes depicting the end of Jesus' life, from his betrayal to his death. Participants can sing hymns and pray as they move from station to station.

Since Christ died on the cross, the Friday before Easter is the most sombre day in the Christian calendar. In many countries, the day is observed as a public or federal holiday. In many English-speaking countries, most shops are closed for the day and advertising from television and radio is reduced or completely withdrawn.

Mode of Fasting

As early as the 2nd century, there are references to fasting and penance on this day by Christians, who, since the time of the early church, had observed every Friday as a fast day in memory of the Crucifixion. Traditionally, Catholics are to abstain from eating meat every Friday of the year as an act of penance, and a mark of reverence to their Lord. Nowadays, this is only a requirement during Fridays of Lent. During Fridays of the rest of the year, other methods of penance may be adopted, for example an extra prayer. As a modern tradition, many Catholics will eat fish on Good Friday but abstain from red meat. In many English speaking countries, Hot cross buns are symbolically prepared and eaten.

CHRISTMAS

Christmas marks the celebration of the birth of Jesus Christ and falls on the 25th of December according to the English calendar in Catholic and Protestant nations. In Eastern Europe, it is celebrated on January 7th because the Othodox church follows the Julian calendar. Armenian Christians celebrate it on 6th of January.

Christmas and other important days are not all celebration, but also include fasting as a remembrance of the penance that Jesus underwent for the sake of mankind.

Mode of Fasting

In ancient times, fasting was the norm one month before Christmas although orthodox Christians fast for 40 days and abstain from eating meat. This was done to cleanse their body and soul before the feasting at Christmas. The fasting period ends on Christmas eve with a midnight mass held in churches and the celebrations begin with family members all dining together on that night.

It was customary to prepare nine meals without meat, using beans, vine or cabbage sarmi, stuffed peppers, turshia, walnuts, apples, honey, ushav, loaf and so on. Everyone had to crack a walnut to see what was in store for them in the year ahead. A well-formed tasty inside meant a lucky or good year while an empty or shrivelled one forewarned of trouble.

Today only a small number of people fast that long before X'mas. It is however, more common for believers to surrender a habit like smoking, drinking or a favourite food and so on till the next Christmas when new vows are taken. Some sacrifice non-vegetarian foods and others eat after noon from the 1st to the 24th of December or Christmas eve, whichever calendar is being followed.

Following popular demand, a church in Thiruvananthapuram has decided to do away with Midnight Mass. Mass is now being conducted from 9 pm to 12 midnight instead of the present practice of beginning at midnight (Dec., 24) and concluding it the next morning (Dec 25). The changes were effected in keeping with the opinion of believers. The laity expressed inconvenience in attending Midnight Mass as a result of which the attendance of believers has been dropping every year. The church believed in the democratic rights of the faithful and respected their sentiments. It also decided to reduce the preparation and fast periods for celebration and reception of the Holy Eucharist from 12 to 6 hours. The church is aware of the hectic schedules and the lifestyles of the believers and thus decided to change with the times.

Message of Christ

The messages of Christ delivered through The Ten Commandments and actually practiced by Him in His life are:

- Believe that God is One
- Be Sincere and Simple minded — Do Right, Speak no Evil and Give generously
- Love Truth
- Observe Purity in Thought and Action
- Be Patient and Understanding — the devil dwells in ill temper
- Trust the Right — Uprightness is the straight way, wrongdoing the crooked one
- Fear the Lord and keep God's commands
- Exercise Control
- Cast off Doubt — Ask the Lord without doubting and you will receive
- Put sadness away as it leads to doubt and bad temper
- Cast off evil Desires

A man who has God in his heart is able to master all things. If one compares the messages of Jesus with those of Allah, Krishna, Sri Sai, Sri Aurobindo, Guru Nanak and other incarnations and philosophers, one finds that the teachings are the same, although the messages are conveyed in different settings suitable to the understanding of people at the time. An example will prove the point.

Mahendra Nath Gupta (M) was a teacher by profession, and had studied the New Testament so thoroughly that he could quote many passages from memory. Long after he had met Sri Ramakrishna, a Christian minister expressed his amazement at the depth of M's knowledge of the Bible. 'M' told him politely, ***Sir, we lived with Christ so we understand his teachings a little.*** To 'M' Sri Ramakrishna and Christ were the same indicating that he had seen Jesus's teachings in practice[20].

MUSLIM FASTS

Muslims follow a religion known as *Islam* preached by the Prophet Muhammad, who appeared in Arabia over 1300 years ago. According to the *Quran*, the holy book followed by Muslims, Islam is as wide in its conception as humanity itself. The Quran is a compilation of the teachings of the prophets of which the last one was *Muhammad*. It is believed that Islam is the religion of *Adam, Noah, Abraham, Moses* and *Jesus;* in fact just every prophet known in the world.

Prophet Mohammad revealed the Quran to the Muslims and was therefore the exponent of the Divine system which was perfected at his advent, in the form of a natural religion for all, just like other incarnations did after him. The Quran states:

> **This nature made by Allah *(God)* in which he has made men; there is no altering of Allah's creation — that is the right religion *(Quran 30: 30).***

Thus, according to the Quran, prophets are raised among different nations in different ages, and the religion of every true prophet is in

[20] Swami Chetananda (1991) p.192.

pristine purity which is the case with Islam. While the fundamental principles remain the same, the emphasis changes with the changing needs of humanity.

Significance of Islam

The dominant idea of Islam is the *making of peace.* According to the Holy Book a Muslim is one who has made peace with God and man. This implies complete submission to His will as He is the source of purity and goodness, it thus advocates doing good to fellowmen.Quoting from the Quran, these ideas are expressed as:

> ***Yea, whoever submits himself entirely to Allah, and he is the doer of good to others, he has his reward from the Lord, and there is no fear for him, nor shall he grieve (2:112).***

In fact *peace* is the greeting of one Muslim to another. Islam can thus be called a religion of *Peace.*

In addition, there is the mystical dimension of Islam which transcends all religions and is referred to as *Sufism.*

Sufism

Sufism originated with the foundation of the *Chisti* order in Khorasam in Persia. This is a way of experiencing truth and self realization, that takes the seeker on the path of serenity, piety and divinity by love and devotion to God, through the medium of poetry and music. Sufi music is therefore evolved, illuminated and enchanting as it is the outcome of the interface between Islam and Hinduism. The word *suf* comes from the Arabic and means *pure.*

The Dargah Sharif at Ajmer in Rajasthan, is the resting place of Saint Khwaja Moinuddin Chisti. It is known for its *Qawwals* and is a popular pilgrimage destination where one can feel the Sufi experience intensely. Particularly on Thursdays, the entire area of the Dargah Sharif is infused with spirituality.

Amir Khusrau created divine musical poetry that reached out to Truth. His interest in Indian ragas created mesmeric blends of Arabic and Iranian compositions. Sufism transcends all boundaries of language and religion. The music has the power to heal, and its philosophy leaves a soothing effect generating tranquility[21].

It is interesting to note that a Quran Institute in South Delhi opened a Sanskrit Study Centre on the eve of Holi, 2006. This is a revolutionary step that escaped media attention. It was stimulating to hear inaugural speakers emphasizing on the importance of Sanskrit for Muslims. Referring to the Islamic tradition that the first Prophet Adham (Adam of the common Jewish–Islamic theology) had appeared on Indian soil and therefore Sanskrit should be regarded as the *father tongue* of the Muslims. Some speakers also pointed out that the Quranic expression *deen-e-qayim* has a remarkably identical expression in Sanskrit – *sanathan dharma* that is followed by so many Indians. This should be seen as the true face of Islam.

An equal respect for each other's faith and a genuine interest in all spiritual traditions was once a part of Islamic culture. This characteristic has been unfortunately eclipsed by the misdeeds of a few fanatics. Alternately it is interesting to know how many in India know that the greatest Urdu poet, Ghalib had composed a long Persian lyric in praise of the city of Varanasi, entitled *Chirage-e-Dair* meaning light of the Temple. Similarly, Mohammad Iqbal too wrote a highly reverential poem for Ayodhya's Lord Ram. Quoting from the latter:

Hai Ram ke wujood pe Hindustan ko naz
Ahl-e-nazar samajhte hain usko imam-e-Hind
Ejaz us chirage-e-hidayet ka hai yahi
Raushan tar az saher hai zamaney mein sham-e-Hind.

Translated in English it reads as:
In the existence of Ram does India take pride
The farsighted see in him India's spiritual guide
The miracle of that Light of Righteousness is here
Brighter are India's evenings than dawns elsewhere.

21 Innervoice@hindustantimes.com

Now, if some Hindu religious institution undertakes to organize teaching of Islam it will be a fine step to the cause of social harmony in the country.

Fundamental Principles

The fundamental principles of Islam which are universally accepted and stated clearly in the Quran are:

- Belief in God and Divine revelation
- Prayer
- Charity and Mercy
- Unity
- Love and Brotherhood

Further the principles need to be practiced in daily life and in dealings with people. Mere belief is no good if it is not practiced through prayer, charity and mercy to bring a sense of unity and universal brotherhood through LOVE.

While Islam recognizes communion with God as the highest aim, as done in all world religions, it refuses to acknowledge the incarnation of the Divine as a Being. Muslims believe that this communion is not attained by bringing down God to man as an incarnation, but by man rising gradually towards God through spiritual progress and purification of life by renunciation of all sensuous desires and motives. Believing in Allah, indicates that the person possesses all the attributes of perfection This, in reality is not seen except in an avatar or incarnation according to the Vedic philosophy. While divinity is present in all human beings to different extents, it is a matter of fact, that no man is absolutely perfect.

Role of Prayer

Prayer is an outpouring of the heart's sentiments to God. The Islamic prayer called *Salat* is a spiritual rendition performed five times a day by Muslims, just as goodness needs to be practiced many times a day, according to the dictates of the Quran. However, if it is performed only as a ritual without sincerity of heart the Holy Book denounces it saying *Woe to (those) who are unmindful of their prayers* (107:4,5). The stated times and manner of praying has also been described for regularity and uniformity all over the world. Table 3.7 summarizes the different prayers and provides the timings and description along with the names given to each prayer.

Table 3.7: The Muslim prayers or salat

S. No.	Prayer	Timing and Description
1.	Salat-ul-Fajr	Early morning, after dawn and before sunrise.
2.	Salat-ur-Zuhr	Early afternoon when the sun begins to decline. Its time extends to the next prayer. This is the normal Friday congregational prayer in mosques.
3.	Salat-ur-Asr	Late afternoon, midway on it its course to setting. The time extends till just before sunset.
4.	Salat-ul-Maghrib	Immediately after the sun sets.
5.	Salat-ul-Isha	Early night when the red glow of sunset disappears in the West. The time extends till midnight.
6.	* Salat-ul-lail	Late night prayer after refreshed from sleep and before dawn. This is specially recommended in the Quran.
7.	* Salat-ul-duha	About breakfast time. This is the time at which the two Id prayers are said.

** These are two optional prayers.*

Moral Teaching

The Quran lays down certain specific criteria for people to follow, in order to ensure a disciplined and good life. These are summarized as:

- Be chaste but not by castration
- Serve God but not as monks
- Be submissive but not at the cost of losing self-respect
- Forgive but not in a manner as to bring destruction upon society by emboldening culprits
- Exercise rights but do not violate those of others
- Preach but not by abusing others

- Spend wealth so as to benefit the poor and needy (Quran – 9: 60)

The Quran also emphasizes *forgiveness* but in proportion to the crime committed. There is a stress on *Truth, Honesty and Good acts,* even to those who have done evil. The importance to *obedience to parents* has also been specified.

Dr. Abdelfattah Badawi a scientist from Egypt[22] made a comparative study between the Quran and Sai Baba's teachings and found them to be exactly the same. He found seven verses in the Quran which stated *Remember God often* while Baba uses the word *always* instead of *often*. There is absolutely no contradiction at all, between the teachings of the great sages, saints and prophets when the latter says:

> ***I don't want devotion to me, I want devotion to my teachings — Love your religion with devotion. Love God.***

If one studies *human values* too from the texts the conclusions are the same. Thus, science is all about searching and achieving in the outer world, while God is all about the inner world. If these teachings are practiced, the world would be a better place to live in, as the same have been preached by all religions, ancient sages, saints and avatars.

Role of Fasting

Wherever there is prayer for seeking God's grace, there is also fasting for atonement of wrong that may have been done. As in other religions, the procedures for fasting and breaking of fasts are also laid out for Islam in the Quran. Fasting is one of the five pillars of Islam being a requirement for every able Muslim from the age of puberty, and is compulsory for those who are mentally and physically fit. Some concessions and alternatives are suggested for those who are sick or travelling during fasting periods to make up for days missed. Through fasting devotees learn discipline, self-purification, self-restraint, generosity and compassion for the less fortunate.

---

[22] *Sanathana Sarathi,* Vol.49, No.8, p. 244-249. Scientific consultant for Ministry of Military Production, Egypt and author of books in Arabic and English.

In Islam, fasting is considered a pilgrimage, because it does not mean just abstaining from food, but from every kind of evil through the journey of life. For this reason the ritual of going to Mecca and Medina for *Haj*, a pilgrimage, is recommended for every believer. In ancient times, fasting was seen as a period of suffering or deprivation in times of mourning or sorrow. Gradually the meaning of Islam has changed, and it is now seen to contribute to ethical, moral and spiritual betterment of man. The noted fasting periods are in the month of *Ramadan* and in bereavements or mourning as at *Moharram* or whenever they occur. These are briefly discussed.

RAMADAN

Muslims fast during the month of *Ramadan* which falls in the 9th month of the Islamic calendar, *Al-Hijrah,* in which the first verses of the Quran were revealed to Prophet Mohammad. The Holy Book calls upon Muslims to observe fasts for 29 or 30 days or till the sighting of the new moon. These fasts are known as *Rozas.*

Being a lunar month, Ramadan falls in different seasons in different years, and according to the days in a particular month, the fasting period may sometimes be too lengthy and impractical for people to observe, in some countries. In such cases, the observance of fasts may be transferred to a season which has shorter days. For example, fasts may be kept in a season when the dawn to sunset would be 15 hours, which is the duration of the fast in *Mecca* and *Medina*. Old people, the sick, pregnant and lactating women are exempted, provided they give food to the poor in charity every fasting day.

Charity in Islam is therefore a permanent feature, a kind of tax on the rich for the poor so that a feeling of brotherhood is established. A 1/40th portion of earnings is payable to the public treasury for the 8 categories of people considered needy, as mentioned in the Quran, for whom the funds could be used.

Observance

Fasting in the month of Ramadan is obligatory for all healthy Muslims. Infants, children below 12 years, pregnant and lactating women, the sick and very old are however, exempt from the observance. Throughout the month, the devotees kneel on their rugs beneath the open sky and jesture with both hands, lifting their hearts to the divine presence which they feel during prayer time. There is an ambience of thanksgiving, hope and piety. Fig. 3.4 presents the view of a congregational prayer setting.

Fig. 3.4: Congregational prayers during Ramadan.

Some people follow the practice of cutting themselves off from all worldly connections during the last 10 days of the holy month by spending day and night in mosques. This is known as *I'tikaf* and is a voluntary practice, not dictated by the Quran. *I'tikaf* helps to control man's passions and once this is mastered, the greed for illegally acquiring what belongs to others also vanishes. Fasting is prescribed in the Holy Quran and its object stated as follows — *Fasting is prescribed for you ... so that you may guard against evil (2:83).* It teaches the ways by which evil tendencies can be suppressed and the good improved.

Early morning *Namaaz* is sounded in mosques at 3 am. and the devout pray while melodious music fills the atmosphere in which peacocks can be heard calling out. They appear to be pleading with man to get rid of prejudices and rise above petty strife and become tuned to nature.

The fast consists of total abstinence from food, water, smoking and other sensual pleasures from break of dawn to sunset on each day of the month. There is however, a greater significance to fasting than mere abstinence, the real objective being to inculcate in man, the spirit of avoidance of sin and the cultivation of virtues. Foods that are forbidden to followers of Islam are indicated in the Quran:

> ***He has forbidden you what dies of itself, and blood and flesh of swine...but whoever is driven to necessity not desiring, nor exceeding the limit, no sin shall be upon him; surely Allah is forgiving, merciful (2:173).***

Once the afternoon prayers, the *Zuhar namaaz*, is over, *Iftar* eateries spring up in every nook and corner in these areas. Film music gives way to Quranic cassettes and traditional hymns. In mosques, the white capped heads rise and bow in a synchronized manner to the rhythm of the prayers inside. A strange calm steals over the areas which are otherwise congested and bustling with activity and noise. The moment of sundown is *Iftar*, a time of bliss, when after a day's hardship the family union takes place. As the siren wails for the final moment, the silence breaks into a mood of fervour and joy.

During Ramadan, study and recitations from the Quran, prayers and lectures in mosques help to strengthen family and community ties. It is accompanied by performance of good deeds and charities throughout the month, in general, fixing the mind on God and refraining from excessive gossip or sinful acts of anger, greed and so on. Thus fasting helps Muslims to be moderate in every thing they do. At sunset the day's congregational prayers are completed either at home with family and friends or in mosques as the case may be and the fast is broken at sundown.

Breaking of Fast

After sunset on each fasting day, the fast is broken by wishing each other well through embraces and expressing happiness at the successful completion of the fast. They then get together in family or friendship groups and partake of the delicacies prepared for the end of the fast. They however, start with a hot or cold beverage, dates and some other snacks, depending on the season and climate at the time in any region or part of the world. After performing *Magrib* or the dusk prayers they have a hearty meal. The food may be prepared at home, bought from outside or families and friends may dine out in restaurants as per convenience. What is enjoyed is the sharing of joy and food, expressed through togetherness and eating.

Daily distribution of food or money in charity is part of the celebration of completing the fast. People also send food to mosques for the breaking of fasts since people congregate there for prayers and break their fast at sundown. Food is also exchanged with neighbours, a practice that encourages neighbourliness and brotherhood.

Thus, the fast is broken by the power of love and bonding, interaction and feasting every day. The prime time of *roza* everyday is called *Iftar*, a time for reunion with family to relish a host of Ramadan delicacies like *Kachalu, khajoor, phenis, sheermal, phirni, pakoris, pulaos* and the like. Today, greeting cards are also available, and the atmosphere is overwhelming from all night foodstalls and the rekindled liveliness of the market.

Ramadan or Ramzan time is marked by evening feasts and spreading of discipline and good cheer. The ambience of Ramadan is only seen in certain areas of the walled city in localities like Jama Masjid, Lal Kuan, Ballimaran, Chandni Mahal, Bara Hindu Rao and other traditional Muslim areas. The lights come on before sunset and the *muezzins* will call the *azaan* from the minarets of the many mosques in these areas. All along Billimaran, Jama Masjid, and Jamia Nagar, people enjoy *Iftar* parties in small or large groups.

MOHARRAM

Moharram is a day of mourning observed with solemnity and fasting, as it was on the 10th day of Moharram that Hazrat Imam Hussain along with many family members and 72 others were brutally killed in public by *Muawiah,* the ruler of *Syria* at the time. Moharram commemorates the martyrdom of Hussain, the younger grandson of Prophet Mohammad, and therefore is observed as a fast day.

Observance

The Shivalla Mohalla of Varanasi makes the most artistic *Tazia* which is a mausoleum-like artifact, taken in procession on the day of Moharram. The first tazia was assembled 600 years ago, and was a contribution from Timur of Persia, who was fascinated by the Indian *rath* or chariot, and on return to Persia encouraged the tradition of carrying chariots in Moharram processions, which got shaped into tazias. The tradition is still prevalent and carried on by Sufi saints who made Moharram symbolic of the demolition of religion, caste and class barriers. Tazia literally means to mourn. The ritual effigies resemble the effigies of evil which are buried on that day, believed to be in the same spirit as burning of the effigies of Ravana and others representing evil at Dussehra[23].

Moharram is observed in India by people belonging to all communities. A tazia procession in Delhi is usually taken out from Imambara, Pahari Bhojla to Jor Bagh enroute the Matia Mahal chowk, Ajmeri Gate, etc.

Interestingly, Varanasi the land of *ghats* and Vedic excellence, has a mixed tradition of observing Moharram, with a number of Hindu families participating in the observance of fast and other rituals to show solidarity with their Muslim brothers.

Need of the Hour

The intelligentsia and priests of the countries with various religions should, using all means at their command, try to spread the message of the Quran, Bible, Vedas as the great sages, seers, prophets and philosophers have done in the past. Jehadis should be rehabilitated in the name of God. They should be infused with the teachings of the Holy Books to make them understand the meaning of Islam, and tell them that employing armed hostilities is completely un-Islamic, and

23 Firoz Bakht Ahmed : innervoice@hindustantimes.com

embracing Islam is not a sanction for destruction of life that God created for us to enjoy.

The Quran and all other Holy Books and prophets of all religions, call for universal harmony between all races, peoples, tribes, sects, clans and so on. Islam even says that if a Muslim ruler is hostile to non-Muslims, he should go. Some quotations will be useful from the Quran:

> ***Let not your own hands throw you into destruction. Do not destroy yourselves; Surely God is most gracious to you. (On suicide)***

> ***Allah dislikes those who indulge in arson, loot and killings. (Sura Al-Bakr, verse 114).***

The youth need to be informed and convinced that today there is only one religion, the religion of Love. Religious leaders have over the years lost the peoples' trust and confidence. This needs to be built back through exemplary practice. The exploitation that people feel leads to frustration, helplessness, anger and violence. People need to understand the positive messages by reading the Holy Books in today's knowledge society and get convinced about the purpose of life.

JAIN FASTS

In the 6th century BC, the vedic religion was getting extinct and Hinduism was at a critical stage. Jainism was at that time not only a mature and living religion but one that claimed antiquity. All its facets had been fully developed by that time and have remained almost unchanged for the last 2500 years.

This religion is important because it has greatly influenced practically all religious thinking of India. Today, it represents a small sect of the Jain community of about 4 million followers mostly belonging to prominent professions.

The roots of Jainism are found in the *Sramanic* movement of the 6th century BC. The wandering monks were the models of religious perfection as opposed to the religious and social order of the Brahmins. Non-Hindu Sramanic faiths with their own set of rules and practices which included some Hindu concepts like *Karma* and *rebirth,* symbolic worship such as the *Stupa*, the *Dharma Chakra, chitya* trees and *Ratna-traya.* Jainism displayed traits of *Ahimsa* and *Moksha.*

Jainism represented extremes of world denial and ascetism and made significant contributions in helping the cultural fusions and assimilation of cultures, beliefs, traditions and concepts of diverse alien races and tribes. Jainism is quite influential in West Bengal, Orissa, Punjab, Rajasthan, Gujarat, Tamil Nadu and Kerala.

Jainism

The word *Jain* is derived from the Sanskrit word *JINA* which means 'conqueror' and thus it means one who has conquered the evils of *raag* or attachment, *dwesh* or aversion, jealousy, greed, passions and desires to attain purity of mind and heart.

According to Jainism, the soul is eternal with infinite knowledge, cognition, power and happiness. It has the ability to expand and contract according to the body it resides in. Its nature is to always go up. It is bonded by material particles called *karmas* which act as insulation and hence does not let the soul achieve and realize its full capabilities. Karma brings about good, bad, pure or other thoughts in a person who acts accordingly. However, the soul has the power to make efforts to change these thoughts for better results or totally eliminate them and ultimately achieve *Moksha. Attachment* and *Aversion* are the main reasons which do not let the soul make such efforts. All religious practices of *Jains* are to make the soul free of material particles of karma, that is attachment and aversion, so that it can enjoy its full capabilities. The *Jains* are the followers of twenty-four *Tirthankars* for whom they have the highest reverence.

Tirthankar

Jains believe that every soul is capable of attaining the state of *Godhood* when it is free from passions, is beyond attachments and aversions and has shed the shackles of karmas, and through the process of purification of the soul, has achieved *Moksha* (salvation), thus bringing to an end the cycle of births and deaths. The entire devotion of the *Jains* is therefore concentrated on *Tirthankars* to become like them and attain salvation. *Tirtha is* the means of crossing over, and *kara* means one who makes it possible. *Tirthankar* is thus a spiritual guide who helps one to cross over the ocean of worldly existence. Hence, they are the personages who delineate the path of final liberation or emancipation of all living beings from the successive cycle of births and deaths.

Tirthankars are the pathfinders, facilitators and the worthiest exemplars, being the conquerors of the Self (*Arihantas*), who have in the evolutionary apothesis attained the transcendental state of body, mind and soul (*Kaivalya),* in which an individual is completely emancipated and endowed with cosmic consciousness.

There are 24 *Tirthankars, Bhagwan Rishabhdev* being the first one, and the pathfinder of the sect. His name also appears in the *Rigveda, Vishnu Purana* and the *Bhagvad Purana. Bhagwan Mahavira* was the 24th Tirthankar and with him Jainism has come to be identified. The crux of Jainism could be defined in three words: *Ahimsa Parmo Dharma.*

Ahimsa

Ahimsa or non-violence is at the core of all *Jain* thought and philosophy. It is not limited to human life, but extends to all life around. To minimize the violence they cause to organisms, some of which they accept as being inevitable, Jains have fashioned a lifestyle which includes covering their mouth when they speak, using only boiled water, sweeping the floor before they tread on it and so on. *Jain* monks and nuns follow this lifestyle religiously. When it rains, monks and nuns do not go out in the rain for fear of harming organisms living in water. So they do not travel during the rainy season. The four months of the rainy season, the *chaturmas*, are spent in one place.

Ahimsa is followed not only in policy but also in aspects of day-to-day living, in which there has not been a single instance reported, of communal riots involving the Jains.

Eating Habits

Jains are pure vegetarians and their food habits are based on the principle of *Ahimsa* or non- violence. They do not take fish, flesh, eggs, honey, and alcohol. They confine their diet to fruits, vegetables, nuts, pulses, cereals and milk. But the degree and strictness to which it is followed, depends on individuals, and their family eating habits. The strict followers avoid vegetables which grow underground such as onions, garlic, potato, and other root vegetables. This is because these vegetables being grown underground are the depository of countless small creatures. Foods generally avoided by Jains have been summarized in Table 3.8.

Table 3.8: Foods avoided by Jains

Description	Foods to avoid
Foods involving injury or death of animals	Meats.
Root vegetables	Potato, onion, garlic and so on.
Intoxicants	Wine, beer, other substances
Foods unfit for human consumption	Stale, infested or infected foods
Vegetables with many seeds	Eggplant

When one consumes food which provides no nourishment it alters the state of mind, and causes disease, leading one to commit violence against self and therefore tobacco, alcohol and drugs are avoided. Stale foods are not eaten as eating such foods would involve consuming bacteria which grow in unpreserved foods. In the monsoon season, a meal would also not include green leafy vegetables, cauliflower, etc as during this season these vegetables get infested with living organisms.

Another common practice among strict followers is renunciation of night meals, for the reason that innumerable creatures come out at night. Besides, there are scientific benefits of day-time eating. Generally it is not recommended to sleep for two to three hours after a complete meal in order to allow time for digestion and to reduce reflux while lying down. It takes two to three hours for a large meal to pass from the stomach to the intestines, and may take even longer if the meal is high in fat content. Food eaten after sunset is not considered conducive to health.

Many emphasize on drinking of boiled and filtered water. The reason for drinking boiled and filtered water is to minimize the consumption of any minute water borne organisms. There is scientific evidence also, to support that boiling of water is safe in order to sterilize it.

Some people argue that just like eggs which Jains avoid, the milk of a cow or goat is also part of the body. However, there is a vast difference between milk and eggs. This understanding is incorrect because an egg represents the progeny of a hen whereas milk does not procreate. In fact, if the milk producing cow or goat is not milked at the proper time, agony is caused to it. By taking milk out of the body of a cow or goat, no harm is done to their lives; whereas egg is avoided because of its potential fertility.

Along with the renunciation of wine and meat, Jain religion also preaches the avoidance of honey because many bees may be killed in the process of its extraction. Gelatin is a common ingredient which is avoided because it is derived from animal bones. The food colouring cochineal present is many fruit drinks is avoided because it is derived from crushing tiny insects.

Vegetarianism is followed not only for its religious and spiritual contributions but also contributes to health. The lower saturated fat, protein and animal protein intake in a vegetarian diet along with high fiber and complex carbohydrates, antioxidant and phytochemical content are the likely reasons for lower rates of cardiovascular diseases, colon cancer, kidney disorders, and so on in vegetarians. In fact, most Jains maintain a healthy lifestyle by avoiding tobacco and alcohol.

Jain Sects

Jainism has two major traditional streams, the *Digambers,* whose monks give up all material possessions including clothes, and *Shwetambers* whose monks too give up all material possessions but they are clad in white. The latter have been further divided into *Deraavaasi* who are temple goers and indulge in idol worship, and *Sthaanakvaasi* who do not worship idols. There is another group among *Shwetambers* called *Teraapanthi* who do not worship idols and emphasize on 13 virtues. Digambers are also divided into 2 or 3 groups. It should be emphasized that these differences are minor and of no consequence to the present times. The doctrine followed by all Jains is identical who believe in the same basic principles and worship the 24 *Tirthankars.*

The Jain community like other communities throughout the world annually celebrates many social and religious functions. The three important festivals are *Paryushan, Deepawali* and *Mahavir Jayanti.* Since austerity is emphasized in Jainism, fasts are strictly observed on the days of their festivals.

Chaturmas

The four months of monsoon or *chaturmas,* as they are known in *Jainism* are considered to be months of abstinence and fasting. The first two months of the monsoon season are known as *Shrawan* and *Bhadharwa* and rituals are observed more strictly in them than in the two latter ones. Stricter believers don't eat any green vegetables at all during the first two months as the high humidity present encourages the proliferation of life which is rampant not only in plants, but also in insects, worms, microscopic bacteria and organisms that thrive on these plants. Hence, the Jains abstain from consuming them. The body's digestive system and metabolic processes too, are sluggish and not functioning optimally during this period.

PARYUSHAN PARVA

Paryushan a major festival celebrated during the auspicious month of *Bhadrapada* of the Hindu calendar which extends from the 5th to the 14th day of the bright fortnight. The festival expresses the celebration through which the *karmic* matter attached to the soul is totally burnt or vanquished (both internally and externally) and thus is known *Paryushan* or self-purification. This festival is also known as *Das Lakshana Parva.*

The *Digambers* and the *Swetambers,* both celebrate the self-uplifting festival with great enthusiasm. The 5th day of the bright fortnight of the holy month of *Bhadrapad* is auspicious for both. The *Digambaras* celebrate this festival annually for 10 days, from the 5th day to the 14th day of the bright half of the month, which then ends on *Ananta-Chaturdasi.* Whereas the *Swetambers* celebrate it only for 8 days *(athai)* and end it with *Samvatsari Parva* on *Bhadrapada Shukla Panchami.* The *Digambar Jains* celebrate *Das Lakshana Parva* starting on the last day of *Shvetambar Paryushan* i.e., on *Samvatsari Parva.*

It is a celebration of spiritual awareness and is known as the festival of fasts. In this period, participants practice self-purification, self-criticism and self-control in order to achieve self- improvement. The festival ordains the Jains to observe the 10 universal supreme virtues in daily practical life. Besides assuring a blissful existence in this world and the other world for every living being, it aims at the attainment of salvation — the supreme ideal for the soul.

Jainism is a prehistoric religion propounded by the first *Tirthankara* Lord Aadi Nath. Upon these grounds, we think that the celebration of *Paryushan Parva* is a holy tradition coming down from the ancient past to the present times.

Significance

Two popular titles of this festival, viz. (i) *Paryushan Parva* and (ii) *Das Lakshana Parva* are in vogue; but the mode of performance and aim of the festival is same.

Devotees during these days rededicate themselves to practice of *dharma* as the scriptures define it. *Jain* literature defines religion in three different ways :

- Nature of a substance
- Conduct of an individual
- Das Lakshana

Every substance has a nature. The nature of fire is to burn, nature of water is to cool, nature of scorpion is to bite, and nature of mother to love and so on. According to the *Jain* philosophy, the nature of every living being is its religion and it is to be happy eternally and not to have pain at all.

The conduct of an individual is his religion. How we live and do our daily duties is religion. The conduct should be right and based on right knowledge about the objective to be achieved. Performing ones duties righteously is religion.

The *Das Lakshana* or the Ten Commandments are the religion and are considered a prelude to attaining *nirvana* or *eternal bliss.* It consists of 10 traits, which have been equated with 10 stepping stones leading towards realization of the goal. Each trait is assigned to one day of the *Paryushan* festivities as shown in Table 3.9.

Table 3.9: Ten commandments of Jainism

Traits	Significance
Mardawa	means gentleness of nature or humility or giving up of pride. Pride leads to immodesty and impropriety of conduct and so should be given up.
Arjava	honesty and righteousness. It implies leading a life free of deceit and craftiness. Our day-to-day dealings and business should be conducted with honesty and uprightness.
Satya	or truthfulness is understanding and believing in the true nature and form of things. Being truthful and behaving ethically with fellow beings is what *satya* is all about.
Shauch	means cleanliness or freedom from defilement. It involves keeping the Atman free of the *Kshayas* and other vices of the world.
Sanyama	means practicing moderation and abstinence in everyday life.
Tapa	means devotional penance. Leading the life of a recluse or hermit while keeping oneself engaged in meditation and study of religion.
Tyaga	is to relinquish or to give away in charity; to donate one's material possessions and wealth willingly for the welfare of the needy.
Akinchan	is applying self-imposed limit for worldly possessions. Even the desire to have more wealth and material gains is kept in check through constant practice of *Akinchan*.
Brahmacharya	or celibacy means maintaining chaste, moral behavior under all circumstances.

(Contd...)

Kshama	The last day of *Paryushan* is celebrated as the day of universal forgiveness among one another for any hurts or offences committed knowingly or unknowingly by them.

These virtues act as buffers in resolving interpersonal conflicts, family feuds and communal tensions and thus can play an important role in promoting communal peace and social harmony. At the individual level, observance of these traits can help us attain mental peace and pave the way for social interaction and all-round prosperity.

Observances

Paryushan Parva is an annual, sacred religious festival of the Jains. All members of Jain community irrespective of social, economic or gender status participate with full vigor and zeal in the various religious rituals and cultural programs. The festival is woven around the need for restraint in food, speech, and other material activities.

Throughout the festival of *Paryushan*, people go to the temples. All the holy places are crowded with followers performing introspection (*pratikraman*). Devotees listen with rapt attention to the holy sermons of the saints and learned Jain scholars arranged during the 10-day festival where tales of *Lord Mahavira* are narrated. The *Namokar Mantra* is chanted everyday. Those who do not fast come back home after worship for lunch and those who fast remain in the temple the whole day meditating or participating in the reading of scriptures or attending religious discourses. In these celebrations lie dormant, the seeds of well being, peace and happiness. On the eve of this festival, all activities, which add to social discord or bitterness are declared taboo from the temple pulpits. These celebrations harbinger social harmony and amity and preach the Jain motto of *Live and Let live*.

The sixth day of *Paryushan* is *Dhoop Dashmi,* a day to clean temples and hold social gatherings. Many married women take vows to observe fasting on this day every year for 10 years. On this occasion, *dhoop* (incense) is offered in temples.

The householders celebrate the festival jointly by suspending all their business, agricultural and commercial activities for the time being. *Das*

Lakshana Parva is the most suitable occasion for giving donations and charities; and on the last day of the festival, the house-holders observe full-day fast and make every attempt to donate to religious and social institutions in cash or kind according to their capacity. For example, donations are given for sick birds that are comforted and deposited for care in the Bird Hospital in *Lal Mandir*, Delhi, which is a landmark religious place for *Digambaras* sect of *Jainas* in the capital. Very often Jain scholars viz. poets and writers get their literary works initiated during the festival days and thus pay their homage to this grand festival.

At the end of the celebration of *Paryushan*, i.e., the day following *Anant Chaudash* or *Samvatsari*, is the *kshamapna* or *kshamabhavo divas*. Everyone asks for forgiveness from relatives, friends and neighbors for any offence which may have been intentionally or unintentionally committed. Practice of forgiving transcends religious boundaries. People also send cards to relatives and friends asking for their forgiveness. They also forgive those who come to them with the same request. *Kshama* is thus twice blessed, by the one who seeks it and the one who grants it. This process is akin to bathing the soul to cleanse it of all impurities caused by attachment and aversion. When the 10 day celebration is over, this festival leaves behind deep impression on the mind and heart of every Jain — young and old.

Mode of Fasting

According to *Jain* tradition, there are four forms of restraints practiced during fasting. These are:

- *Anshan*—complete fasting
- Unodari—eating less
- V*ritti-sankshepa*—selective restraint
- *Rasa-parityaga*—taste-selection

Some Jains observe fast for the entire month of *Bhadrapada* in which the festival falls, while others fast for 1 to 8 or 10 days during *Paryushan*. The last day of fasting period is known as *Samvatsari* or *Anant Chaudash*. All *Jainas* are expected to observe fast on this day.

Anshan

The Jain fast lasts for 24 hours from one sunrise to the next and is a complete *nirjal* fast or adapted to one's own devotional prowess and physiological capacity. Extreme followers do not even brush their teeth with paste, or take medicines of any kind. Only intake of boiled water in limited quantities may be consumed, and that too only during daytime, since renunciation of night meals is observed during the period. During the festival days, the Jains drink boiled water at home and abstain from drinking in a restaurant or in the houses of non-Jainis.

Unodari

Those who cannot fast, practice *unodari*, that is, eat less than what is needed to satisfy one's hunger. It is a proven fact that by eating less, one can lead a healthy, long life. Continuously stuffing the stomach is the cause of many illnesses — it can even reduce one's lifespan. *Unodari* is not less important than fasting. Temperance in eating is a very important formula for good health.

Vritti-sankshepa

Restraint in eating was the main component of Mahavira's self-mortification. A controlled diet helps us conserve energy. Energy is reduced in persons who overeat. Over-eating and constipation have a close connection because food does not get digested, as it should have. This leads to other problems like sleeplessness, depression and restlessness. Bhagvan Mahavira explained in the language of his times that the food intake of a healthy person consists of 32 morsels. The number of items to be eaten can be limited in many ways. One may decide not to eat more than five items. Many Jains decide to eat a fixed number of items during *Paryushan* e.g., some decide to eat only two cereals throughout the festival, one could be wheat flour and the other could be any one pulse preparation.

Some avoid certain foods or not eat on certain days. For example, it is a common practice to abstain from eating fruits and vegetables on *Chaturdasi, Panchami,* and *Ashtami* falling during days of *Paryushan.* The devotees either fast or take one meal on these days. However, some strict observers follow this practice throughout the year. One could opt to eat only at select places. During *paryushan,* Jains eat and drink at home and abstain from eating or drinking in a restaurant or in the houses of non-Jains. As a matter of fact, some do not eat anything from the market be it bread, butter or cold drinks.

Rasa-parityaga

Sensory restraint is to avoid eating foods of a certain taste. It involves renouncing foods that evoke passion/*rasa*. The six foods, oil, ghee, curd, sugar, salt and milk, which provoke excitement are avoided. Interestingly, all these foods are rich in fat and contribute to the unhealthy *part* of the vegetarian diet. Hence, reducing them is not just a step towards spirituality but also towards better health. It's a common practice during *paryushan* festival. Devotees sacrifice one taste for each day of the week as indicated in Table 3.10.

Table 3.10: Sensory restraints followed by Jainas

Week day	Taste/Foods	Foods avoided
Monday	Green (Fruits & vegetables)	All fresh fruits and vegetables
Tuesday	Sweet	Sugar, jaggery, artificial sweeteners
Wednesday	Ghee	Ghee, vanaspati
Thursday	Milk	Milk, porridge, *kheers*, ice creams
Friday	Curd	Curd, *raitas*
Saturday	Oil	Oil
Sunday	Salt	Salt

Note : The taste of a particular food is to be avoided e.g., on Thursday milk is avoided. But the person observing the fast can have curd because milk and curd have different tastes. All the preparations containing milk in its original form are avoided.

This is a festival of self-discipline through fasting and other ascetic practices. An extraordinary feature of the Jain fast is that all sexual contact between couples is forbidden for the duration of the fast, even if only the wife or the husband has refrained from food. Although the vow of celibacy, *brahmacharya* does not demand the vow for fasting, the Jains seem to perceive the latter incomplete without the former.

Ancient sages laid down the *sadhna* or practice of *maunam* i.e., silence to maintain purity of speech believing that excessive talk could lead to sins and abuses that hurt others through speaking of untruths or creating emotional excitement. *Maun* does not mean absence of speech alone but also absence of thoughts. If thoughts are removed, the mind gets dissolved. Many people observe silence while having their meals during this festival.

The Jain fasts are of different kinds and while there are individuals in the community who subject themselves to severe forms of penance by forsaking food for days on end, for the general householder, it is the shorter fasts, which are undertaken. These are attempted even by younger groups. A fast may involve eating only at one sitting, or once a day. Prescribed food items are consumed after sunrise and before sunset. Fasts like the *Ekasana* and *Ayambil* are undertaken on a large scale. During the *Ayambil*, for instance, the observer concentrates on partaking simple bland food and abstains from eating green vegetables, milk and spices. *Ekasana* means eating once a day. Even those who do not observe the fast abstain from eating root vegetables, tobacco, drinking and smoking and refrain from eating after sunset.

Breaking of Fast

Fasting for a day only is considered child's play among the Jains. Many, especially women during the sacred week of *paryusana-parva* undertake fasting extending between 1 to 10 days. Even small children observe partial fast for 8 to 10 days without experiencing any ill effects. The formal conclusion of a fast takes place long after sunrise, with a sip of boiled water, usually after an offering of food is made to a Jain monk or nun visiting the household for collecting alms. The breaking of fast especially after longer periods of fasting, are occasions for joyous celebrations by the relatives and friends of the person who has completed the vow faultlessly and cheerfully. Along with the fellow members of the community, they gather to feed such a person with spoonfuls of boiled water or fruit juice. The participating community shows in this manner its delight in the spiritual progress made by one of its own and also earns merit by the act of giving food to so worthy a person. They also give gifts to the person as a token of their appreciation of the effort made to observe the fast. Those who have not kept long fasts also break the fast after going to the temple usually with a sip of water.

To sum up, *Paryushan Parva* is a Jain festival of self-introspection, self-enlightenment and self-achievement, which ultimately leads to the one and only one final goal of liberation or salvation.

Present Scenario

As a community, Jains need to be mindful of what is served in restaurants. McDonalds recently admitted that it used beef fat in its French fries preparations and also settled a lawsuit for the same. Cheese can contain rennet which comes from cow's intestines. Jelly has gelatin which comes from animal bones, though these days some companies are manufacturing it synthetically, one can never be sure. Many cakes, cookies and ice creams may contain eggs. These days, the inclination to use ready-made articles of food and drink is gaining popularity. In the use of such articles, knowingly or unknowingly the use of meat and wine is involved. The people who are totally vegetarian they too knowingly or unknowingly eat and drink these articles, and are thus involved in the use of wine and meat in some form or other.

Restaurants and supermarkets need to be more responsible in what they serve. In India, packaged vegetarian foods are marked with a green dot which makes choices easier for the consumers.

Organic foods are those that are produced without pesticides, fertilizers, growth hormones, ionizing radiations, food colorings and are not genetically modified. In many ways, some organic foods follow the principle of non-violence and are also pure and natural and can be recognized on the market shelf by the Organic India symbol. The symbols which indicate vegetarian packaged foods and organic preparations are shown in Fig 3.5.

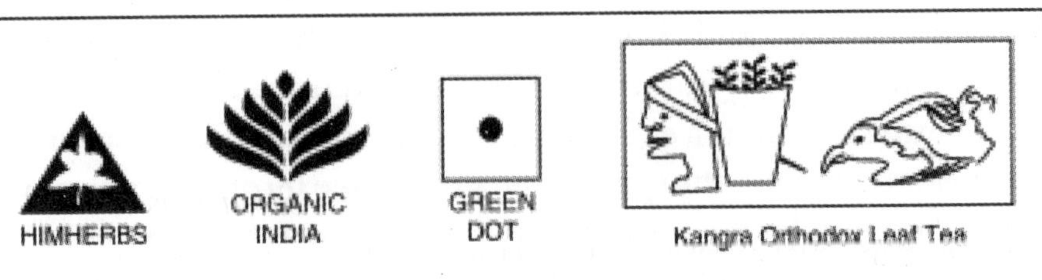

Fig 3.5: Symbols indicating acceptable foods for Jainas

The symbols shown in Fig 3.5 expand food selection possibilities for Jainas who otherwise are hesitant to eat anything from market shelves.

OTHER FASTS

There are many other fasts which are observed in different communities all of which cannot be documented here. Some are being discussed briefly for their salient features, rituals if any and observances.

SWAMINARAYAN FAST

These are very strict fasts observed by the monks or *sadhus* of the *Swaminarayan* religious order. They are called *vrats* of *paramhansas* since He practiced great austerities during his life for the sake of the salvation of mankind.

The most important feature of the *vrat* austerities were *Bhiksha* or receiving alms. The peculiarity was that all alms consisting of cooked items, raw flour and grain were to be collected in one cloth. This was then dipped in water several times to render the contents tasteless. From this, an amount which filled half a coconut shell was eaten once a day.

The second was *shadrastyag* in which monks have to avoid food with the six tastes — salty, sweet, chilly hot, sour, bitter and oily. This is observed for periods long enough to cause night blindness which came to light from an incident in which Brahmanand Swami once requested sadhus in his group thus — *anybody who can see please bring my sarangi,* to sing in front of Shri Maharaj.

Bhagwan Swaminarayan also enjoined other fasts during either *Shravan* or *Chaturmas,* the four holy months of monsoon season for mastering *brahmacharya.* These are indicated in Table 3.11.

The above fasts have been and are still performed by *sadhus* today. The harshest and seemingly impossible is *Parakkruchchhra,* which stymies today's physicians, since they believe that it would certainly cause kidney failure. It gets precarious if the weather in *Ashadh – Shravan* is hot and dry, rather than usual rainy and humid monsoon, when the body's water loss is less.

Table 3.11: Vrats of Paramhansas

Vrat	Details of observance	Remark
Pakwa (Pukka) Dharna Parna	*Dharna* means fast and *Parna* means having food. One meal is eaten on the first day and a *nirjal* fast is observed on the next day.	15 fasts and 15 meals
Apakwa Dharna Parna	As above, except three meals may be eaten on *Parna.* Both these fasts were observed during *Chaturmas.*	Total 15 fasts and 45 meals in a month.
Chandrayan	*Chandra* means moon. *Chandrayan* fasts involve eating food balls whose number coincides with lunar waxing and waning. Each food ball was rolled to a size of a large *amla* fruit, approximately 1.5 inches in diameter.	
Yavmadhya Chandrayan	*Yav* is barley. A barley grain is thick in the middle and pointed at both ends. Hence, the sequence of eating is 1 ball on first *shukla paksha*, 2 on second increasing to 15 on *Punam*. Then in *Krishna paksha* (14th to 1st *tithi*) this is decreased sequentially from 14 balls to 1 ball.	240 balls.
Pipilikamadhya	*Pipilika* in Sanskrit means an ant; thin in the middle	15 – 0 – 15.

(Contd...)

Chandrayan	and thick on both ends. 14th of Krishna *paksha* downwards to *amavasya* when a *nirjal* fast is observed. Then 1 ball is eaten on 1st of *shukla paksha,* increasing to 15 balls on *Punam.*	240 balls.
Yati Chandrayan	8 balls once at midday for 1 month.	240 balls.
Shishu Chandrayan	*Shishu* means baby. Hence only 4 balls twice a day; at midday and after sunset, for 1 month.	240 balls.
Rishi Chandrayan	3 balls once at midday only, for 1 month.	90 balls.

Some more severe *vrats* that Lord Swaminarayan enjoined young *sadhus* for mastering *nishkam vartman*. They are:

Vrat	Details of observance
Taptakruchcchhra	A 12 day *vrat*: 3 days on warm water – three *palis* once only i.e., 340.5g. (One *pali* is ¼ *sher* i.e., 113.5g. 1 *sher* = 454g). Then 3 days on warm milk — 2 *palis* once only. Then 3 days on warm ghee — 1 *pali* once. Followed by 3 days of *nirjal* fast.
Parak Kruchchhra.	12 days of *nirjal* fast. This fast was advocated to young *sadhus* during *chaturmas.*
Padkruchchhra	A fast of four days, which is repeated four times in a month. Day 1: one meal at midday Day 2: one evening meal Day 3: one meal if it arrives without request. Day 4: *nirjal* fast.
Kruchratikruchchhra	A 12 day fast. 9 days on warm water, once daily and three days of *nirjal* fast.

Note : Reproduced with permission from Vachanamrut Handbook by Sadhu Mukundcharandas

SATYANARAYAN VRAT

The word *Satya* means Truth, *Narayan* represents that which is abiding in everybody and everything. Lord Satyanarayan, a form of Lord Vishnu recommends, that in order to overcome difficulties and problems either caused by this life or previous births, one has to begin worshipping truth. Worshipping truth means being truthful to oneself and to others. The *Satyanarayan vrata* is one of the most common ritualistic prayers that are offered to the Lord.

Enthusiastic devotees, from time immemorial, have performed it with greatly beneficial results. It has been observed that after the performance of this *puja* with faith and devotion, devotees benefit by getting their problems and difficulties resolved. Thus, the sick regain health and those with other worldly problems find that help suddenly comes in from unexpected quarters. This *puja* is conducted to ensure abundance in one's life. The *Satyanarayan puja* can be performed on any day. It is not a *puja* confined to any festivities. But *purnima* (full moon day) or *sankranti* is considered to be the most auspicious day for this *puja*.

Observance

Satyanarayana is worshipped commonly by Hindus in their homes with family and friends. In this *puja*, called *Satyanarayana puja,* people worship by reciting the gracious story of Lord Satyanarayana. This story was originally told by Lord Vishnu himself to the sage Narada for the benefit of humankind. Many people carry out this *puja* immediately after or along with an auspicious occasion like a marriage or moving into a new house or any other success in life. This fast is observed in reverence to Lord Vishnu and observed on a *purnima* or full moon day. Devotees wake up before dawn, bathe and then start the fast which begins with the lighting of the lamp, a symbolic gesture of lighting the lamp of devotion in one's heart. Then special offerings are made in the evening and the fast is broken with prasaad.

The items for the offerings include saffron, *kum kum,* beads, beetelnut, milk, curd, honey, *shakkar* (sugar), ghee, flowers, sweets and fruits. People may invite priests for performing the *puja* with rituals as required and then offer charity on completion. The *prasaad* for this *vrat* is known as *Sapaad* which is a preparation of *rava,* milk, ghee, banana and sugar.

WEEKLY FASTS

As the name suggests, each day of the week is attributed to a certain deity for the purpose of prayer, fasting and ritual observance. Many people choose the day(s) on which they wish to observe fast and follow the rituals laid down for the assigned deity of that day. The methodology is laid down in small publications available from temples or the printers of the leaflets. Priests have copies which they distribute at the time of the prayer and offering for the devotees to follow. Stories or anecdotes of the power of the Gods are narrated in these publications.

Monday Fast

Monday fasts are not very strict observances but are attributed to Lord Shiva and Parvati to whom *puja* is offered at the end of the fast. The fast lasts only up to sunset after which prayers are offered to the deities and *prasaad* of fruits and or sweets is distributed to all present. There are no specifications for the observance except that only one meal is eaten in the day usually the evening meal. White colour is given special significance on this day.

There are however three version of the observance:

- Simple Monday fast
- *Saubhya Pradosh*
- Sixteen Mondays fast

The *kathas* or narrations built around each of these versions is different and specific for each fast.

The 16-Mondays vrat is observed during the monsoon season for removal of difficulties in body and mind, and for that fervent prayers are offered to Lord Shiva. Specific food offerings are specified which include *atta, ghee, gur, bael leaf,* sandal wood powder, flowers, *janyeyu,* clothes and so on usually under the guidance of a priest or *pandit.* There are two types of restrictions followed that is only sweet or only salty foods are offered and eaten.

Tuesday Fast

This fast is observed to worship Lord Hanuman and is kept for obtaining lasting happiness, gain respect, status and progeny. It is also supposed to improve blood circulation and general health. This fast is believed to destroy all evils associated with *mangala graha.* The food cooked in wheat and jaggery *(gur)* alone should be consumed only once during the day. The fast is recommended to be kept for 21 weeks. Flowers usually used for *puja* are red in color which is the significant color for the day.

Wednesday Fast

Lord Shiva is worshipped on this day, the fast being kept for peace, tranquility and to fulfill all dreams. The prominent colour which is supposed to be significant is green on this day, therefore people wear green clothes, eat green vegetables, offering them at *puja* and after the *aarti* is over, taking them as *prasaad.* During this fast only one meal a day is taken. This fast is said to provide protection against evil and is generally observed if one needs to travel on a Wednesday. However, the *puja* should not be left midway.

Thursday Fast

This fast is observed in reverence to Lord Vishnu. The significant colour for the day is yellow and therefore yellow flowers are offered and yellow clothes worn. The banana is worshipped on this day. The offerings at worship comprise roasted bengal gram, *gur* and banana which are later eaten as *prasaad.* The meal is cooked without salt, being eaten only once in the day. Meals are consumed only after the worship is completed.

Friday Fast

The fast is observed to remove all obstacles and is observed till evening with one meal taken at night. The predominant color for the day is *white* reflected in the clothes which people choose to wear and it is recommended that white colour flowers be offered and similar coloured foods like rice, puddings, milk, cashew nuts, etc. be offered and consumed. The condition is that no sour foods are prepared even for the household irrespective of whether all the members observe the fast or not.

This fast is for *Santoshi Maa*, daughter of Lord Ganesha. It is also observed for Goddess Padmavati among the Jains. The fast is also called *Annapurna Vrat* and supposed to grant one wealth and prosperity. A pot of water is kept along with the offerings which after *puja* is sprinkled in the house and the remaining water is given to the *tulsi* plant, which adorns almost all homes in India.

Among the Christian community, Friday is a significant day for abstaining from eating non-vegetarian foods which they love the most in remembrance of the crucifixion of Christ.

Saturday Fast

The Lord Shani is worshipped on this day. The planet Saturn/*Shani* is traditionally known to act as an obstacle in people's life. Whether it is true at all times is unconfirmed. The observance requires that only one meal be taken in the evening after the *puja* is over. The colour for the day is black and therefore *black til* or sesame seeds, whole black gram or *urad* is offered although salt is avoided. Worship is performed to ward off evil and the fasts are kept for a period of one year.

Sunday Fast

This fast is observed with the hope of fulfilling desires and only once during the daytime before sunset, a salt free meal is consumed. Lord Surya is worshipped on this day which starts by offering salutations to the sun through a *Surya Namaskar* as it rises. Golden colour is considered auspicious on Sundays.

Other religions which originated in India and preached the same Vedic teachings of Hinduism and Oneness are, *Buddhism* and *Zoroastrianism* both ancient in their origins.

Buddhism

Buddhism is a religion founded around 563 BC by the great God Brahma Sahampati who in his first sermon delivered to 5 monks in Benaras (now Varanasi) said ***Come close O monks, live in holiness and put an end to misery.*** From this day, there were 6 saints in the world and the Buddhist community had been founded. The essentials of Buddhist teaching are contained in the Canon of the Sacred Scriptures, written in *Pali* and *Sanskrit*, that is the Chinese and Tibetan versions. In both it is made up of three parts hence the name triple basket or *Tripitaka*. The *Sutras* are an enormous collection of sermons and moral fables uttered by the Buddha himself who had achieved enlightenment through meditation for seven long years in Gaya under a *Bodhi* tree. Buddhism gradually spread and greatly impacted South and South East Asia.

Zoroastrianism

Zoroastrianism originated in Persia and was therefore more prevalent in Arabia. It is the religion of the migrant Iranian and Parsi community in India. The scriptures compiled and retrieved through the turbulent wars and destruction in Iran through history are known as *Gathas*, which contain the spiritual messages of their founder *Zarathushtra* or *Zoroaster* as the Greeks named him, Prophet of ancient Iran. He is believed to be the first in human history to have founded a religion based on the ethical values of Truth and Justice named *Asha* (Vedic *Rta*) in the *Gathas*, a poetic rendering of the scriptures. He preached about One Supreme God, *Ahura Mazda*, Lord of life and wisdom to be worshipped through word and deed for the protection and evolution of man and nature. His followers are known as *Zoroastrians* in the West and *Zartoshtis* in East Iran and India.

Sikhism

When the founder of Sikhism, *Guru Nanak* arrived on the Indian scene, Muslim invaders had ruled for over three centuries in the Punjab. As a result, a large Muslim population had a presence in many parts of the country due to conversions of Hindus. Guru Nanak was Punjab's chief propounder of the *bhakti* sectarian tradition. Born in a rural middle class family in south-west Lahore, his place of birth has now come to be known as *Nankana Sahib* which has Sikh temples or *Gurudwaras.* Nanak wrote hymns and set them in music, expressing the spirit of love and things holy with complete indifference to material things. These form a part of the Sikh's sacred books. Devotees do not worship idols but the holy book known as *Guru Granth Sahib.*

The teachings of all religious leaders and prophets are basically the same and relevant for the period in which they were incarnated or born and enlightened. Since these three religious streams have no mention of fasting as a ritual in observances, they do not fall within the purview of this text. Therefore, only a brief introduction has been provided.

SOCIAL FASTS

Chapter 4

All fasts undertaken that permit people to get together are termed as social fasts. Fasting and breaking of fasts together in groups or in the community or in temples can be classified as *social fasts*, since they bring people together in the spirit of oneness, and this is more often than not, followed by sharing food in the form of *prasaad*, and then breaking the fasts at dinner time or after sunset as required, in an atmosphere of feasting and joy. Women and children particularly, convert every fast day into one that they look forward to because of the special food offerings and the socializing involved. The men may join in the prayers or festivities but few keep fasts religiously.

Regular fasting say *weekly* or f*ortnightly* is a traditional practice in India, but the success of frugal eating needs to be blended with a lifestyle in which fasting is neither seen as a punishment nor a discipline, but on the contrary, a respite from daily routine activities. The time being spent quietly allowing the body to feel rested, peaceful and rejuvenated after the fast.

Social fasting thus helps to come back to routine work with greater vigour of both body and mind. Social fasts can basically be divided into three categories:

- Festivals
- Celebrations
- Unexpected events

These categories are being briefly discussed with examples.

FESTIVALS

Some festivals have already been discussed along with their required observances, some of which include fasting which may be *partial* or *complete,* but the real focus is on the social aspect of the festival. Some examples are *Karvachauth, Teej* and the like, in which fasting is optional and people look forward to the festival for the anticipation, pre-preparation, excitement and fun it provides, in addition to the opportunity of meeting people whom they may see only infrequently in the year.

KARVA CHAUTH

Karva Chauth falls about nine days before *Diwali* on the fourth day of the dark fortnight of *Kartik* (fourth) day of the waning moon) some time in October – November. It is the most important fast observed by married women of North India to renew and celebrate the special bond between husband and wife. A woman keeps such a fast for the long life and well being of her husband, who becomes her protector after she leaves her parent's home.

Observance

Karva Chauth is an occasion which all married women look forward to, but more so the newly married ones, who enjoy the special attention they get from parents and in-laws, in terms of gifts, special food and sweets. Preparations for this festival start a few days before the festival. Markets come alive and women prepare for the day by buying bangles and applying *henna* patterns on their hands. The festival is almost incomplete without henna, which is auspicious as on a wedding day and is considered an essential ritual. The huge queues at henna shops clearly reflect the mood. It is believed that if the henna leaves a dark color on the hands, it symbolizes love.

A day before Karva Chauth *sargi* is given by the mother-in-law to her daughter-in-law. It consists of *mathri* (both sweet and salty), *pheni,* fruits, or money to buy *shringar* (cosmetic and accessories) items like bangles, *bindi, kajal,* etc. Following a bath early in the morning on the day, well before dawn, the women wear new clothes, bangles on their henna-decorated hands and pray, offering food to the deity and then takes a small meal from the *sargi* which is prepared and given to her by her mother-in-law. The mother-in-law is also expected to take a bath, pray and then enter the kitchen. The *sargi* is eaten before sunrise. New brides wear their bridal outfits and others wear bright dresses woven or laced with gold during the ritual starting an hour before sunset. The important rituals include worshipping *karvas* or spherical clay pots with a spout and *legends* associated with the festival are narrated. The goddess known as *Gaur Mata* is worshipped along with *Lord Shiva* and *Parvati.* Women make *diyas* out of wheat flour dough and put pure ghee and wicks and place them in their *thali* along with the dry fruits, sweets and gifts for the mother-in-law. These are later exchanged with other married women who sit in a circle before sunset and pass the trays around several times. The women go to their homes after the *karva puja* and wait for their husbands to come and the moon to rise. The women also give a *baaina* consisting of fruits, sweets, nuts, gifts and money to their mothers-in-law as a mark of respect, and take their blessings.

Mode of Fasting

The fast of Karva Chauth is a very tough fast to observe, as it starts before sunrise and ends after worshipping the moon, which rises at night. Those who observe it abstain from food and even water for the whole day. Some keep a partial fast and sip some juice or coke during the fast as the younger generation is not very particular these days and according to them it is tough fasting for the whole day especially while on a job.

Breaking of Fast

Once the moon rises, women see its reflection in a *thaali* of water, after which they do a pooja for their husband's safety and long life. They see the moon through a strainer on the edge of which a *diya* is lighted. This is done along with their husbands whose face they equate with that of the moon. *Aarti* is then performed of the moon and the husband. The husbands help their wives to break the fast by giving them the first sip of water and the first bite of food with their own hands.

Present Scenario

The importance of Karva Chauth can be gauged by the fact that this fast is kept even in modern homes, as a symbol of a woman's love for her husband. Even girls who are engaged to be married, keep it for their fiances or for their boyfriends, whom they think they will marry sooner or later.

It has become the ultimate symbol of role alteration, where men and women fast together as a mark of love for each other. It is no longer considered out of place for the men to keep a fast with their wives or girlfriends. More and more men across all ages, be it 16 or 50 year old are getting ready to do the same to show their partner that they care and love or to impress them. A new outlook is that if women are taking on the responsibility of helping out with the finances of the house, its only fair that the men pitch in by doing their bit to strengthen their relationship.

The latest trend is feasting as you fast and thus paving the way for designer parties in South Delhi farmhouses. Traditionally Karva Chauth was a busy day for sweetshop owners, henna designers and bangle shops, but now event management firms and restaurant owners have also joined the wagon. Booking and plans are made well in advance as to what to wear, choosing which Karva Chauth party to attend, planning shopping for gifts and so on.

Gifts also form an important part of the festival. Many look forward to the fast because of the reward at the end of the day. Today the market is flooded with unique gifts especially for the occasion. One can also present hand-made gifts, flowers, cakes or chocolates. Husbands generally gift their wives new clothes or exquisite jewellery. Max Healthcare offers a health checkup package as a gift from wives to their husbands.

Many have also taken it up as a business opportunity. From neighborhood beauty parlors to mega shops, every store is offering a Karva Chauth package. From Botox shots to slimming packages, the festival means a boom time for all parlours. Some customers demand a complete makeover to match the look that their favorite film heroine sported in a movie or serial. Few leading fashion stores offer discounts if you wear bangles, *bindi, sindoor* and *mangalsutra.* Karva Chauth special *suhaagan thalis* are available online, consisting of Ganesha idol, *haldi-kumkum*, 1gm *kesar, mehndi* cone, one dozen bangles, red *chunari.* New designs for jewellery and sarees are also introduced specially for Karva Chauth.

While the nature of the celebrations may have changed, the sentiments remain the same. Karva Chauth was traditionally a reminder of the wedding day fast and rites to give an annual boost to the married life. But today people celebrate their wedding anniversaries in addition, with or without the fast or prayers, influenced by the western world.

TEEJ

Teej is an ancient festival celebrated to mark the reunion of Lord Shiva and Parvati, who were united after 100 days of severe penance. It also marks the onset of the monsoon season which is a relief from the intense heat of summer which often created dry and drought laden conditions. India being a largely agricultural economy dependent heavily on the rains for its production and prosperity, people used to fast and pray for the monsoon.

Teej is a *Jaya tithi*, during which period any work that one takes up meets with success or victory. The festival is celebrated over two or three days as there are three types of Teej observances. These are usually practiced in Haryana, Punjab, Madhya Pradesh and Rajasthan amidst fasting and great festivity.

It is still celebrated but in a modern way often without the fasting. Women and girls enjoy it more as a festival than for fast and prayer, by enjoying outdoor activities of shopping for bangles, jewellery and clothes while also decorating hands and feet with henna. They also participate in the festive spirit of Teej by visiting fairs where *jhulas* or swings of different types are installed for all ages. Sweet offerings are not made at home as they used to be, but special foods associated with the festival which are available are bought, shared and relished with joy. The three types of Teej are briefly discussed.

Akshaya Teej

This falls in the month of *Baisakh* (April-May) and is so called because on this day the *Satyug* is supposed to have started, known as *akshatra yatritiya* in the sacred texts. The day is considered so auspicious that marriages, any kind of contracts, celebrations are all enjoyed on this day. *Chandan* paste which has natural cooling properties is applied to deities in temples.

Haritalika Teej

The *Haritalika Teej* falls on the third day of the second fortnight in the month of *Bhadrapada*. On third day only married women observe a *nirjal* fast for the whole day and night breaking it only the next morning after prayers and offerings to Lord Shiva and Parvati. It is believed that invoking Parvati's blessings on this day results in continued marital bliss. The special foods offered are *Ghevar, Anares,* a fried preparation of rice flour topped with sesame seeds, *Gujia* and sweet *pheni.* These are then used to break the fast.

Haryali Teej

Hariyala Teej is celebrated on *Shravan Shukla Tritiya*, the third day of the second or bright fortnight in the month of *Shravana* (July-August). It is also known as *Swarna Gauri Vrata.* On this day, both young girls as well as married women may observe a fast, and offer *Mathris* and sweets to Goddess Gauri or Parvati. There is a grand fair held at the temple of Naina Devi, and a 2-day fair at Jaipur and Udaipur in Rajasthan.

All the fasts are accompanied by prayers and charity activities, seeking blessings and grace for the family, and end in festivities that are organized by communities for the welfare and happiness of all around.

These festivals were a way of socializing, removing attention from the environmental discomfort of the summer heat, and gaining knowledge of the cooling and heating effects of natural substances which abound in nature, through the rituals laid down.

Today, less emphasis is laid on the fasts or rituals preceding the festival and more on the festivities. People have lost the significance but still want to keep in touch with tradition for the fun that it provides. Instead of the silence and concentrated prayer, the youth now enjoy loud non-devotional or folk music and festivity and fairs have lost their natural ambience and sanctity.

CELEBRATIONS

These include occasions for rejoicing with family and friends as in the case of marriages, thread ceremonies of adolescent children, naming ceremonies of new-born infants and the like. There are so many occasions for celebration in India that are shared and enjoyed with extended families and friends, that it is impossible to list them all, but what is common is that some austerity and prayer precede each celebration. *Pujas* are performed in specially arranged areas of worship called *mandaps,* conducted by religious priests, *prasaad* offered to the Lord and then distributed to the invitees. Ceremonies are then accompanied by music suited to the occasion with or without dancing, fun and games.

Marriages

On such occasions, the immediate family of the bride and bridegroom fast on the day of the marriage and pray for the couple's happiness and prosperity in their new life. They look forward to the celebration, but the bride and bridegroom also fast traditionally so that the first morsel of food is fed to them at the completion of the religious ceremony when the groom puts the first morsel of food, usually sweets, in the mouth of the bride and vice versa. The people present wish the couple with gifts, flowers, and blessings for a happy married life.

This marks the beginning of the celebrations for both the families involved, and a new bond between the families is established, which they enjoy for the rest of their lives.

Similar celebrations are held for other occasions mentioned, the norm being to propitiate the Gods by performing religious rites and then blessing the persons for whom the ceremony was designed. Fasting is optional as per the beliefs and traditions of the family are concerned.

UNEXPECTED EVENTS

These include sudden calamities that result in a drastic change in the lives of people, such as a serious accident of a family member or friend, death in the family, even martyr's day for remembering those who lose their lives for the country or a natural disaster that may cause large-scale dislocation of people in society.

All the above reasons lead to a state of helplessness or deprivation and fasts get imposed on those involved, as a result of people losing their appetite or having to reorganize their lives and therefore have little time or even resources to think of food or themselves. Those who feel completely shocked with the unexpected turn of events can only pray for help, as in the case of accidents and critical conditions. Such events therefore naturally make people fast both physically and mentally and observe *maun vrat* till prayer gives them the mental strength to clear their thoughts and get into action in an attempt to salvage the situation. For example, on martyr's days and death anniversaries, it is a practice to observe two-minutes silence as a mark of respect to the departed souls.

Most such events result in the community visiting the affected persons to offer all kind of help possible, and mental support through sharing the sorrow of their neighbours, friends, associates in the community. Examples of this are seen often in the case of bereavement or during disaster situations such as the Tsunami, droughts, earthquakes, floods and now terrorist activities or blasts which has become the modern-age disaster.

The unity seen in such situations is exemplary as everyone rises above caste, creed, religion, enmity, jealousy and so on in an attempt to help normalize life for their affected brethren. If this single thread could bind people together for all times, what a peaceful and happy world we would be in!

CIRCUMSTANTIAL FASTS

As the term suggests circumstantial fasts are imposed on people by changes in their circumstances, which therefore impact their living environment and lifestyle. There are basically three reasons for these changes, namely:

- Old age
- Health status
- Economic status
- Other

OLD AGE

When people get to the age of retirement they start to feel unwanted because they are no longer required in their jobs. This feeling is carried into their lives at home and outside. Depending on how positively they think and whether they have developed hobbies during their working lives, they learn to adjust themselves to lowered physical activity, more rest and less socialization. These can result from a change in their economic situation as well.

The change in the circumstances make women especially, cut down on food when they begin to relax and follow all religious rituals that they could not do when at work. These are accompanied by regular fasting according to their choice, which may vary from weekly, fortnightly to monthly fasts. These help them to develop new friends and social contacts too. This is very important as the number of elderly and old persons in the population have increased enormously due to increased longevity. The elderly are now making efforts to remain fit physically and mentally, using all techniques at their disposal to prevent disease.

HEALTH STATUS

Overweight or sickness brings a change in circumstances that requires restricted food intakes or enforces partial fasting to enable a cure, depending on the severity of the illness, and the kind of physical activity that a person can engage in. In such cases healing can be facilitated by focusing the mind away from food and eating, by indulging in leisure time activities or rituals involving fasting and prayer. Thus, focusing away from the body and its ills, to one's divinity through meditation and simple yogic techniques such as *pranayama* everyday, helps to relax the mind and body enabling it to go through the imposed fasting with ease, and assisting successful recovery of the body to health.

ECONOMIC STATUS

There are a large number of poeple in the country below the poverty line, but it is common to see them eat one scant meal of cereal with potato or green chilli and be happier than the millionaires of the country. Sometimes the women of the family skip meals altogether in order to feed the others. In India, it was traditional for women to feed the bread winner first (men) and children next and then themselves. This however, has changed because the women too are bread winners today.

Low incomes drive people to work hard to earn their food and share it with the family, and their minds are turned towards God, and to seek His blessings resort to celebrating festivals and performing rituals occasionally. But those with high incomes tend to become greedy for more, rather than turn their minds inward to thank Him for His grace and share it with those who have less. That is why our traditions always emphasized on charity in every ritual, festival or celebration. It is because our ancient teachers, fore fathers and gurus taught the human values of Austerity, Truth and Dharma by exemplifying them in their own lives.

OTHER

Fasts imposed by circumstances on people may take the form of penance, protest or retaliation against injustices meted out to people, by the family, community head or even government, making people resort to fasting to press their demands. Such observances are termed as *circumstantial* and may not always be sudden or unexpected as in the case of some social fasts.

Sudden turn of events caused by factors beyond one's control can also be called circumstantial as they lead to penance, prayer and fasting for long periods in an effort to survive the vagaries of nature as well as man-made by the ills of society.

FASTING AND HEALTH

Fasting impacts our health in a number of ways, physically, physiologically, mentally, emotionally and spiritually. As already discussed, fasting methods and duration vary widely and therefore health effects will vary. Some factors which impact health are:

- Tradition, religion and culture
- Reasons for fasting
- Type of fast
- Period of fasting

TRADITION, RELIGION AND CULTURE

Fasting patterns vary with the traditions, religion, culture and practices followed within a family, community, region and country. In most traditional societies, fasts were related to some socio-religious event such as thanksgiving, seeking a boon from God through prayer, celebrating success, memorial services and so on. It was a way of inculcating self discipline, purification, connectivity with one's inner conscience and getting peace and satisfaction through austerity. According to the Mahanarayana Upanishad (79/3):

Austerity is the source of strength and also the means of liberation. By the power of austerity Gods attain Godhood, sages achieve perfection and human beings overcome obstacles and attain success in life.

REASONS FOR FASTING

Fasts may be observed for many different reasons such as:

- Social
- Health
- Circumstantial
- Economic
- Psychological
- Spiritual
- Environmental

Each of the above are briefly discussed in the light of their health implications.

Social Fasts

Fasting and breaking of fasts together in groups, families or community is a type of *social feasting* or meeting that brings people together in the spirit of oneness. Women and children look forward to such occasions, as they are usually bound by household and working routines with little time or incentive for meeting others and sharing joy and love. The relaxed and happy experience also improves their mindset positively and returning to routine jobs charged with renewed energy. Such occasions thus improve on the mental health of families, leaving no room for loneliness or depression. People then look forward to the next fast day and festivity. Although socializing is tiring especially in crowds in temples or holy places, it provides sound sleep after the day.

Health Fasts

Health induced fasting is the result of sickness when the appetite naturally declines as a result of the body's natural reaction to fight the infection by resting the processes not needed for immediate healing. Such infections may be disturbances of the gastrointestinal tract leading to discomfort from eating, such as diarrhea, vomiting, stomach pain and so on. In such cases fasting helps recovery. Dr. Dewy once said, *When a patient stops taking food the disease and not the patient dies of starvation.* In fact, feeding a patient against his desire does not nourish him, but provides strength to the disease microbes to grow faster and therefore the cure takes longer.[24]

Conditions in which fasting is not desirable are pregnancy, cancer, tuberculosis, diseases of malnutrition, glandular disturbances such as diabetes, thyroid problems, hyper or hypo functioning of the adrenal gland, diseases of liver and kidneys. Fasting helps with all minor chronic diseases, although there is hardly a disease which will not be controlled in its progression, partially or completely with fasting, unless the organs of the body are malfunctioning or the body resistance is very low. Using fasting as a total cure would however be foolish if the symptoms are not controlled.

Another reason why people resort to fasting for reasons of health, is to reduce weight, in an effort to ward off chronic disease. This however is wise only under medical supervision or with the expert advice of a qualified clinical nutritionist. Although routine weekly or monthly fasts would be helpful, they cannot be used solely for the purpose. Weight reduction regimes require self-control, discipline and determination coupled with well worked-out advice on diet and exercise routines advised on an individual basis.

Circumstantial Fasts

Apart from the many reasons for religious and other types of fasting, some of which have been discussed in Chapter 2, there are many others that can motivate people to fast as a means of penance, protest or retaliation. In such cases, fasting is used as a tool to exert pressure on peers, family, society and governments to achieve personal or group goals or express strong feelings about an issue.

There is enough evidence of this when children refuse to eat meals because a demand is not fulfilled by parents, and subject themselves

24. Dhiren Gala (2003), p.7

and their parents to mental stress affecting health thereby, if continued routinely.

Another case in point is the group protests against suppression by employers which bring about trade protests, hunger strikes and so on which can prove fatal if carried on for months at a time. Although such protests are not strictly called fasting, they do amount to abstinence of food and impact health adversely, physically, mentally, emotionally and spiritually. Some examples are being cited below.

Sometimes unexpected circumstances like a disaster, war or bereavement force people into fasting situations when food is either not available, or appetites wane because of emotional or mental distress. A case in point is the fasting carried out by social activists against the building of the Narmada Dam because of the displacement of families it caused. Similarly, the fasting by professionals for better living and working conditions, justice and autonomy of institutions was another such notable demonstration of circumstantial fasts. All such circumstances do impact health adversely and in some cases may even prove fatal.

Economic

Sometimes due to economic reasons, people are compelled to consume only one meal a day, as is done in most routine fasts. This implies that they fast all their lives, especially women who ensure that the men of the family eat first, then the children and lastly themselves. This means that the leftovers are eaten by them, and this may amount to not even one square meal in the developing countries. There is a fine line between this category and those suffering from dire poverty who in any case eat cereals or *chapatti* with an onion or green chillies. Even if salaries are increased experience tells that the men use up the extra money on alcohol and gambling instead of food security for the family. This is the reason for abuse of women, suicides, foeticide and infanticide of female offsprings especially in Lower Income Group (LIG) families.

The health implications of the above are serious as the women and children are subject to prolonged malnutrition and its consequent diseases. The situation has not improved even after government intervention for the last 5 decades. The present scenario holds little hope for improving the situation unless knowledge and money trickles down to the grassroot levels in rural communities and the women and would-be mothers get empowered with entrepreneurial skills to improve their economic and educational status. More hospitals and medical centres are not the answer.

In fact such enforced fasting leads to starvation of the body, mind and soul and needs to be tackled by each and everyone on a war footing. People who fast should part with the food they abstain from and feed the less fortunate people in their surroundings. Some NGOs are doing excellent work in this area of health and education, and as equal citizens the haves should help the have-nots through these agencies, that can and are trying to make a difference in the lives of the under-priviledged.

Psychological

Some women resort to fasting to draw attention of the family, be it their husbands or other members. Children do not eat if their demands are not fulfilled by their parents or elders. In this manner, psychological advantage is gained. Of course most fasting and breaking of fasts result in friends and family getting together for special feasts after the ritualistic offerings in temples and provides a change from routine work and meals. This increases connectivity, participation and enjoyment resulting in relaxation and positive psychological benefits.

Spiritual

Most fasts are observed for religious purposes, and the methods of observance are guided by priests in temples, who are involved with *pujas*, rituals and readings from the sacred texts on special days. There is devotional music and chanting carried out at fixed times and *langar* is served to all as *prasaad* irrespective of caste, creed, religion or economic level. Fasting helps spiritual development in many ways as discussed under religious fasts in Chapter 2. It is important to state however, that once ignorance is removed, desires and thoughts controlled, the mind gets harnessed too. This leads to a clear perception, subtle discrimination, correct judgments and precise and wise comprehension of situations in life.

Fasts are also observed in thanksgiving to the Lord, when a lot of effort has gone into the achievement of a desired goal. Gandhiji kept a 24-hour fast in this spirit, on Independence Day in 1947, when India freed itself from 100 years of colonial rule which involved great sacrifices of the people at the time.

Further, with the focus shifted from food to prayer and devotion, the silence observed during the period leads to experiences of higher consciousness and oneness, bringing peace and joy that generates love, goodwill and unity.

Environmental

Fasts help to preserve the environment in many ways. As mentioned earlier, on fast days non-vegetarian food, alcohol, tobacco or other stimulants are prohibited. Vegetarian food remains are easily biodegradable and therefore enrich the soil as well as do not form non-biodegradable wastes. Also household food preparation is minimized and fuel use decreases leading to less pollution. Important religious and festival days are usually declared as national holidays and therefore traffic and the ensuing pollution is also reduced. The breaking of fasts together is not done with lavishly laid out food but with that offered to the chosen deities and regarded as *prasaad,* which is usually taken in disposable containers that are eco-friendly in nature.

TYPES OF FAST

The nature of the fast determines the impact it will have on health. If it is a religious fast it will involve more effort in the act of preparing for it and performing the necessary rituals. This requires more energy in its preparation and conduct making people involved feel hungry. If the fast is a partial one involving abstinence from cereals, pulses etc. but one meal is permitted everyday after prayers and *puja*, usually after sunset or moonrise as the case may be, the effects on health are not marked and may prove positive in terms of physical, emotional and mental health.

If the person is fasting with great devotion, the focus will shift from food to prayer and fasting becomes a joy leaving the devout in a blissful state at the end of the day, with positive mental vibrations. Such fasting does not involve excessive denial in terms of food and eating and is therefore easier to observe. It is advisable to give in charity the cereal or other foods abstained from during fasting. This further enhances mental and emotional health. It is said that feeding a hungry child is the greatest service one can render to Krishna.

SEASONAL FASTS

Seasonal fasts are observed every 2-3 months, mainly to rest the body processes and increase vitality to counteract illnesses that are experienced at the change of seasons especially in tropical climates. In India, it is observed that fasting days are increased during the monsoons, all related to religious festivals by our sages. Since this season is fraught with infections due to less sunlight and high humidity, fasting helps to decrease the incidence of disease by slowing down body processes and increasing immunity. Further, the time that people cannot spend outdoors reduces their physical activity and therefore reducing intake of food through fasting helps to keep the balance of the body in terms of health. Mental health too improved because more time was spent in devotional activities and freedom from routine jobs.

ROUTINE FASTS

Regular and routine fasting such as weekly, fortnightly or monthly observances is positively helpful to the body and mind. Such fasts provide rest to the organs of the body particularly the mouth, stomach, intestines, liver, kidney, heart, and lungs, enabling them to function with increasing efficiency. The body processes especially involved after meal ingestion are mainly digestion, absorption, storage of energy and fat to be used by the body when required, removal of toxins and so on. These get rested during fasting and activated after its completion, thus improving and maintaining health by increasing the efficiency of the body. It is for this reason that one feels good after a fast day, and even though the food eaten may be routine, it tastes and smells better because of improved sensory acuity and better glandular secretion.

However, too much austerity or prolonged fasting is not recommended as it can be detrimental to health. Sri Ramakrishna used to keep a watch on his devotees and when he observed any disciple performing austerities excessively, he would say – ***please eat your meals regularly and then practice japam or meditation.***[25]

Spiritually too, fasting increases connectivity with the inner consciousness and establishes clear signs of value inculcation through development of a sensitive conscience. It thus enables people to control emotions such as anger, greed, hatred, jealousy, compassion and so on and live with love towards all humanity. Sai's message to humanity is expressed in the phrase *Help Ever, Hurt Never.* This is the index of spiritual health to be guided by, practiced and attained in our daily lives.

Period of Fasting

The length of the fasting period and the nature of the fast, whether complete or partial, determine the reaction of the body and its systems to the absence of food and eating. The health effects of partial fasts are different from those of *nirjal* or total fasts. If fasting is prolonged, the body starts using its cell proteins for energy and the internal processes get affected, pressurizing vital organs, which then cannot function optimally. Occasional fasts however are good for maintaining health, because the body processes which are slowed down provide rest to all organs, which then get revitalized.

The period of fasting may extend from 1-12 or more days depending on the aim and type of the fast. In prolonged periods of austere fasting extending up to 12 days or more, the body tends to adapt to lower levels of nutrient intake and often no physiological impact on the vital organs are observed. However, in such cases vigorous activity is not recommended and the body should be well rested at short intervals. This also implies that the mind should be at rest, listening to devotional or other soft music or reading light literature not involving stress or anxiety of any kind.

During prolonged fasting the appetite too gets depressed and people are unable to ingest enough food to provide their requirements for

25 Chetanananda (1991).

energy, protein and vital nutrients like minerals and vitamins thus compromising their nutritional status. They become weak, susceptible to infections, mentally stressed, all leading to different metabolic responses in the body, depending on individual attitudes to fasting.

Metabolic Response in Prolonged Fasting

The normal healthy person adapts to fasting by utilizing the body's energy reserves in the liver and muscle in preference to the greatest stores available in the form of fat. These however get exhausted in less than 24 hours, after which protein from the skeletal muscle becomes the primary source of energy for meeting the needs of the body. This may represent a loss of about 75g protein per day. After a few days the body tries to conserve protein for maintaining the health of the vital organs, and fearing disaster shifts its energy source to body fat. In this process, blood insulin levels fall. If fasting or deprivation continues too long the brain adapts to using ketones, the breakdown products of fat, for energy.

Stress Response

With the body subjected to physiological stress moving towards starvation, one can notice an increase in metabolic rate and accelerated tissue breakdown. This brings weight losses, headache, giddiness and even fever, hormonal and other changes that are similar to the body's response in the case of an infection. A state of malnutrition results along with its multiple deficiency symptoms. Thus, a vicious circle of malnutrition, reduced resistance to infection and more malnutrition sets in affecting performance and productivity leading to economic deprivation.

Therefore, it is important to monitor physiologic, nutritional and mental or behavioral symptoms in the case of very prolonged fasting extending to months as Gandhiji resorted to for the independence of the country. His emaciated body was evidence of the stress that the body had to undergo for the great sacrifice, which he was determined to make for us. It is not for nothing that he is revered as the *Father of the Nation.*

It is therefore important to emphasize that fasting is good for healthy people in short bursts but is not recommended for chronically undernourished people as their resistance is already low, and they can succumb to illnesses that may take very long to recover from or even prove fatal. Fortunately, most fasts followed for whatever reasons are broken by feasting in less than 24 hours, or eating and drinking is allowed with specified exclusions under each fast.

Breaking Fasts

Fasting is much easier than breaking the fast as far as its effect on the body is concerned. It is therefore important to understand the significance of breaking fasts sensibly. The hunger pangs in a normal person indicate the body's need for food, therefore during fasting, it is natural to feel hungry at the time when the first meal is denied. This is completely habitual and when the body gets no food till the next meal the hunger pangs become weak and gradually disappear. Breaking a fast therefore, should be done very slowly with light foods taken at short intervals, starting with water, then fluids, soft diet and restricting the quantity eaten at one time, till the body recovers to its normal digestive capacity and physiologic activity.

Advantages of Fasting

The advantages of fasting can be summarized as:

- Improvement of digestive efficiency
- Increase in natural resistance
- Reduction of toxicity in the body
- Enhancement of mental powers
- Inculcation of discipline—physical, mental and spiritual

Disadvantages of Prolonged Fasting

If fasting is prolonged for over a month, serious effects occur in the body. These are:

- Loss of weight leading to emaciation
- Gastrointestinal disturbances — diarrhoea, vomiting, stomach pain and the like
- Accumulation of acids in the blood and urine when proteins are broken down for energy

- Kidneys have to work harder to excrete waste products
- Dehydration
- Increased heartbeat and low blood pressure
- Rapid deep breathing because of lack of oxygen
- Life gets endangered
- Changes in consciousness

Some of the symptoms can be delayed if during fasting one takes salts or soda with water and fruit juices periodically. Also symptoms do not occur in all people equally. In fact, a lean person may suffer from protein breakdown for energy, because his body fat is limited, and this may prove fatal.

However a fast of 10-12 days is considered safe although a fat person can observe it safely for 30 days. Prolonged fasting should however, not be extended with the aim of just reducing body weight. If this is resorted to, the body systems may breakdown enough to hamper recovery from many illnesses since hormonal and glandular imbalances may set in which are beyond repair. Hence, fasting for weight watching too, should be medically monitored if prolonged for whatever reason.

It is also important not to fix the fasting period beforehand, because this will depend on the body's reaction, necessity and circumstances.

FASTING AND DISEASE PREVENTION

The relationship of fasting with disease prevention has been established through the experience of sages, seers and avatars, whose longevity was a common occurrence in ancient times. Interesting age-related figures have been recorded about Sri Krishna and others after him[26].

As far as health is concerned, the necessity for fasting only arises when eating, drinking and living habits are not regular, balanced or in the right proportion, and the body builds up enough levels of toxic elements to cause disease. A number of diseases are the result of the way

---

[26] Sadhu Mukundcharandas(2005), p.147

we conduct ourselves in everyday life, and are termed as *lifestyle diseases.*

The main causes are:

- Stress
- Overeating
- Excessive exertion
- Boredom

Stress

Stress can be mental, physiological or physical but all or any type causes symptoms of illness and if prolonged can lead to disease.

Mental stress — This includes fear, anxiety, excitement, overwork, hurry and so on. One cannot avoid this kind of stress completely in our daily lives, but can make an effort to reduce it to a level that will not cause tension or stress-related discomfort to our body. The levels of stress should only be at levels that will motivate us to act, for solving day to day anxieties and problems instead of ignoring them completely and becoming indifferent to them. Remember that causes once identified need to be removed to enable the mind to relax. Basically it is a matter of mind control and fasting is an important tool for achieving it.

Physiological stress —This can be caused by continuously eating out, socializing, entertaining and so on. The result is a constant working of the body's internal organs and systems, without rest. This can be tackled through regular fasting routines to rest the organs, thus increasing immunity for detoxifying and revitalizing the system.

Physical stress — Once mental and physiological stress is controlled, physically the body also gets rested through fasting.

Overeating

Habitual overeating leads to overweight and sluggishness of the body and its processes resulting in progressive inactivity and lethargy. Overweight also places a physical burden on vital organs reducing their efficiency and causing chronic diseases, and if allowed to go unchecked, depression, heart problems, diabetes and other chronic problems can result leading to serious consequences.

Excessive Exertion

Overexertion is as hard on the body as extremes of anything in life, be it mental or physical. Crossing thresholds of body capacity as far as exercise routines, or mental work is concerned can result in fainting, severe headaches, blackouts, spinal or other injuries as a result. These can lead to the other extreme, the inability to exercise for long periods till recovery is complete. So every activity should be performed only in moderation and sensitivity to body signals is very important.

Boredom

Boredom causes undue stress since activity gets reduced along with body processes, leading to a depressed state of mind. This can lead to a number of problems both mental and physical that not only results in physical ailments but also leads to ills in society. Young people who are jobless, and cannot sit idle because they have the energy, mental capability and intelligence may be driven to mental depression and physical ill-health, leading to low self-esteem and a complete sense of worthlessness. Because of extreme frustration they may adopt measures to draw attention which we are witnessing today in the form of suicides, accidents, and the like. Sri Sathya Sai has declared that[27].

> ***Illness is caused more by malnutrition of the mind than the body. The treatment recommended is repeating the name of God. A regulated life and habits are two-third the treatment while medicines contribute only one-third.***

The youth today are increasingly using their energies, creativity and intelligence in antisocial ways, by getting involved in gambling, murder, theft, terrorism and the like, all for the sake of money. This is what we are witnessing today in all societies; mental ills that are difficult to cure, because FEAR is the biggest cause of illness.

Love and not retaliation appear to be the only means to rebuild the mental health of people, and re-establish faith in our youth. In addition, fasting and prayer can bring about a change of heart to help them to discover their own divinity and that of others around them. In this way, people can free themselves and others from the ills and consequent

---

27 *Sanathana Sarathi,* Vol 39, No. 3, March 1996, p.75.

destruction of such a beautiful world. God does help those who help themselves.

Thus in healthy individuals, fasting prevents onset of disease by revitalizing the body processes. In those who are sick, it controls the progression of the disease, and is an important tool to use in preventive medicine along with other alternative natural and medical therapies. While food provides energy and heat, fasting leads to health and purity of the body, because it helps in eliminating body toxins quite effectively.

FEASTING

Feasting always triggers a connection with celebrations be it a mere social get-together or for celebrating festivals, birthdays, anniversaries or any other event. Some hint of feasting as part of breaking fasts has been dealt with in the chapters on Fasting. Other festivals in which fasting precedes the festivities, such as Durga Puja, Christmas, Easter, Eid and so on, have been included under Fasting as well as in this section for the fervour they create and the feasting that follows the ritual.

This section covers 6 chapters:

- ❐ Feasting
- ❐ Religious Feasts
- ❐ Social Feasts
- ❐ Circumstantial Feasts
- ❐ Feasting and Health
- ❐ Way to Peace

FEASTING

Chapter 7

Feasting means creating a spirit of celebration and is the sign of sharing joy arising from any event in life be it enjoyment of a festival in the family, commemoration of a national day, important person or Prophet, or the festive activity associated with family or social events. In India, feasting plays a very important role in the life of people and therefore there are so many holidays in the year, that foreign visitors or business associates often wonder when we Indians work. It has been estimated that 50-60 days off work in a year is the norm, which can be even more for some professions than others. Tables 7.1 and 7.2 give a fair idea of the calendar indicating holidays granted for festivals and other occasions not accounted for on a regular basis.

The holidays included in Table 7.1 are issued through a notification of the State government in every region of the country. The list presented has been issued by the government for the National Capital Territory of Delhi, for the year 2006 (Saka Era 1927-28). The names of festivals and celebrations may vary slightly in lists of other states depending on the local festivals they celebrate. It will be noticed that the approved holidays add up to 18 days in the year. In addition to this, there are a

Table 7.1: Annual gazetted holidays for year 2006

S. No.	Name of the Holiday	Month (Solar Calendar)	Month (Lunar Calendar)
1.*	Id-ul-Zuha (Bakrid)	January 11	Pausa 21
2.	Republic Day	January 26	Magha 06
3.*	Muharram	February 09	Magha 20
4.	Holi	March 15	Phalguna 24
5.	Ram Naumi	April 06	Chaitra16
6.	Mahavir Jayanti	April 11	Chaitra 21
7.*	Id-Milad-un-Nabi (Birthday of Prophet Mohammed)	April 11	Chaitra 21
8.	Good Friday	April 14	Chaitra 24
9.	Buddha Purnima	May 13	Vaisakha 23
10.	Independence Day	August 15	Sravana 24
11.	Janamashtami	August 16	Sravana 25
12.	Gandhi Jayanti	October 2	Asvina 10
13.	Dussehra (Vijaya Dashami)	October 2	Asvina 10
14.	Maharishi Valmiki's Birthday	October 7	Asvina 15
15.	Diwali	October 21	Asvina 29
16.*	Id-ul-Fitr	October 25	Kartika 03
17.	Guru Nanak's Birthday	November 05	Kartika 14
18.	Christmas Day	December 25	Pausa 04

*Subject to appearance of the moon.

number of restricted days off work, given for special celebrations of non-nationally established holidays as for minorities, tribal or local festivities and so on, in the various regions of the country. These have been presented in Table 7.2.

Table 7.2: Restricted holidays in 2006

S.No.	Name of the Holiday	Month (Solar Calendar)	Month (Lunar Calendar)
1.	New Year's Day	January 01	Pausa 11
2.	Guru Govind Singh's Birthday	January 05	Pausa 15
3.	Makara Sankranti	January 14	Pausa 24
4.	Pongal	January 15	Pausa 25
5.	Basant Panchami	February 02	Magha 13
6.	Guru Ravidas's Birthday	February 13	Magha 24
7.	Maharishi Dayanand Saraswati Jayanti	February 23	Phalguna 04
8.	Mahashivaratri	February 26	Phalguna 07
9.	Holi (Holikadahana/Dolyatra)	March 14	Phalguna 23
10.	Chaitra Sukhladi	March 30	Chaitra 09
11.	Vaisakhi	April 14	Chaitra 24
12.	Mesadi	April 14	Chaitra 24
13.	Vishu	April 15	Chaitra 25
14.	Vaisakhadi (Bengal)/ Bihu (Assam)	April 15	Chaitra 25
15.	Rath Yatra	June 27	Asadha 06
16.	Hazrat Ali's Birthday	August 08	Sravana 17
17.	Raksha Bandhan	August 09	Sravana 18
18.	Parsi New Year	August 20	Sravana 29
19.	Ganesha Chaturthi	August 27	Bhadra 05
20.	Onam	September 05	Bhadra 14
21.	Dussehra (Maha Saptami)	September 29	Asvina 07
22.	Dussehra (Maha Ashtami)	September 30	Asvina 08
23	Dussehra (Maha Navami)	October 01	Asvina 09
24.	Jamat-ul-Alvida	October 20	Asvina 28
25.	Deepawali (South India)	October 20	Asvina 28
26.	Govardhan Puja	October 22	Asvina 30
27.	Bhai Duj	October 24	Kartika 02
28.	Chatt Festival	October 28	Kartika 06
29.	Guru Teg Bahadur Martyrdom Day	November 24	Agrahayana 03
30.	Christmas Eve	December 24	Pausa

As seen from Table 7.2, these account for 30 days taking the total to 48 days in the year. The dates may vary if the festivals follow the lunar calendar. To this are added days due to unexpected circumstances like sickness, emergency, disasters or national mourning. Since everyone does not observe all the days as expected, one can imagine the amount of festivity or leisure time that is granted and paid for by employers.

Thus, feasting is an important aspect of life in India and in every country and is being discussed under three main heads namely, Cultural, Social and Circumstantial Feasts. These are further subdivided into various types of celebrations as indicated in Fig. 7.1.

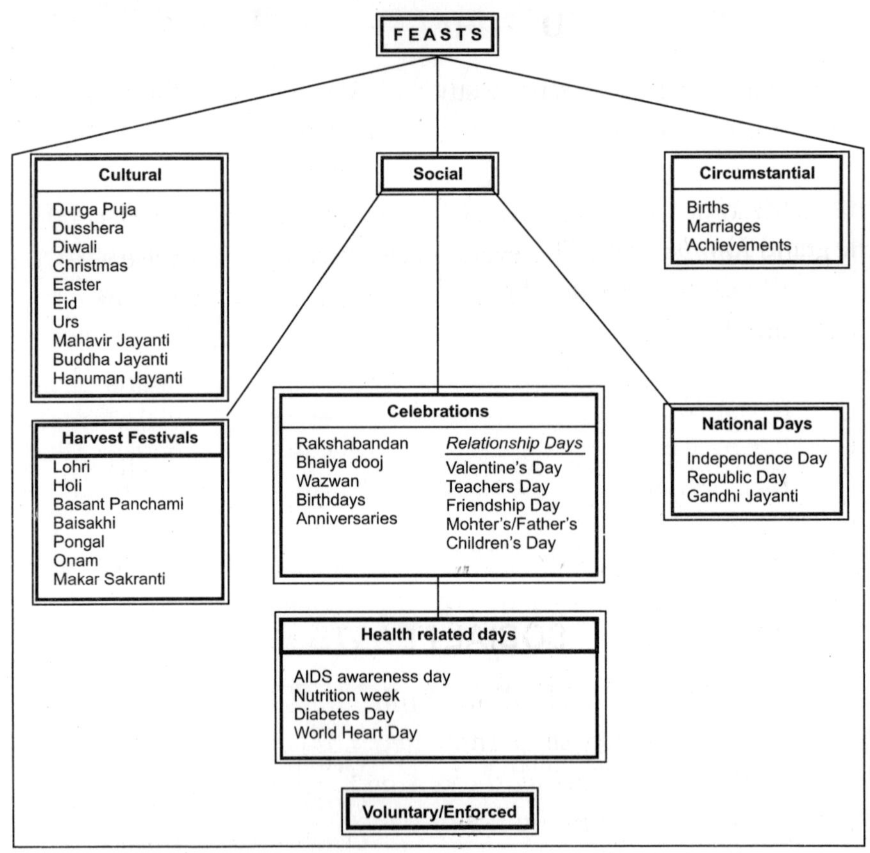

Fig. 7.1: Classification of feasts

It will be seen from Fig. 7.1, that cultural feasts cover celebrations built around the veneration of the concerned deities. It must however be stressed here, that all religious rituals which do not include fasting as a major component, or in which fasting is optionally observed, or may not be practiced everywhere are being included under feasting. This is because they are celebrated with great fervour after a lull in activity that results after the festival and its accompanying feasting is over, as in other nonreligious celebrations, such as social and circumstantial feasting. Feasting also includes birth anniversaries of Gods, Goddesses and Prophets but since all of them cannot be discussed in detail some have been listed and briefly described.

CULTURAL FEASTS

Traditional celebrations were mostly built around religious functions and family get-togethers to share joy and feasting irrespective of the reason for doing so. Most festivals in India have a cultural basis and are celebrated in honour of some God or Goddess, or the commemoration of a legend as is the grand *Kumbh Mela*. This event is celebrated once in twelve years, and mythically it recalls the coming up of the vessel of *amrita* at the churning of the ocean of milk by Lord Shiva. Festivals are enjoyed for a number of reasons varying from mythical and cultural connections, seasonal changes and the delight of culinary excellence with which each celebration is linked.

Each celebration has its own traditions of fairs or *melas* in which people participate wholeheartedly be it a holy dip in the Ganges, pilgrimages or festivities built around commemoration of Prophets, Gods and Goddesses.

SOCIAL FEASTS

Social feasts include celebrations built around the harvest festivals throughout the country since India depends greatly on nature for the bounty of its harvest. Further the getting together of people for family occasions and celebrating by feasting related to the specific nature of the occasion is common practice.

There are certain National days which are celebrated with zest and a feeling of patriotism such as Independence Day, Republic Day, commemorative days like Gandhi Jayanti and the like.

Further, certain days have been declared by the agencies of the United Nations for health improvement and development of countries around the world. Some of them are AIDS Awareness Day, Nutrition Week, World Heart Day, Diabetes Day, Elders day, International Day of the Child, Obesity Day and so on. Most developing countries celebrate these days with the focus desired through organizations, who plan specific awareness programmes and set up fairs or exhibitions, specially arranged for public participation. These special days are also added to the celebrations in every country, since they are meant for spreading knowledge to the common man as well as providing enjoyment for the whole family through games and food stalls.

CIRCUMSTANTIAL FEASTS

As the name suggests, these are celebrations connected with expected or unexpected changes in circumstances related to living styles, economic and social status. Some examples are the birth of a child in the family, achievements for which hard work has been put in, the announcement of an engagement or wedding and so on.

It will be observed that in India, every occasion is marked by some kind of celebration and feasting, whether it is passing an examination or building a house.

Present Scenario

Today, a lot of festivals are celebrated for a cause since the country faces so many natural disasters, the Tsunami of 2005 having shaken the country and the world to the core. Since then there have been so many devastating earthquakes as well as man-made disasters.

It is heartening to see that festivity is getting a positive direction and inculcating good feelings of unity through concern and care, which is our national heritage. All the cash collections accompanying celebrations are diverted to causes and charities that assist people in distress. Such celebrations are held as cultural or social events in clubs, farmhouses, homes, hotels, all of which have open spaces and yet remain exclusive.

CULTURAL FEASTS

India has always been known for its colourful festivals with their celebratory fervour, religious feasting therefore is all about celebrating festivals, each with its different aura and emphasis on regional menus, eating and sharing customs, spiritual focus and the like. What they all have in common however are fresh flowers, exchange of gifts, new clothes, meeting new and old friends and offering sweets all summing up to a typical celebration. Although the significance of these festivals varies with each occasion, all of them are observed with great pomp and show, and joy without any exception. The basic characteristics of Indian festivals are gaiety, enthusiasm, feasting, customs, rituals and prayers to God, most of them related to relationship bonding or connectivity.

Culture and tradition dictate that every occasion is marked by feasting. There are however, some feasts which may or may not follow fasting such as harvest festivals. Most festivals in India follow the lunar calendar and therefore fall on different dates each year, shifting by a few days within the same lunar month.

Six cultural feasts are being described as celebrated in their ritualistic finery, along with three *Jayantis* or birth anniversaries of prophets which form important national holidays. These are all depicted through Fig. 8.1.

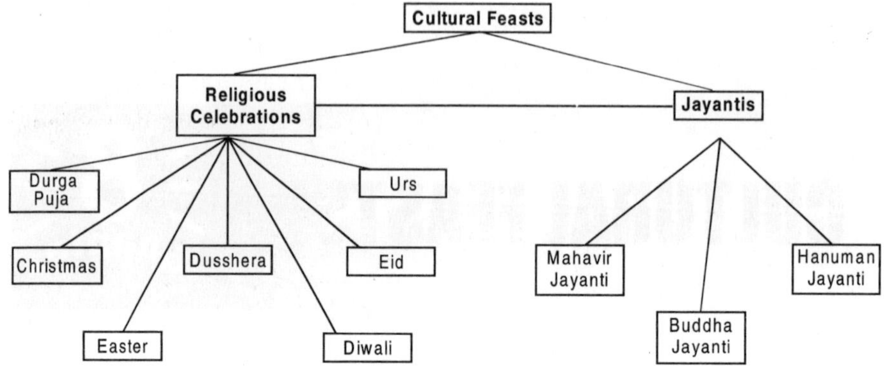

Fig. 8.1: Cultural feasts and Jayantis

A few festivals which are celebrated annually on a regular basis are being briefly discussed. There may be many others which are local to tribal areas or remote regions of the country that are celebrated with equal fervour but are not well documented.

DURGA PUJA

The celebrations of *Durga puja* are being highlighted as a festival that is the most looked forward to, especially in Bengal, which is known as the land of festivals. Bengal is supposed to have 13 festivals in 12 months in addition to a host of other occasions for celebrations. The year starts with *Baisakh* and ends in *Chaitra.* Table 8.1 summarizes the festivals as they occur during the lunar year.

Table 8.1: Festivals of Bengal

Month	Festival	Celebration
Baisakh	*New Year*	Known as *Poila Baisakh,* it is the most significant day for traders who open new books of accounts called

(Contd...)

		halkhata wrapped in bright red colour. At dawn, traders rush to temples, offer puja and seek blessings for a prosperous new trading year. Shops are decorated with mango leaves, flowers and lights and every town reverberates with festive music. Patrons offer sweets and roses to all who visit the shops. Householders too get absorbed in prayer for health of the family, exchange gifts and enjoy festivities throughout the day.
Ashad and *Shravan*	*Rathyatra* and *Raas*	Decorated chariots carry the Goddess in processions throughout the city rejoicing in prayer and festivity.
Ashwin	*Durga Puja*	Prayer accompanying the celestial chime of puja and festivity in *pandals* erected at open spaces, under a cloudless azure sky. After the immersion, there is a lull in the atmosphere and life gradually returns to normal.
Paush and *Magh*	Preparation of sweets	Markets flooded with choicest sweets in festive spirit.
Phagun	*Holi*	Played with natural colours and flower petals.

Bengali festivals thus, start with the New Year in the hot summer months of Baisakh, followed by the Rathyatra and Raas during the monsoons, the celestial chime of Durga puja in Ashwin followed by Holi the festival of colours in Phagun.

History

According to the *Puranas,* King Suratha, used to worship the goddess Durga in spring and thus *Durga Puja* was also known as *Basanti Puja* or *Saradotsav*. But Lord Rama conducted an untimely worship of Durga in autumn, prior to His quest to avenge Ravana for kidnapping Sita, and is therefore also known as *Akal Bodhon*. It is believed that Rama performed the *Chamundi Homa*, following which the Goddess divulged to Him the way to kill Ravana. Myth has it that *puja* was performed when the Gods and Goddesses were awake, a period known as *Uttarayan* and was not held when the Gods and Goddesses rested, known as *Dakshinayan* as was the traditional practice.

A period follows during which prayer is offered for the peace and welfare of ancestors which represents a fortnight before *Mahalaya* known as *Pitri-paksha*, a period also known as *Shraadh* in many northern regions of the country.

Pitri-paksha

Pitri paksha is the time to express reverence and gratitude to deceased elders, and is also a means of instilling reverence for them in the minds of the younger generation. According to Hindu belief, it is one of the important duties of every person to perform the rituals according to the *shastras,* during this fortnight which holds great religious merit.

Rituals

The rituals involve the worship of ancestors in the presence of a temple priest invited to every home especially on the last day of the *paksh.* Every effort is made to satisfy whatever the ancestors had wished for, during their lifetime, in the belief that they will rest in peace. In fact most traditional homes still have a family priest who presides over all the family functions, be it the *puja* for marriages, naming ceremony of a newborn, death or other. On each day of the fortnight, special offerings, including favourite food items of the departed souls, are specially prepared and offered to the *pandits* or priests who are invited to perform *puja* in the homes and thereafter fed. Balls of rice and flour, called *pinda*, are prepared and offered, along with the sacred *kusha* grass and flowers, amidst sprinkling of holy water and chanting of *mantras* from the *Sam Veda*. A small portion of the *prasaad* is also fed to the crow, considered as a connection between the world of the living and the dead. Charities are given to the needy thereafter.

The *Shraddh* rituals performed during *Pitri paksha* are not funeral ceremonies. They are rather *Pitru-Yajna* of the ancestral forms, kept along with the deities normally worshipped in homes at prayer time. *Shraddh* is mainly performed for three generations of *pitrus,* namely the father, the grandfather and the great grandfather. When performed for all the ancestors, seven generations of ancestors are believed to benefit from it. Departed spirits who may be dwelling in heaven or hell as well as those who may have been reborn as humans or as any other form of life, all benefit from oblations offered during *shraddh* rituals.

Shraddh must be performed with full faith, devotion and reverence for those who are no more. According to Hindu scriptures, a son who does not perform *Shraddh* for his ancestors is an ungrateful son. The scriptures condemn such a person to a life of misery and poverty.

The final day of *Pitri paksha* is the new moon day called *Mahalaya Amavasya*. It is believed that on this day, the departed souls leave their abode and come down to the world of mortals to visit the homes of their descendants.

It is the day when many throng to the banks of river *Ganga,* clad in dhotis to offer prayers to their relatives and forefathers. People in the pre-dawn hours pray for their demised relatives and take holy dips in the Ganges. This ritual is known as *Tarpan* and bears immense significance for the Bengalis. According to Muktipada Bhattacharya, chief priest, Shivmandir, *Mahalaya* literally means the house of happiness. On this day, departed spirits are supposed to descend on earth to be close to their loved ones. *Tarpan* is our way of satisfying them through offerings.

Mahalaya

Mahalaya starts seven days prior to the pujas and indicates the end of *Pitri-paksha* and start of *Devipaksha* or *Durga puja* celebrations, when the Goddess Durga visits the earth for only four days. Mahalaya is the traditional six-day countdown to *Mahasaptami* and is the first day of the commencement of the Durga puja rituals.

Devipaksha signifies the waking up of the Gods and Goddesses to prepare themselves for Durga puja. The predawn hours of the day is marked by devotional recitals on *Akashvani* or All India Radio, and signals the start of the countdown to Durga Puja.

In the year 1930, Mahalaya was first broadcast over the radio through *Akashvani*. The programme of devotional music was sung by a number of artists among whom Birendra Krishna Bhadra's voice became associated with Mahalaya and still rings in the air from dawn during the entire period.

Puja Days

The five festive days of Puja welcoming Devi Durga overlap with the *navratras* and are aplomb with rituals. According to Hindu mythology, the trilogy of Brahma, Vishnu and Maheshwara created the ultimate sources of light and power called *shaktis*. These were female forms and created with the purpose of killing the demons, Rahu and Ketu. Though known by various names, these *shaktis* were actually different manifestations of Goddess Durga also known as Shakti. The festival thus enforces that women are stronger than men.

In fact Shakti is the *Devi* considered closest to Shiva and in the South there are temples dedicated to this form of the goddess known as Shakti temples or *Pithalayas*. Durga however, is the most important among the various manifestations of Shakti.

The sixth day after Mahalaya when Goddess Durga is welcomed is known as *Shasthi*.

Shasthi

On Shashti day, Goddess Durga is welcomed with much fanfare and zest when Her beautifully sculpted face is unveiled through a ritual called the *Bodhon* ritual. Right above the image of Durga is Lord Shiva, who represents cosmic consciousness. Elaborate rituals and *bhajans* start from dawn till dusk when the *aarti*-performer, holding a mud pot with blazing coal, dances to a trance with the rhythmic beat of the drums, as aromatic fumes permeate the air creating a mystic ambience.

Saptami

Saptami is the seventh day which coincides with the first day of Durga puja when the *Kola Bow* ritual commences with pre-dawn bathing. In the early hours, some twigs of white *aparajita* plant along with nine bunches of yellow threads are used to tie the *Navapatrika* or nine plants. The nine plants comprise banana, colocassia, turmeric, jayanti, wood apple, pomegranate, arum, rice and the ashoka tree. The nine plants of *Navapatrika* represent the nine forms of the Goddess and therefore, are symbolically bathed with waters brought from eight different holy places. This bathing ritual is accompanied by varied *mantra* recitations accompanied by diverse musical instruments, for the different forms of the goddess.

Forms of Durga

Goddess Durga is a symbol of the Universal Mother who protects, provides, instills respect, devotion, love and care in the hearts of all. Since ancient times, women have upheld the dignity and honour of the family and community and earned the grace of the Goddess. *Varalaxmi* is the form who grants all the boons that women pray for. While she is referred to by numerous names in every region of the country, her nine forms as spelt out in the *Puranic* Encyclopedia are indicated in Table 8.2.

Table 8.2: The nine forms of Durga Ma

Puranic Forms	Navdurga Forms
Nilakanthi	*Shailputri*
Ksemankari	*Brahmacharani*
Harasiddhi	*Chandraghanta*
Raudra	*Kooshmanda*

(Contd...)

Vana	*Skandmaata*
Agni	*Katyayani*
Jaya	*Kaalratri*
Vindhyavasini	*Mahagauri*
Ripunasini	*Siddhidatri*

She is commonly addressed as *Lakshmi, Saraswati, Shakti, Sharada, Sheranwali Ma, Paharanwali Ma, Jyotir Ma, Durga Mata.* Various other titles have been used for expressing Her glory, talents and the grace she bestows on all.

Ashtami

Ashtami the eighth day, celebrates the victory of the Goddess over *Mahishasura,* the demon, the day when devotees recite the sacred mantras and offer flowers or *pushpanjali* to Devi Durga and ritualistically offer animal sacrifices while praying for her blessings. The animals have now gradually been substituted with *chalkumro,* a type of pumpkin, cucumber and banana.

Navami

Last and ninth day of Durga Puja marks the commencement of *Sandhi Puja* which signifies the end of *Ashtami* and the beginning of *Navami* the day on which 108 earthenware lamps are lighted. At this time, Devi Durga is believed to have transformed into Devi Chamunda, her ferocious form, to kill *Chando* and *Mundo*, the two generals of *Mahishasura,* the Buffalo Demon. *Navami Bhog* is a traditional ritual on this day in which Goddess Durga is offered food which is later distributed among the devotees as *prasaad.*

In Kerala, Tamil Nadu and Mysore, Navami is observed as *Ayudha Puja* day when people exchange greetings by offering *shami* leaves to each other. Even today, it is a matter of faith that our army and police forces lay down their weapons on this day and take them back after the ritual puja.

Ayudha is applied in a wider sense to include all tools that are used to earn one's livelihood. Pens, books, tractors, cars, agricultural implements are all decorated with flowers and worshipped on *Vijay*

Dashmi for invoking God's blessings. This ancient belief and concept is expounded in the *Bhagavatam* where *Prahalad* fearlessly remarked that the Lord is omnipresent, and dwells in pillars as well as in dust particles.

Dashami

Dashami is the tenth day and the last day of the celebrations when the Goddess Durga is united with Shiva after her play is over, and accompanied by her children sets out for *Kailash*, her husband's abode. *Sindur Khela*, the vermillion game, considered a major event of Dashami is enjoyed by married women who apply vermillion on each other and exchange greetings and sweets.

In the evening with a heavy heart, the devotees immerse the clay idol of Durga in the sacred Ganges, symbolizing the immersion in the ocean of consciousness of Lord Shiva which marks the culmination of the spiritual process. Devotees thus bid her goodbye and earnestly wait to see her again the following year.

When the immersion is completed with the accompanying recitations and fanfare, people greet each other with *vijaya* greetings and men follow the customary *Kolakuli* by embracing each other. Durga Puja is celebrated without religious inhibitions as it is a socio-cultural festival that tends to renew kinship with friends and relatives year after year.

The Dashmi day is also linked with the Mahabharata since the *Pandavas* after 12 years in exile had to spend one year *incognito.* When they entered the kingdom they left their weapons concealed behind a *Shami* tree. After a year they collected the weapons, offered thanksgiving and then commenced the war with the *Kauravas* on Vijay Dashmi.

The presence of the four offsprings of the Goddess in the battlefield is symbolic. When subtle intelligence represented by Ganesha is applied to nurturing nature, wealth in the form of Lakshmi evolved. Material prosperity begets learning and fine arts as symbolized by Saraswati, and military prowess for protection and preservation is represented by Kartikeya. All four are worshipped for worldly achievements.

All round material prosperity follows a God-demon principle. These are to be accepted as gifts of the divine, as stepping stones for further progress following the law of nature. But, the pernicious ego sheltered under the veil of beastly ignorance, identifies itself as omnipotent and breaks the natural law of harmony and peace. At this spiritual crisis, the primordial nature in the form of Goddess Durga intervenes to vanquish the ego and makes it surrender to her. With her 10 hands wielding weapons and the wisdom of the third eye, she transcends the 10 human senses of perception and action, to bring about the lost harmony in creation.

Present Scenario

Festive fervour takes over the cities at least one month before hand, when shops display their wares for a shopping bonanza before the puja days arrive. During Durga Puja people throng to *Durga Puja pandals* to revel in fun-filled, devotional extravaganza. It is the time of the year when the community in the city virtually drops every work at hand and starts preparing for welcoming Goddess Durga to her earthly abode.

By now the shopping is done, the local theatre production rehearsals completed and the schedule packed for four days of celebrations. The only decision left to be made is, which pandal should be visited and which can be ignored. These days, there is keen competition between pandal makers and sculptors of the Goddess, as prizes are awarded for the best pandals and their innovative goddess forms and displays.

Old timers have seen puja celebrations in the city shift gears from night long screening of classic films and early morning preparation for *pushpanjali* to rock shows and empty pandals. Perhaps keeping in touch with the times is the only way out for the city's vintage pujas.

With mushrooming of pujas and big ticket corporate sponsorships ruling the roost, puja committees are going all out to outdo each other on the innovation front. The budget of these pujas range from 5 lakh to 25 lakh. The special attractions of these are *dhakis* dancing to welcome the Goddess at a traditional pandal. The more affluent also invite *Bollywood* singers, rock bands, comedians and so on. Folk theatre and *Jatra* are also in store in few cases.

Jatra, a folk form of East India, was the backbone of Durga and Kali Puja celebrations in the capital for over three decades from the 1960s. It is still extremely popular in West Bengal, Orissa, and Assam. Jatra is a stage presentation of a play or a storyline on a grand scale, which comes across as a movie being enacted in front of an audience. There is a full budget script interspersed with song and dance sequences, lighting, actors and actresses and loads of props. The basic themes of Jatras in Delhi revolved around historical and mythological tales.

With the new forms of entertainment, like movies and discs, gaining popularity among the youth, the Jatra tradition has faded. Apart from an occasional performance in two to three years, Jatra has disappeared from the city's cultural calendar, though it is still popular in West Bengal, Orissa and Assam.

Beautiful idols are made to attract devotees to the pandals. Recently, a society made an idol of thermocol, in contrast to the religious diktat that the idol should be made in clay only. The society felt that the idol is an attempt at infusing something new in the proceedings. There is also the convenience factor. The new generation does not take such keen interest in the puja anymore, so there is always shortage of manpower and thus the light weight thermocol idol, is easier to transport.

The pandal makers are also in a spirit of competition with each other to be judged the best. Three prizes are awarded for the best pandals in the state. Though the outward ruffles have increased, the puja has been preserved in its purest form.

DUSSEHRA

Dussehra is a popular festival in India and is celebrated with great fanfare in most places of India, including *Kullu, Varanasi, Mysore* and slightly differently as *Durga Puja* in Bengal.

Worship of the Goddess is the oldest tradition, representing the female deity's supremacy over the male Gods who were unable to destroy the demon. The worship of Durga also has social implications. As goddess of war, she is a particular favourite with *Kshatriyas*, the warrior caste, once constituting the ruling elite and aristocracy of the country.

Significance

Dussehra is the day in *Satyayuga*, on which Ram, the eighth incarnation of Lord Vishnu, killed the great demon and King of Lanka, *Ravana*. Therefore, this day is also known as *Vijay Dashmi*, because of the victory of Ram over Ravana. The *Puranas* also state that on this day Goddess Durga in her warrior form, killed the buffalo demon *Mahishasura*. The celebration thus marks the victory of Lord Rama over Ravana and the triumph of Goddess Durga over the buffalo demon Mahishasura, both symbolizing the victory of *good* over *evil*. It is recorded that Ram prayed to the Goddess before going to war with Ravana although it was not the scheduled time of the year for the Durga Puja. That is why the navratri fasts and celebrations come twice in the year instead of only once, when the Goddess supposedly visits the earth to redeem the evils facing mankind.

Vijay Dashmi is also known a *Vidya Aramban Day* when children and adults are initiated into learning. This ancient practice is still observed in Kerala and Tamil Nadu, where initiation of children to knowledge is reverentially made by a priest or eldest family member making them write the first alphabets and numerals on raw rice spread over the floor before a lighted lamp.

In Karnataka, where the Goddess of learning presides, thousands of parents with their children flock to temples for the initiation ceremony. It is believed that any new venture started on this day is bound to succeed.

Observance

Preceding Dussehra, the *Ramlila* is enacted for nine days, which depicts the life of Lord Rama through theatrical performances everywhere. On the tenth day which is Dussehra, larger than life clay models or effigies of Ravana and his brother Kumbhkarana and son Meghnath filled with crackers are erected in large spaces for all to see. These effigies are then set on fire using a long flaming pole to ignite them from a distance. Today methods of remote control are used for greater safety.

People watch the three effigies which are a sculptural delight, amidst cracker bursting, as the effigies come crashing down one by one and the sky is filled with light sprayed all over the skyline. It is a source of great delight for children and adults to watch the mammoth cracker display for which they travel long distances to metropolitan cities to watch, in spite of the pollution it creates as seen from the rise in the pollution levels after the festival.

During Dussehra and Durga puja, people decorate the entrances of their homes with *rangoli,* buntings and flower strings. Before sunset, villagers cross state borders, a ritual known as *Simoilanghan*, and worship the *Shami* tree. The leaves of the *Apta* tree are collected and exchanged among friends and relatives as gold.

In many households, sisters apply a sacred *tika* or vermilion mark on the forehead of their brothers, and pray for their health and long life. Brothers bless their sisters and promise to protect them from the hardships in life. After applying *tika*, the sister gives her brother a few eatables along with a coconut. On this occasion, sisters are lavished with gifts, sweets and blessings from their brothers.

The Puja

Dussehra puja varies from region to region and place to place depending on local myth and religious beliefs.

Northern India

In Northern India, the festival is celebrated as Ramlila, in which interesting and important episodes from the Ramayana are enacted in schools, colleges in regular theatres or those built for the festivities temporarily, in huge grounds that resemble fairs. The enactments organized by professionals, depict parts from Rama's life such as the destruction of Ravana and *Bharat Milap,* that is, the reunion of Rama with his estranged brother Bharat, on the former's return to *Ayodhya* after 14 years in exile. These draw large crowds from neighboring states to Delhi every year, and thus the Dussehra night passes in an enthusiastic and enchanting fair-like ambience, although today, under heavy security and police presence.

Himachal Pradesh

In Himachal Pradesh, a week-long fair is held in the hill town of Kullu, as part of the Dussehra celebrations. From the little temples in the hills, deities are brought in procession to the maidan in Kullu, to pay their homage to the reigning deity, Raghunathji. As per tradition, the celebration begins 10 days in advance.

Punjab

In Punjab, Navratri is considered as a period of fasting for nine days, in which only one meal is eaten after prayers at sunset. All cereals, pulses and non-vegetarian foods are avoided during the fasting period. On the 10th day Vijay Dashmi is celebrated.

West Bengal

In West Bengal, the 10 days of festivity are celebrated with intense fervour and zest. Of the ten, nine days are spent in worship and therefore called Navratri or nine nights. The tenth day is celebrated with devotion to Goddess Durga, who occupies a special place in the pantheon of Hindu Gods and Goddesses. She is considered as *shakti* the cosmic energy in all beings.

Beautiful idols of the Goddess Durga are worshipped in elaborate *pandals* for nine days, after which they are carried in procession for immersion or *visarjan* in a river , pond or the sea, depending on where people are located geographically.

Gujarat

In Gujarat, the days are occasions for the colourful and fascinating *garba* dances and music that goes on in the day and night, to lift the spirit of the people and the festival. The women dance around an earthen lamp while singing devotional songs accompanied by rhythmic clapping of hands in which all present participate. The men too join later in the evening.

Karnataka

In Karnataka, the Mysore palace is illuminated for a whole month during Dussehra, and caparisoned elephants lead a colourful procession through the decorated streets of the city. The celebration is known all over the world for its beauty, majesty and the aura and delight it creates.

Tamil Nadu

In Tamil Nadu, the first three days are dedicated to the worship of Lakshmi, the goddess of wealth and prosperity, the next three to *Saraswati,* goddess of learning and arts, and the last three days to Shakti or *Durga.*

Andhra

In Karnataka, Tamil Nadu and Andhra, families arrange dolls or *Bommai Kolu* on artificially constructed steps and decorate with lamps and flowers, all set up on the first day of Navratri. Traditionally the women exchange gifts of coconuts, clothes and sweets.

After the *Saraswati puja* is completed on the ninth day, all the sets are taken down on *Vijay Dashmi* or tenth day, which is considered highly auspicious for children to start their education in dance and music, and to pay their homage to their teachers.

GANGA DUSSEHRA

During the festival of 10-days devotees worship the holy river *Ganga* or Ganges venerated by the Hindus as a mother and goddess. Places like *Rishikesh, Haridwar, Garh-Mukteshwar, Prayag, Varanasi* and so on through which the river flows, hold special significance. Devotees go to these places, to touch the Ganga waters or to bathe in them through the special *ghats* made for the purpose at these places of pilgrimage. Priests too are available for performing puja, when and if desired.

In Haridwar, *aratis* are performed at twilight and the little earthenware lighted lamps placed on dried leaf platters with flowers, are set afloat in the river during and after the *arati* as offerings to the

Mother. The devotees sit on the river banks and watch the lamps till they go out of sight. Many concentrate on the aura of the river and meditate. It is a practice to bring home *Gangajal* or Ganges water which they take after their daily prayers as *charanamrit* or grace. It is used as a means of purification when sprinkled around the house or on other auspicious occasions. The *Gangajal* or water is sprinkled as a benediction of peace and used as a last sacrament when a person leaves his body.

The Ganges

The river holds a special place in the life and consciousness of Indians. It rises in the Himalayas at Gangotri, cascades down mighty boulders, and flows down into the hot plains of Uttar Pradesh, Bihar and finally meets the sea in the Bay of Bengal. At Allahabad, the Ganges merges with the rivers Yamuna and the mythical Saraswati, where their confluence known as *Prayag*, is considered one of the most sacred spots on earth.

The Ganges is the largest river in India, and considered the most sacred river since the ages. Regarded as the celestial river originating in the heavens, the Ganga is a gift to mankind in answer to the great *sadhana* undertaken by *Bhagirath*, a descendant of the *Sagara* dynasty, who prayed for the Ganga to descend onto the parched earth and bring life. This is why she is also called the *Bhagirathi* which comes down with great force and levels off in the plains becoming calm and steady. It is believed that Brahma and Vishnu asked Siva to accept the Ganga into his matted hair. That is why the Ganga is shown flowing from the hair of all Shiva deities. The river thus lost its destructive force and became a placid, calm, life-giving river. The Ganges is therefore, believed to be the Mother who washes away all the sins of mankind. The water of the river is naturally sanctified and pure even though it may appear dirty.

Tourists and researchers have bottled the so-called dirty water of the river at places of pilgrimage, and found that if it is kept for a time, the suspended impurities settle to the bottom and when decanted gives crystal clear, pure water. Another property that needs to be highlighted is that the water never develops a foul odour, no matter how long it is kept, which is not so with municipal water supplies to the cities. Despite the pollution, the Ganges is a symbol of purity, bestowing salvation to the dying and new life to the living.

Present Scenario

People may not perform all the rituals of fasting at Navratri or take part in the Dussehra celebrations but the focus is certainly on the feasting aspects. Special foods are not made at home but bought today, except in the more traditional homes. The spirit of a festival is however, kept alive by the media and so people prefer to watch them in their own comfortable surroundings on television.

DEEPAVALI

Deepavali is a Sanskrit word meaning *rows of lights*. The festival is commonly called *Diwali,* celebrated by rows of lighted lamps and therefore the festival is also known all over as the *Festival of Lights*. Deepavali is a festival of inner enlightenment, an occasion to eradicate one's inner darkness by renouncing addictions and base instincts. It is observed all over the country as well as in those countries which have a sizeable Indian presence. In the USA, Diwali is celebrated every year in the White House.

Deepavali is a 5-day Hindu festival, which occurs on the 15th day of the month of *Kartika,* usually 20 days after *Dussehra*. Traditionally earthenware lamps called *diyas* in which a wick and mustard oil is placed, are kept ready for lighting in the evening.

In fact Diwali falls in the month of so many festivals and celebrations that it is a time when in India everything comes to a near standstill as far as work is concerned and nothing but celebration one after the other, seems to be in the air. Some festivals that come during this month are Guru Nanak's birthday which is celebrated with great fervour and devotion. Delhi has the flower festival *Phoolwalon ki Sair* which dates back to the *Moghul* period, in which all communities take part. Sharad dances depicting *Krishna-Radha* dances with the *gopis* are staged at this time for all to enjoy their *leelas*.

Significance

As with other Indian festivals, Diwali signifies different things to different people across the country. In north India, Diwali celebrates Rama's return from his 14-year exile in the forest and defeat of Ravana, to his kingdom in *Ayodhya* for his coronation as king. In other regions, there are slight variations even among communities, although the mode of celebration and the meaning of the festival remains the same.

Gujarat

In Gujarat, the festival honors Lakshmi, the goddess of beauty and wealth; and lamps are lit because Lakshmi shuns darkness. She visits every home that is lighted. She has been transformed into a Goddess of wealth because of her bounteous nature, but actually *Kubera* is the God of wealth, who has almost been forgotten.

Bengal

In Bengal, the festival is associated with the Goddess *Kali*. Everywhere, it signifies the renewal of life by vanquishing evil, and heralds the approach of winter and the beginning of the second sowing season. For some, Diwali marks the beginning of the New Year for their trade and business. It is therefore common for people to wear new clothes on the day of this festival, pray for prosperity and good tidings and rejoice.

For the Jains, Diwali is an important festival, because on this day *Mahavira,* the last of the Jain *Tirthankaras,* is supposed to have attained *nirvana*. In many *Digambara* temples *laddoos* are offered on Diwali morning. According to the Jain tradition, the chief disciple of Mahavira, Ganadhar Gautam Swami also attained complete knowledge on this very day, thus making Diwali a really special occasion for the Jains to celebrate.

Punjab

The Sikhs also celebrate Diwali to commemorate the laying of the foundation stone of the Golden Temple in 1577. It is also known as *Bandi Chhorh Divas* because the Mughal emperor Jahangir arrested the Sikh Guru Hargobind and imprisoned him in Gwalior although he relented later and released him. The Guru asked that 52 rulers imprisoned with him should also be released. To the joy of the Sikhs when the Guru returned to Amritsar on Diwali the followers were prompted to celebrate the day with lights, and share much joy and happiness.

On Diwali, the Sikhs illuminate their Gurdwaras and homes and decorate them with fresh mango leaves, flowers, buntings, lamps and candles. Early in the morning, Sikh pilgrims take a dip in the sacred tank while reciting the *Japji Sahib* while they circumambulate the tank, and then pray at the Golden Temple.

Uttar Pradesh

In many Krishna temples, Diwali is celebrated as a day of feeding and venerating cows. In Nathdwara, for instance, there is a day-long feast for cattle called *Annakoot*. The sacredness of the cow goes back to the belief of the churning of the cosmic ocean by the gods. Of the 14 jewels which the ocean gave to the gods, *Kamadhenu*, the celestial cow, was one. She was venerated as the mother of the universe. A cow is the constant companion of Sri Krishna, who lived his life as a cowherd boy.

South India

In the South, Diwali has two more legends connected with it. The first legend again concerns the victory of good over evil. *Narakasura* the demon of hell, challenged Krishna to battle. After a fierce fight lasting two days, the demon was killed at dawn on *Narakachaturdashi*. To commemorate this event, people wake up before sunrise and make imitation blood by mixing kumkum or vermillion with oil. After crushing underfoot a bitter fruit as a symbol of the demon, they apply the blood triumphantly on their foreheads. They then have ritual oil baths, anointing themselves with sandalwood paste. Visits to temples for prayers are followed by large family breakfasts of fruits and a variety of sweets.

The second legend is about King Bali, the benevolent demon king of the netherworld. He was so powerful that he became a threat to the power of celestial deities and their kingdoms. Intimidated by his expanding empire and taking advantage of his well-known generosity, they sent Vishnu as the dwarf mendicant *Vamana*, to dilute Bali's power. Vamana shrewdly asked the king for land that would cover three steps as he walked. The king happily granted this gift. Having tricked Bali, Vishnu revealed himself in the full glory of his godhood. He covered the heaven in his first step and the earth in his second. Realizing that he was pitted against the mighty Vishnu, Bali surrendered and offered his own head inviting Vishnu to step on it. Vishnu pushed him into the nether world with his foot. In return Vishnu gave him the lamp of knowledge to light up the dark underworld. He also gave him a blessing that he would return to his people once a year to light millions of lamps from this one lamp so that on the dark new moon night of Diwali, the blinding darkness of ignorance, greed, jealousy, lust, anger, ego, and laziness would be dispelled and the radiance of knowledge, wisdom and friendship prevail. Each year on Diwali even today, one lamp lights another and like a flame burning steadily on a windless night, brings a message of peace and harmony to the world. Diwali is considered a huge family festival, a time to usher in the New Year of love and unity.

In the south of the country people celebrate Diwali usually one day before they do so in the north, although in some years the dates may coincide.

North India

Diwali is celebrated over five days in most of North India on a new-moon day which marks the last day of a 15-day period or *parva* in the month of *Kartik*. The first day of Diwali is *Dhanatrayodashi* or *Dhanteras* the13th day of the first half of the lunar month of *Ashwin*, celebrated to seek the blessings of Goddess Lakshmi, the goddess of wealth.

Dhan means *wealth* and *Trayodashi* means *13th day* and is an auspicious day for shopping for new utensils. The custom was important for households who used this day to change their old cooking utensils, especially for those who could not afford to spend throughout the year. Festivals allowed them something new to look forward to once in a year. There are legends behind *Dhanteras* too, giving reasons why lamps are kept lighted for two days at Diwali.

Western India

Diwali is of great importance to the merchant community too, a time when even the rich decorate and renovate their shops and offices. The *Dev Diwali parva* begins with the *Devprabodhini ekadashi* or the 11th day and ends on *Kartik shukla* 15, known as *Dev Diwali, Kartik Purnima* or *Tripurari purnima.*

Torans of mango leaves and marigolds are hung on doorways. *Rangolis* are drawn with different coloured powders, flowers or dried grains to welcome guests. The traditional motifs in red, blue, green and orange on the doorsteps not only add colour to the festival but are meant to attract the Goddess Lakshmi into the house or shop. A pair of small footprints are drawn too, which symbolize the entry of the goddess of wealth and prosperity, and are often linked with auspicious symbols drawn for good luck. Oil *diyas* are arranged in and around the house. On this day, people buy something for the house or some jewellery for the women and children, along with new clothes for everyone working or living in the establishment. It is auspicious to buy something metallic, silver or steel.

Genesis of Rangoli

Rangoli is the art of painting designs with coloured rice powder, sand , dried flowers and leaves or even other staple grains depending on the region where it is done. It can be traced back to *Chitralakshana,* the earliest Indian treatise on art. Rangoli goes by different names in different regions being referred to as *alpana, aripana, madana, kolam, chowkpurana and muggu.* Diwali infuses a new life into this fast disappearing art form.

Traditionally, rangolis were made at the entrance of homes to welcome guests, who in India are considered divine and revered and honoured as *Atithi devo bhava,* the basis for the exemplary hospitality of India. Rangoli designs vary from the simple, innovative to intricate, the popular ones being the *Swastika, Om* and the *trident*, may or may not be interspersed with floral motifs. Rangoli is symbolic of different family members coming and mingling together like the colours of the art form, to celebrate the festival of colour and lights. Traditionally rangolis were made using natural auspicious ingredients but today, wet paints are also used for brightness and to preserve the decorations for longer periods.

The next day is called *Chhoti Diwali, Kali Chaudas or Naraka Chaturdasi. Narak* means a new era of light and knowledge. *Chaturdasi* implies the fourteenth day on which Kali, the Goddess of strength, is worshipped. This day also focuses on abolishing laziness and evil.

The actual day of Diwali, is celebrated on the third day of the festival, when the moon completely wanes and total darkness sets in the night sky (*Amavasya).* It is the last day of the year in the lunar calendar on which *Lakshmi puja* is performed after which lamps and candles placed in rows everywhere adorn the home, shops, government buildings, monuments and the like. People go out for long drives around the city to witness the sight, the illumination being awesome against the pitch dark skyline.

The entrances to all homes are lit up and decorated with *rangoli* patterns to welcome Lakshmi, the goddess of wealth who shuns darkness. Tiny footprints are drawn at the entrance to symbolize the entrance of the Goddess, and all the lights of the house remain switched on the whole night to attract the Goddess into the house. The illumination on Diwali signifies the end of darkness which stands for ignorance, and marks the beginning of knowledge symbolized by lights that shall enlighten all.

The houses which are not lighted are those in which there has been a bereavement, and in that case, none of the festivals are celebrated for a year. Only the prayer room is lit by a single lamp and prayers offered for the grace of the Goddess in the future.

The festival ends with a mega cracker-bursting session of 5-6 hours, which creates deafening noise and air pollution, yet every family burns fire crackers worth thousands of rupees. Popular fire crackers are sparkling pots, bombs, rockets which burst into coloured stars in the dark night making it a delight to watch. The explosion of fireworks forms a major part of the celebrations especially for kids.

Families dress in new clothes and jewels, exchange Diwali greetings, through gifts and sweets with friends and loved ones and prepare and eat festive meals. It is a time to forget quarrels and make up with people. During this time, homes are thoroughly cleaned and windows are opened to welcome Lakshmi, the goddess of wealth. Candles and lamps are lit as a greeting to Lakshmi.

Playing cards is extremely popular on Diwali day as it is believed that by doing so the goddess of wealth smiles upon the players and ensures her goodwill. The tradition of gambling on Diwali also has a legend behind it. On this day, Goddess *Parvati* played dice with her husband Lord Shiva and she decreed that whosoever gambled on Diwali night would prosper throughout the ensuing year. It is therefore considered auspicious to play before Diwali. Those who lose are believed to be extra blessed as they now make a new beginning on Diwali when they pray for Lakshmi or wealth. Losing also symbolizes that money is not important and it will come and go.

The fourth day of Diwali, *Varsha-pratipada* or *Padwa* falls on the first day of the lunar New Year. Diwali is the last day of financial year in traditional Hindu business organizations, therefore all business accounts of the previous year are settled and new account books are started. The new books are offered in prayer and worshipped along with the image of Lakshmi in silver or gold at a special ceremony. Pledges are taken by participants of *pujas* for removing anger, hatred, and jealousy from their lives. Diwali is considered auspicious for shopping, inaugurations of new homes, business deals or for starting any new ventures and projects.

The fifth day is *Bhaiyya Duj* or *Bhai Duj* also called *Bhaubeej* or *Bhayitika* and falls two days after Diwali. On this day, brothers and sisters meet to express their love and affection for each other. The celebrations vary in different regions.

On *Balipratipada*, the final day of the festival, Bali, an ancient Indian king, is also remembered as he destroyed the centuries-old philosophies and traditions of the time. However, he is remembered for being a generous person and so the focus of this day is to see the good in others, including those whom one does not like, and to see the divinity in all.

Present Scenario

As the festival of Diwali nears, shops stock up on *diyas*, figurines of Gods, Goddesses and eco-friendly goods of all kinds for shoppers as well. Cracker bursting has been somewhat reduced, the children being taught in schools about the harm that they can do through the noise and air pollution they cause, and the resulting diseases that ensue. Besides, there is now greater awareness about the children working in the cracker factories, who should be in school instead of endangering their health with exposure to explosives. This has reduced though only slightly, the pollution levels during the Dussehra–Diwali season. Now especially in cities and urban environments, the traditional *diyas* have been largely substituted by electric lighting, with fancy and attractive bulbs and blinking lights.

Diwali is the brightest festival but has a dark side too, in the high stake gambling that people resort to in the name of Deepavali.

As against simplicity in traditional worship where the same *puja thali* was used for all year round prayers, today pretty *puja thalis* are available, specially decorated for the festive season of Diwali. They come in all shapes and sizes, and make pretty festive gifts. The Diwali *puja thali* contains all the essential accessories for a puja: a bell, small *katauri,* a *matka,* an *om* coin and a leaf-shaped tiny box to hold *roli chawal.* Idols of Ganesh and Lakshmi, the deities associated with wealth and prosperity, which are included in the set, are all ready to use at prayer time.

Diwali has become commercialised as the biggest annual consumer festival because every family shops for sweets, gifts and fireworks. There are numerous discounts offered by companies to attract the customer.

There is a ever-rising demand for a wide variety of beautifully packed and decorated gift options available in the markets. The gifts could range from simple candies to silver and gold jewellery.

The tradition of playing cards — *flash* and *rummy* with stakes on this particular day continues even today, except that home sessions have given way to *casinos* and local gambling houses, which do brisk business during the Diwali week. In most homes, people invite their friends and relatives to play cards. Lavish card parties are thrown and people play cards throughout the night, drink and feast on the most sumptuous food.

To add to the festival of Diwali, fairs called *Diwali Melas* are held. Girls and women especially dress attractively during the festival. Wearing colourful clothing, new jewellery with their hands decorated with innovative henna designs.There are plenty of activities that take place at a mela which include cultural performances, fortune tellers, puppet shows, dance competitions, lucky draws and many more. Food stalls are also set up, selling sweet, and spicy foods. A variety of rides are present during the fair, which include Ferris wheels and rides on animals such as elephants and camels.

Since Diwali is no fun without crackers, community celebrations organised by Resident Welfare Associations and clubs have taken the place of family cracker bursting, towards which everyone contributes, to reduce the pollution levels in every street. Children can then safely enjoy the display of fire crackers and the elders can even participate in candling them off.

By the time the autumn festivals end, the spirit of Christmas takes over the greeting and gifting. The merry mood goes on till the New Year is rung in, and then the cycle of festivities is repeated. It is as though, the Gods are showering all their blessings in India for the world.

EID

The sizeable Muslim community has its festivals in common with the Muslim communities across the world. Basically, there are three festive occasions celebrated by the Muslims in particular, called *Eid-ul-Fitr, Eid-ul-Zuha,* and *Eid-milad-un-Nabi,* all of which are celebrated in India.

Eid comprises three days of celebration after the holy month of *Ramadan*, but the main activities occur on the first day which coincides with the first day of *Shawwal* in the Muslim calendar, when people dressed in new clothes and in their best attires greet each other, friends, family and acquaintances by saying *Eid mubarak.* Children play with dyed hard-boiled eggs and open their gifts much like at Easter.

Eid-ul-Fitr

Eid-ul-Fitr is popularly known as the festival of *the breaking of the fast*, and is celebrated on sighting the new moon, which marks the end of the long fasting period of Ramadan. The festival is a joyous occasion marked by feasting on special foods and delicacies prepared for the occasion and later distributed to neighbours and friends while greeting them.

During *Eid-ul-Fitr* an obligatory charitable gift from every Muslim called *Zakat* is given to the poor and needy. The purpose is to purify oneself from all types of indecent acts — be it of thoughts, words or deeds while fasting.

People engage in charitable ventures having distributed *alms* to all assembled at the *Idgah*, where the prayers and distribution are led by the *Imam*. The *Idgah* is a large place especially set aside for large congregations who attend the special Eid prayer early in the morning. It can be an open ground or field where people can pray together in large numbers. On other occasions, the proper place for prayer is considered the mosque.

The holy month of Ramadan is auspicious for all Muslims because the *Quran* was revealed to Prophet Muhammad during this sacred month over a period of 23 years. The celebration of Eid-ul-Fitr after Ramadan therefore, is truly spirited and very significant.

Eid-ul-Zuha

Is also called *Bakrid* or *Eid-ul-adha* and is a festival of great rejoicing, celebrated with traditional fervour and gaiety in India. On Eid-ul-

Zuha, thousands of devotees gather in mosques to offer special congregational prayers, after which greetings and gifts are exchanged. It is basically referred to as a *festival of sacrifice*. It is a four-day celebration during which Muslims all over the world offer a sacrifice by slaughtering a sheep, cow or goat following traditional Islamic customs. The major part (share) of the sacrificed meat is firstly distributed to the poor and needy and the rest is then distributed to relatives and friends. This meat is a *prasaad* or *Tabarruk* which is shared by friends, neighbours and family.

Eid-ul-Zuha is a commemoration of *Hazrat Ibrahim's* great test of obedience to Allah, who ordered him to sacrifice the thing dearest to him. Ibrahim decided to sacrifice his son Ismail at Mina, near Mecca. As the great religious leader was on the point of applying the sword to Ismail's throat, it was revealed to him that the exercise was merely a test of his faith in Allah, which he successfully passed and a ram was sacrificed in place of his son Ismail.

Eid-ul-Zuha is a reminder of Prophet Ibrahim's readiness to sacrifice his son for God's sake. It also marks the completion of *Haj*, the pilgrimage to Mecca and Medina. On this day special *dua* is recited in one voice by crores of Muslims for peace and prosperity. The pilgrimage is the largest annual congregation of Muslims from all over the world and is the greatest conference of peace known in the history of mankind. The theme of the pilgrimage is peace with each other, one's soul and with God.

On *Bakrid*, Muslims go to the mosques in the morning to offer prayers to Allah, and then sacrifice the animal after coming back home. *Bakr* means sheep and it is common for the affluent to sacrifice one animal per member of the family, and distribute two-thirds of the meat among the poor. A full grown camel, cow, goat or sheep, free from disease, is sacrificed as desired. Bakrid is also a day of feasting and visiting friends to wish them *Eid Mubarak*.

Eid-Milad-un-Nabi

Eid-Milad-un-Nabi is also called *Barrahfaat* since it is the day when the prophet Mohammad was born and also died. It falls on the 12th day of *Rabbi-ul-Awwal,* the third month of the Islamic calendar. Since the day is also the death anniversary of the Prophet, the word *Barah* is used, standing for the twelve days of the Prophet's sickness, before He left his body.

In some parts of the country, a ceremony known as the *sandal rite* is performed over the symbolic footprints of the Prophet engraved in stone. A replica of *buraq*, a horse on which the Prophet is believed to have ascended to heaven, is kept near the footprints, and anointed with sandal paste or scented powder. The house or casket in which these are placed is elaborately decorated. *Elegies* or *marsiyas* are sung in memory of the last days of the prophet. The 12th day or the *Urs* is observed quietly, in prayer and almsgiving.

The most orthodox Muslims, called *Wahabbis* as in Saudi Arabia, do not celebrate Eid-Milad-un-Nabi as it is also the death anniversary of the Prophet. Besides, they do not believe in God with form. However, the birth of the Prophet is celebrated in India, Pakistan and the Far East, as is done for other prophets and *avatars,* not only by the Muslims but by the other communities too. No special feasts are prepared or celebrations visible on this day but the Prophet and his messages are heard by groups where, eminent speakers are invited to address the audience, on the life and preachings of the Prophet.

Islam follows an unique approach to celebrating Eid. After *namaz* or prayer, Muslims are required to celebrate in a responsible manner, greeting one another at home and or in the neighbourhood. People visit each other's homes and partake of festive meals comprising special dishes, beverages and desserts. Children receive gifts and sweets on this special occasion.

During the religious feasts of *Eid-ul-Fitr* and *Eid-ul-Adha*, the old and the young wear brand new clothes, families get together, gifts and money called *Eedi* are distributed among children and joy and cheer fills the air. These two feasts are very special and accompanied by strong religious sentiments and meaning. The beginning of both Eids are marked by morning prayers or *Salat-ul-Eid* in praise of God, after which the eldest family members are visited first followed by others, to seek forgiveness for any wrongdoings of the year gone by, and reinforcing the feelings of brotherhood.

Present Scenario

With the introduction of speedy means of communication, people today need not visit others to greet them, as e-cards, mails, wireless phones and mobiles are available. They can hear, see and wish their family and friends who may be in far-off places or countries. What is lost however, is the personal touch of the embrace, time spent together celebrating, gossiping, preparing delicacies which cannot be shared at a distance and relished. Well, development and ambitions have their sacrifices too.

URS

The *Urs* or *Ziarats* is a typical Kashmiri festival held annually at the shrines of Muslim saints on their death anniversaries. It is said that it snows when the Urs of Meesha Sahib is held: it is windy when the Urs of Batamol Sahib takes place, it rains on the occasion of the Urs of Bahauddin. These Urs are popular despite the rigours of the weather, and are celebrated in different parts of Srinagar, by Muslims, Hindus and Sikhs alike. An interesting feature of Urs in Batamaloo, the locality in Srinagar named after the saint *Batamol* Sahib, and in *Anantnag,* and at *Rishi Mol's* anniversary, is that both Muslims and Hindus abstain from taking meat during the course of the festival.

The inter-communal participation is the main feature of the Urs celebrations. The anniversary of *Rishi Pir,* a Hindu saint, is held on the 5th day of the full moon of *Baisakh,* at his home in Srinagar and attended by Muslims also.

Muslim festivals which are celebrated nationally are *Shab-e-Meraj* which is followed by *Shab-e-Baraat.* The dates of these festivals change according to the appearance of the moon and shift by 10 days every year. During the night of Shab-e-baraat, the Muslims keep vigil. Legend goes that on this night the holy Prophet visits each house and relieves the pain and suffering of humanity.

The *Urs* is held at Ajmer in Rajasthan every year during the first six days of *Rajab,* the 7th month of the lunar calendar. Obeisance is offered at the tomb of the sufi saint *Khwaja Moinuddin Chisti,* commemorating his symbolic union with God. The *khwaja* came from Persia and established the *Chistia* order of the *fakirs* in India. The Urs is held in a solemn ceremony in memory of the saint who is fondly remembered and revered as the benefactor or protector of the poor, and therefore called *Gareeb Nawaz.* His spartan life spanning almost a hundred years was dedicated to the service of mankind.

At the end he died in solitude having withdrawn to his cell for six days before he embraced death asking not to be disturbed. The *Dargah Sharif* in Ajmer is the place where the mortal remains of the saint lie buried, and is the site of the largest congregation held on Urs. Pilgrims from all over the world gather there to pay homage, and it is said that more than five lakh devotees belonging to different communities gather there from all parts of the subcontinent to offer their homage to the khwaja on Urs, his death anniversary. The Urs fair in India is the largest ever witnessed in the world.

Offerings

Pilgrims who come to seek the blessings of the ***khwaja*** make rich offerings called *nazrana* at the holy spot where the saint has been entombed. Offerings of rose and jasmine flowers, sandalwood paste, perfumes and incense contribute to the fragrance in the atmosphere inside the shrine. Devotees offer *chadar, ghilaph and neema*, which are the votive offerings placed at the tomb of the saint.

The offerings are brought by the devotees on their heads and handed over to the *khadims* inside the sanctum sanctorum. Outside the sanctum professional singers called *qawwals* are seated in groups with their instruments, and sing the praises of the saint in a characteristic high-pitched voice, which people hear attentively, sometimes clapping to the rhythm of the music.

Mehfils, qawaalis and *mass prayers* are held which call for the eternal peace of mankind. An interesting ritual is the looting of *kheer* or milk pudding, which is cooked in two large cauldrons called *degs* and distributed to the devotees as *tabarruk* (prasaad) or blessed food.

Celebration

The Urs is initiated with the hoisting of a white flag on the dargah by the *Sajjada Nashin* or representative successor of the Chishtis. On the 6th of *Rajab*, after the usual mehfil and cracker bursts accompanied by music, the *Sajjada Nashin* performs the *ghusal* (bathe) of the tomb, at which the *Fatiha* or group recitations and *Salamati* (thanksgiving) are read. A poetic recitation called the *mushaira* is arranged in which poets of all communities arrive to recite compositions dedicated to the Khwaja. The *Qul* marks the end of Urs on this day.

At night, religious assemblies or *mehfils* presided over by the *Sajjada Nashin* of the dargah, are held in the *mehfilkhana,* a large hall meant for this specific purpose. *Qawaalis* or poetic renderings in song are presented in the saint's honour, in the hall which is packed to capacity. The mehfil terminates late in the night with a mass prayer for the eternal peace of the khwaja in particular and mankind in general.

The lakeside town of Ajmer also called *Ajmer sharif* meaning holy, comes alive during the Urs which attracts lakhs of devotees irrespective of caste, creed or social status.

During this time, the largest Muslim fair is organized and religious books, objects, rosaries, embroidered carpets, silver ornaments, and various other articles are available on sale. During the Urs, special buses ply from cities all over India to enable devotees to pay their homage at the shrine, in Ajmer.

EASTER

Easter is considered as one of the oldest and most joyous days on the Christian calendar.

Along with Christmas, the three days from Good Friday through Easter Sunday have become a traditional observance, as Christians believe that the crucifixion, burial and resurrection of Christ occurred during that period. Easter Sunday marks the completion of Jesus' crucifixion, burial and His resurrection.

Observances

Religious services and other Easter celebrations vary from country to country throughout the regions of the world. In the United States, many *sunrise services* are held in the open on Easter morning. These early services are symbolic of the empty tomb that was found early that Sunday morning and of arrival of Jesus in Jerusalem before sunrise on the Sunday of His resurrection.

People observe Easter Sunday by going to church, and later enact plays based on the *Last Supper*. Christians don't mourn His death but celebrate because it is believed that He resurrected to be united in heaven with God, His father.

Every year as Easter approaches, the stores are filled with jellybeans, candy eggs, egg-coloring kits, stuffed, real and chocolate bunnies (a symbol of fertility), of all types arranged in baskets for carrying the Easter bounty. In addition to the religious celebrations and observances of Easter, many countries also celebrate Easter with sweets and baked eatables. Cakes and breads are baked and beautifully decorated, along with chocolate candies of all shapes and sizes, which_are bought for the occasion.

Eggs, a traditional symbol of new life, are hard-boiled and painted usually in bright colors to represent the sunlight of spring. There are Easter-egg rolling contests and bright and colorful eggs are also exchanged as gifts. In many homes, families celebrate Easter with a gathering of family members welcomed to an elaborate Easter dinner.

CHRISTMAS

The fasting that precedes Christmas has already been dealt with under religious fasts. Christmas being basically a celebration of the birth of Christ, is being briefly described here as an important feast day for the Christians. It is declared a national holiday in all countries and today considered a world holiday when children around the globe can enjoy the spirit of the occasion. The word Christmas comes from the words *Cristes maesse*, which literally means mass celebration while *Christ* is a Greek word meaning, anointed or one set apart by God for a special purpose. Christmas is celebrated on 25th of December every year practically all over the world.

Celebrations

Originally, the celebration of Christmas, involves a mass in church on the eve of the celebration, followed by a special lunch with family and friends at home, prepared on December 25, by the members themselves. Over time however, a full 10-day to 2-week vacation is granted in schools in many countries for people to take off and travel far and wide to enjoy a prolonged vacation with family and friends.

Christmas is both a *holiday* and a *holy* day. It is one of the biggest events of the year for the members of the Christian community and especially for kids. During the Christmas season, people take their children to malls where they can meet Santa Claus, who distributes various gifts to them on Christmas day, and the Christmas tree is beautifully decorated in all shopping areas with lights and ornamental buntings, to mark the start of a season and not only a day. It is the focal point of people's holiday decoration. Christmas shopping starts far ahead of the celebration, with shoppers being offered heavy discounts on items they buy during the period. Even in homes, trees are similarly decorated and gifts piled under the family trees while members gather around the tree to sing Christmas carols and drink eggnog on Christmas day.

Gift giving is a near-universal part of Christmas celebrations. The tradition of gifts seems to have started with the gifts that the wise men brought for Jesus. As recounted in the Gospel of Matthew:

On coming to the house they saw the child with his mother Mary, and they bowed down and worshipped him. Then they opened their treasures and presented him with gifts of gold and of incense of myrrh.

Exchanging elaborate gifts was not a habit until late in the 1800s. The Santa Claus story combined with an amazing retailing phenomenon that has grown since the turn of the century has made gift-giving a central focus of the Christmas tradition.

The concept of a mythical figure that brings gifts to children derives from *Saint Nicholas*, a bishop of Myra in fourth century Lycia, Asia Minor. The Dutch recognized Saint Nicholas, or *Sinterklaas*, who gave gifts on the eve of his feast day on December 6, when his birthday was celebrated. He became associated with Christmas in 19th century America and was renamed *Santa Claus* or *Saint Nick.*

Santa Claus is a cultural derivation of *Sinterklaas.* In the Anglo-American tradition, this jovial fellow arrives on Christmas Eve on a sleigh pulled by reindeers, and lands on the roofs of houses. He then climbs down the chimney, leaves gifts for the children, and eats the food they leave for him. He spends the rest of the year making toys and keeping lists on the behavior of the children.

One belief passed down through the generations is the idea of lists of good children and bad children. Throughout the year, Santa supposedly adds names of children to either the good or bad lists depending on their behaviour. When it gets closer to Christmas time, parents use the belief to encourage children to behave well. Those who are on the bad list receive a booby prize, such as a piece of coal, rather than presents.

Children leave empty containers for Santa to fill with small gifts such as toys, candy, or fruit. Some hang a Christmas stocking by the fireplace on Christmas Eve because Santa is said to come down the chimney the night before Christmas to fill them.

Family members and friends also bestow gifts on each other. In most of the world, Christmas gifts are given at night on Christmas Eve or in the morning of Christmas day. Many people also send Christmas cards to their friends and family members. Many cards are customized with messages such as *season's greetings* or *happy holidays*, so as to include senders and recipients who may not celebrate Christmas.

In India too, Christmas is an official holiday for devotees to attend the church services on Christmas eve finishing at midnight. All schools are closed from 24th December to 5th or 8th of January in the New Year. This vacation is given for the celebration of the New Year too, before returning to serious work. Schools hold their celebratory activities before they close, to set the tempo for the vacation. Children of all religious communities actively participate in the programmes. This involves enacting dramas or plays related to Christ, singing carols and so on.

The President of India officially celebrates Christmas at the Rashtrapati Bhavan. The celebrations continue and get merged with New Year celebrations. Christmas is also known as *bada din* (the big day) in Hindi, and revolves around Santa Claus, shopping, gifting and feasting.

In many countries, offices, schools, and communities have Christmas parties and dances in the weeks before Christmas. Christmas pageants may include a retelling of the story of the birth of Christ. Groups may visit neighborhood homes to sing Christmas carols. Others do volunteer work or hold fundraising drives for charities.

Tradition and Food

On Christmas day, a special meal of Christmas dishes such as turkey roasts, brussel sprouts and Christmas pudding topped with brandy sauce are usually served. In some regions, particularly in Eastern Europe, these family feasts are preceded by a period of fasting. Candy and treats are also part of Christmas celebration in many countries.

The menus of course would differ from country to country and region to region, depending on the favourite foods eaten there. However, *turkey* is special and particularly associated with Christmas or X'mas lunch. The meat that remains unconsumed is stuffed into patties or sandwiches and used for the next meal. Turkey dishes are relished and considered delicacies at X'mas time.

The interior of houses is decorated with garlands and evergreen foliage, particularly holly and mistletoe. Some decorate the exterior of houses with lights and sometimes with illuminated sleighs, snowmen, and other Christmas figurines. Christmas banners may be hung from streetlights and Christmas trees placed in the town square. The Christmas festive period has grown longer in some countries. In the U.S., the pre-Christmas shopping season begins on the day after *Thanksgiving*. In the Philippines, radio stations usually start playing Christmas music during September and October.

Present Scenario

The Christmas - New Year season has been totally secularized in India. Everybody displays such joyous fervour in the year-end festivities that the small number of Christians in the metropolis feel that the entire city is celebrating with them.

The weeks leading up to Christmas are one of the biggest shopping weeks of the year for many nations. Therefore, retailers hype the event beyond belief. Sales increase dramatically in almost all retail areas and shops introduce new products as people purchase gifts, decorations, and supplies. Rolls of paper with secular or religious Christmas motifs like Christmas trees, Santa Claus, stars, reindeers, are imprinted on wrapping papers or as stickers for use on all gift items, greeting cards and visiting cards much before Christmas.

Christmas tree is the focal point of people's holiday decoration. The growing and selling of fresh Christmas trees is a big business. Millions of Christmas trees are produced each year. The majority of these trees come directly from Christmas tree farms or plantations. Among the best-selling Christmas trees are the Douglas, Fraser, Noble and Balsam firs, and the Scotch, Virginia, Fraser firs, white pine trees and Colorado blue spruce.

And for those synthetic-focused shoppers who don't want a natural tree, everything from snow-covered limbs to pre-lit branches to fully decorated trees are available. Fiber-optic trees and models that come complete with an MP3 player and speakers are the latest in synthetic Christmas trees.

In North America, film studios release many high-budget movies in the holiday season, including Christmas films, fantasy movies or high-tone dramas with rich production values. This helps the studio, to capture holiday crowds and position themselves for the Academy Awards. Christmas-specific movies are generally screened in late November or early December, as their themes and images are not nearly as popular once the season is over.

Because of the focus on celebration, friends and family, people who are without these, or who have recently suffered losses, are more likely to suffer from depression during Christmas. This increases the demand for counseling services. It is widely believed that suicides and murders spike during the holiday season. Because of holiday celebrations involving alcohol, drunken driving related fatalities rise sharply.

Many orthodox Christians, as well as anti-consumerists, decry the commercialization of Christmas. They accuse the Christmas season of being dominated by money and greed at the expense of the holiday's more important values. It is felt that frustrations over these issues and others, can lead to a rise in social problems at Christmas time.

Need of the Hour

With much emphasis on celebration and feasting especially among the youth, it would be appropriate to shift the focus back onto the message of Christ in whose reverence Christmas is celebrated. His message was:

- God is One
- Unity and equal mindedness
- Forgiveness
- Love

Adhering to these guidelines would keep people away from sinful thoughts, words and deeds thus preserving the spirit of Christmas.

CHHATH

Chhath is a festival celebrated on the sixth and seventh day after *Diwali* in which Hindu women pay obeisance to both the rising and setting sun. The word *Chhath* denotes the number six and thus the festival begins on the sixth day of the Hindu month of *Kartik* which falls in October - November. It is one of the holiest festivals for *the* people of Bihar and extends for four days. It is dedicated to the worship of the Sun God and therefore, is also known as *Surya Shashti.* Chhath is considered to be a means to thank the Sun for bestowing the bounties of life on earth, as also for fulfilling particular wishes.

Celebrations

The festival of Chhath has a greater significance in Bihar and is celebrated in a unique manner. It is marked by 4-day-long celebrations and rituals. The first day of Chhath is marked by taking a dip in a waterbody, preferably in the holy river Ganges by the devotees to wash away their sins. The river water is used to prepare the offerings. On the second day, the devotees observe a fast for the whole day, which is broken in late evening, after performing worship at home. The offerings usually consisting of a rice porridge, *puris* (deep-fried puffs of wheat flour) and bananas are distributed among family and visiting friends and relatives. The third day of the festival is spent in preparing the offerings at home during the day. In the evening the devotees move to the water body. There, the offerings are made to the setting sun. At nightfall, the devotees along with the family and friends return home where another colorful celebration takes place. Under a canopy of sugarcane sticks, clay elephants carrying earthen lamps, and containers full of the offerings, are placed and the Fire God is worshipped. On the final day of the festivities, the devotees, family and friends, move to the waterbody and offerings are made to the rising sun. Strict saltless vegetarian menu prepared without onions and garlic is offered during the entire festival period and food is cooked and served in earthen vessels. The festival is concluded after offering prayers to the Sun God and other forces of nature. The sunrise on the fourth day signals the conclusion of the festival. The devotees believe that the Sun God and mother earth bless those who follow the rituals.

Chhath is a very joyous and colorful festival. All the people dress up in their best and loud devotional music reverberates in the air, purifying the whole atmosphere. Folk songs are sung both at home and on the banks of the waterbody. Millions of people throng the banks of river Ganges, forgetting all the barriers of caste, creed and colour, to offer their prayers to the Sun god.

The streets are kept spotlessly clean by bands of volunteers, who also decorate all streets leading to the river with colorful festoons, ribbons, and banners.

Present Scenario

Large numbers of people go to Bihar to celebrate this festival. There is a popular belief that all the desires of the devotees are always fulfilled during Chhath. Also, an element of fear is present among the devotees who dread the punishment for any misdeed during Chhath and therefore no crimes are committed during the days of Chhath.

The biggest festival of Bihar, Jharkand and eastern UP has become a part of the religious and social calendar of Delhi in recent years with migrants from Bihar and eastern UP comprising around 40 lakh of the total population. From a symbolic celebration by a selected few at India Gate's Boat club and the mass gathering at ITO *ghats* till a few years back, Chhath has gone much further today with about 24 ghats constructed on the banks of the river Yamuna this year for this specific purpose.

Organizations like Poorvanchal Gana Sangh (PGS) and Poorvanchal Kranti Sangh (PKS) contribute to the festivities by making arrangements for first-aid, providing volunteers at many of the ghats and organizing cultural shows on the occasion of Chhath.

The city wears a different look with hoardings and posters carrying Chhath greetings from politicians, *Bhojpuri* music ringing on streets and in markets with shops selling puja material and sweets.

MAHAVIR JAYANTI

Mahavir Jayanti or the birthday of Lord Mahavira is celebrated by both the *Digambar* (sky-clad) and the *Shvetambar* (white-clad) *Jains* on the 13th day of the bright half of the month of *Chaitra* (March-April).

The 24th and last Jain *Tirthankara,* Mahavira was born in 599 BC and lived for 72 years. He was the son of Siddhartha, the king of Kundalpura and Queen Trisala. It is said that the expectant mother had 16 auspicious dreams before the child was born. Astrologers interpreting these dreams had stated that the child would be either an emperor or a Teerthankar. *Maha* means great and *Vira* means a hero.

Mahavira was more a reformer than the founder of the faith. In Jain metaphysics, time is divided into cycles. It is claimed that in each half-cycle, 24th Tirthankaras, at long intervals, preach the doctrines. Mahavira was the 24th and like the others, was omniscient. He revived the Jain doctrines.

Mahavira was also known as *Vardhamana* meaning *ever advancing* and *Sanmati* or wisdom. At the age of eight he observed the 12 spiritual vows mentioned in the Jain scriptures. He was obedient to his parents and served them with great devotion.

Vardhamana resolved to give up everything worldly at the age of 30 years. He gave up attachment to his parents, friends and relatives. He thought over the 12 *Anupreksha*s or matters of deep thinking according to the Jain scriptures: He believed that:

- All worldly things are temporary.
- The soul alone is the sole resort.
- This world is beginning-less and crooked.
- There is nothing to help the soul, but the soul itself.
- Body and mind are essentially separate from the soul.
- The soul is essentially pure and the body impure.
- The soul's bondage is due to the inflow of *karma* to it.
- Every being ought to stop this inflow.
- Emancipation is attained when there is no *karma.*
- Emancipated souls remain fit for the absolute stage at all times.
- In this world, to be born a human being and to meditate on the nature of the soul are the greatest blessings.

Distributing all his wealth among the poor, Mahavira went to the forest and became a monk. He achieved enlightenment under an Ashoka tree after fasting and meditation. Mahavira practiced rigorous austerities, including fasts that lasted many days. He meditated on the pure nature of the soul and lived a life of absolute truthfulness, perfect honesty and absolute chastity. He lived without any material possessions, finally attaining omniscience in 557 BC and Nirvana in 527 BC.

Mahavira established the rules of religious life for Jain monks, nuns, and the laity. Mahavira taught people that they can save their souls from the contamination of matter by living a life of extreme asceticism and by practicing non-violence towards all living creatures. This advocacy of non-violence encouraged his followers to become strong advocates of vegetarianism.

Mahavira's followers were aided in their quest for salvation by the five vows he taught in practice, which were the renunciation of killing, speaking evil, greed, sexual pleasure and all attachment to living and non-living things.

Celebration

The birth anniversary of Lord Mahavira is celebrated with a special fervour by the entire Jain community, throughout the country, especially in Rajasthan and Gujarat, where the community is much greater concentrated than in other states. This religious event is celebrated by visiting sacred sites and worshipping the Teerthankars.

Jain pilgrims from all over the country congregate at the ancient Jain shrines at *Girnar* and *Palitana* in Gujarat, at *Mahavirji* shrine in Rajasthan, *Pawapuri* and *Vaishali* in Bihar and other such centres of pilgrimage. Vaishali being the birth place of Mahavira, a grand festival is held there popularly known as *Vaishali Mahotsava*. On this auspicious day, grand chariot processions with the images of Mahavira are taken out, rich ceremonies are held in the temples, fasts and charities are observed, Jain scriptures are read, and at some places, grand fairs are organised as the main attractions.

BUDDHA JAYANTI

Buddha Jayanti celebrates the day when *Lord Buddha* was born, attained enlightenment and Nirvana. It falls on the full moon in the month of *Vaisakha* and has a three-fold significance for Buddhists or devotees of the faith called Buddhism.

History

Siddhartha, the only son of Shuddhodana, the King of Kapilavastu situated at the foot of Himalayas, was prophesied by the royal astrologer to become either a famous emperor or a world-renowned ascetic. The father, anxious that his son should not take to the thorny path of a recluse, took extraordinary precautions to avoid every situation which would provoke such thoughts in his son's mind.

Siddhartha grew of age in comfortable, royal surroundings without ever knowing what misery or sorrow was. One day, the prince desired to see the city, so the King ordered that the city should be all cleaned and decorated, so that everywhere his son went he would see only pleasant sights. During his sojourn in the city however, his eyes fell on an old and crippled man by the roadside. It was a sight never witnessed before by the prince: a sunken face, a toothless mouth, all the limbs emaciated, the whole body bent and walking with extreme difficulty.

The innocent prince asked who that creature was, so Chenna, the charioteer, replied that he was a human being who had become old. To further enquiries of Siddhartha, Chenna informed that the old man was of fine shape in his young age and that every human being had to become like him after the youthful days are over. The perturbed prince returned to the palace, deeply engrossed in anxious thoughts.

King Shuddhodana, in order to cheer up his spirits, again ordered for his son's procession in the capital, but on subsequent rounds, Siddhartha came across a sick man and a corpse being carried to the funeral ground. Again it was Chenna, the charioteer, who explained that human beings were prone to illness and that death inevitably awaited man at the end. As luck would have it, on his final round, Siddhartha saw a person, his face beaming with joy and tranquility, and heard from Chenna that he was an ascetic who had triumphed over the worldly temptations, fears and sorrows and attained the highest bliss of life.

That changed the thoughts of the young prince at the time, although he was then hardly 29 years of age. In that full bloom of youth, in the midnight of a full-moon day, he bade good-bye to his dear parents, his beloved wife Yashodhara and sweet little child Rahul and all the royal pleasures and luxuries, and departed to the forest to seek for himself answers for the riddles of human misery.

Renunciation

For seven long years, Siddhartha roamed in the jungles, underwent severe austerities and finally, on the *Vaishakha Purnima Day*, the supreme light of Realization dawned on him. He thereafter became Buddha, the *Enlightened One*. When he was an itinerant monk, he was called *Gautama* and later became popular as Gautama Buddha. Buddha's overflowing love for the downtrodden and destitute acted as one of the greatest factors for social harmony and justice to the weaker sections in the society.

The *Bodhi* tree in Gaya under which Buddha attained his supreme enlightenment, has since provided the common man with peace and succour. Gaya has since been known as *Bodh Gaya* to commemorate the event and has to this day remained one of the most sanctified places of pilgrimage for the Buddhists and Hindus in particular and the world at large.

Buddha's philosophical analysis of the basic problem of human suffering and misery was communicated to the common man through a purified and simplified *Eight-Fold Path of Salvation.* The messages therein withstood all logic and reasoning which were therefore readily accepted by the people. These elaborated a view of the right type of:

- Life-view — life was to be viewed with equanimity, considering that everyone is divine.
- Intention — his intention was to ensure that no one is hurt or miserable.

- Speech — must be soft and sweet for it is sourced from the primordial sound, that comes from within, and pervades through the entire creation.
- Action — all actions need to be helpful to others, hands being for performing good acts, the throat for upholding truth, the ears for listening to the sacred and expressing love to all.
- Livelihood — people must work for their livelihood, or depend on nature to provide it.
- Effort — without effort nothing can be achieved. Whether failure or success effort should not be abandoned, because the fruits of our labour are not in our hands.
- Frame of mind — all thoughts, actions and speech get reflected, reacted to or create resound or echo back therefore should be treated as divine and used resourcefully for positive thoughts, good actions and pleasant and useful words.
- Concentration — thoughts and actions should be focused towards preset goals to ensure they are attained. Further, there should be no doubts in the mind and all actions should be offered with humility to the divine to ensure their fruition.

Like Mahavira, Buddha denounced animal sacrifices in the *yajnas,* and himself stood as the very embodiment of compassion to all living beings. His teachings have been scripted in the *Dhammapada,* the sacred book.

Message of Buddha

The foremost message of the Buddha to the world was that of *Ahimsa*, meaning not to hurt or harm anyone. Non-violence has been described as the highest form of *Dharma* in every religion. Non-violence is not merely refraining from inflicting injury on others with limbs and weapons, it has to be practiced with purity of mind, tongue and the body. In the texts this is known as *Trikarana shuddhi* or triple purity. Even ill feelings is a form of violence, and unthoughtful speech too can really hurt, therefore one needs to take care that what the mouth utters is sweet, pleasing and wholesome.

If one concentrates on the body to the neglect of the mind and soul one becomes endowed with animal-like qualities. If the body and mind are allowed to prevail to the exclusion of the soul, one becomes demonic in nature. If all the three work in harmony, then humanness is manifested. If the soul dominates over the mind and body, the person shows divine qualities in his life.

In fact, the violent environment of the world today is the result of people not leading righteous lives. People perform rituals, observe fasts, chant the name of the Lord, and engage in other forms of penances, yet still do not have peace. This is because they are misusing the body and their talents and the qualities given to them.

Celebrations

On the day of *Buddha Purnima*, Buddhists arrange *Panchasheel, Ashtasheel, Sutrapath, Sutrasraban*, collective prayers and various other religious ceremonies. Many Buddhists organise three-day festivities including organized social and cultural events and fairs for children and so on. The *Bodhidham Mela* is held at the village Baidyapara in Chittagong and is one of the most popular fairs. Some people visit the famous ruins of the *Mahasthan, Paharpur* and *Mainamati,* which are relics of the finest specimens of Buddhist civilization and culture.

Various *melas* are organized in villages and *viharas* including those of the tribal communities living in forests, tea gardens, plains, and the hill tracts who have their own festivities centering round different deities. Through these, Buddhist organizations distribute souvenirs, magazines and books to people. The radio and TV provide broadcasts of special programmes and newspapers bring out special issues or supplements on the occasion of Buddha Jayanti. Pilgrims come from all over the world to Bodh Gaya to attend the Buddha Purnima celebrations. The day is marked by congregational prayer meetings at which sermons on the life of Gautam Buddha, religious discourses, continuous recitation from Buddhist scriptures, group meditation, processions, worship of the statue of Buddha and symposia in commemoration are held.

The Mahabodhi Temple is decorated with wide range of beautiful flowers and flags. On Buddha Purnima, Buddhist followers bathe and wear only white clothes, a symbol of purity. They collect at one place and pray together and give alms to monks. Some of the followers just spend the entire day listening to teachings and preachings of Lord Buddha. They even invite Buddhist monks at their *viharas* and listen to the discourses on the life of Lord Buddha.

Food and Customs

On Buddha Jayanti, Buddhists eat rice cooked in milk and sugar which is also known as *kheer.* They even share this rice pudding with friends, relatives and the poor. Much emphasis and significance is given to preparing rice pudding to commemorate the sacred memory of Sujata's offering to Buddha shortly before he attained enlightenment. Stalls are set up in public places to offer visitors and devotees clean drinking water and also show kindness to animals. Buddha Purnima is celebrated and observed around the world in different ways with each country of South East Asia having its own distinctive Buddha style.

In India (Gangtok), the roaming monks walk through the streets in processions carrying the sacred scriptures, as part of the general festivities described.

In Burma , believers of Buddhism set a day apart every month in honour of the Buddha. Since the Buddha attained enlightenment sitting under a Bodhi tree, special care is taken while watering and tending to Bodhi trees as part of their regular activities.

In Sri Lanka , houses are brightly illuminated and even the poorest people light at least one oil-lamp in their porch. Buddhists make *Vaisakh vakats* out of bamboo, decorate them with stars and arrange them in their houses. Some people drape the walls of their homes with paper or cloth depicting incidents from the *Jataka* tales that are based on incarnations of the Buddha prior to his birth as prince Gautama.

In Japan, replicas of shrines are made out of spring flowers and an idol of the Buddha is bathed and consecrated with great reverence before it is placed on the flowers in each shrine. These shrines are then visited by all on that day with great devotion.

A lot has been written about the Buddha Purnima celebrations in various poems, novels and it has also been depicted in various paintings. Buddha Purnima holds a special significance in the lives of the Buddhists because it is the day when one reflects on the life and teachings of one of the greatest practical teachers, the world has known.

HANUMAN JAYANTI

Hanuman *Jayanti* falls on *Chaitra Shukla Purnima* and is a celebration of the birth of Hanuman, the stalwart devotee of Lord Rama, and one of the most revered deities of the *Sanatana Dharma.* His idol is that of a typical *daas,* when he is seen kneeling down with joined palms in *pranam* at the feet of Lord Rama and Sita. Occasionally he is depicted holding Rama and Lakshmana on his shoulders. Hanuman is revered for His ability to provide protection from evil and diseases, and for removal of obstacles that may occur in the performance of auspicious events, resolving the problems with finesse and devotion.

In Allahabad near the Prayag, a Hanuman temple exists where a life-size sculpted Hanuman lies in a sleeping posture, in a deep grove, surrounded by iron grills and one has to look down as if in a well to see Him. The idol is supposed to have been brought to shore by the rivers Ganges, Yamuna and Saraswati when they were in spate. The idol was left behind on the sand when the waters receded. According to the priests, the temple had to be built around the idol since it was on sand and in danger of being washed away again. The walls were raised to prevent water entering the place. This temple is specially sanctified, since this is the only one known, in which Sri Hanuman is lying straight, stretched out on his back, and one, which the rivers brought to its designed destination.

Throughout the Ramayana, Valmiki lauds Hanuman as a confluence of virtues, and his greatness as a devotee and *daas* or servant of the Lord are exemplary. The qualities exhibited by Hanuman throughout the Ramayana which need to be emulated are:

- Humility
- Tranquility

- Purity of Heart
- Truthfulness
- Flawless Service
- Patience
- Equal Mindedness
- Implicit Faith
- True Devotion
- Obedience
- Self-confidence

Humility

Whenever Hanuman had anything to say to anyone, he was known to either look at their feet and speak, or kneel down with folded hands. When sent to rescue Sita from Lanka he never looked at her face, but only watched her from behind, although he was sent to take care of her, and give her the Lord's message.

Tranquility

No problem or success ever disturbed his emotions, as there is no reference in the text that Hanuman was excited or in despair. He was always calm and thoughtful about what the next step would be to tackle any situation.

Purity of Heart

He was an epitome of Purity, never suspecting anyone's word or intention, and even when he found out that Ravana had abducted Sita, he never lost his temper or talked avengefully. He only prayed to Rama for instructions, and without thinking of the consequences carried them out.

Truthfulness

Hanuman was always true to his word. His thoughts and actions proved this and he was the supreme exemplar of speech — truthful, pleasing and well-meaning. Truth does not carry meaning if it hurts anyone, and therefore it was never spoken in a harsh language by Hanuman. His speech was always soft, sweet, pleasant and conducive to peacefulness. Dauntless, sweet and persuasive words promoted friendship between Rama and Sugriva.

Flawless Service

When Sri Ram and Lakshmana met Hanuman, he was living an ordinary simian life in *Kishkinda.* When asked who he was, Hanuman replied: ***O Prabhu! From the body's point of view I am your daas or servant and from the jiva's view I am your bhakta.*** It was this reply that made Rama accept service from him.

He served His master Rama like a true *daas,* obeying His commands without question, and carrying them out till the end with great devotion, integrity and humility without seeking any rewards for his services.

Patience

He performed all tasks allotted to him by Rama with great devotion and hard work, and then waited patiently for the next command without bothering about the results of his actions.

Equal Mindedness

Equal mindedness is exemplified in Hanuman's life when knowing that Ravana and his clan were involved in evil activities against his Lord, he still spoke very respectfully with them, and told them who he was and why he was in Lanka. He helped everybody he could that came his way with a problem.

Implicit Faith

Such faith in the Lord can be seen nowhere else in life. The texts and spiritual leaders ask devotees to have faith but where has it been adhered to, so single pointedly? What needs to be understood is that God is without attributes, whereas everyone who is born has form and name, but the divinity within them has no name or form. Swami Chetanananda has said:[28]

> ***Doubt contracts the heart and causes stagnation whereas faith expands it and creates motion. Faith brings joy, without which it is hard to live in this world.***

---

[28] Chetanananda (1991), p. 303.

True Devotion

Hanuman's devotion is exemplary, never has a single instant been recorded in the texts where a doubt ever occured in his mind about Lord Ram, Sita or Lakshman's intentions. He blamed Ravana for his evil designs to kidnap Sita, but never for a moment blamed Lakshman for not being there to protect her as commanded by Ram. So simple and pure was his devotion. A true devotee offers everything to God saying — ***Nothing is mine it all belongs to you.*** The *gopis* also declared, ***Krishna we are yours,*** while the people of Dwaraka developed pride and egoism over their kinship with Krishna. In many ways perception of the one without a second is supreme knowledge.

Obedience

There will never be a greater example of obedience in anyone's life than Hanuman. Children obey their parents, students their teachers, but there always are times when they disagree and strive to disobey them. Not so in Hanuman's life, who regarded whatever Rama said as Gospel truth (*Ved Vakya*), and never questioned whether it was bad or good, right or wrong. He felt himself incompetent to judge the words of the Lord, although he was highly intelligent in matters relating to the Divine. He said ***it is my duty to carry out whatever Rama says.*** The *Gita* also refers to duty as being yoga, and further describes yoga as *excellence* in the performance of duty. It thus proclaims that all actions should be carried out according to Divine injunctions.

Self-confidence

Hanuman had tremendous confidence in himself to achieve any thing he was asked to do. This showed what purity of heart, devotion to duty, unstinting faith in the divine and humility can do to one's self-confidence. Can an ordinary person lift a mountain and bring it to Ram because he did not recognize the plant that was needed to cure Lakshman?

To seek self-realization without self-confidence is a wasted effort. Realisation is not discovering one's lineage or roots that are related to the body, but realizing that you do not belong to any family or clan.

The nearest approach to realization is to consider divinity as being all pervasive.

Detachment

Detachment or *Vairagya* does not mean renouncing hearth and home and retiring to the forest. True detachment means giving up worldly feelings and developing Godly thoughts.

Hanuman was completely detached to material things, he had no object however valuable, which did not proclaim the name of Rama. He once discarded the pearl necklace Sita presented to him as a gift, saying the pearls do not recite Rama's name. He was not attached to anyone either although it may seem that he was attached to Lord Rama and Lakshmana, but in fact it was his devotion that made him serve them selflessly. In fact Rama praised Hanuman as being one of the greatest devotees, declaring:

> ***Hanuman! No material object is fit enough to be given to you as a present. You live in the world of the spirit, you have no attachment to the things of the world. Let you be present wherever my glory is sung.***

Egoism or *Ahamkara* and possessiveness are the cause of one's pleasure and pain, happiness and sorrow. Hence everyone needs to curb these tendencies as Sri Hanuman did. Those without ego are totally free from the consequences of their actions. And this makes them completely fearless as Hanuman illustrated throughout his life.

Lord Swaminarayan exhorts every devotee to imbibe Hanumanji's three important virtues, be an ideal *bhakta*, devotion and *brahmacharya.* He advocates *Hanuman puja* on *Aso Vad* 14, and enjoins those afflicted with evil spirits to chant the Hanuman *strotam* or *chalisa.*

Hanuman is the sole Hindu deity to be equally venerated by believers and non-believers, non-Hindus, Jains, Parsis and Muslims.

One can go on and on with the qualities that Hanuman had exemplified in his life to mankind. The unity of the body, mind and spirit needs to be understood. If we can imbibe even a fraction of the qualities of Hanuman and practice them in our day to day dealings with people what a wonderful, safe haven our world would be.

Present Scenario

Today, everyone is full of doubts in the mind in every sphere of life. *To do or not to do* is the perpetual question. To meditate on God why should there be any doubt? There should be no doubt. Jesus once told his disciples who complained of being ridiculed: *If a person hits you on one cheek, offer the other.* In the same vein Buddha was asked why he did not answer to people who criticized him, and his reply was: ***If a person is unkind or abusive recognize the divinity in him.*** He also said:

> ***When you react to wrong doing you are accepting it, but when you keep silent and think of the divinity, what is said goes back and hits the person who sent it.***

Hence service needs to be rendered to all without distinction and with full and unstinting faith.

There are millions of people in the world who recite the Lord's name, but when doing so do not realize its greatness and glory. Whatever name you recite, you should also be active in the service of the form associated with the name. Take part in social service activities with dedication to the Lord. By rendering help to fellow beings and helping the needy one becomes eligible for His grace.

SOCIAL FEASTS

As the title suggests, social feasts comprise those celebrations that provide an opportunity for the family, community and country to get together and enjoy the spirit of special occasions. Besides having special foods on such occasions, they present an environment in which people can socialize with friends, make acquaintances and useful contacts. Social feasts can be categorized as indicated in Fig. 9.1.

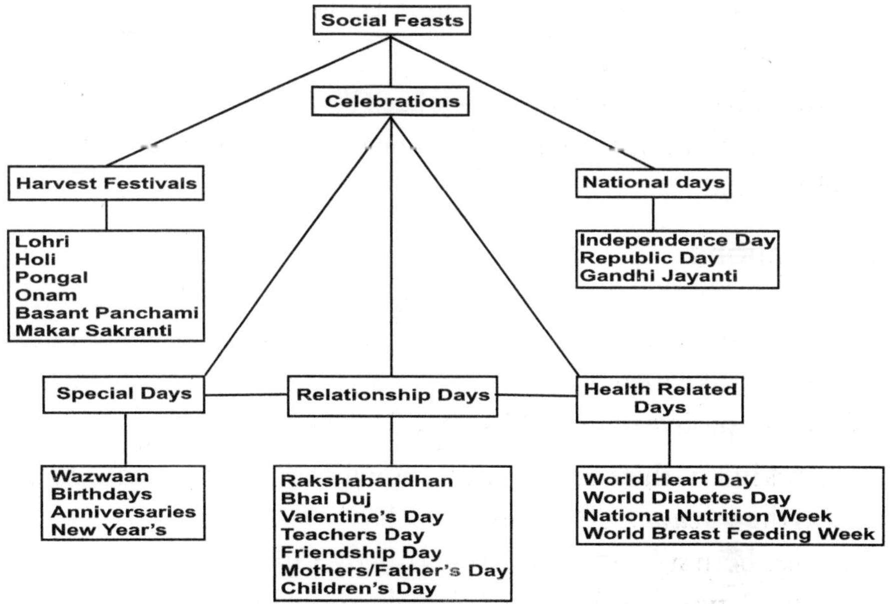

Fig. 9.1: Classification of social feasts

The classification in Fig. 9.1 shows that social feasts are built around celebrations for good harvests, family occasions, special days like birthdays, marriages and so on, national and international days related to independence, national achievements and memorials, health-related days declared by the United Nations through its reading of world situations and its impact on health of its people and overall development.

Each of the categories, have been discussed with respect to tradition, rituals and celebrations.

HARVEST FESTIVALS

Since India is a country with different climatic conditions in each region, harvest seasons and staple crops differ and so do the eating habits of people. In addition there is great dependence on natural sources of irrigation and soil conditions. In a good year of rains the harvest is plentiful and in a year of low or no rainfall the harvest is poor. Also when rains are not timely they can wash away crops or destroy them completely. Some regions are prone to droughts, earthquakes and other unexpected disasters and therefore when harvests are good, people get into a celebratory mode, built around traditional harvest festivals of each region.

Some of the harvest festivals have been discussed in detail to indicate their similarities and differences in the performance of rituals and mode of celebration.

Celebrations

As indicated in Fig. 9.1, celebrations are of three main types namely, *special days* of the year such as New Year's Day, birthdays or anniversaries on which special menus are planned, prepared and served to invitees or guests, irrespective of the venue where the feasts are held.

In addition, there are certain regional feasts with specific names such as the *wazwaan* of Kashmir, which is so special in its preparation that it has been subsequently covered briefly. Other regions too may be having such typical feasts served on really special and formal occasions like weddings, golden jubilee celebrations of anniversaries or platinum jubilees of Institutions or events, but not as well documented as the waazwan.

Relationship Days comprise the next category of celebrations and are usually family occasions involving feasting that strengthen familial bonds between members of the family or friends and community. Their celebration is almost like those of a festival, except that people do not necessarily congregate at temples for performing rituals. These include Rakshabandhan, Bhai dooj, Valentine's day, Teacher's day, Friendship day, Mother's Father's, Children's days and the list can go on and on depending on the event people want to create for a celebration.

The next category includes *Health-related Days* which have been created by national and international agencies to increase the awareness of the citizens about certain epidemic, endemic and chronic diseases. Some examples are National Diabetes Day, World Heart Day, Aids Awareness Day or Week, Nutrition Week and so on. Some of these days are celebrated internationally, but every country decides their programmes according to their literacy levels, regional incidence of the particular disease, funds available, the urgency felt and therefore the thrust given according to laid down national priorities. The dates are fixed for these days in the calendar by the national departments or the World Health Organization or WHO.

The celebrations may be in the form of exhibitions and lectures on the relevant disease by doctors, nutritionists, extension workers, NGOs and others, through holding of 2-3 day's *melas* or fairs to expose the public to the need for prevention, free check ups through camps for early detection, methods of screening available, and distribution of printed material in more than one language for people to read, understand and become aware about, in terms of the hazards that can result from lack of awareness and timely action.

National Days

These include country-specific days such as Independence and Republic Days, or days attributed to the advent of national figures like the founder of a nation as was the case of Mahatma Gandhi who came to be known as the *Father of the Nation* in India. For all national days, the citizens have to make great sacrifices just as in the case of India's independence from centuries of colonial rule. Hence, they are celebrated with patriotic fervour and joy. Other countries may have more national days on the calendar to celebrate and therefore mark achievements for that nation.

Social feasts have been discussed in detail under harvest festivals, celebrations and national days as they pertain to the different regions of the country and some worldwide as well.

MAKAR SANKRANTI

Makar Sankranti is the most important day for the celebration of harvest festivals, when according to Hindu astronomy, the sun enters the zodiac sign of Capricorn or *rashi* of *Makara*, which is considered the most auspicious day as it signifies a new beginning. Makar Sankranti is celebrated in the month of *Magha* when the sun passes through the winter solstice, from the Tropic of Cancer to the Tropic of Capricorn. This day is celebrated throughout India as a harvest festival. It is a way of giving thanks to the elements of nature that help man to a good harvest. This is a period when the winter recedes and paves the way for the summer. It is the time the farmers bring home their harvest. In coastal regions it is a harvest festival dedicated to *Indra,* the God of rain.

Rituals

These vary slightly from region to region depending on the nature of the harvest and are called by different names too, depending on the regional languages, customs, traditions and beliefs.

North India

In Punjab and Haryana, the festival is known as *Lohri* and is one of the most celebrated, with bonfires that keep people warm on the wintry day. It falls on 13th of January each year as it is connected with the solar year, and is celebrated on the eve of Makar Sankranti. This festival marks the departure of the winter season. Earlier it was celebrated mainly in Punjab but today, it is celebrated throughout the country as a harvest festival named differently in each region such as *Bihu* in Assam, *Bhogi* in Andhra Pradesh, *Pongal* in Tamil Nadu and *Sankranti* in Karnataka, Bihar, Maharashtra and Uttar Pradesh. In the north a ritual bath in the river, pond or lake is important on this day. The special dish prepared is *khichri*, a soft rice–pulse preparation to celebrate the new harvest coming in.

Maharashtra

In Maharashtra, *tilgul* or *laddoos* made of jaggery and *til* or sesame seed, are distributed among family friends and neighbours, to spread the message of love and brotherhood. In Gujarat, it is celebrated as the kite-flying day.

Assam

In Assam, the harvest festival is called *Bihu,* celebrated to mark the end of the winter paddy harvest. On the night before people fast and pray, and thatched pavilions are erected around the countryside. As a sign of the festival having begun, these pavilions are set on fire at dawn. Bull fights and celebrations mark the day.

On the Sankranti day, sweets, puddings and sweet rice are prepared in every home especially in South India. The pot in which the rice is cooked is beautifully adorned with turmeric leaves and roots, the symbols of auspiciousness. The cooking is done by the women of the household with great devotion and faith, the food offered to the Lord first and then eaten by the family.

LOHRI

Lohri is the first festival of the year and falls on the 13th of January every year. It is celebrated over two days in the northern parts of India especially in the Punjab where it is symbolic of their love for celebrations. Lohri is essentially a festival dedicated to *Agni* or Fire and *Surya* or Sun and is therefore known as the *bonfire festival.* It is the time of the year when the temperatures vary between 0°C and 5°C, with dense foggy conditions prevailing. This is also a time when the Sun transits the zodiac sign *Makara* or Capricorn and moves North, which astrologers in India term as *Uttarayan* that lasts from 14th of January to 14th of July.

Origin of Lohri

The origin of Lohri is related to the central character of most Lohri songs, Dulla Bhatti, a Muslim highway robber who lived in Punjab during the Moghul emperor Akbar's reign. Besides robbing the rich he rescued Hindu girls being forcibly taken and subjected to the slave trade of the Middle East. Bhatti arranged their marriages to Hindu boys with the customary rituals and dowry. Understandably, though a bandit, he became a hero for all Punjabis. Therefore, every other Lohri song has words of gratitude to express to Dulla Bhatti. The clan singers claim that Maharaja Ranjit Singh is a Bhatti scion.[29]

Some believe that Lohri has derived its name from *Loi,* the wife of Sant Kabir for in rural Punjab, Lohri is pronounced as *Lohi.* Others believe that it comes from the word *Loh,* a thick iron sheet *tawa* used for making chappatis for community feasts. Another legend says that Holika and Lohri were sisters. While Holika perished in the Holi fire, Lohri survived.

Eating of sesame seeds or *til* and *rohri* or jaggery is considered to be essential on this day, and that is how the word *Tilohri* was coined and later became shortened to Lohri to give the present name to this festival.

Significance

Lohri marks the culmination of winter, and is celebrated according to the Lunar calendar, in the month of *Paush* or *Magh* a day before Makara Sankranti which is considered an extremely auspicious day. It is celebrated with gusto in Punjab, Haryana and Himachal, but for *Punjabis,* it is more than just a festival and is an example of a way of life. Lohri celebrations are associated with fertility and the spark of life. People make preparations for Lohri many days in advance and set the spirit for the festival.

The Bhagavad Gita deems it an extremely sacred and auspicious time, when Lord Krishna manifests Himself most tangibly (Ch.10 and 11).

---

29 C.D.Verma, Innervoice@hindustantimes.com

Hindus bathe in the Ganges and other holy rivers to celebrate the month and the prodigious harvest it brings.

Observance

It is celebrated as a harvest festival, since the winter crops are harvested. It coincides with the harvest festivals of *Pongal* in Tamil Nadu, *Bihu* in Assam, *Bhogi* in Andhra and *Sankranti* in Karnataka, Bihar and Uttar Pradesh.

Ceremonies that usually comprise Lohri are making of small images of the Lohri Goddess with cowdung, decorating it and kindling a fire beneath it, while chanting its praises. This was the practice in rural India since dried cowdung mixed with fibrous stalks of plants or coal dust, were used as fuel for kitchen fires. The final ceremony is to light a bonfire at sunset and offer sweets, nuts and seeds to it while dancing around the fire till it dies out. People take the embers of the dying fires to their homes to light their home fires to keep themselves warm.

Lohri is an occasion which generates bonhomie and warmth as bonfires are lit in the harvested fields after sunset, and in the open spaces outside homes. People gather around the fire and circumambulate or do *parikrama* around the bonfire singing *aadar aye diladar jaye* along with folk songs, and dancing to express their joy and brotherhood. The phrase means *may honour come and poverty vanish.* This is a sort of prayer to *Agni,* the fire God to bless the land with abundance and prosperity. After the parikrama, people distribute *prasaad,* meet friends and family and exchange greetings and gifts.

It is customary to throw jaggery and sesame seed preparations called *rewari,* puffed rice, unshelled peanuts or groundnuts and popcorn into the lighted fire. Such foods put into the fire along with popcorn and freshly harvested groundnuts, not only helps the fire to keep burning and giving warmth on a wintry night, but is an expression of thanksgiving to God for the good harvest. Charity to those who are less privileged, forms a part of the festival observances, and all old usable clothes and furniture are kept outside to be given or taken away.

Lohri also enables all old and broken unusable furniture to be burnt in the fire, helping to clear the house for new things to come. The festival marks the beginning of the end of winter which lasts through February and people look forward to the coming spring.

The festival coincides with *Sankranti* in Maharashtra, *Pongal* in Tamil Nadu, *Magh Bihu* in Assam and *Tai pongal* in Kerala all celebrated on the auspicious day of *Makara Sankranti* on January 14th, a day after *Lohri.*

Food and Customs

Lohri is the day when women and children get special attention. The first Lohri of a bride or a newborn irrespective of the gender is considered extremely important. In the morning of Lohri, children go singing from door to door in the neighbourhood where they get money or sweets like *gajak, rewari* or others made of *til* and jaggery or groundnuts. Winter savouries are served around the bonfire with the traditional dinner of *makki-ki-roti* and *sarson- ka- saag*. The typical sweets of Lohri are *gujia, laddoo, burfi, gulabjamuns, petha, khandavi, thandai* and the like.

The men start the *bhangra* dance after the offering to the bonfire, which continues till midnight with new groups joining in from time to time amid the beat of the drums. Traditionally, women do not join the bhangra. They have a separate bonfire in their home courtyards orbiting it with the graceful *gidda* dance.

In Maharashtra, it is customary for people to exchange food made from *til* and *gur* as a gesture of goodwill when greeting. Offering sweet snacks is symbolic for blessing and wishing that people should speak only sweet words.

In addition, Lohri fairs or *melas* are held to bring cheer to all irrespective of caste, creed, status and so on. The fairs market all types of articles from household goods to bangles, glassware, handicrafts, food and fun with music, games, races, bouts, folk instruments like the *vanjli* and *algoza,* swings and games to enable all age groups to participate in the fun and frolic.

Today, with busy schedules for both men and women, Lohri is an opportunity for people to come together socially, and enjoy the ambience with their neighbours, friends and extended family. The rich and famous celebrate Lohri with pomp and show in the form of farm parties with decorations of marigold strings, *bhangra,* music, barbeques, wine, champagne, and other alcoholic drinks followed by sumptuous meals. The open spaces are interspersed with *angithis* and bonfires which set the mood for relaxation and enjoyment till the wee hours of the next morning.

An expression of the host's charitable tendencies is seen when all waiters, drivers of guests and other workers are well fed and given gifts in cash and kind.

Message of Lohri

The message of Lohri can be summarized as:

- Friendship
- Bonding with Love
- Unity and Oneness
- Goodness
- Sharing

Friendship

Getting together of neighbours, passersby, and family around the bonfires of Lohri is a symbol of extending friendship to one and all in the same spirit as that of the family.

Bonding with Love

This bonding does not only refer to family relationships but to all humanity and therefore we are reminded of it one or more times a year at festival times. The most important message is to find the love within you and spread it to others, bringing about bonding between people. When vibrations are felt between people they get drawn to each other, even if there is no festival being celebrated.

Unity and Oneness

Unity too, is to be seen in the same spirit of oneness, not only through friendships or associations in the external arenas of life, but unity through the heart and a feeling of divine oneness with others.

Goodness

Goodness reflects from upholding of Truth and being righteous in all actions, decisions and judgements while dealing with people and situations. Speaking in a loving, kind voice, hearing positive things from people and lifting one's own thoughts, helps to spread positive vibrations even if it involves personal sacrifices.

Sharing

Sharing connotes helping others by sharing their joys and sorrows, be it sharing material resources such as food, clothes, money and so on. The message conveys relieving others of pain in sickness, or poverty and inculcating charitable tendencies. Thus, imploring the *Haves* to serve the *Have-nots* and establishing an order, that strives for equitable distribution of wealth.

Since Lohri coincides with harvest festivals all over the country, it communicates the message of oneness while at the same time providing an opportunity for thanking God for a bountiful life on earth for one and all.

PONGAL

The word *pongal* has two meanings, first it is the name of a dish cooked on this day, and second *ponga* means overflow. So the word Pongal means 'that which is overflowing'. Traditionally the dish is prepared by boiling the ingredients, in a new mud pot called *Pongapani* on which artistic designs are drawn. Pots of various sizes, shapes and designs are available at village fairs, which are an aesthetic treat. The pot gave the harvest festival its name.

Pongal falls in the month of January after the winter solistice, the festival marking the favourable course of the sun. It is a festival celebrated as *Makar Sankranti* all over South India, but in Tamil Nadu, it has an additional significance as Pongal welcomes the occasion of the incoming harvest. It is in all probability a Dravidian harvest festival that has survived the influence of the Indo-Aryan religion in the South.

It is a festive time for nature too, because with the end of the rainy season, the trees flower with the *kaya* blossoms, *konrai* flowers which shower their golden pollen on the ground and white *kandal* flowers. The deers are found running about in the fields providing an elated feeling.

There is the mood of anticipation and excitement in the people of Tamil Nadu, which gets its rains from the north-eastern monsoon in October and November, while the harvest is gathered in the period before the Pongal festival.

Pongal is celebrated over four days, the first is called *Bhogi Pongal*, the second is *Surya Pongal* and the third is *Mattu Pongal.* The fourth day is *Kaanum Pongal,* celebrated outdoors as an excursion or picnic day in total harmony with nature. It promotes harmony, universal brotherhood and peace.

Bhogi Pongal

This day is usually meant for prayer to Lord Indra, the rain God, to whom homage is paid for the plentiful harvest, and prosperity to the land. The rest of the day is spent in family get-togethers, special meal preparation and enjoyment at home, followed by family activities.

Observance

On this day before sunrise, a huge bonfire is lit in front of the homes and all useless household articles are thrown into the fire. The burning of all that is old is symbolic of the starting of a fresh New Year. The bonfire is kept burning throughout the night while boys beat little drums or *Bhogi Kottus* made from the hides of buffaloes.

Homes are thoroughly cleaned and decorated with *kolam* designs drawn with the white paste prepared from newly harvested rice, the outlines being drawn with red mud.

In the villages yellow pumpkin flowers are set out in cowdung balls in the middle of the designs. The harvest of rice, turmeric and sugarcane is brought in to be used for the next day's festivities.

Surya Pongal

This day is dedicated to the Sun God. During this period the sun shines brightly, the granaries are full, trees are in full bloom, the air is filled with chirping and singing of birds and hearts overflow with happiness seen through colourful and joyous celebrations.

Observance

A plank is placed at the centre and beautiful *kolam* designs made on the sides. In the centre of the plank is drawn the figure of the Sun God with its bright rays. Farmers harvest paddy only after performing *puja* to the Sun God.

The puja starts after the auspicious moment of the birth of the new month *Thai,* and prayers and offerings to the Sun God are made to seek His benedictions. While the puja is being performed the neck of the *pangopani* is tied with fresh turmeric and ginger saplings bearing tender green leaves.

The green leaves is the symbol of prosperity, the turmeric of auspiciousness and ginger for the spice of life. The special dish called *Sarkkarai Pongal* is cooked in the mud pot. After the rituals are over, sarkkarai pongal with sticks of sugarcane are offered to the Sun God as a thanksgiving fo=r the plentiful harvest. Sugarcane offered symbolises sweetness and happiness in life.

It is said that on this day Lord Sundareshwar in the Madurai temple performed a miracle and breathed life into a stone elephant who could eat sugarcane. The carving of this event can be seen in the Meenakshi temple. From this month of *Thai,* the marriage season starts in Tamil Nadu.

Mattu Pongal

The *Mattu pongal* is the festival celebrated as a day for thanksgiving to the cattle, the cow being the giver of milk and he buffalo the plougher of the land. The cattle are bathed, their horns painted and fitted with metal caps, then adorned with multi-coloured beads, bells, sheafs of corn and flower garlands around their necks. They are fed pongal and taken to village centers, the entire atmosphere is festive and full of fun and revelry.

A game called *Manji Virattu* is played in which young men chase the running bulls with their bells tingling. In some places a bull fight is arranged called *Jallikattu* in which money bags are tied to the horns of the animals, and unarmed young men are asked to wrest them from the bull's horns.

On the Mattu Pongal day, Lord Ganesh and Goddess Parvati are worshipped and Shakkarai Pongal is offered in the puja, with faith and sincerity. This day is also known as *Kaanum Pongal.*

Kaanum Pongal is celebrated much like *Rakshabandhan.* On this day coloured balls of cooked rice, are placed in the open air by girls, for the birds to eat. With each ball of rice the sister makes, she prays for her brother's happiness and he too remembers her well being wherever he may be. Sisters visit their brothers, apply tilak on their foreheads and give them sweets made of sesame and jaggery, praying for their health and prosperity and getting gifts in return.

Observance

Community dinners are also organised where the rich and the poor, landlord and peasant, old and young, women and children all share food together in a spirit of bonhomie, forgetting all caste or creed. Old vices are washed away and all that is good is welcomed in the New Year, looking up to heaven in joy and thankfulness to God, for everything from beasts, birds, crops and all life, especially peace, happiness and a feeling of brotherhood.

Present Scenario

Today, pongal is celebrated purely as a harvest festival and therefore not much mention is made of the *Surya Pongal.* The *Bhogi* and *Mattu Pongal* are however, celebrated as they are directly linked with the harvest.

BAISAKHI

Just as *Pongal, Bihu* and others, *Baisakhi* is a harvest festival of north India which always falls on the 14th of April in the month of *Baisakh* every year and marks the beginning of the new year. Just before the festival, farmers return home with their bumper *rabi* crops, the fruit of a whole year's hard labour, and this day is therefore celebrated with great fervour, zest and revelry, in Punjab, Haryana and Himachal Pradesh especially in the rural areas which are basically farming zones.

Observance

The celebration is a thanksgiving to God, for the good harvest of the year and people pray for a repeat in the following year too. Early morning on Baisakhi day, people take a dip in the holy rivers, lakes and tanks, to cleanse the body and purify souls. Celebrations are held on river banks and in the fields. One can hear cries of *Jatta aai Baisakhi* filling the air, as people dressed in their best clothes break into the *bhangra* dance to the beats of the *dholak*, and express their joy.

The dancers and drummers challenge each other to continue the dance. The scenes of sowing, harvesting, winnowing and gathering are depicted through the dance movements articulated with zest to the accompaniment of ballads. The women celebrate the day with more delicate but rhythmic movements than those of the men, in dances called the *Gidda*. The children and youth demonstrate their skills in martial arts to the accompaniment of musical bands.

A Sikh Festival

Baisakhi has a special meaning for the Sikhs, since Guru Amar Das first institutionalized Baisakhi in 1567, as one of the special days when all Sikhs would gather to receive the guru's blessings at *Goindwal.*

On this day in 1699, the 10th Guru, *Gobind Singh*, organized the order of the *Khalsa*, and discontinued the tradition of Gurus in Sikhism by declaring the *Granth Sahib* as the eternal Guru of all Sikhs. To form the *Khalsa Panth* he asked his followers to be ready to lay down their lives to save others. Five volunteers of five different castes were made the *Panj Piaras*, who would lead the rest. These came from Punjab, U.P., Andhra Pradesh and Bihar. The Panj Piaras in turn baptized Guru Gobind Singh into the Khalsa brotherhood.

There were five requisites required for being a true Sikh which were required to be adhered to as follows:

- *Kesh* - not to cut hair or beard
- *Kangha* – to carry a comb always
- *Kirpan* – carry a sword, always ready for battle
- *Kachha* – wear an underwear
- *Kada* – wear an iron bangle

These five *Ks* were considered mandatory and are till today followed by devout Sikhs.

Guru Arjan Dev was martyred by the Muslim rulers who, in barbaric cruelty threw him alive into a cauldron of boiling oil on this day. The Sikhs therefore, celebrate *Baisakhi* by visiting *gurudwaras* and distributing *kada prasaad*. Processions led by the *Panj Piaras* or the five religious men are taken out. *Kirtans* and recitations from the Guru Granth Sahib are also organized in the gurudwaras, where people line up to receive *prasaad* and perform *kar sewa*, that is, offer their help in the daily chores of the gurudwaras. The most sacred place of pilgrimage is Amritsar, where the Golden Temple is situated. Devotees are offered *lassi* and sweets on Baisakhi.

It is basically a community festival but is celebrated in homes too, when friends and relations visit to greet each other. Special puja is performed with recitations from the texts, after which the day ends with special meals and sumptuous feasts. Consumption of meats and alcohol is not prohibited, and sweets and fruits are sent to the families of married daughters.

Children are taught to perform acts of charity and are expected to continue them throughout the year. Many Sikhs choose to be baptized into the Khalsa brotherhood on Baisakhi day. The wrappings of the Nishan Sahib flag post are changed on this day at most of the gurudwaras.

On Baisakhi in1875, Swami Dayanand Saraswati founded the *Arya Samaj,* a reformed sect of Hindus devoted to the *Vedas* for spiritual guidance, and rejected the concept of idol worship.

This day is also of immense importance to Buddhists because Gautam Buddha attained enlightenment or *Nirvana* under the *Mahabodhi* tree in the town of Gaya on the same day. The day is also celebrated as *Buddha Purnima*, and is declared a national holiday.

Baisakhi is celebrated by the organization of fairs all over the northern region especially the Punjab. These fairs offer recreational activities, in the form of sports, competitions and bouts, apart from shopping bonanzas, handicrafts, bangles and festive food of various kinds. The occasion is celebrated with great gusto at Talwandi Sabo, where Guru Gobind Singh stayed for nine months and completed the recompilation of the Guru Granth Sahib. The celebrations however, vary slightly from state to state.

Kashmir

In the middle of April or on Baisakhi day, the New Year of the *Vikrami Samvat* starts. The day presents a grand spectacle of colour and gaiety on the Dal lake in Srinagar, and areas surrounding it.

Himachal Pradesh

In Himachal, Baisakhi is celebrated twice in a year in honour of Goddess *Jwalamukhi*, in the months of Baisakh (April-May) and Kartika (November). People from Himachal worship the Goddess whose image near a hot spring issues forth flames.

Bihar

In Bihar, the sun God is worshipped on Baisakhi. People offer flowers and water from the Ganges. Cattle fairs are held in villages, which bear a festive look. Vendors sell ice cream, flossy sugar pops and *chaat* of all description in addition to handicrafts and household goods.

Present Scenario

While Baisakhi was traditionally a harvest festival celebrated in rural farming communities, it travelled with the communities migrating to urban areas for jobs other than farming, as the land began to shrink in size after industrialization. Today almost all festivals are celebrated in the cities too, and recognized as national holidays to encourage the celebrations.

Most working people make it a point to visit the gurdwaras on this day, and pray for harvests to be good always, so that every one can eat to live comfortably. A way of offering thanks to God too is by partaking and distribution of prasaad. All the poor can eat free from the gurdwara *langars* on these special days and celebrate the charity devotees offer for the purpose.

ONAM

Onam is an annual harvest festival, celebrated mainly in the Indian state of Kerala which falls in the month of *Chingom* or *Aso-Bhado* according to the lunar and August-September as per the solar calendar. Preparations for Onam start on the *Atham* day and *Thiruvonam* is the most important day of the festivities. It brings ten days of colour, feasting, boat races, song and dances to the state. According to legend, onam celebrates the golden age of King Mahabali, the mythical ruler of Kerala.

Observance

For ten days, women and children decorate their home courtyards with elaborate circular floral decorations, known as *Athapoovu,* in the centre of which is placed a clay image of *Thrikkakkara* or *Appan* Lord Vishnu. This points to both the aesthetic and devotional aspects of the festival.

On Thiruvonam day, people bathe and offer worship in temples, after which it is traditional for the whole family to get together and enjoy special foods associated with celebration and festivity.

Cultural programmes comprising plays, music concerts, dances, mock fights, ball and card games, and sports are enjoyed. Women participate in *onjalattam* or swings, and different types of group dances, locally known as *Thumbithullal, Thiruvathirakali* and *Kaikottikali.*

For Keralites, rivers are objects of reverence and therefore *Jalotsavams* or water festivals are held with great enthusiasm by men, women and children of all communities. Boat races form an important part of Onam celebrations and thousands of tourists are attracted to Kerala to witness them. The most famous water festival is the Aranmula Snake Boat Race named after the Aranmula village, which houses the famous Parthasarathi temple, which is dressed up like a bride for the occasion. The race starts on the Pampa river, which commemorates the crossing of the river by Sri Krishna on that day.

In fact, the common belief is that God travels in all the boats on this occasion, and so these are expected to reach their destination simultaneously. It is not a competition but just for the joy of the celebration. People line up the river banks for about three kilometers to watch the colourful races. It is called the Snake Boat Race since the boats, 100 metres long, are so constructed to provide a raised hood-like appearance at the rear end, which appears like the raised hood of a snake. Each boat has a strength of 150 oarsmen, singers and ruddersmen. Huge ornamental umbrellas and banners are held aloft to create a spectacular display. Besides Onam, other festivals of Kerala include the *Thrissur Pooram* and *Vishu.*

Thrissur Pooram

This is another colourful festival of Kerala celebrated in *Medom* (April-May) every year. The best elephants from South India are requisitioned for the event by the parties along with the most attractive parasols, which are raised on the elephants during the display. Utmost secrecy is maintained by the parties during the preparations in their attempt to excel.

Celebration

Spectacular processions of richly caparisoned elephants from various temples congregate in Thrissur for the event. The celebrations include fireworks display in which two rival groups representing the two divisions of Thrissur, namely Paramekkavu and Thiruvambadi, vie with each other to excel. The festivities start at dawn and continue till dawn the next day.

At the close of Pooram, the elephants in all their glory enter the temple through the western gate and exit through the southern gate to array themselves into two groups, which stand facing each other in silent confrontation, and providing an awesome spectacle. All the spectators stand transfixed by a magical feeling, and the magnificent sight of caparisoned pachyderms with their shimmering, glittering umbrellas. Tourists from all over come to visit this magnificence accompanied by the roar, clang, crash and blare of percussion and wind instruments, as fly-whisk bearers twirl and swirl their plumes.

Vishu

This festival is celebrated by the people of Kerala on the first day of *Medam*, and falls on the same day each year unlike other festivals which are determined by the lunar asterisms. As the day on which Vishu falls is the astronomical new year day, Malayalis believe that the fortunes of the coming year depend on the nature of the first object one sees on waking up on this festival day.

To ensure that family members see an auspicious object on waking, a *kani* or auspicious sight, is prepared the night before for viewing.

Observance

Some raw rice is spread in a circular bell metal urn, called *uruli,* which is covered with a clean folded cloth. Then a metal mirror, a palm leaf book or scriptural text, yellow *konna* flowers (Cassic fistula), betel leaves, golden ripe cucumber and a few gold coins are arranged pleasingly on the cloth. Two halves of a coconut with oil and lighted wicks are placed in the *uruli* to illuminate the articles placed in it. A bell metal lamp is then kept beside the uruli.

Early on Vishu day the eldest female member of the family gets up and lights the lamp and looks at the *kani.* She then wakes the other members and the kani is shown to each of them, taking care to see that they do not cast their eyes on anything before they view the kani. Sometimes the kani is carried to each bedside, or each member is blindfolded and led to the kani. Even the cattle are made to view the kani which is taken to their shed. Later silver coins are handed over to the youngsters, relatives and servants in a ritual called *kaineetom.* A feast is prepared and served to all after they have bathed, worn new clothes and greeted their elders.

Of all the festivals of Kerala, Vishu symbolizes the simplicity and unostentatious ways of the people. Athough it is observed with solemnity it has no religious connotations. Most *Keralites* believe that the fortunes of the coming year depend on what they first see on that day howsoever modern they may be in their outlook.

BASANT PANCHMI

Basant Panchmi is the fifth day of spring falling in the month of *phagun-chaitra*, and is celebrated by worshipping Goddess *Saraswati* as she symbolizes the constant flow of wisdom, while representing the full blossoming of nature and kindling the light of inspiration and hope. All music lovers and those involved in cultural activities, specially pray to her for her blessings. The yellow colour is of special importance during *Basant Panchmi* as is the coming of spring after the long winter. Yellow is the colour of energy-giving sun and the mustard fields in bloom, which warn of the coming of spring. People therefore wear yellow or orange coloured clothes, and are seen with radiant faces, happily enjoying the spirit of the occasion. The radiance is also symbolic of Goddess Saraswati associated with knowledge.

During this time, the bird-loving Kashmiris cook yellow rice, prepare small balls of it and throw them on the roof of their homes for crows and other birds.

During the eight phases of the day, Saraswati manifests through speech at least once. Everyone has experienced that sometimes what is uttered even casually comes true. It is possible to attain this state where one's speech is consistently governed by *Kamalasana* or the one who is seated on a thousand petalled lotus, each petal representing a particular quality.

Saraswati's *vahan* or vehicle is the *hans* or swan, which has the ability to hold a mixture of milk and water in its beak and spew out pure water from one side and milk from the other. This is known as *neerkshir vivek* or the water-milk wisdom. In philosophical terms, it means a wise person is one who, like the swan is able to pick out the peals of wisdom from the vast spread of knowledge.

Each string of the *Veena* that Saraswati holds in her hands represents the body, food, humaneness, work, intelligence, religious and spiritual cultures. Besides these, the seven colours, glands, chakras, skies, *rishis* or holy wise men and, also the seven steps of consciousness are to be experienced to be understood in the right perspective.

Whosoever has accomplished these symbolic seven *swaras* or notes, will be safeguarded from drowning in the *samsara sagara* or worldly ocean by the two *tumbas* or globes on either side of the veena. The strings should be in perfect tune to hear and experience the sweet music of life. Thus, the message of Saraswati who is also called V*eena Vadini* is that, seven years of *sadhana* or penance are required to complete the transformation for manifesting divine qualities.

The Goddess is always clad in white, the colour of purity. The red border to her sari represents sensitivity and desires in life so that it can blossom creatively for joy in life. The *Tulsi mala* or rosary made of tulsi seeds which she wears, represents perseverance and consistency in *sadhana* or *bhakti.* The Vedas she holds in her hand signify knowledge and wisdom, which form the basis of the 64 art forms. These represent and express the evolved nature of our ancient civilization and culture.

Saraswati holds a pen in one hand representing the power to manifest the truth through words, to dispel ignorance, foster compassion, wisdom and authenticity in speech and spread light. The Saraswati *Gayatri* is an invocation to the spirit of knowledge.

Offering

The Goddess's food is made up of *panch magaz,* or five varieties of ingredients that provide essential nutrients for the brain. These are *banslochan* or nodes of the bamboo shoot, *misri,* nuts, *elaichi* or cardamom, lotus stems and seeds or *makhanas.* Prayers are offered and then the food offerings distributed as *prasaad.* A quote of the prayer from Swami Paramananda is very appropriate for this occasion:

... make my life full of Divine inspiration,
That it may become productive only of good.
Free me from all pettiness and narrowness.
Help me to keep my thought fixed on
That which is vast and majestic.
Expand my heart and enlarge my mind
That I may be able to contain Thee
And give myself up wholly to Thee.

Basant was once an important day in North-western India, with fairs being held in many places with men seen in yellow turbans and women in yellow clothes. They merrily imitated nature as the yellow mustard fields were in bloom. Floral and fruit trees were in bud or blossom. At many places in Punjab, colourful kites are flown on this day.

Present Scenario

The partition of the country took half the fun out of the celebration; the turbans have gradually gone out of fashion, although the kite flying and music concerts are still held. In Delhi, some groups do organize fetes and sell clothes, accessories, food and kites. It is believed that the tradition of kite flying is still prevalent in Lahore, which is now in Pakistan.

HOLI

Holi is known as the festival of colours, mirth and friendship. Colors got associated with Holi because the festival falls in spring when flowers are in full bloom spreading their fragrances all around. It is about celebrating nature and the country goes wild with joy, people smearing each other with brightly hued powders and coloured waters. Holi falls on *ekadashi* in March every year on the full moon day and is therefore referred to as *Rangbhari ekadashi*. The festival marks the beginning of spring and the weather is usually pleasant and dry, a season ideal for experiencing love and happiness. But, in exceptional years Holi can be very wet and cold for enjoying a specifically outdoor festivity. It is celebrated in different ways in different regions, although the spirit remains the same.

Holi coincides with the harvesting of the rabi crop, and was traditionally celebrated using natural colour extracts from seasonal herbs, flowers and other parts of plants.

Origin

The festival of Holi is ancient in its origin and celebrates the triumph of *good* over *evil*. While colours associated with Holi is the external face of the festival the original reason lies in its soul. Literally, Holi means *burning* and is associated with the legend of Hiranyakashyap, a demon king who wanted to avenge the death of his younger brother, who had been killed by Lord Vishnu. Hiranyakashyap performed severe penance and prayer for many years to gain enough power to be granted a boon by the Lord. In arrogance he asked his people to worship him instead of God, because he thought that he had become invincible. But his young son Prahalad was an ardent devotee of Vishnu and continued to pray to Him. Hiranyakashyap therefore decided to kill his son and asked his sister Holika to help him, as she was immune to fire because of a boon granted to her. He asked Holika to sit young Prahalad in her lap and lighted a fire, but to his dismay Prahalad came out unscathed while Holika was burnt to ashes.

The festival is therefore celebrated and enjoyed over 2 days — on the first day, a bonfire is lit to symbolically destroy Holika and therefore all evil and the second day is celebrated with colour and water with great fervour and rejoicing. Holi is celebrated differently in the different regions of the country as briefly discussed.

North India

Holi fell on March 15th last year (2006) and was a wet and cold Holi. In fact, the Met. department records showed that a wet Holi had occurred only twice in the past eight years, in 1998 and 2000, and the temperatures recorded showed the festival of 2006 was the coldest in many years. Recordings showed that a minimum temperature of 14°C and a maximum of 27°C dampening the spirit of people a little, since Holi is enjoyed only by sprinkling coloured water on each other on a dry sunny day. To make up for it however, it is a time when the annual exams are over for students who really take to the streets with their friends, drenching each other and whosoever they see. There may be few cases of rage but the spirit of the festivities makes people only laugh, enjoy and forgive anything that went wrong in the past.

In Mathura and Vrindavan, where Lord Krishna spent most of His childhood, Holi is celebrated for over a week with great gusto. Each Radha-Krishna temple is decorated and people throng there to get drenched in coloured water considering it a blessing from God.

Krishna was from the village of Nandgaon and Radha from Barsana so at Holi, men come from Nandgaon to Barsana to celebrate with the women who are ready to beat them up with sticks instead of playing with *gulal,* the holy red powder.

Haryana

In Haryana, the celebration involves the making of a human pyramid, by men getting on to the back of each other till the topmost person can reach the pot of buttermilk suspended high up in the streets and break the pot to spill and or share the contents. There is also a tradition of the Hindu undivided family where the brother's wife beats her brother-in-law with her saree rolled up into a rope in a mock rage. This is all enacted in good humour, and in the evening the brother-in-law brings sweets for her.

Western India

In Maharashtra and Gujarat, a grand procession of men soaked in coloured water walks through the streets with a mock alert call that asks people to take care of their pots of milk and butter as they come in, referring to the stealing of butter and milk by Krishna from homes. The custom of hanging a pot of butter and milk high up in streets is also observed. Men making a human ladder try to break the pot and whoever succeeds is crowned the Holi King of the year.

All these traditions come as mock shows to relive the acts of Krishna who popularized Holi in its present form.

Eastern India

In Bengal, Holi is called the *Dol yatra* or the swing festival, traditionally celebrated with Krishna and Radha on the swings and devotees taking turns to swing them. Women dance around the swings and sing devotional songs while men spray coloured water and red powder called *abeer* on them.

Orissa too has similar traditions but replace Krishna–Radha by Jagannath and his consort, the deity the Oriyas worship. Jagannath is considered as Lord of the universe, another name for Krishna.

North East

In Manipur, Holi is a 6-day festival starting on the full moon day of Phalgun. The traditional and centuries-old *Yaosung* festival of Manipur was amalgamated with Holi in the 18th century, with the introduction of Vaishnavism. Traditionally, folk dances are performed to the tune of folk music in the moonlit night, to the beat of the drums. People collect money well in advance to spend on the festivities so everyone felt involved and a feeling of kinship and unity prevailed.

A thatched hut of hay, twigs and sticks is built and then set ablaze, equivalent to the burning of Holika one night before Holi. The next day, the boys get collected in groups to play Holi with the girls using dry powders. In return for playing with them, the girls take money from the boys. Devotees dress themselves in white and yellow turbans play Holi with *gulal* or red powder in front of Krishna temples and sing devotional songs.

On the last day of the festival, hundreds of devotees join in procession to go to the main Krishna temple, 3 km west of the state capital, Imphal, where cultural activities are performed as well.

This year in Varanasi, *Holi* began with even greater gusto than usual, five days earlier, just as the embers of the blasts at the *Sankat Mochan* Temple were dying out. The spirit of the festival, *Rangbhari ekadashi*, was not allowed to be dampened at the colourful religious ceremony performed at the *Kashi Vishwanath* Temple in Varanasi. The hues and spirit of Holi even covered the footprints of terror and erased the darkness of Varanasi's *Black Tuesday*. A local unsung and unknown poet announced:

> ***Bomb phuta hai mare hamare, yeh sab kuch hum jhelenge;***
> ***Ugravad ki aisi- taisi, Hum sab Holi khelenge***

We will bear the agony of the bomb blast which killed our kin, we will celebrate the festival of Holi shunning the terrorism.[30]

Present Scenario

The traditional methods however have been gradually replaced by modern musical bands and fluorescent lights. Colours used in the celebration are a mix of natural and synthetic hues, some to be used dry

---

[30] Binay Singh, Times News Network, 7th March, 2006, Varanasi.

and others dissolve in water and used as pastes and sprays.The safety from such colours has become an important feature today, when these are bought in unpacked loose forms, and not branded.

Safety of Colours

The traditional herbal and natural colours have gradually been replaced by synthetic dyes which contain harmful chemicals that damage the skin and cause allergic reactions.

Unpacked and non-branded colours sold at Holi may be toxic whether dry, pastes or waters, since many of them are made of cheap and hazardous materials. Majority of the colours are made from cheap materials like acids, crushed pieces of glass, mica and alkalis which lead to skin abrasion, itching and irritation as well as respiratory, vision and other serious problems. Once you mix the colours with oil and apply them, the chemicals get into the body through the pores of the skin. Holi colours contain chemicals that can cause severe health effects which have been summarized in Table 9.1.

Table 9.1: Toxic effects of colours

Form	Chemicals	Colour	Possible Health Effects
Pastes	Lead oxide	Black	Renal failure
	Copper sulphate	Green	Eye allergy, puffiness and temporary blindness
	Aluminum bromide	Silver	Carcinogenic (cancerous)
	Prussian blue	Blue	Dermatitis
	Mercury sulphite	Red	Skin cancer
Gulals (powder)	Asbestos or silica as toxic base	All colours	Silica — dry and chapped skin Asbestos — cancer; gets built into body tissues even in micro amounts.

(Contd...)

Gentian violet	Blue, purple	Skin discolouration, dermatitis, and allergies of mucous membranes. In concentrated form gentian violet can lead to kerato-conjunctivitis and dark purple staining of the cornea.
Heavy metals	All	Systemic poisons

Gulals are made up of mostly heavy metals known to be systemic toxins. They get deposited in the kidneys, liver and bones and disrupt metabolic functions. Table 9.2 outlines the effects of each metal.

Table 9.2: Effects of heavy metals on the body

Metal	Effects
Lead	Affects the nervous system, kidneys and reproductive system. Can cause learning disabilities in children
Chromium	Bronchial asthma and allergies
Cadmium	Leads to fragile bones, an affliction called *Itai Ita*
Nickel	Dermatitis and or pneumonia
Mercury	Disorder of the nervous system called *minimata* disease
Zinc	Causes fever
Iron	Makes one sensitive to light.

In fact lead can affect the physical and mental growth of children, even the foetus, if a woman in pregnancy is exposed to it. It may even lead to premature birth, low birth weight, miscarriage or abortion. Cadmium has been classified as a probable human carcinogen.

Today, the awareness of the public and children towards toxicity of colours has increased, because of schooling, higher literacy levels and the media. We see a shift back to organic colours which are not only health friendly but also ecofriendly. Ways of making safe colours was first initiated through the introduction of the *Basant Utsav* or Spring Fest by Nobel Laureate Rabindranath Tagore in his school at *Shanti Niketan*, opened to keep the Indian traditions alive without polluting the environment. Today Shanti Niketan is a full-fledged University but still lives up to the tradition of greeting the spring every year. The festival is observed in the midst of the spring flowers with traditional music and dance.

Some ways of making safe Holi colours are suggested in Table 9.3 using *nature* as the guide:

Table 9.3: Making safe Holi colours

Colour	Ingredients	Method
Yellow	- Turmeric *(haldi)*, flour, talcum powder, water colour	Mix together in water to make paste or liquid
	- Turmeric, *besan*, marigold flowers and water	Soak flowers overnight with haldi and besan. Use as paste or liquid.
Green	- *Mehndi* or *henna* and flour	Mix together to make green powder
	- Leaves of any plant, water	Boil leaves and use green water
Magenta	- Beetroot, water	Chop beetroot, soak in water for a few hours, strain for magenta water.
Brown	- Tea or coffee, hot water	Pour hot water over tea or coffee, then cool and use decoction
	- *Katha* and water	Use as such or dissolve in water
Red	- Sandalwood powder, lime,	Mix together with water and use water
Orange	- *Tesu* flowers, water	Soak the flowers overnight and use the water
Reddish pink	- Beetroot, water	Cut and boil beetroot in

(Contd...)

		water till all colour is leached out. Cool, strain and dilute.
Deep red	- *Choona* (lime), turmeric	Mix to get deep red color.
Mehroon	- Rose petals	Dry and grind to powder and use.
Saffron	- Flowers from trees	Flowers may be boiled in water, left overnight, strained and used

As far as is possible natural dyes or sources for materials should be used for playing Holi. These ideas may help one to become more creative and safe in your festivities. Colours have a lot of power over moods, personalities and behaviour of people too. Some of these effects have been listed in Table 9.4.

Table 9.4: Effect of colour on personality and behaviour

Colour	Significance	Personality and behaviour
Blue	Expresses emotion through creativity with art, music and literature	Trustworthy, healer, artist or diplomat.
Red	Indicates conviction and zest for life	Dynamic, generous, competitive and passionate.
Orange	Initiates motivation and creativity	Dynamic, creative, ambitious and focused, passionate.
Yellow	Signifies communication and	Confident, extrovert and
Gold	counseling skills.	influential, optimist.
Purple	Endorses interest in mystical and	Religious, philosophical and self confident.
Lavender	metaphysical and nature related aspects of life	

(Contd...)

Green	Signifies an appreciation for detail and averse to sudden surprises	Love nature, despise vio lence, peaceful and calm
Brown	Signifies love, harmony, loyalty.	Steady, reliable, down to earth, with subtle sense of humor.
Black Grey	Expresses despair and negativity	Rebellious, revengeful or depressed.
White	Expresses purity and will to start afresh	Calm and adaptive

Since colours are so deeply linked to personalities, they also hold potential to add or take certain characteristic away. Artist Niladri Paul says that each colour symbolizes a positive mental state and can counteract a negative one. He recommends the following colourful remedies :

- Emerald green and ultramarine blue for stress relief
- White and cobalt blue for short temper
- Purple for creative stimulation
- Orange for rejuvenating
- Cerulean blue for toning down hyperactivity
- Neutral tones such as black and white for combating jealousy

Spirit of Holi

The celebration of *Holi* is not complete without its official traditional drink called *bhang* which accompanies all other special foods eaten after the colour spraying is over, and every one gets ready to make merry in the evening. When and how the association began is anyone's guess, but elders always insisted that there in no *Holi* without bhang. Perhaps because it was Lord Shiva's nectar or because bhang gives a long and sophisticated high that goes well with a day-long celebration.

Bhang

Bhang is the herbal drink without which *Holi* is not complete in Kashi or Varanasi. It is India's official festival drink. Since 1000 BC, bhang has been prepared by crushing the dried leaves and buds of the cannabis plant, *Cannabis sativus*, commonly grown in North India. It is also eaten in the form of sweet marble-sized balls made from crushed leaf of the plant and mixed with ghee, sugar and milk. It is also made into *ladoos* or simply swallowed as balls called *antas* or marbles. It however, takes half an hour before its effects set in. If however, it is mixed with other intoxicants like smoking marijuana the effects are felt soon after ingestion.

The bhang is characterized by a feeling of euphoria, which increases the perception of colour and sound giving a pleasant feeling of well being. It increases appetite, spurs creative or philosophical thinking and appreciation of music. Overconsumption however has negative effects, seen as headaches, drowsiness and a sense of complacency. Among first timers, it may cause paranoia, hallucinations, lethargy and drowsiness. The psychoactive substance is Tetra Hydro Cannabinol (THC) associated with energetic cerebral high. The effects of bhang vary with individual's physiological status, environment and the state of mind. There have however, never been reported any medically established ill effects or fatalities.

Not only the bhang, but also the spirit of Holi is intoxicating with friendship, love and bliss. Holi inspires creativity, music, joy and unity.

Recent Trends

Children and adults have started buying colours after reading labels on packets. Most people avoid playing wet Holi any way, and prefer to remain indoors. Doctors advise not to play with water balloons as they can damage health if struck on the head, eyes or chest.

RAKSHA BANDHAN

Raksha Bandhan falls on the full moon day of the month of *Shravan* (August-September) and celebrates the love between brother and sister. On this day, sisters tie a sacred thread, the *rakhi* on the wrists of their brothers to protect them against evil influences, and is therefore also called *Rakhi*. The festival is unique to India and creates a feeling of belonging and oneness amongst the family and brotherhood within the community at large.

Significance

The sibling relationship is nowhere so celebrated as in India. It is the celebration of the bond of love and care between brothers and sisters. It is the day when the siblings pray for each other's welfare and happiness. *Raksha* means protection, and *Bandhan* means bond or bonding and hence *Raksha Bandhan* signifies the bond of protection. It is a pledge from the brothers to protect their sisters from all harm and troubles and a prayer from the sister to protect the brother from all evil. In North India, the occasion is popularly called Rakhi, the name adopted for all the different colourful threads used to express sibling sentiment.

While this festival is now celebrated for brothers and sisters, it was not always so. There have been examples in history where *rakhi* was tied for *Raksha* or protection. It started as a tradition amongst the warrior clan when wives, daughters, mothers or sisters after offering prayers tied a sacred thread called *rakhi* on the wrist of their husbands, fathers, sons and brothers going to war with a wish that they come back victorious. Gradually this changed and sisters started tying *rakhis* on the right wrist of their brothers praying for their protection from evil influence and any situations that may taint their character. The solemnity and meaning of the occasion strengthened the bond of love between them.

The *rishis* tied *rakhi* to the people who came seeking their blessings. The sages tied the sacred thread on their own wrists as a safeguard from evil. According to the scriptures it is by all means the *Papa Todak, Punya Pradayak Parva* or the day that bestows boons and ends all sins. Even today, priests tie the sacred thread on the wrists of their devotees who in return present their offerings to them.

Significance

There are regional differences in the observance of the festival, each state indicating its cultural and geographic traditions and adding meaning to their ritual. These are being briefly outlined.

Maharashtra

The festival of *Rakhi* is also known as *Narial Purnima* or Coconut Full Moon. On Mumbai's famous beaches, coconuts are thrown into the sea to propitiate the Sea God, *Varuna*, who is the chief object of worship on this occasion.

South India

In Southern India, *Rakhi* is called *Avani Avittam*. This is the time of *upakaram* and is celebrated in various ways. Thus *Raksha Bandhan* forms an important Hindu festival that fosters love, peace and goodwill.

For Brahmins, the festival is also known as *Balev* and has special significance as it is an occasion for the thread changing ceremony, when young Brahmin boys discard their old sacred threads and don new ones ritualistically. While changing the sacred thread, they rededicate themselves to the study of the Vedas and take a fresh vow to the path of spiritual upliftment.

Kashmir

Rakhi or *Raksha Bandhan* is the day for brothers and sisters to renew their affectionate ties. On this day, Kashmiri Hindus climb to the temple of Shankaracharya on a hill top, believed to be an abode of Lord Shiva. The more revered abode is in the glacier-bound cave-shrine of Amarnath, which pilgrims from all parts of India behold as sacred. Those who cannot trek to Amarnath go to Thanjivara cave to worship the Shivalingam. The belief is that three pilgrimages to this shrine equal the merit of the Amarnath Yatra.

Traditions & Rituals

Traditionally the ceremony of *Raksha Bandhan* is very simple but it means a lot to siblings who have great faith in the festival as it helps them to reunite mentally, emotionally and physically to remind themselves of their duties to each other.

The day of *Raksha Bandhan* starts with a festive mood in every Indian home. The preparations begin much in advance. Some 20 days ahead of the festival colourful *rakhis* are available in the market. *Rakhis* are made or bought before the festival. New clothes are bought and *rakhis* are sent to the brothers staying away from home. Traditional dishes are prepared early in the morning. Women wake up early in the morning and take a bath, to purify mind and body, before starting any preparations and then wear their finest clothes. In some households the brothers go to the sister's place and in some, sisters go to their brother's place to tie the *rakhi*. A *thal* (plate) is prepared on which they put the *rakhi*, a *diya* (earthen lamp), water, vermilion or turmeric powder, *kaleva* (red sacred threads), raw rice, coconut, and some sweets. Then offering of *puja* (worshipping of God) takes place. In some parts of the country, it is customary to draw the *swastik* symbol and other figures on the walls of their home and worship them with offerings of vermilion, *kaleva* and *kheer*. The imprints of palms are also put on either side of the entrance and *rakhis* are stuck on them as part of the Rakshabandhan ritual in some households. The sister performs *pujan* of her brother by applying traditional *tilak* (vermilion or turmeric mixed with 2-3 grains of rice, sugar and water) on his forehead. The *tilak* is put on the forehead between the two eyebrows. It is said that the *tilak* indicates the point at which the spiritual eye opens. After this she offers *aarti* (a traditional way of worshipping) to her brother and ties the *rakhi* on his right wrist. Then she gives him sweets and gifts. In return the brother gives her a gift as a token of his love and affection and vows to protect her. The tradition of giving gifts and presents is also an important part of this festival.

In many households, rakhi is tied after the brother does *pranaam* to the sister usually by touching her feet to take her blessings in the traditional manner. Blessings are always taken from saints, gurus in this manner. It teaches humility and was part of education given by the sages and seers who also respected women highly from ancient times.

In a few households, sisters observe a fast on the Rakshabandhan day and only when they have tied the *rakhi* to their brothers do they eat. The rituals may differ a little from region to region but generally carry the same aura.

Mode of Feasting

The relationships are the essence of the celebration. This holds true for any Indian festival. Each festival brings the families together. The family reunion itself is the reason for celebration. The celebration of one such relationship is Rakshabandhan, the brother–sister relationship. Treating her brother along with her entire family with the tasty dishes, sweets and other eatables that have been prepared as an important part of the festival.

Present Scenario

It is not the rituals, customs and traditions that change over time but the celebration styles and perspectives that become contemporary. For centuries, this festival has been celebrated in the same way. The traditions are followed with the same enthusiasm. The gaieties have only grown up to a large scale. It is the celebration of the chaste bond of love amongst siblings.

The market is flooded with the fanciest of *rakhi*s ranging from a colored cotton string to exquisitely decorated balls of various sizes and materials such as fluffy cotton, *zari*, paper, tinsel, beads and so on, to batman and spiderman embossed threads. What used to be a celebration of sibling bonds has come a long way to become an occasion for the exchange of expensive gifts and throwing of lavish parties. *Pooja thalis, rakhi* greetings, special gift packs are mass manufactured to meet the demand. The gift, garment and sweet shops, etc. are all flooded with things to attract people. It has now become an extravagant affair where both parties expect the most expensive gifts. At the end of the day, sisters compare their gifts.

For those siblings who because of distances are not able to meet, it is a day for remembering the time when the day was celebrated together. Emotions are expressed through e-mails, e-cards, *rakhi* greeting cards, and *rakhis* can now be sent through Internet or mail. Nothing on this day can stop the overflowing emotions.

Rakhi for many centuries encompassed the warmth shared between the siblings but now it goes beyond it. If the sister is out of the country then the daughter ties the *rakhi* to her father. If the siblings do not have a brother, then the sisters tie *rakhi* to each other to strengthen the chord between them. Some tie *rakhi* to neighbours and close friends who are not related, but whom they consider to be like a brother, in a way, signifying a peaceful co-existence of every individual. Congregations like *Rakhi Mohotsavas*, started and popularized by Rabindranath Tagore, promoted the feeling of unity and a commitment to all members of society to protect each other and encourage a harmonious social life. He started this to propagate the feeling of brotherhood amongst people. This invoked trust and feeling of peaceful co-existence. The festival is thus a symbol of harmony. The tradition continues as people tie rakhis to their neighbours and close friends. It is a festival denoting national sentiments of harmony.

The day has a deeper perspective in today's scenario. The occasion stands for a life-long pledge to practice moral, spiritual and cultural values. The values and the sentiments of harmony and peaceful coexistence attached to the rituals of this festival are worth inculcating by the entire human race.

The face of the festival may have changed but the essential sentiment it celebrates is very much intact. While Rakshabandhan may not hold literal significance for those who celebrate it, it still reaffirms the bond of love between brothers and sisters.

In a world full of crises, these kinds of rituals hold the key to peaceful existence. The auspicious day of Rakshabandhan can be used as a potent tool for social change, which could ultimately envelop everyone in a permanent bond of love and friendship.

BHAI DOOJ

Bhai or Bhaiya-Dooj as the name suggests is celebrated between brothers and sisters. *Bhaiya* means brother, and *dooj* indicates the timing of the celebration, which comes two days after new moon in the month of *Kartika* every year. Thus, Bhaiya Dooj comes every year on the fifth or last day of *Diwali.*

This festival is called by various names such as *Bhai-Bij* in Gujarat and all Marathi-speaking communities, *Bhai-Tika* in Nepal, whereas in Bengal this event is called *Bhai Phota*, which is performed by the sister who religiously fasts until she applies a *phota* or mark with sandalwood paste on her brother's forehead, offers him sweets and gifts and prays for his long and healthy life. The festival may have different names according to regional customs and languages but the observance and meaning of the festival is the same.

Bhaiya Dooj is also called *Yama Dwiteeya* as it is believed that on this day, Yamaraj, the Lord of death and the custodian of hell, visits his sister Yami, who puts the auspicious mark on his forehead and prays for his well being. So, it is held that anyone who receives a *tilak* or *tika* from his sister on this day would never suffer hell.

Significance

Like all other Hindu festivals, Bhai Dooj too has got a lot to do with family ties and social attachments. It is a good time, especially for a married girl, to get together with her maiden family, and share the post-Diwali joy with her brothers and parents.

There are various legends behind Bhaiya dooj which lay stress on the significance of the pious relationship between a brother and his sister, making it an extremely important festival. Bhaiya dooj is a restricted holiday in India and those who have to travel far off for the festival take leave from work.

According to another legend, on this day Lord Krishna, after slaying the *Narakasura* demon, went to his sister Subhadra who welcomed him with the lamp, flowers and sweets, and put the holy *kum kum tilak* on her brother's forehead wishing him protection from evil.

Another story behind the origin of Bhai Dooj says that when Mahavir, the founder of Jainism, attained *nirvana*, his brother King Nandivardhan was distressed because he missed him, and only his sister Sudarshana succeeded in comforting him. Again when Lord Vamandev was pleased with Bali Maharaj and appeared as Vishnu, Bali asked a boon that Lord Vishnu would be on every door at *Patalaloka*. Lord Vishnu agreed and became a *Dwarpalaka* of Bali. When this news was given to Goddess Lakshmi by Narada, she was greatly distressed. In order to make her husband return back to his original place, Laxmi played a trick on Bali. She went to him as a poor woman seeking help and said that she does not have a brother and would dearly like one. When Bali accepted to be her brother and told her to ask anything that she wants, *Laxmi* asked him to release Lord Vishnu. Thus, Lord Vishnu was released from the service of Bali. Since then, women have been revered during Bhai Dooj.

Observance

On this day, sisters apply a sacred *tika* or vermillion mark on the forehead of their brothers, and pray for their long life. Brothers bless their sisters and promise to protect them from the hardships in life. On this day every girl or woman invites her brother to come and share food with her to consolidate the sibling bond.

The *Bhai dooj puja* is carried out in the puja room, or on the same platform that was decorated for Diwali. The sister arranges a silver or other precious metal *thaali* with the *mithai, batashas, roli* and rice along with a coconut. The puja lamp is lit and after the puja is performed by every member of the household, the sister applies the *tilak* or a vermilion mark and rice on the forehead of the brother and performs an *aarti* of him by showing him the light of the holy flame as a mark of love and pray for his protection from evil forces. After applying *tika,* she gives him a few of the eatables along with the coconut. On this occasion, sisters are lavished with gifts, goodies and blessings from their brothers and they in return receive her blessings for health and longevity.

Traditionally brothers and sisters do not eat till the ceremony is over. While it is a simple ritual it is charged with love and affection. Every brother eagerly waits for this occasion that reinforces the bond between brothers and sisters and their affectionate relationship. It is an opportunity for a good feast at the sister's place, coupled with an enthusiastic exchange of gifts, and merriment.

Married women staying nearby, visit their parents' place early in the morning to greet their brothers, and those staying far-off either take a few days off to visit their brother or express their love and blessings through posting greeting cards or e-cards and sending their good wishes. After the rituals are performed, brothers give gifts to their sisters. Generally, the girl of the house is given presents of clothes, utensils, and lots of *mithai* and fruits at festivals, before she returns from her parent's or brother's home.

Present Scenario

Nowadays, sisters who are unable to meet their brothers send their *tika* in an envelope by post. Virtual *tilaks* and Bhaiya Dooj e-cards have made it even easier for brothers and sisters, who are far away from each other, to specially remember their siblings on this propitious occasion and convey their greetings.

In India, even today, no auspicious occasion in the family like a wedding takes place without the presence of the siblings no matter how far they may be living from each other.

MOTHER'S DAY

Celebrated every year on the second Sunday in May, Mother's Day is the day when every child expresses thoughts and feelings of love and respect that they have for their mother. It is celebrated slightly differently in different countries according to their traditions and cultural and traditional associations with their children. Mother's Day is a holiday honouring mothers, celebrated on various days in many places around the world.

Greece

Mother's Day celebrations can be traced back to the spring celebrations in ancient Greece in honour of Rhea, wife of Cronus and mother of gods and goddesses. In Rome, a festival, was dedicated to the worship of Cybele, another mother goddess, in whose honour ceremonies began about 250 years before Christ was born. This Roman religious celebration was known as *Hilaria* and lasted for three days, the ceremonies believed by some, to be adopted by the Church to venerate Mary, the Mother of Christ. Others believe that the Mother Church was substituted for mother goddess and custom began to dictate that people visit the church of their baptism on this day, which they did laden with offerings.

England

During the 1600s, England celebrated a day called *Mothering Sunday* celebrated on the 4th Sunday of Lent. It was so named to honour the mothers of England. As Christianity spread throughout Europe, the celebration changed to honour the Mother Church, the spiritual power that gave them life and protected them from harm. Over time, the church festival blended with the *Mothering Sunday* celebration and people began honoring their mothers as well as the church. The day is now commonly called *Mother's Day* in the United Kingdom, and has no direct connection to the American practice. It falls on the fourth Sunday of Lent in March or early April. Most historians believe that young apprentices and young women in servitude were released by their masters that weekend in order to visit their families for the celebration.

A special cake, called the mothering cake, was often brought along to provide a festive touch. Sometimes *furmety* was served consisting of wheat grains boiled in sweet milk, sugared and spiced. In northern England and in Scotland, the preferred refreshments were *carlings*, that is, pancakes made of steeped pease fried in butter, with pepper and salt. In fact, in some locations this day was called *Carling Sunday.*

United States

In the United States, Mother's Day started nearly 150 years ago, when Anna Jarvis, an Appalachian homemaker, organized a day to raise awareness of poor health conditions in her community, a cause she believed would be best advocated by mothers. She called it *Mother's Work Day*. In other countries of the West too, the day was celebrated on different dates because of varying reasons. These are indicated in Table 9.5.

Table 9.5: Mother's Day celebrations in different countries

Second Sunday in February	Norway
Shevat 30, falls between January 30 and March 1	
March 3	Georgia
March 8	Bosnia and Herzegovina, Serbia, Montenegro, Slovenia, Macedonia, Albania, Bulgaria, Romania, Belarus, Russia, Ukraine, Vietnam. The date coincides with the International Women's Day.

(Contd...)

Fourth Sunday in Lent (Mothering Sunday)	England, Scotland, Ireland and Wales.
March 21	Bahrain, Egypt, Lebanon, Syria, Palestinian
(first day of spring)	Territories,
	Jordan, Kuwait, United Arab Emirates, Yemen
April 7	Armenia
May (First Sunday)	Hungary, Lithuania, Portugal, Spain
May 8	South Korea, Albania (Parents' Day)
May 10	South America, El Salvador, India, Mexico, Oman,
	Pakistan, Qatar, Singapore
May (Second Sunday)	Most of the world.
May 26	Poland
May 27	Bolivia
	France (except if it coincides with Pentecost day, in which case Mother's Day will be shifted to the first Sunday of June),
May (Last Sunday)	Dominican Republic, Haiti, Sweden
May 30	Nicaragua
August 12	Thailand (the birthday of Queen Sirikit Kitiyakara)
August 15 (Assumption Day)	Antwerp in Belgium, Costa Rica
October (Second or third Sunday)	Argentina — *Día de la Madre*
November (Last Sunday)	Russia
December 8	Panama
December 22	Indonesia
20th Jumada al-thani (*Women's Day*)	Iran and among other Muslim peoples, especially Shias. The date is the disputed birthday of Fatima Zahra. The Islamic calendar is lunar so it cycles, relative to the Western calendar and dates change each year.

In Western countries in general, familial norms are very different from those practiced in Indian and Far Eastern countries. As soon as children become teenagers they begin to get independent and earn their pocket money doing odd jobs after school, varying from distributing newspapers, to working in grocery stores or cafes. At this time, they start contributing to household expenses for their food, services and so on.

Sometimes even parents ask them to earn for their food, which they willingly do since all their friends and peers do the same. This makes them leave their mothers sooner than children in India or Asian countries where children enjoy the company and care of their mothers for longer periods.

The children therefore do not get that attached to their mothers, and tend to drift away from them, physically, emotionally and mentally. It is for this reason that individual days are allocated in the year for all kinds of relationships to keep in touch with, and hence Mother's Day is treated as a special day.

Mother's Day is therefore the time to honour one's mother through greeting cards, gifts and flowers and make the day joyous for her, to make her feel wanted, cared for and very special. It is the time to award *moms* for being the most loving, kind-hearted, understanding and caring persons in the world. It's time to post Mother's Day messages through loving quotes around the house on *moms* and their love. It's time to treat her like a queen and treat her with a royal buffet prepared by one's own hands, to give her promise-cards and coupons that she may use, when she needs your help the most.

India

In India, traditionally everyone lived in undivided or joint families in which all members belonged to the same family, whether children, cousins, parents, uncles, aunts, grandparents or others, who would normally be called extended families today. This resulted in bonding with all the members and relations, irrespective of the extensions to which they belonged. The children were lucky in such an environment, because being the young ones they were always loved by so many members in the family.

Today, with families having become nuclear and dispersed for reasons of study, jobs and the like, the western concepts have made Mother's Day an infrequent once-in-a-year day to remember her, and show that they still love her. But, in spite of the physical distances that have cropped up, the Indian traditions remain deep rooted and children do follow the festivals in their own way, wherever they are, and remember to take their mother's blessings on each festival day. Mother's Day for Indians has become one additional reason to remember her.

Those who live with their mothers are treated as children till they leave home irrespective of their age or gender. The girls get married and separate from them physically, while the boys in many families remain with their mothers, for a long time.

The roles however, may get reversed when mothers grow old, tradition expects that the boys will look after them and now protect and care for them, everyday of their lives, just as the mothers did for them, when they were young. This is not however always possible, and gradually parents end up looking after each other. However, mothers look forward to their children visiting them and still feel very loving, loved and happy.

In India, mothers are happy when they see their children happy and pray for them with every breath, because they feel that children specially, are God sent. Traditionally, every day is mother's day and from ancient times mothers have been highly revered, the sages having given her the position of a Goddess.

Symbolically, Goddess Durga or Shakti represents the universal principle of energy or holy vibration of the cosmos and is worshipped as Mother by one and all. The scriptures have documented her various qualities from love, compassion to strength and destruction for upholding Truth and destroying evil. This reminds one of a writing on the wall which said:

Mothers were sent because God could not be everywhere. **(Physically)**

Mother's love is the only unconditional love in the world, not expecting anything in return. Experience tells us that the first word a baby speaks is *Ma*, *Mom*, or other similar words refering to the mother, and not papa. The same happens when a child is hurt or in pain, without any conscious effort the first uttering is *Ma*, knowing unconsciously that she is always by the side when needed.

The Vedas teach us Matru devo bhava, Pitru devo bhava, Acharya devo bhava, which means revere your mother, father, preceptor or teacher, and guest as God. Unfortunately, such love, respect and devotion to parents is fast declining due to the flooding of consumerist attitudes and increasing desires. Parents too, do not set moral and ethical standards which children can imbibe. Those who see their parents looking after the elders in the family, will surely learn to do the same for their parents when they grow old, and require help. Thus by example alone, can parents teach youngsters the greatest of human qualities which is Love.

Above all, it is important to communicate that the purest form of Love in the world is a mother's love for her children. Everyone needs therefore, to take all her blessings that one can get, for these will go a long way in life to bring success, prosperity and happiness, remembering that blessings of elders are the one thing that money cannot buy. These have to be earned by giving Love and not by building old-age homes for parents but converting cold, desolated houses into warm and loving homes with your hearts. Quoting Mother Teresa[31] :

> ***...one cannot understand, what is meant by talking of the impermanence of worldly joys. For one would renounce them so much the more gladly, could they but be eternal.***

Mother Teresa was and still stands in the hearts of people in India and the world as the epitome of a mother's love.

CHILDREN'S DAY

Children's Day was first celebrated in the year 1954, as decided by the UN General Assembly. It was basically instituted with the sole aim of promoting communal exchange and understanding about and among

31 Now Saint Teresa.

children, as well as to promote their welfare all over the globe. In 1959, the Declaration of the Rights of the Child was adopted by the United Nations General Assembly on 20th November. This date was therefore selected for a Convention on the Rights of the Child in 1989 which has been sanctioned by 191 states, ever since. Today, 20th November is universally celebrated as Children's Day since it marked the anniversary of its adoption. Subsequently, all countries changed it to the day that represented their children's welfare best, and organized various activities on that day.

India

In India, Children's Day is celebrated on 14th November, coinciding with the birthday of Jawaharlal Nehru, the first Prime Minister of Independent India. This was a tribute to the love and passion he had and exhibited for children, and the dreams he put before them for building a great nation in the future. He was therefore lovingly called *Chacha Nehru* (uncle) by all of them, and is still remembered by that name.

Children's Day is celebrated with great zest all over India, where activities are planned not only in schools but at the national level too. Shankar's on-the-spot painting competion was the start of the national level activities and today fan out into competitions for poster making, dances, music, debates, quizzes, fancy dress and the like. Schools enter the children for these contests and lots of prizes are given and covered by the media. The day is really involving for children, their parents, schools and the media, bringing much joy and excitement for all. Today even the corporates are participating in offering or sponsoring activities and prizes to encourage talents in children.

Japan

The National Children's Day has been celebrated in Japan since ancient times, and was declared a national holiday in 1948. The 5th day of May was traditionally called *Tango no Sekku* and was initially a festival for boys. The girls had their own festival, the *Hina Matsuri* or doll festival, held on 3rd of March. Today the Children's Day is known as *Kodomo no Hi* and is celebrated on 5th of May every year for all children. Families celebrate the day with special dishes like *Kashiwamochi,* which are rice cakes filled with red beans and wrapped with oak leaves, and *Chimaki,* rice cakes in bamboo leaves. They thus, celebrate the healthy growth and development of their children.

The boys celebrate the day by flying huge carp-shaped streamers called *koinobori* outside the house while dolls are displayed of national heroes, famous warriors and the like inside the home. The carp was chosen because it symbolizes strength and success, and according to a Chinese legend a carp swarms upstream to become a dragon.

In recent years as the people have moved into smaller apartments, the carp streamers have also become smaller, and there are now miniature versions available for decorating the indoors of the homes. On Children's Day, families take baths in water sprinkled with iris leaves and roots, because iris is thought to promote good health and ward off evil.

At the National Kasumigaoka Stadium in Tokyo, tens of thousands of children and their parents participate in a *Kids Olympics.* Many other activities involve arts, theatre, music, *kyogen* recitals involving about 18 young actors, the youngest being a second grader and the oldest a seventh grade student.

Thus, Children's Day is celebrated as *Childhood Day* and a tribute is paid to all children of the world, as they are loved by all, and win over the hearts of people with their angelic eyes full of love, and innocent smiles reflecting simplicity and purity, a way that we were always required to be by nature.

TEACHER'S DAY

Teacher's day, also known as Teacher Appreciation Day or National Teacher's Day, is celebrated in many countries.

Since ancient times, Indians have respected their teachers or *Gurus,* as they were addressed with reverence and devotion, since the students truly believed that their *Guru* will be able to shape their life for *good.* Nonetheless, the role of teachers has remained the same and the Teacher's

Day celebration was called *Guru Purnima*, a day on which the student gave the teacher a gift of flowers, milk sweets and clothes that were worn at the time, like the *dhoti* and *cloth* which was placed around the neck. They were and they are still our guides, creating conditions conducive to the overall development of their students, who will always be thankful to them for their valuable guidance and support.

Teachers mould the lives of those they influence in very subtle ways, so that lessons learned from teachers remain with the students throughout life. Teachers break down any existing barriers and reach into the hearts of the students, who then start vibrating with them. There are however, exceptions on both sides depending on the goals of the teachers as well as the learners. Today, true Gurus of the ancient calibre are few but nevertheless Teacher's Day is celebrated all over the country and students enjoy thanking their teachers, who in return express their happiness and appreciation for the tokens presented to them and the good words spoken. A thought rightly expressed by Dr. A.P.J. Abdul Kalam, the President of India as follows :

> ***A student spends 25,000 hours in the campus. The school must have the best of teachers who have the ability to teach, love teaching and build moral qualities.***

In India, Teacher's Day is dedicated to Dr. Sarvepalli Radhakrishnan, who was a staunch believer of education and was one of the greatest scholars and teachers of all times, as well as a former President of India. When Dr. Radhakrishnan became the president of India in 1962, some of his students and friends approached and requested him to allow them to celebrate his birthday which fell on 5th of September. In reply, Dr. Radhakrishnan said:

> ***Instead of celebrating my birthday separately, it would be my proud privilege if September 5 is observed as Teacher's day.***

Since then, as a tribute to this great teacher, philosopher and guide, his birthday has been observed as Teacher's Day, and signifies the appreciation of teachers by their students and therefore, celebrated as a tribute to the hard work that is put in by the teachers all round the year.

On Teacher's Day, school students dress up and act as teachers and take lessons in classes that are normally assigned to the teachers, who on this day behave as students in the class. Sometimes teachers sit in their classes as students, reliving the time when they themselves were students. Thus, both students as well as teachers get to understand each other's position. Functions are also organized in schools, colleges and universities on Teacher's Day, when students present various programs for the entertainment of their teachers. In addition to being the day when the efforts of teachers are recognized, it provides a chance for an *out of class* healthy interaction between students and teachers in a casual and happy environment.

However simple the celebrations may be, they reflect the fact that teachers are cared for and never forgotten even when the students are far away physically or in years.

In **India,** Teacher's Day is celebrated on September 5, in honour of Dr. Sarvepalli Radhakrishnan, the second President of India as his birthday falls on that day . At some schools on this day, the senior students take up the responsibility of teaching as an appreciation for teachers.

Teacher's Day around the world is not celebrated on the same day. However, the day of celebration, itself, holds no significance, what matters, is the feeling behind the celebration.

In **China,** Teacher's Day was founded at National Central University in 1931. It was adopted by the central government of Republic of China in 1932. In 1939, the day was set on August 27, Confucius' birthday. The People's Republic of China government abrogated it in 1951 but reestablished it in 1985, and the day was changed to September 10. Now more and more people are trying to revert the Teacher's Day back to Confucius' birthday. In Russia, Teacher's Day is on October 5. Before 1994, this day was assigned to the first Sunday of September.

In the **United States,** Teacher's Day is a non-official holiday on the Tuesday of the first full week of May.

In **Thailand** January 16 was adopted as Teacher's Day by a resolution of the government on November 21, 1956. The first Teacher's Day was celebrated in 1957.

In **Iran,** Teacher's Day is celebrated on May 2. It commemorates the assassination day of Iranian professor Ayatollah Morteza Motahhari on May 2, 1980.

In **Turkey,** Teacher's Day is celebrated on 24 of November. Kemal Atatürk dedicated November 24 to teachers.

In **Malaysia,** May 16 is celebrated as Teacher's Day.

It is said that an average teacher teaches, a good teacher explains, a superior teacher illustrates, and a great teacher both learns and inspires students. Students can never thank their teachers enough for their efforts. Teacher's Day is celebrated to show the acknowledgement and recognition of the hard work put in by teachers towards the development of their students.

FRIENDSHIP DAY

Human beings are social creatures and have always valued the importance of friends in their lives. To celebrate this noble feeling it was deemed fit to have a day dedicated to friends and friendship. Through a Proclamation made by US Congress in 1935, the first Sunday of August was declared as a holiday in US in honour of friends. Since then, World Friendship Day is being celebrated every year on the first Sunday in the month of August.

Friendship Day is the time to recognize your friends and their contribution to your life. It is a day to let our friends know they are truly appreciated. This beautiful idea of celebrating Friendship Day was joyfully accepted by several other countries across the world. And today, many countries including India, celebrate the first Sunday of August as Friendship Day every year. Celebrating Friendship Day in a traditional manner, people meet their friends and exchange cards and flowers to honor their friends. Even if the friends cannot meet they make it a point to talk to each other on phone or send e-cards. Many social and cultural organizations too, celebrate the occasion and mark Friendship Day by hosting programs and get together to appreciate their donors, mentors and friends. One might have fun, or do something together with a friend for the welfare of the community, in terms of helping to clean up the environment, assist elders in shopping, give charity, or do some good deed or service. This should not be done only on one day of the year, but on every single day of one's life. Doing things to help create a clean, more peaceful, just and sustainable world with friends is doubly rewarding as we move in a better world, while at the same time strengthening the bonds of existing friendship and extending it to those we never even knew.

It may be noted that some associations celebrate Friendship Day differently and at entirely different times of the year. For instance:

- **National Friendship Day** is on the first Sunday in August.
- **Women's Friendship Day** is on the third Sunday in August
- **International Friendship Month** is February
- **Old friends, New friends Week** is the third week of May

However, what is remarkably similar is the idea behind the celebration of the day. Everywhere, people express love for their friends and cherish their presence in life but, our endeavour should be to expand that friendship and love to all who come in contact with us, by seeking opportunities to serve them. It is said that service to man is service to God, as the same spark of Divinity pervades all life in nature.

If we simply greet people lovingly even if we do not befriend them, we set up vibrations of love in them, that will ultimately spread itself. Love always expands, it never contracts so the more of it we give and share, the greater it rebounds and also spreads in all directions just as the rays of the sun.

Many forms of devotion have been described in the Puranas but the two relevant here are *Sakhyam* or friendship and *Seva* or service. Both friendship and service go hand in hand and if spread through mankind, can result in experiencing of bliss in the heart. Sri Ravishankar has so aptly said:

> ***Again and again remember that you are peace, you are love, you are joy and that you host the creator. If you don't realize that you are the host, you live like a ghost.***

Like the birds returning to their nests, again and again come back to your source; only then can you realize that you host the Divine.

When this realization comes, friendship with one and all will spread and lead to lasting contentment and happiness.

VALENTINE'S DAY

Saint Valentine's Day or *Valentine's Day* as it is usually called, falls on February 14 every year and celebrates friendship, romance and love in life. It has its origins in Europe although some argue that it is a western concept.

The Day became associated with romantic love in the Middle Ages, when the tradition of courtship and romance flourished, prior to marriages being fixed in families. The courtship period was meant for prospective couples to get familiar with each other and learn the family traditions into which they would finally get married and settle. It also provided young people the space and time to see if that is what they want for life. This system made marriages last, instead of being based on instant, fickle decisions or on parental or familial pressure, without the partners having seen or understood each others personalities and needs.

St. Valentine's Day contains vestiges of both Christian and ancient Roman tradition. Today, the Catholic Church recognizes at least three different saints named Valentine or Valentinus, all of whom were martyred.

One legend contends that Valentine was a priest who served during the 3rd century in Rome. At this time, Emperor Claudius II decided that single men made better soldiers than those with wives and families, he outlawed marriage for young men who would serve his army in the future. St.Valentine, realizing the injustice of the decree, defied Claudius and continued to perform marriages for young lovers in secret. When his actions were discovered the Emperor ordered that he be put to death.

Other stories suggest that Valentine may have been killed for attempting to help Christians escape from Roman prisons where they were often beaten and tortured.

While in prison, it is believed that Valentine fell in love with a young girl, who may have been his jailor's daughter and visited him during his confinement. Before his death, it is alleged that he wrote her a letter, which he signed *From your Valentine*, an expression that is still in use today. Although the truth behind the Valentine legends is murky, the stories certainly emphasize his appeal as a sympathetic, heroic, and, most importantly, romantic figure. It is no surprise that by the Middle Ages, Valentine was one of the most popular saints in England and France.

Present Scenario

Since the 19th century, hand-written notes have largely given way to mass produced greeting cards not only in Europe but throughout the world. The Greeting Card Association estimates that approximately one billion valentines are sent world-wide each year, making the day, the second largest card sending occasion after Christmas. It is estimated that women purchase 85 per cent of all valentines in the form of cards. In fact the tradition has expanded so much that even in India and in the Asian region candies, flowers and gifts are exchanged between loved ones, on Valentine's day a practice that has also spread in every other country across the globe.

In **India**, some argue that the concept of Valentine's Day is alien to Indian culture, values and its *sanskriti*. The younger generation however, celebrates it with passion as they adopt global cultures in every sphere. Tokens such as flowers, cards, candies and gifts of every possible description are exchanged. The colours of the flowers and gifts sometimes coincide with the favourite colours of the loved ones, since different colours are expressions of love, creativity, trustworthiness, passion and so on. The effect of colours on personality has been summarized under the festival of Holi.

In addition, eating out and holidays have become common, as a way of spending time together, with gala events being organized by hotels, restaurants, resorts and the like, and companies sponsoring programmes of dance and music while offering Valentine Day promotions.

Sufi poets compare Love with wine because both intoxicate, although wine leads to self-forgetfulness, to subterranean darkness and denial, whereas love leads to self-realization and gives wings to the soul for freedom.

Celebration is all around and people join in the festivities, because the average person does not believe that they are turning their back on Indian traditions and values. It is a day for fun and frolic and passes off like any other festival day like *Holi, Diwali* and others which also augur love, friendship and unity.

Friendship, romance and love has been ingrained in our mythology and the scriptures, very much a part of India's rich cultural heritage. An understanding of this can be gained by learning about the different forms of the Goddess Lakshmi who is credited with eight forms as follows:

- *Adi Lakshmi* — the source of wealth
- *Dhan Lakshmi* — material
- *Vidya Lakshmi* — education
- *Dhanya Lakshmi* — health
- *Dhairya Lakshmi* — courage
- *Santaan Lakshmi*— friendliness
- *Vijaya Lakshmi* — victory
- *Bhagya Lakshmi* — dignity and destiny

If one is able to strike a perfect balance between all the aspects of the Goddess, she makes you her *lakshya* or goal and remains with you in all her forms. In the absence of balance she will continue to elude you even if you spend your whole life praying to her.

Santaan Lakshmi, the wealth of friendliness is an essential component of our cultural heritage. If one has this wealth it should be celebrated, using the opportunity of Valentine's Day.

In general, if we follow nature as our guide, we should be celebrating all the time. The trees, birds or any other life, in fact our very existence is an eternal celebration. Only man is serious, because he does not want to be a part of the whole creation. He does not want to disappear, seeks an identity, name, fame, form and power over all else and that is what creates misery in the world. A genuine saint always sees happiness and therefore has to enjoy celebration. Eckhart Tolle[32] says:

> ***We depend on nature not only for our physical survival, we also need nature to show us the way out of the prison of our own mind.***

Nature is full of magnetic power in some form or other which can only be experienced with joy. The flowers attract by their colour and fragrance, the bees are attracted by the honey in the flower and love is the most powerful magnet in the heart of man as seen through the attraction between a husband and wife.

This power of love has been seen in our sages, prophets and *avatars* that attracted devotees and still do from all over the world. Lord Krishna's love attracted the *gopis*, Sri Aurobindo's love attracted the Divine mother from France along with other devotees, Mother Teresa's love for destitute children attracted them to her and provided her an opportunity to better their lot; Sri Ramakrishna, Swami Vivekananda, Sri Sathya Sai all have attracted the attention of the world as seen from the spread of their teachings globally.

Their power of attraction lay in the Divine love that they gave to all, irrespective of colour, caste, creed or gender although they were all born of very humble families in small villages of India. The opening of spiritual centres all over the world to further their messages of love and peace bear testimony to their magnetic power.

According to the *Puranas*, love is connectivity, and there are nine forms of devotion that have been described, among which *sakhyam* or friendship and *seva* or service are mentioned. The texts state that everyone needs to develop respect and regard for others in their hearts and promote love and affection for all.

In the modern progressive world of today, this opportunity is provided by St. Valentine and therefore should be used as an opportunity to sow the seed of love in the hearts of people, in the same spirit as is intended through all the prophets of the world. Fill your hearts with

---

32 Eckhart Tolle. In his book *Stillness Speaks.*

love, so that loving thoughts and actions should blossom and spread to all mankind.

The day is now mostly associated with the mutual exchange of love notes in the form of *valentines* without having any deeper meaning or purpose. Modern Valentine symbols include the heart-shaped outline and the figure of the winged Cupid.

WAZWAN

The *Wazwan* is a traditional feast that came to Kashmir 400 years ago from Iran and Central Asia, and is celebrated by the *Kashmiris* in India. It is possibly the biggest feast known that is celebrated in the country.

Observance

Preparations begin months in advance, while the actual cooking starts 36 hours before the commencement of the feast. Traditionally, at least 15-30 meat dishes are served, some of which are cooked throughout the night and involve the cooking of whole sheep, including its intestines. An average Kashmiri consumes one kg of meat and probably one chicken at a Wazwan. A thriving trade in meat supports several Kashmiri families in Delhi and neighbouring towns.

The actual feast is still held in the traditional way in which the dishes may vary from 4 to 30 and the seating and serving patterns, which have trickled down from the Arabs, have also not changed over the years. The meals are served on a *dastarkhaan*, which is a large white sheet spread on a carpet, while the guests sit around the meals which are placed in the centre.

Each dish is brought in, covered with a lid called the *sarposh* and only after all the dishes are placed on the *dastarkhaan* does the feast begin. Curd and chutney are served in small earthen pots. Then one of the elders says *Bismillah* and the feast begins. First comes the thick but fragrant Kashmiri rice decorated with a piece of chicken or *kababs,* followed by *rista* or minced meat balls. The *Roganjosh* and *Gosht* or meat cooked in milk are followed by *Marteswagan korma*, *Haaq* and *Yakhni*. The last dish is always the *Goshtaba*. The guests serve themselves from the serving bowls onto platters placed in the centre of the *dastarkhaan.*

Present Scenario

Earlier, even the poorest threw at least a couple of Wazwans in his lifetime, while the rich threw one at any excuse. But now Wazwans are restricted to marriages and with the ongoing instability in Kashmir, the feasts are in danger of being relegated to history.

A visit to the *Wazwan mohalla* in Srinagar, where the famous *waza khandaans* or traditional family cooks live, is enough to reveal that business is definitely on the decline. In the past few years, everything from marriages to parties and festivals is being celebrated on a low key. *Wazwan* may soon be a thing of the past with Kashmiris unable to afford the elaborate cuisine, and the qualified staff to prepare and serve it gradually facing extinction.

Today practically all Kashmiri pundits have migrated to various regions of the country and the world, gradually adapting their meals and eating habits according to the geographic, climatic, regional, cultural needs, and activity patterns of their new environments.

NEW YEAR

The coming of a New Year is an occasion to be celebrated, as it signifies the end of one year of mixed blessings and the beginning of the next. All over the world, everyone introspects on what went wrong in the past year and makes promises and resolutions to improve matters and make new beginnings in the year that arrives. New Year celebrations vary only slightly in the time of the year during which the festivities are held since different countries and regions in the same country follow different annual calendars. Usually the New Year falls at the same time each year, irrespective of the calendar followed. For example, if the New Year starts with a harvest festival it will fall in the same month and if the solar calendar is used it will be exactly on the same day each year. It really depends on how the dates for the year are calibrated for a particular country.

The first day of each year in the Gregorian calendar used by most countries is 1st January marking the beginning of a New Year. Its celebration is the oldest of all holidays in every country. Where the lunar calendar is used the dates differ somewhat, because every country starts its year corresponding to a festival or its harvest season. Brief descriptions of celebrations in some countries is presented along with their history where documented.

Babylon

The New Year was first observed in ancient Babylon about 4000 years ago, where the celebration lasted for 11 days. Each day had its own particular mode of celebration, but it is safe to say that modern New Year's Eve festivities pale in comparison. In the years around 2000 BC, the Babylonian New Year began with the first visible crescent after the Vernal Equinox or the first day of spring. The beginning of spring is a logical time to start a new year. After all, it is the season of rebirth, of planting new crops, and of blossoming. January 1 on the other hand is purely an arbitrary date and has no astronomical or agricultural significance.

Other traditions of the season included the making of New Year resolutions, a tradition that dates back to the early Babylonians, whose most popular resolution was to return borrowed farm equipment.

Rome

The Romans continued to observe the new year in late March, but their calendar was continually tampered with by various emperors so that it soon became un-synchronized with the sun. In order to set the calendar right, the Roman senate, in 153 BC, declared January 1 as the beginning of their new year. But, tampering continued until Julius Caesar, in 46 BC, established what has come to be known as the Julian calendar. It again established January 1 as the new year, but in order to synchronize the calendar with the sun, Caesar had to let the previous year drag on for 445 days.

USA

The New Year is celebrated on the 1st of January in various ways with popular modern resolutions including the promise to lose weight or quit smoking, alcohol or drugs.

The Tournament of Roses Parade dates back to 1886. In that year, members of the Valley Hunt Club decorated their carriages with flowers. Although the Rose Bowl football game was first played as a part of the Tournament of Roses in 1902, it was replaced by Roman chariot races the following year. In 1916, the football game returned as the sports centerpiece of the festival.

In California, the ripening of the orange crop is celebrated in the New Year. In Georgia, it is a tradition to eat black-eyed peas and turnip greens. The peas represent copper and the greens are for dollars. It is said that each pea eaten equals one dollar's worth of earning, and each portion of turnip greens equals one thousand dollars. Some people say that it brings good luck and prosperity. This may be founded on truth because a 3-ounce portion of black-eyed peas and turnip greens is supposed to be good for the digestive system.

Greece

The tradition of using a baby to signify the New Year began in Greece around 600 B.C., to celebrate their God of wine, *Dionysus*, by parading a baby in a basket, representing the annual rebirth of the God as the spirit of fertility.

Egypt

Early Egyptians also used a baby as a symbol of rebirth, although the early Christians denounced the practice as pagan, the popularity of the baby as a symbol of rebirth forced the Church to re-evaluate its position. The Church finally allowed its members to celebrate the New Year with a baby, which was to symbolize the birth of baby Jesus.

Germany

The Germans brought an image of a baby on a banner carrying the symbolic representation of the New Year to early America. They had used the symbol since the 14th century.

Spain

For a long time, the people of Spain have had a traditional custom to celebrate New Year's Eve. On the last day of the year, that is, 31st of December, they wait until midnight , ready to usher in the New Year with 12 grapes ready in hand to eat at the stroke of 12 (midnight), when the clock begins to chime. It is traditional to listen to the clock from Puerta del Sol in Madrid and put one grape in the mouth with each chime. By the time the clock has finished chiming, everybody has to have finished their grapes and the New Year starts, but nobody finishes eating the grapes on time.This tradition started in Spain because one year when there was a big grape harvest, the king of Spain decided to give grapes to everybody to eat on New Year's Eve.

China

The Chinese New Year, also known as the Lunar New Year, occurs every year on the new moon of the first lunar month, around the beginning of spring called *Lichun*. The exact date can fall anytime between 21 January and 21 February of the Gregorian calendar. Because the lunisolar Chinese calendar is astronomically defined, unlike the Gregorian calendar, the drift of the seasons will change the range. Each year is symbolized by one of 12 animals and one of five elements, with the combinations of animals and elements (or stems) cycling every 60 years. It is the most important Chinese holiday of the year.

Paper cuttings are one of the most popular folk arts in China. They are properly framed or simply pasted onto the windows. Traditionally, they were only made of red paper. Most elderly women would make them just with a piece of red paper and a pair of scissors. They made them as decorations for their own families for celebrating the Chinese New Year. The Chinese believed that these paper cuttings could scare away the evil spirits, so they could not get into the house through the windows. The cuttings were also believed to bring luck for the New Year.

The cuttings have now changed from red to all colors. Today, there are factories that manufacture them in bulk. It is not only a custom to have them displayed all over, but they are also a beautiful art form representing Chinese culture. Many are still made completely by hand, and then hand painted in bright colours.

Vietnam

The Vietnamese New Year is the *Têt Nguyên Đàn* which is at most times the same day as the Chinese New Year. Nowadays, Vietnamese still observe this as a traditional holiday.

The New Year holiday comes in February, but a month before hand, people clean and whitewash their houses. They buy fresh flowers and a peach blossom to put in the house which is a Vietnamese custom, and receive their relatives with cakes and fruits, such as watermelons, sweetmeats of ginger, coconut and plum, along with lotus seeds.

On the midnight of the New Year's Eve, people go together merrily to *pagodas* to pray to Lord Buddha. After that, the old and young alike go to the park to see the Chinese dragon, dances and fireworks following which people greet each other, bringing in the new year. The Vietnamese have fun and are always happy on New Year's Day.

The next morning, children wish their grandparents, parents and relatives a *Happy New Year* and seek their blessings. After the children wish their parents good luck, they receive a red envelope from them with some money in it as a gift. The family then shares cakes and watermelons, considered special fruits during the New Year, after which they all return to their homes. The Vietnamese holiday is important because everyone still follows the customs of their ancestors.

Japan

On New Year, the Japanese have a tradition of making rice cakes called *Mochi* made from glutinous rice which when steamed and pounded with *a Kine* and *Usu* becomes *mochi* .

Korea

Like many other Asian countries, Korea has two different New Year days according to solar and lunar calendars. The more widely preferred one is the lunar day called *Sol-nal* , a day of reunion for the whole family for a refreshing start to the new year. The day has many special meanings and events. On *Sol-nal* eve, people prepare special sieves made with straw called *bok-jori* and hang them outside doors to protect their family from evil and bad luck. Often, kids try to keep awake all night because they believe that if they sleep, their eyebrows will turn white. On the morning of *Sol-nal*, everyone dresses in specially prepared, traditional new clothes, generally decorated with five colors. They are called *Sol-bim*. Early in the morning, every family gathers at their eldest male member's home to perform *Cha-rye*, the ancestral memorial rites. Bowls of *Ttok-kuk* are served. This is a soup of thinly sliced white rice cake, boiled in a thick beef broth topped with bright garnishes and green onions. *Ttok-kuk* means adding age by one more year. Koreans traditionally add one to their age, not after their birthdays but after *Sol-nal*.

Afterwards, the young boys go outside to fly kites, spin tops and the girls enjoy playing on the seesaw. Inside, people play *Yut-no-ri*, a game played with four wooden sticks and checkers. They eat, talk, and play all day long and enjoy their large family reunion extending from great grandfather to great grandchildren.

India

In India, New Year, is celebrated with gusto, the celebrations taking the form of a cultural bonanza in each region, being accompanied by dances, music, shopping through the organization of fairs, beauty contests and so on. Being secular the country exhibits a mix of all religions and their cultural , artistic and other talents along with traditional foods.

The Hindu New Year starts with the harvest festivals all over the country, in spring, that is, March-April. In South India, the main harvest crops arrive in January and therefore the new year sets in around the 12th of the month. Because of the different regional languages, geographical and climatic conditions the new year has various local names in each State of the country, but starts when the main harvest is to be celebrated.

In Gujarat, the 1st day of the lunar month is celebrated as New Year's Day and is called *Padvo*. It is believed that whoever remains happy on this day will experience happiness throughout the year. A large variety of foods are prepared and offered to deities in thanksgiving and people pray for the Lord's grace through the year. The offerings are enjoyed with well wishers, friends and family.

All over India the solar calendar is used for the holiday period from Christmas through the new year, when schools and other educational institutions are closed. Therefore 1st of January is celebrated as the new year. Exchange of greetings through cards, phone calls and e-mail along with gifts for personal contacts and local family members is the norm.

The lunar year which begins at harvest time in spring and at *Diwali* in autumn, marking the start of winter in the north, is celebrated with traditional fervour amidst crackers, lights and much fanfare. The media now highlights all celebrations all over the country and globally. Some regions therefore celebrate two New Year days, one at harvest time and the other at Diwali.

India's hospitality is known the world over, so it is famous for its celebrations and feasting, sharing their joys and food with one and all. People in this country need any excuse to celebrate, and at new year too every community is found celebrating their new year in their own traditional ways and sharing their food with others in the community. Some examples are given in chapters 13 and 14 through recipes.

Jewish New Year

The Jewish community is small comprising of about 2000 persons who have settled in India for about 5000 years without persecution. According to the rabbi:

India is our motherland or karmabhoomi while Israel is in our heart – its our dharma bhoomi. We are Indians first and Jews later.

The Jewish New Year is celebrated on September 23 and is called *Rosh-ha-shana*. According to Ezekiel Isaac Malekar, the rabbi and secretary of Judah Hyan Synagogue, the only Jewish synagogue in Delhi, Rosh-ha-shana is a solemn day of soul searching and self examination, devoted to congregational prayers in the synagogue during which the blasts of *shofar* (horn) are heard as a clear call to repentance. The prayer, he says, is followed by sanctification over wine, with traditional food comprising of dates, pomegranate, apple dipped in honey, gourd, leek, beetroot and sheep or fish head. The rituals also include *Taschlich*, a prayer performed at a sea shore or banks of a river. Here, bread pieces are thrown into the water for fish to eat. It is believed that by doing this, one is casting off all sins into the water.[33]

Parsi New Year — Jamshed-E–Navroz

The Parsis celebrate their New year called *Navroz*, or nine-day festival, which starts on the first day of the first month of the Zoroastrian year. Over 3000 years ago, Shah Jamshed of the Peshadian dynasty ascended the throne on Navroze - *nav* meaning new and *roze* meaning day. It was the day of the Equinox — a day when light and darkness stand equal on the scale of space and time and the length of the day equals that of the night. That particular day came to be known as *Jamshed Navroz* and is celebrated even in modern times with lot of feasting. Apart from new clothes, all Parsis wear their gold or silver *kustis* and caps. Auspicious symbols like fish, birds, butterflies and stars, are patterned on doorways with metallic moulds. Guests are welcomed with a sprinkling of rose-water and rice.

The most traditional drink for Navroz is *falooda*, which is prepared with milk and flavoured with rose water. The traditional lunch consists of *sev* and sweet yogurt, followed by *pulao*. The meal would end with *ravo*. A copy of the *Gathas*, a lit lamp, an *afrigan*, a bowl of water containing live fish, a shallow earthenware plate with sprouted wheat or beans for prosperity, flowers for colour, a silver coin for wealth, painted eggs for productivity, and sweets and rosewater in bowls for sweetness and happiness, are kept on a table. Apart from these, the table also has seven foods beginning with *sh* and *s* as these are meant to symbolise creation.

This new day is the beginning of a new year, a new awakening into an inner sphere of spiritual consciousness and a new vision of life. Thus, Navroz is a new dawn in everyone's life, and is a day of celebration.

---

33 Megha Suri, Times of India, September 23, 2006.

The Navroz festival of the Shia Muslims comes a week after the New Year's Day which they celebrate with feasting and other activities that show the spirit of gay abandon, in contrast to the recitation of religious *dirges* that characterize most of their festivals.

Kashmiri New Year

For Kashmiris the New Year Day falls on the 1st Navratra, that is, the 1st day of the new moon in the month of *chaitra*. In every Hindu home it begins with an invocation to Lakshmi, the Goddess of bounty. In every family, a young lady, lays a large plate with paddy, sugar, curds, fruits, walnuts, coins, mirror, inkholder and a new scroll. Early morning she shows the plate to every member of the household and thus seeks the blessings of the Goddess for moral and material prosperity of the family.

Luck and the New Year

Traditional New Year foods are also thought to bring luck. Many cultures believe that anything in the shape of a ring is good luck, because it symbolizes coming full circle, equivalent to completing a year's cycle.

It was thought that one could influence one's luck in the coming year by what they did or ate on the first day of the year. For that reason, it has become common for folks to celebrate the first few minutes of a brand new year in the company of family and friends. Parties often continue into the middle of the night after which the ringing in of a new year is celebrated greeting each other with love and hope, dancing and singing, or reciting emotional poetry and so on.

It was once believed that the first visitor on New Year's Day would bring either good or bad luck the rest of the year. It was particularly lucky if that visitor happened to be a tall dark-haired man. The Dutch believe that eating donuts on New Year's Day will bring good fortune.

In many parts of the U.S. people celebrate the New Year by consuming black-eyed peas. These legumes are typically accompanied by either hog jowls or ham. Black-eyed peas and other legumes have been considered to bring good luck in many cultures. The hog, and thus its meat, is considered lucky because it symbolizes prosperity.

Cabbage is a good luck vegetable that is consumed on New Year's Day by many since its leaves are considered a sign of prosperity, being representative of paper currency. In some regions, rice is a lucky food that is eaten on New Year's Day.

In India, people believe more in praying for prosperity in the new year rather than depending on luck. Every new venture too is started with prayer, offerings in a temple or home prayer room seeking God's grace for all occasions and people. The Vedas teach us to recite after our prayers *Loka Samastha Sukhino Bhavantu* which means, may all the people in the entire creation be happy and at peace, a wish for God's grace not only for ourselves but for His whole creation.

The social feasts are also built around celebrations of special days like birthdays, anniversaries and so on. The celebrations on such may vary from going to temple, giving charities, going out with friends and family to giving lavish parties. Birthday parties are among the highlights of a child's year when they look forward to blowing the candles and opening presents.

HEALTH RELATED DAYS

Health related days are also celebrated with an aim of bringing about an improvement in the health status of the masses. Some of these are :

- World Hcart Day : 24th of September
- National Nutrition Week : 1st – 7th of September
- World Breast Feeding Week : 1st – 7th of August
- World Diabetes Day : 14th of November

Many celebrities now hold cultural and sports events on the various days to support the causes for alleviation of poverty, malnutrition, education, awareness and eradication of disease, which is taking on epidemic and endemic proportions.

NATIONAL DAYS

National days are celebrated to mark special events that take place through the history of the nation. For example, when a country becomes independent of foreign rule and becomes a republic with its own constitution. Further, there are the days to remember such as those when, soldiers or freedom fighters laid down their lives for the country. These are celebrated as martyr's days, birthdays of great people who have guided and led the nation to independence by non-violent means. The nation celebrates Mahatma Gandhi's birthday as a National day since he guided the nation to independence. He is known as the Father of the Nation and his compatriots are revered for their sacrifices made in honour of the country.

National awards are also given every year on such days, for excellence in nation building, through music, cultural events, education, sports, industry and the like, to honour people for being ambassadors of the country in their special fields. Their names are printed in golden letters and the lists of honoured persons maintained at the Rashtrapati Bhavan (President's House), the highest office in the country.

INDEPENDENCE DAY

The Independence Day of India falls on the15th of August every year and is celebrated throughout the country with great zeal, and is declared a national holiday. The day reminds every Indian about the dawn of a new beginning, the beginning of an era of deliverance of the country from British colonial rule that lasted for more than 200 years. It was the fateful morning of 15th August 1947 that India was declared an independent nation, when the reins of control were handed over to the leaders of the country. India's gaining of independence was a tryst with destiny, as the struggle for freedom was a long and tiresome one, witnessing the sacrifices of many freedom fighters, who laid down their lives for the sake of freedom.

The first President of independent India was Dr. Rajendra Prasad, and Pandit Jawaharlal Nehru held the position of the Prime Minister. They formed the Indian National Congress, in 1947, where Sardar Vallabh Bhai Patel was made the Home Minister. He is referred to as the *iron man* for his determination, strong will and action.

Celebrations

The Independence Day celebrations start with devotional music in the early hours at Rajghat, followed by politicians paying homage to Mahatma Gandhi through wreath laying and offering rose petals on his *Samadhi,* which is then circumambulated with reverence led by the President, Prime Minister, Chiefs of Staff and other dignitaries. They then leave for the Red Fort where the Prime Minister hoists the National Flag among sprinkling of rose petals and music with singing of the National Anthem and the *Vande Matram* in front of a standing audience who salute the flag and the country.

The Prime Minister then addresses the nation, from the ramparts of the Red Fort, through which he greets the nation on this historic day, and highlights the achievements of the country while placing before the people his visions for the future. The ceremony concludes with the slogan *Jai Hind* repeated by the audience after the Prime Minister, three times.

In the evening, the President hosts a reception at the Rashtrapati Bhavan for selected invitees which include dignitaries representing all countries, politicians, freedom fighters, Chiefs of staff, senior government officials, awardees and civilians who have contributed to nation building in exemplary ways.

It is the practice to carry out *flag hoisting* ceremonies in all institutions, on the eve of Independence Day. The premises are decorated with colours of the national flag and *rangolis* to celebrate the event with visitors, invitees and staff. This tradition was started because it is a national holiday and all institutions are closed on that day. However, schools and colleges arrange debates, speeches and national song competitions among students to mark the occasion and prizes are awarded to the winners by the chief guest invited for the occasion. Colourful dishes are presented and served to mark the occasion and make it festive, enjoyable and happy.

REPUBLIC DAY

India became a Republic when the Constitution of the country came into force on 26th January of 1950, thereby defining it as a sovereign, socialist, democratic republic with a parliamentary form of government. The Indian Constitution, which was adopted by the Constituent Assembly after considerable discussions represented the framework of the government of the country. Henceforth, 26th January has been recognized and celebrated as India's Republic Day with great patriotic fervour, pride and joy, a day on which its achievements, culture, traditions and unity are on display for all to see and enjoy, as it is a national holiday. The event is a constant reminder of the selfless deeds of all martyrs of the country, who laid down their lives in the freedom struggle and various succeeding wars against foreign aggression, to defend and maintain the sovereignty of the country.

On the eve of the Republic Day, the President addresses the nation through a live broadcast on radio and television for all to hear his thoughts and present the vision he has for the future of the country.

Celebrations

The beginning of the celebration is always a solemn reminder of the sacrifices made during the freedom movement, when the President, Prime Minister and the three military chiefs lay down wreaths in reverence and gratitude, at the *Amar Jawan Jyoti,* a monument that carries the names of all the *jawans* who sacrificed themselves for the country's honour. After this the celebrations take off.

Today, the Republic Day is celebrated with much enthusiasm all over the country and especially in the capital, New Delhi. Then, the President comes to the venue of the parade at Rajpath where he is received by the Prime Minister and chiefs of staff and meets invited dignitaries. He then takes the salute of all the contingents passing the saluting base offering their salutations to the President, before the tableaux pass the saluting base with their cultural performances. After the parade, the President awards medals of bravery to selected officers from the armed forces for their exceptional courage and also to civilians, who have distinguished themselves by their different acts of bravery in various fields of achievement.

The Republic Day celebrations are marked by a grand parade held in the capital every year, which starts from the Vijay Chowk through the Rajpath and terminate at the Rajghat. The different regiments of the Army, the Navy and the Air Force march past in all their finery and official decorations as do the school children from various schools in the capital in their colourful clothes. People come from various neighbouring states and line up along the route of the parade to watch the spectacle.

The parade is followed by a pageant of spectacular displays from the different states of the country. These moving exhibits depict scenes of activities of people in those states and the music and songs of that particular state accompany each display. Each tableau brings out the diversity and richness of the culture of India and the whole show lends a festive air to the occasion. The parade and the ensuing pageantry is telecast by the National Television and is watched by millions of viewers across the country.

The patriotic fervor of the people on this day brings the whole country together even in her essential diversity. Every part of the country symbolises the occasion in its own unique manner, which makes the Republic Day the most popular of all the national holidays of India.

GANDHI JAYANTI

Gandhi Jayanti is celebrated as the birth anniversary of Mohandas Karamchand Gandhi. He is also known as *Bapu* or *Father of the Nation* and was born on the 2nd of October 1869, in Porbunder, Gujarat. He was instrumental in acquiring independence for India and this day serves to remind all Indians of the sacrifices he and others made, to secure independence to the country.

History

After his early education in India, he was sent to London where he qualified as a barrister. He practiced law in South Africa and continued to do so till 1914, leading the Indians there against the apartheid of the British. His stint in India took a decisive turn when national leader Gopal Krishna Gokhale introduced him into the Indian Freedom Movement. He returned to India to join the Indian freedom struggle.

Gandhiji was a preacher of truth and *ahimsa* or non-violence. He started the *Satyagraha* movement for the Indian freedom struggle, and believed in living a simple life as a *Swadeshi* using everything Indian. He proved to the world that freedom could be achieved through the path of non-violence. He was a symbol of peace and truth. From then onwards, till India gained independence, Gandhi gathered an entire nation behind him in his relentless quest.

Gandhi was not just a political leader. In fact, he was never a keen politician, but a leader of the masses with whom he always identified himself. In fact, Gandhi took pains to learn to sign his name in all the major Indian languages. All his actions had the power to galvanize the will and spirit of people. When others walked out of the Assembly in protest, Gandhi walked 100 km to the sea at *Dandi* to make salt illegally. He worked extensively for the social upliftment of the untouchables, whom he called *Harijans*, and was the leader of the *Quit India Movement*, which served as a final signal of discontent to the British dominion in India.

Gandhi was also deeply spiritual, and believed that all religions show the way to ultimate enlightenment. He also wrote a commentary on the Bhagavad Gita, a book that influenced him deeply.

Gandhiji used to say that giving alms to the poor is an insult to them and expresses contempt from the donor and only acts as a palliative to his own conscience while reinforcing poverty. For the poor to be freed from the debilitating impact of charity, it is the responsibility of the donor to lift the poor out of dependency on alms.[34]

But *partition* was a big blow to his dreams and ideals, and Gandhi was in extreme pain during the night of the nation's partition as Pakistan and India. Five months after independence, Gandhiji was assassinated by Nathuram Godse while going to his daily prayer meeting. He was 78 when he left his mortal frame.

Celebration

Mahatma Gandhi believed in simple living but possessed high ethical values. Respecting that, even though Gandhi Jayanti is a national holiday,

34 *Jamaica Gleaner*, a Jamaican newspaper.

the festivities are simple and low key. Those with devotion pay their respects to him at the Rajghat, or observe two minutes silence wherever they are in reverence to a great and selfless man.

A prayer meeting is held at the Gandhi samadhi at Rajghat, in New Delhi. To mark the respect that Gandhiji had for all the religions and communities, representatives from different religions take part in it. Verses and prayers are read out from the holy books of all the religions. Gandhiji's favourite song, *Raghupati Raghava Raja Ram*, is invariably sung at all the meetings associated with him. Prayer meetings are held in various state capitals as well. Gandhi Jayanti is observed all over the country, both in government and non-government forums. All the offices and schools, throughout the country, remain closed on this day as a mark of respect.

His ideas of resistance through non-violent means, to the British colonial rule, has never failed to inspire later generations to live a life of brotherhood in a peace loving country. And this has been proven by the success of a latest Bollywood movie *Lage Raho Munnabhai* that is based on the use of his principles to solve everyday problems.

Mahatma Gandhi represents a concept, and is recognized by the world as an icon. In fact the press recently reported that the Nobel Prize Committee failed in their decisions in the 1940s to award the Nobel Peace Prize to Gandhiji, even though his name appeared in the list three times. The present head of the committee offered an apology and also said Gandhiji's name missing in the prizewinner's list till date takes away the glory of the prize. He also admitted that when the next committee decided to finally award the Nobel to the Mahatma there was no clause permitting it to be presented posthumously.

Gandhiji however is the Father of our Nation, which no generation can deny. Gandhiji stood for non-violence, democracy and equality, other principles on which he lived his life were simplicity, courage of conviction, determination, truth, love and faith. His messages should be a guiding force for many generations to come, provided they imbibe his qualities in their lives.

Houston in the U.S.A. celebrates Gandhi week and prompts people to make a commitment to practicing peace in their personal lives and promoting Gandhi's message of non-violence.

A time has come when the country is again under siege by both internal and external forces of destruction, which need to be tackled using the principles of Gandhiji. What we need is strength of character and the determination to succeed using the way that has been successfully shown to us by his life and deeds.

A few quotes of the *Mahatma* from various sources are presented to enable a understanding of a man who spoke few words but did much for the country.

⇒ *Strength does not come from physical capacity, it comes from an indomitable will.*

⇒ *There is no way to peace, peace is the way.*

⇒ *There is surely something wrong with a person who is supposed to be highly spiritual and yet is always ailing physically.*

⇒ *Change is a condition of progress. An honest man cannot afford to observe mechanical consistency when mind revolts against anything in error.*

⇒ *God never made man that he may consider another man as an untouchable ... To say that a single human being because of his birth, becomes an untouchable, unapproachable or invisible is to deny God.*

⇒ *Freedom is not worth having if it does not connote freedom to err. It passes my comprehension how human beings, be they ever so experienced and able, can delight in depriving other human beings of that precious right.*

⇒ *To befriend the one who regards himself as your enemy is the quintessence of true religion.*

⇒ *God alone can take life because He alone gives it.*

⇒ *The highest honour my friends can do me is to enforce in their own lives the program that I stand for or to resist me to their utmost if they do not believe in it.*

To limit Gandhiji's quality to the little that he said would be an injustice to his greatness, for a lot was not recorded. As Albert Einstein aptly said :

> ***The true value of human beings is determined by the measure and the sense in which they have obtained liberation from oneself. We require a substantially new manner of thinking if humanity is to survive.***

Gandhiji's last words were: *Hey Ram* !

CIRCUMSTANTIAL FEASTS

Circumstantial feasts result from circumstances that bring happiness, joy and excitement and therefore call for a celebration for which a feast is arranged, to share the event with others within or outside the family. Such events may be expected or unexpected, and are celebrated by one and all according to their economic status and the degree to which they feel the joy and excitement over the event. This also depends greatly on the amount of egoism or humility in the people concerned. The pompous, feast at the drop of a hat as they want to show off their wealth and find any excuse to do so, while the humble may celebrate by offerings at temples or giving in charities as a gesture of thanksgiving to the Lord for his blessings. The types of expected and unexpected events are presented in Fig. 10.1.

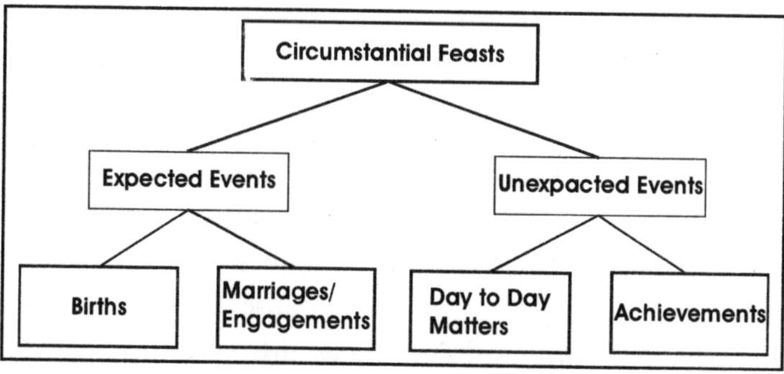

Fig. 10.1: Circumstantial feasts

Figure 10.1 suggests that these feasts are connected with expected as well as unexpected events that occur in life, and people need to cope with them according to their social and economic status as well as their personality traits. These are being briefly discussed.

EXPECTED EVENTS

The expected events that lead to feasting include the birth of children in the family, engagements, marriages and related activities and many others which are either planned or desired. Jubilees like silver, golden and platinum are also occasions for celebration. Individuals, married couples or institutions might celebrate these jubilees. When our dreams come true for whatever reason, they give joy, that is shared through feasting first within the family by offering thanksgiving and then formally in the form of celebrations with family, friends and associates. Being expected, these events can usually be planned and the family or host knows when, where and how the feasting related to each event needs to be organized. Expected events are a source of great joy that everyone is anxious to share with family and friends and the guests too enjoy the feasts thoroughly since these have been planned with finesse, in advance.

However, the extent to which parties and feasts are planned depends on a number of factors:

- Social status
- Economic level
- Profession
- Personality

Social Status

Social status is usually judged by the locality and house one lives in, some areas in a city carrying a stiff collar compared to other colonies which house middle income or lower income families. Further, the type of clothes one chooses to wear, the jewellery, footwear, educational institutions to which children are sent, memberships of clubs and so on all point to a sense of status and indicate wealth, whether earned honestly or otherwise. Designer clothes and jewellery, or the brand of the car which if more expensive, are associated with a higher social status as also the area for shopping visited on a daily basis or the number of staff employed as domestic help. Club memberships too, are a prestige issue whether their facilities are regularly utilized or not. Let us see how social status affects feasting.

Usually people like to show off their wealth since they cannot or do not have the desire to utilize it for non-visible means like charities and so on. So they like to celebrate at the drop of a hat, just for the most insignificant reason. They get involved in kitty parties planned in homes or clubs where the ladies spend time and money ordering lavish menus. They come home tired, but satisfied, because their egos are satisfied. There is no plausible reason to celebrate at all except to show off and be noticed. Such people are generally termed *socialites* who go out to parties every other day and then reciprocate the invitations of their friends and family by returning their hospitality by organizing a feast at home or outside.

This category of people celebrate family events like engagements, marriages, births and even examination success of children so lavishly that people would be talking about the menu or arrangements for some time to come. Without doubt they require a lot of money for their lifestyle.

Middle-class families live more frugally and do not indulge in luxuries but enjoy their earnings with family and friends in a more informal and friendly manner. The children too, imbibe a sense of discipline and work sincerely for achieving what they most desire. They are more content, have a higher sense of values and are grateful to parents and God for what they have. They also value time, money and friendships which they enjoy on special occasions by feasting at home or with friends. They also value leisure time for outdoor activities and through them build team spirit and bring happiness to themselves and those around them.

The lower income category spend most of their time trying to make both ends meet, so their children adopt simple leisure time activities like running, *kabbadi* and indoor activities. Most of them go to government schools if at all or else help the parents to look after their younger siblings. But, this category has a lot of love in their eyes and heart, which they go all out to share, and so develop into good human beings, valuing the little that can be provided for them. Parties and regular feasting is not for them, but they do enjoy family functions like marriages, even if they have to borrow money to celebrate a wedding in the house with joy and happiness for all in the family and community.

Migration of villagers to urban environments, has however changed life for them and they have begun to imitate the ways of the urbanites whether they can afford them or not. This has taken them away from community participation and greener cleaner environments to a more polluted and relatively individualistic society. They are therefore destined to hard labour, few amenities for a comfortable living and often resort to child labour practices to be able to afford one meal a day. Feasting for them is getting intoxicated in the evening to forget their tiredness and woes leading to aggressive and often criminal behaviour to fight the odds.

It is a sensible step that the government and industry is now resorting to taking facilities to the rural areas to stop the migration and try to provide basic facilities to improve the economic status of the less priveledged in the country, within their own natural living environment.

Economic Level

Social status directly affects the economic status of families and what they can afford. Celebrations and feasting do require a certain amount of money in hand to enjoy them, and one really cannot resort to these activities if money is loaned for such festivities. Feasting for social purposes is the privilege of the rich and therefore today people are faced with anti-social ways of acquiring more money by any means possible, ranging from corruption, theft, crime, assault and kidnapping for ransom or even scams and frauds occuring in unimaginable ways.

Profession

The amount of feasting occasions and the manner in which they are celebrated and enjoyed are also determined by the profession one follows for day-to-day living. For example, friendships develop within professions, according to their even economic and social status. Feasting also is enjoyed only among one's own associations which offer common ideas for sharing together. It is a common experience that an academic is happy being among other academics, for they share common values, just as businessmen enjoy feasts with other business families or senior officials with whom they wish to maintain cordial social relations for the benefit of their business ventures.

Personality

Some people have extrovert personalities and love to invite and be invited so they can have fun with others both at home and outside, feasting at the slightest excuse even though they may not be throwing lavish parties, but only arrange social get-togethers to share joy and be happy. Introvert people prefer to remain in protected company and feel uncomfortable with strangers in parties. They are happier among a few friends in informal environments and usually shun even family celebrations, avoiding unfamiliar people.

UNEXPECTED EVENTS

Unexpected events cover achievements in the form of successes for which a lot of hard work is put in, but the outcome is not expected, such as an honorary degree by a foreign university, or a national or international award, such as a Padamshree, Bharat Ratna, Arjuna award, a Booker's or even a Nobel Prize. You can imagine the joy that Amitabh Bachchan's family and friends felt when he was honoured in France or invited by Madame Tussaud's in London for making a wax model of him. The event was certainly not planned, but worth the welcome and the feasting that would have followed among family and friends on return. Well, he is a celebrity in any case, but the same can happen in the case of a sports person who has come to the limelight from a poor village family, or whose son has cleared a medical entrance exam that was always a dream and a far cry. The only difference in the mode of feasting and expression of joy would be, that the parents would offer special *prasaad* or charity at a temple in humility, thanking God for His grace, and after distributing *prasaad* to all who visit to felicitate the family for the event, they hug each other in joy and excitement and offer sweets to them. Similarly, an unexpected promotion at work or simply an unexpected exam result would call for a celebration.

In day-to-day life, events which may appear very insignificant to those are used to planned parties, can lead to an environment of feasting. Some examples are an unexpected gift on one's birthday, the sudden arrival of a friend who had not been in touch for years, and was therefore totally forgotten. Sometimes a longing to go abroad which was stalled by the refusal of a visa on account of an unfavourable medical report, may be granted unexpectedly. The joy such events kindle in the heart is beyond description, and people coming together itself, results in the organization of impromptu celebrations. Such feasting is not tiring and at the same time it is exhilarating and lifts the spirit, irrespective of social status or economic considerations.

Similarly, there are many such occasions that call for celebration and feasting all of which cannot be documented, also they differ with the circumstances and the environment in which people live. What is important though, is to remember that where there is devotion and humility in the heart of people the joy such events bring is much greater than when the sharing of joy through feasting results only in fanning people's ego and exhibiting their wealth through whatever means.

FEASTING AND HEALTH

Health is all about the body being in a state of physical, physiological, mental, emotional and spiritual well being in an effort to maintain the body in a state of equilibrium. The WHO also defined it similarly but without the word *spiritual* in its definition.

The main ingredient for maintenance of good health is the food we eat, and hence the phrase, *we are what we eat.* Therefore, it is evident that feasting will have some impact on health for good or worse.

WHAT IS FEASTING?

Feasting is usually associated with plenty of food and drink, consumed in an atmosphere of gaiety and joy that makes people generally overeat and drink in company. If this happens once in a while its effect on health goes unnoticed, because the body is so adaptable that, its natural internal mechanisms and processes adjust to the changes bringing back the equilibrium.

Body Adaptation

When feasting or overeating and drinking goes on continuously as during complete seasons of parties, the body gets no time to adapt to the burden forced on it, so it reacts in three ways, such as:

- Adapting to the increases in the level of food intake and storing the extra energy inputs as fat, gradually leading to weight gain, which is apparent by measuring on a weighing scale.
- Creates a habit of overeating by adapting to the excess intake through expansion of stomach size, and the body begins to get obese, throwing extra weight on the internal organs, which thus become gradually sluggish and chronic diseases set in, destroying health.
- Body processes breakdown and imbalances set in, which start reflecting through changes in mood, behaviour, personality, self-esteem and health status. The problems that arise may not only be physical, but physiological, psychological, emotional and mental too.

The equilibrium of the body having been disturbed, over time mental problems of loss of concentration, memory and so on also set in. Then drastic steps need to be taken to bring the body back to health, which may mean taking strong medicines, restricting foods which were previously enjoyed, doing more exercise for which the body is too heavy to respond easily without strain and so on.

Men do not adapt very easily to changed circumstances in their lives whether health related or otherwise. To cope some may start overeating and others may cut down on food intake. In both cases they fall a prey to sicknesses and diseases. Thus a viscous cycle of disease and enforced fasting gets set up, leading to physical, physiological, emotional, mental and spiritual apathy.

Physical Health

Physical health refers to the normality of the body and all its parts, which are the wonders of creation all from the fusion and multiplication of a few cells. The cells multiply to millions of cells, forming organs with specific functions, myriads of fine arteries, veins and nerves supplied to all the parts of the body. In addition, there are the glands and their secretions which respond to any changes that may occur in the body or its environment, trying to maintain it in equilibrium and proper functioning. Further, the body is supplied by ductless glands that inject chemicals straight into the bloodstream to help the different organs to work in tandem and coordinate with each other in a masterly manner.

It would be interesting to note that a foot is made up of 26 bones constituting 1/4th of the bones in the body, 33 joints, 107 ligaments and 19 muscles. In addition there are 250,000 sweat glands in both feet. The average person takes 8-10,000 steps a day or 115,000 miles over a lifetime. Women have four times more foot problems then men. So, if any one of these systems pack up or do not communicate or cooperate with each other, the body suffers and ill health results.

Thus by nature, all the organs of the human body and its internal processes work in coordination to keep it physically and physiologically healthy. If any of the parts or processes are disturbed, consciously or by accident the equilibrium is lost, although even then, the body warns us through very subtle inbuilt mechanisms that it is being stressed. If the deviation from normality is slight, the body takes care of it through adjustment of its internal processes, by secreting the needed quantities of hormones and so on.

However, if we are sensitive to our body signals then corrective action can be taken in time before illness develops. The most important signal is *pain* indicating that some disturbance has set in, that the body cannot cope with on its own and needs attention.

For example, if one experiences a headache it is not generally related to the stomach or eating, but often exercise or yoga can relieve the problem if it is due to gas in the stomach or flatulence. Sometimes headaches indicate a low level of sugar in the blood in which case taking a sweet drink can help to bring relief. This is so because the only form of energy that the brain can use is the circulating glucose in the blood, which does not reach the brain in sufficient quantities if the circulating levels are low.

Similarly, a pain in the stomach can occur due to overeating that is generally relieved by resting the stomach through fasting or eating soft food in limited quantities till the body recovers. Pain can also be due to flatulence, eating wrong foods or imbalanced diets, toxicity or extreme hunger.

A family physician of old, Dr. Bhagat Ram, used to say *all illnesses start from the stomach, and overeating is the root cause of all problems.* His main diagnostic tool was the temperature chart for a week because he believed that body temperature was indicative of a problem in the body, even if there were no visible or obvious signs of illness. Some ailments related to unbalanced eating are indicated in Table 11.1.

Table 11.1: Ailments resulting from imbalanced eating

Ailment	Reason	Remedy
Constipation	Overeating or wrong foods	Increasing water and fibre intake.
Diarrhoea	Eating or drinking infected food	Medicine and clean home food, plenty of liquid.
Stomach ache	Constipation, gas, infection	Light food at short intervals according to appetite, digestive aids, and rest. Medicine as required.
Fatigue	Heat, over exertion, anemia	Cooling liquids, rest, nourishing food and supplements as required.
Fever	Over exertion, infection	Rest, soft food as required. Medicine if it persists.

It is important to avoid physical discomfort after a feast or party, which the body signals through headache, stomach ache, bloating of the stomach, chest pain and the like. All these symptoms signal either overeating, or imbalanced food and eating habit.

Level of Food Intake

With lifestyle changes there is an increased level of social feasting and the consumption of high calorie foods. It is imperative that when eating out frequently becomes the norm, especially during festive seasons that never seem to end in India, one loses control of the amount eaten in company. In addition there are the additional calories from sweet and alcoholic drinks. Moderation is the key, and this too can be monitored by becoming sensitive to body signals, which make us aware that we are going overboard in terms of consumption. A few guidelines important for preventing imbalances and illnesses are.

- Eat out in moderation to the stage of *less than fullness*
- Choose foods that will bring balance to the day's diet. For example if one meal is heavy, eat light at other times or skip a meal.
- Observe fast to help the body to recover from overdoses of eating.
- Eat slowly by proper mastication of foods.
- Have fruits or salads first so that energy dense foods are not consumed in large amounts.
- Do not refill your plate, with practice you will know how much you need to eat in order to feel just good.
- Check the menu for any favourite desserts you might not want to miss, and adjust your meal on the plate accordingly.

If uncorrected for a long time such habits can lead to chronic diseases, the beginnings of which are seen in overweight leading to obesity, which starts a vicious cycle of chronicity that can cause other diseases like diabetes, heart problems, hormonal disturbances which could have been prevented. It is therefore important to keep weight in check on a regular basis, especially if eating energy dense fast foods or resorting to uncontrolled feasting on a regular basis.

Since people are always in a hurry for work, school, play, and so on, often missing a meal, it would be useful to know that missing a meal can cause imbalances in the body especially if it is the breakfast, which in any case is eaten after a gap of 10-12 hours. It would be better to avoid this by simply eating a fruit, say, a banana. This gives satiety and helps to get rid of not only immediate hunger, but can relieve a lot of minor ailments because of the balanced nutrition it provides and the ease with which it can be carried safely and consumed. It contains approximately 70% water, 27% carbohydrate, 1.2% protein, 0.3 % fat and supplies 116 kcalories of energy. In addition it provides 5 vitamins and 11 minerals and fibre, all essential for the normal functioning of the body.

In India, the banana used to be called the poor man's food, which he may not be able to afford today as the prices have been constantly rising, as indicated by starvation and malnutrition deaths that are reported in the press, even from places where they were never heard of before. So eating a banana can prevent blood sugar from falling, causing weakness and giddiness and even blackouts when a meal is missed, and help to tide over the energy needs till the next mealtime. Table 11.2 presents some of the effectiveness of the fruit in alleviating minor ailments.

Table 11.2: Effectiveness of banana as a substitute for missing a meal

Ailment	Effectiveness
Anemia	Contains iron that stimulates the production of haemoglobin in the blood.
Blood Pressure	High in potassium and low in sodium (salt), which is a perfect combination for regulating blood pressure.
Constipation	High fibre content helps normal bowel action.
Diarrhoea	An overripe banana helps to bind stools and alleviate the symptoms of diarrhoea by supplying moisture and salts for rehydration.
Hangovers	Banana milkshake with honey soothes and rehydrates the system, which is dehydrated by alcohol and drugs.
Mosquito bites	Rubbing the affected area with the inside of a banana peel relieves the itching and spread of the toxicity.
Pre-menstrual syndrome(PMS)	Vitamin B_6 in banana regulates blood glucose levels, and enhances mood.
Ulcers	Banana neutralizes acidity and reduces irritation by coating the stomach lining.
Warts	The inside of a banana peel placed on a wart can destroy it.

Drinking and overeating are the outcome of excessive feasting occasions, because of the celebratory atmosphere and the great variety of high calorie snacks and foods served to tempt the diner. This can lead to overweight and obesity no matter how much it is counteracted by missing meals, fasting and exercise. Some of the chronic diseases that affect health for life and make people dependent on medical aid are briefly discussed in the light of today's lifestyles.

Medical research has established that meat eaters are more prone to arterial blockages, and by the age of 23, three out of four have arterial blockage in America, where people live on steak and hamburgers, and at the age of 60, one in four persons are found to be completely impotent. But there is hope, since turning vegetarian can reverse the process of blockages because the average person becomes leaner. This is because plant foods are low in calories and their natural starches stimulate two catabolic hormones which lead to calorie burning.

It has been found that in Japan, as the traditional diet became westernized with increase in consumption of meat and fat, baldness became more common in younger men. Excess meat-based diets also lead to increased production of testosterone in the body, that causes overstimulation of cell production in the prostrate gland and its ensuing health problems. On the other hand, vegetables provide more fibre in the diet improving intestinal health and toning down aggressive and dominant behaviour in people.

Obesity

Overweight is a serious problem in middle and old age with men putting on excessive weight around the abdomen and women at abdomen, thighs, hips and other places in the body. Excessive overweight is called *obesity* which is a real health hazard, difficult to control with diet alone and requires drastic changes in lifestyle and eating habits, which die hard at this age. Extra fat deposition puts a further burden on the internal organs and precipitates chronic diseases of the heart, kidneys, liver and so on. The whole glandular and hormonal secretory mechanisms get disturbed and complications of thyroid and other glandular functions get imbalanced leading to diabetes, high blood pressure, joint pains, lethargy and chronic fatigue. Once these set in, there is little one can do to reverse them completely.

What is disturbing however, is that today even children are victims of the overweight syndrome. While obesity is consistently increasing in urban populations, current reports suggest that almost 40% adults, and 15% children are overweight, further classified as 50-70% women, 27% young girls and 22% boys as being obese.

A recent study reported from New York suggests that the amount of time people spend sleeping affects their weight. Loss of sleep has been found to increase rate of obesity in the US. Shorter sleep duration may affect levels of two weight control hormones, the levels of *leptin* which is associated with satiety had reduced, and the levels of *ghrelin* associated with hunger were increased. Populations studied had a higher prevalence of suicide and a greater propensity towards other risky health-related behaviours too.

These days with awareness of health, nutrition and wellness increasing, people can easily monitor their own weight at home, and calculate the index of obesity called Body Mass Index or BMI when the scales tip too much to the right of their normal average steady weight. Men in particular can control their abdominal size and women their waist and hip measurements, with suitable exercises and monitor the progress by using a simple tape measure as a tool.

Calculating BMI

This can be done by any literate person using the following simple calculation:

Weight in kilogram divided by height in metres, squared. So if your weight is 60 kg and height is 5.2 metres the BMI would be 60 divided by (5.2 × 5.2) or 60 divided by 27.04 = 22.18.

According to the WHO the normal range for BMI is between 18.5-25, whereas values between 26-29 are considered overweight and 30 and above indicates obesity. For Indians 18-23 is considered normal. So it is very easy for everyone to monitor their weight and know when you have to start taking steps to be within the normal range to prevent health problems leading to chronic diseases. A little modification in eating habits and exercise patterns can go a long way to promote health and wellness.

Among Indian women the easiest way to control eating is by regular fasting and prayer, taking the mind away from food, and setting up disciplined routines for walking and exercise or yoga, which not only relaxes the body after a day's work but also balances the systems within, to promote health. In fact statistics show that children too, are becoming overweight and obese these days because of our new living styles. Let us compare the lifestyles of old with present-day routines to answer why we are suffering more today in terms of health, than our elders who in fact have increased lifespan, leading to a shrinking of the working population of the country. This comparison is presented in Table 11.3.

Table 11.3 indicates a sea change in homes, living and working styles of people and their environments over the last 3-4 generations. Whatever the different reasons, the changes have affected the health of people in general, especially of younger persons and children in particular.

Thus, physical and physiological health go hand in hand, and one cannot be maintained without the other being normal. Some general *dietary guidelines* to maintain the body in health are:

- Start the day with one glass of water. Traditionally this was keptovernight in a copper utensil in the prayer room and then taken in the morning.
- No water should be taken with meals, but half an hour earlier or two hours after a main meal. This aids in digestion by bringing the food eaten in contact with the digestive enzymes and staying with them longer, instead of getting quickly flushed out or diluted with water or liquids. This is why soups or drinks are used as appetizers much before a meal is served.
- Use of salt should be minimized, as it is hygroscopic and draws water into the body. If taken in excess it can bring about blood pressure changes, or cause water retention in tissues.
- Minimize use of sugar, especially refined sugars as they over stimulate the pancreatic glands to produce insulin for maintaining blood sugar levels. Refined sugars can be substituted by jaggery

or honey or used in the form of natural products such as fruits, sweet corn, beetroot, sweet potato, milk and so on.

- Use minimum fat in cooking foods. It is much healthier to take a spoon of ghee on top of steamed foods like *idli*, rice, vegetables and so on than to cook in it. Use of natural unrefined oils are a good source of essential fatty acids especially linseed oil.
- Low fat milk containing upto 2% fat, is desirable for all milk and its products.
- Vegetarian balanced diets are best, but if meats are important to you, then avoid red meats.
- Consume foods in their natural form, like whole cereals, pulses, fruits and vegetables.
- Consume organic foods, the extra expense is not more than medical expenses of illness.
- Restrict tea and coffee to not more than 2 cups a day if it must be had, or switch to herb teas.
- Avoid refined foods in the diet or minimize their use.
- Eat less quantity and more quality, avoid fullness.
- Do not make it a habit to eat out.
- Masticate food properly, enjoy the experience of eating.
- Adopt regular and moderate eating habits.
- Say no to alcohol, smoking or chewing tobacco.
- Maintain moderate but regular physical exercise, hard work, yoga and positive mental attitudes.

To maintain health some cues for healthy living can be taken from traditional practices and fitted into present day lifestyles without much effort. It is important to remember that children imitate adult habits, so care is required to set good examples about what they see or hear at home. Sound eating habits are learnt early in life and so effort is required to expose children to a variety of healthy foods and diets. Overeating or overburdening the body with excess fat through fast foods or nutritionally unbalanced diets slows down the body processes resulting in disease.

Table 11.3: Lifestyle changes affecting health, then and now

Lifestyles	Then	Health effects	Now	Health effects
Waking time	Pre-dawn	The predawn vibrations in the atmosphere help to improve memory.	After sunrise	Missing out on predawn benefits.
Activity	*Suprabhatam*	At sunrise *Suprabhatam* prayer done in yogic postures enable intake of oxygen and ozone while contributing to vitamin D content of the body.	Exercise indoors and in a hurry	Facing pollution and its ill-effects along with stress.
	Walking	The morning walk provides exercise to activate the body for the day.	Outdoor	Sunburn+harmful rays
	Active work	Walked/cycled to work– healthy body and mind	Indoor in homes and air conditioned gyms	Lack of fresh air, low immunity to weather changes. SedentaryAllergies Overweight and related diseases.
Bathing	Early morning	Inculcate clean habits and disciplined routines.	No fixed time	Not bothered about orderliness.
Prayer	After bath	Starting work with devotion and faith	No norms – may not pray at all.	Always short of time and delayed.

(Contd...)

Lifestyles	Then	Health effects	Now	Health effects
Cooking	After prayer	Preparing own food with ingredients of love and devotion.	No norms– Cooking done by servants	Taste, flavour, appetite and eating habits affected. Cleanliness not ensured.
Eating	Served with love and care	Enjoyed with the family in peace with focus on food.	Served by servants or self served, eaten in a hurry.	Digestion, appetite affected and family bonding absent.
	Eat to live	Good health	Live to eat	Excessive eating disorders.
	Eating freshly cooked food.	Good health	Stored, reheated food	Lacks nutrition and taste
	Ate less; physical activity more	Good muscular development	Eat more and physical activity reduced.	Poor health
Eating out	Home food only—eating out taboo	Traditional balanced diets with sound health	Frequent eating out	Quality variable. Eating disorders and gastrointestinal disturbances.
Mental health	Respect for elders, faith and devotion	Sound ethical values, development of humility, obedience, trust and bonding.	Elders not cared for, institution of old age homes and NGOs.	No support system to fall back on leading to depression, frustration and anxieties.

(Contd...)

	Sound character	Built by imitation of elders who practiced what they preached in terms of sharing, giving and guiding.	Individualistic, egocentric, selfish and non-caring, materialistic	Lack of understanding, adjustment, demanding, aggressive and even violent.
	Sensitive conscience	Preserved through divinity and charity	Battered conscience Ethical values at their lowest	Mental illness due to increased self-induced stress.
	High self-esteem	Leading to increased confidence, self worth and dignity.	Low self-esteem	Depression, aggression and anti social tendencies.
Interaction	Only among elders, No discussions. Only receiving instructions	Decision making simple but younger members of the family suppressed. Variable mental and emotional health.	Healthy discussion, debates, shelving of decisions.	Confusion, chaos and little solution to problems. Shirking of responsibilities, tensions/anxieties, variable mental and physical behaviour.

(Contd...)

Lifestyles	Then	Health effects	Now	Health effects
Financial	Controlled by head of family.	Disciplined spending and consuming within means. No mental stress. Contented	Uncontrolled spending and consuming, easy loan facilities and insatiable desires.	Stress, anxieties because of high cost of borrowing yet insufficiency and lack of contentment.
	Money was used as a means for living happily.	Less stress, happy, satisfied.	Money is used not only to buy commodities but also to buy people.	Lack of understanding and basic virtues leading to anti-social tendencies, demanding, violent.
Travel	Light with few things	Physically comfortable.	Heavy	Physically uncomfortable travel and yet not contented.

The daily diet needs to have at least 2 teaspoons of honey, 2 lemons, 3-4 g fresh garlic, 20-25 g raw onions and sprouts in addition to raw vegetable salads using seasonal foods. For a high protein vegetarian diet, soya products may be added to the diet. Controlled eating, exercise and occasional fasting helps the sick body to regain its health, while at the same time helping to maintain the physical health of the body.

Recent Findings

Researchers at the Scripps Research Institute in California found that the active ingredient in cannabis, delta-2 tertra hydro cannabinol or THC can prevent the neurotransmitter acetylcholine from breaking down more effectively than commercially marketed drugs. THC is also more effective at blocking clumps of protein that can inhibit memory and cognition in Alzheimer's patients.[35]

It has been an ancient practice to use *bhang* while feasting at Holi. The story goes that the gods helped by demons churned the ocean of milk in order to obtain *amrit* or nectar and where a drop of that nectar fell on the earth, the first cannabis plant sprouted. This story is quite consistent with history. In fact it is believed that the use of cannabis in India dates back to 1000 BC. It is believed that Lord Shiva spent most of his time at Mount Kailash, his abode, in deep meditation or smoking marijuana. Rituals involving the use of bhang or marijuana frequently accompany festivals that revolve around worshipping Shiva. The drinking of bhang at Holi feasts is believed to bring about a high sense of Divinity in people, as they consider it as Shivji's prasaad used in the form of a drink called *thandai*, or added to food or sweets. People believe that all living beings are kept healthy by the kindness of Shiva.

The marijuana plant is believed to have originated in Asia, and is very much an essential folklore and tradition. The flowering bud is harvested and dried and usually smoked with tobacco in a *chillum* or rolled into a cigarette or *bidi*.

New research shows that smoking pot may stave off Alzheimer's disease, the active ingredient of which may prevent its progression by

[35] J. of Molecular Pharmaceutics.

preserving levels of an important neurotransmitter that allows the brain to function.

Today, marijuana is used to relieve glaucoma and can help reduce side effects of cancer and AIDS treatments, although modern forms of alcohol are now being imported into the country and consumed by all ages at all celebrations and feasts with only harmful effects.

Mental Health

Ailments that originate in the mind are aberrations of the mind which set up reactions in the body that result in various diseases. Even a slight disturbance in the mind can trigger a reaction in the physical body because the body and mind are closely inter-related. It is for this reason that negative or bad thoughts create bad feelings, which if not weeded out immediately can precipitate physical ailments and diseases varying from indigestion, variations in blood pressure, heart rate fluctuations and so on. Worries, anxieties or mental stress of any kind if not nipped in the bud with positive, progressive and good thinking can lead to chronic diseases like diabetes, heart disease, asthma and many pulmonary diseases. As Sri Sathya Sai has said:

Illness is caused more by the malnutrition of the mind than the body. He calls it ***a deficiency of vitamin G, and recommends the repetition of the name of God.***[36]

It is important to understand that the state of mind changes with the changes in the body processes and vice versa, resulting in psychological states that are seen as lowered self esteem, depression, boredom and sometimes complete withdrawal from other people and social interaction. Sometimes these kinds of mental states lead to conditions such as binge eating and anorexia with no control over instincts, making people prone to illness. A regulated life and habits are two-thirds the treatment and medicine only one-third.

In fact, studies have shown that depression can lead to brittle bones in which case anti-depressant drugs could be used to treat osteoporosis.

---

36 *Avtar Vani, Sanathana Sarathi,* 43:8, August 2000, p. 249

A study conducted at Jerusalem's Hebrew University maintained that anti-depressants increase bone density and hence level of activity and social interaction. The new findings for the first time point to depression as an important element in causing bone mass loss and osteoporosis.[37]

Stress

Any imbalance in thought, word or deed leads to a situation that becomes stressful, and requires to be managed with care to prevent illness. There is no doubt that life is full of stress, causing anxieties at all levels — physical, physiological, mental, emotional and spiritual.

Physical

Physical stress can be due to a number of factors such as poverty, environmental change, illiteracy, epidemics and natural disasters, each impacting health in some way or other. Most of these circumstances which require rehabilitation lead to enforced fasting, making people resort to eating whatever they can get, and often consuming only one meal a day, either due to unprecedented changes in their life or if they are destined to poverty. This has its toll on the body due to the physical stress exerted on its organs, which affects its physical capacity to work.

Physiological

This is the stress placed on the functions of the internal organs and processes of the body as in food poisoning or toxicity, short duration, acute or chronic illnesses which often precipitate symptoms of diarrhoea, head and stomach aches, vomiting, fevers and so on. Physiological stress can also be a result of poverty, starvation and malnutrition, the latter being caused even by overeating or regular feasting in affluent societies, called the *malnutrition of affluence.*

However, chronic undernutrition as in poverty or in the elderly who cannot help themselves as much as they used to, makes people succumb to infections more readily through lowered immunity, and recovery from illness is also unduly prolonged.

---

37 Prof. Raz Yirmiya, Hebrew University, 2006.

Mental

Mental stress results from pressures created at school, work, tension in relationships, lack of leisure time, deviation from tradition, custom and practice, generation gap affecting interpersonal communication and peer and parental pressures. As you think so you become, *Yad bhavam tad bhavati,* so it is important to think positively and make every failure a stepping stone to success. Negative attitudes indicate a weak personality that also vitiates the environment with negativity for every one around.

However, the circumstances in which people are subject to conditions of poverty impose partial fasting on them making them resort to consuming only one meal a day routinely because they cannot afford any better. But, when one compares the mental health of poor people to that of those who can afford three meals per day, the former are much happier and at peace than the latter, accepting their lot and constantly praying for better times.

Emotional

Emotional stress occurs due to anger, lust, greed, attachment, pride and other *tamasic* tendencies in people. It is common to see perfectly young and energetic people lying the whole day with remotes in hand watching TVs or sleeping, these are signs of mental and emotional illness. They must be encouraged to spend time outside the house and play team games if possible or participate in any outdoor activity as close to nature as possible. The greater the body is used the more efficient its processes become leading to balance and mental stability. Sports activities are excellent means of managing stress situations, as they teach people to bond with each other, and enjoy success and failure with equanimity.

Emotional strength is gained by putting all logic aside because no problems can be solved through logic alone, since life is not always logical. Instead it is useful to have an anchor in life that helps to release stress from the heart such as a guru, an ideal or goal to focus on, or God to whom we can surrender all situations in full faith. We cannot therefore separate the emotional part of ourselves from our understanding of why we become ill.

Spiritual

Spiritual stress is caused when actions are performed against one's conscience or inner guidance. Sanctify time by good speech, good mind and good heart making *love* the basis of life in order to remove spiritual stress.

When all round health is gained through consistent effort, an inner strength develops, and positivity becomes the foundation of our expressions, which shows in a well balanced personality equipped to cope with any challenge in life instead of succumbing to it in the form of illnesses.

Traditional methods of fasting and prayer not only help to keep the body healthy but the mind and the spirit too, undoubtedly improving mental health. The importance of forgiveness has been extolled for centuries, but only recently has its health benefits been demonstrated. Control of the senses helps to eliminate anger, frustration and the like, and fosters tolerance, empathy, togetherness, self-sacrifice and charitable tendencies leading to social justice and peace.

Spiritual Health

This is the dimension of health that has reached rock bottom in the country and the world. People proudly announce that they do not believe in God, and yet turn to something within themselves for help when in trouble, or commit an act that is performed against their conscience which hurts them. The stress in people is increasing because they are constantly running after what their external eyes can see. A very interesting anecdote reported in the *Sacred Space* in the *Times of India* daily, is worth a thought.

A group of highly established alumni visited their old professor, and their conversation turned to stress in work and life. Offering his guests coffee, the professor went into the kitchen returning with a large pot of coffee and an assortment of cups made of plastic, porcelain, glass, crystal, some plain looking others exquisite. He told his guests to help themselves to hot coffee. When all of them had a cup in their hands, the professor said:

> ***If you noticed all the nice expensive cups were taken up, leaving behind the plain inexpensive ones. It is but normal to want only***

> ***the best for yourselves, that is the source of your problems and stress. What all of you really wanted was coffee, not the cup, but you consciously went for the best cups and were eyeing each other's cups.***
>
> ***Now if life is coffee, and the jobs, money and positioning in society are the cups, they are just tools to hold life, but the quality of life doesn't change. Sometimes by concentrating only on the cup, we fail to enjoy the coffee in it. So don't let the cups drive you...enjoy the coffee instead....***

This is a lesson in spiritual health in the light of modern education, but what was taught by our sages and prophets was the development of ethics, and living life with morality and simplicity. They taught techniques like *japa,* meditation and discipline in daily living, by which people developed faith in them and devotion to duty. Faith expands the heart and gives joy contributing to mental health. Being rich in values like truth, renunciation, love and selfless service, dedicating actions to good causes all build character. If one goes by the dictates of the conscience no wrong can ever be done, for the conscience is the teacher which tells us right from wrong, and actions decide the results. As Sai Baba has said:[38]

> ***Be firm in your faith that your hriday (heart) is Easwara, mind is Vishnu and speech is Brahma. Make the best use of speech, the mind and the heart and you will surely attain the goal of supreme blessedness.***

One who imbibes this teaching will never harbour evil thoughts and feelings and therefore will exhibit purity of speech and action through always adhering to truth and *Dharma*. Unfortunately, the cleverer the man, the less faith he has because he applies his mind and intellect to the understanding of nature and God who cannot be understood by the limitations of the mind and intellect. This is because He is the creator of both and therefore beyond any comprehension while still being all pervasive.

A concept that has evolved is that of *walking meditation* in which the Lord's name is chanted with each step walked, and this remains in the mind throughout the day, thus nourishing the body and the spirit. On the contrary when we walk early in the morning with anxiety and sorrow in our minds and heart, it can be compared to eating junk food.

---

[38] Sanathana Sarathi. Vol. 41, No. 3. March 1998. p.58.

Walking must be done slowly while enjoying the bouquet of peace that results from the chanting.

Present Scenario

Many people try to maintain physically healthy by following weight reduction programs that restrict certain foods, but do not get expected results. There are certain reasons for this:

- The process of weight reduction is very slow.
- Strict discipline is required to follow the regimen because it is easier not to eat at all than to eat less.
- Restriction has to be followed for long periods till the weight reaches normal levels, and this requires constant monitoring and effort.
- The levels have to become constant by sustained effort, which is difficult without determination and a strong will to achieve the levels, for life.
- Eating habits die hard and come back after some time, therefore most people put on weight even after they succeed to lose it initially.

This is why weight management programs with auto management tools and techniques are now offered by companies all over the country, although, fasting regularly rather than feasting, is still the best method of weight management. No saint or prophet has ever been seen to be overweight or obese, in ancient or modern India, and neither have they ever advocated feasting after a fast, in the sense in which feasting is seen today, even when associated with religious festivals.

What we see today is, that people have more resources than their parents had when they brought up all the family including relatives, but today not even one child has the time or inclination to look after their old parents, whom they consider a burden to care for. This is, in spite of parents getting their pensions and having savings to live by.

It is sad to see that the quality of education, technology and development are taking us away from our real wealth, the character building, which the *shastras* and teachers of old taught us. In fact, there is an influx of foreigners into the country who are coming to learn our ancient scriptures and healthful techniques, and imbibe the values of that education from the Gurus, whose legacies are still practiced in the ashrams, institutions and universities which they founded for the purpose. This is mainly because we have lost touch with our inner selves and shifted our focus to the glamour of the outside world away from self discipline and towards feasting and ill-health. A regulated life and habits are two-thirds the treatment for all illnesses and medicines only one third. According to the Buddha:

> ***Excessive eating is submitting the body to violence and therefore emphasizes on moderation. There is no meaning in dedicating conscious acts of violence to the Divine, which the conscience will not approve.***

Mental health leads to emotional health, that is, the heart feels good. The only barrier to mental, and emotional health is man's ego which exists only if you take yourself and everything else in life seriously. Nothing kills the ego like playfulness and laughter. When a person starts taking life as fun, the ego is destroyed. The ego is an illness and needs an atmosphere of sadness to exist and that is what makes a person depressed and wanting.

A genuine saint is never serious because he enjoys life as a continuous celebration. If we turn towards nature we find no seriousness at all. The trees, birds, rivers, mountains and everything existing around us appear to be in a state of eternal celebration sharing whatever they have with one and all. Only man is serious because he does not want to be part of the whole but craves for identity, name, form and so on, even if it creates misery for him. Man's psyche is well illustrated by George Bernard Shaw, when asked:

> ***Where would he like to go after death, heaven or hell ?*** and his reply was ***wherever I can be the first, and not second.***

This only shows the ego's strength in polluting our thoughts and creating unrest in the mind, leading to hurt in life for ourselves and those around, by creating negative vibrations. Egoism or *ahamkara* is a disease that needs to be prevented, because there is no reason for conceit or pride which comes with worldly success, money or power of position.

The only thing to feel proud of is one's goodness which stays in the world always and inspires others.

Ills of Today

In terms of health, the ills of today are lack of a disciplined life leading to mental reactions of irritation, anger, frustration leading to increase in assault, fear and terror with little or no regard to physical, physiological, mental or spiritual health. Everyone today, is familiar with wife beating, infanticide, rape and other forms of social ills indicating diseased mental and emotional health, that lead to the lack of control of the senses. The increase in the incidence of suicides, homicides, murders and so on, are all signs of extreme imbalance of the mind and the degradation of the spirit, brought about by alcohol, smoking and today's lifestyles which hinder the development of body, mind and soul.

The need of the hour is to follow the teachings of the prophets and stick to the principles of truth, *dharma* and relearn the art of controlling the senses and desires to bring back discipline in life for all aspects of health. This can only be done by adopting techniques of *japa*, yoga, meditation and looking into ourselves for sometime every day, and offering all our achievements as well as problems to our Creator, for if we call upon Him we can never be lost in the wilderness of life.

Devotion is a quality which means single-pointedness, and has the power to create the Creator. However, thinking minds have always shown an allergy to devotion only because devotees have made fools of themselves by passing off fear as devotion. In fact, devotion is for the truly intelligent and not for the stupid because without devotion there is no meaning to life. Devotion does not mean visiting the temple and chanting the name of God. Anybody who can give himself single-pointedly to whatever he is doing is a natural devotee. It is not because there is God that devotion has come, but because there is devotion that God happens. Knowing and experiencing devotion just as an emotion makes life sweet. Devotion in its true sense dissolves the ego and leads to bliss.

People going out to enjoy a feast in the metros never reach their destinations happy because of the hazards of driving, road rage, being late and always in a hurry. They only pretend to be happy on reaching, establishing the fact that life is a stage, on which each one acts their roles. One can do that only if one is genuinely healthy in body mind and soul.

Statistics show that there has been a spurt in health and diet counselling clinics, weight management centres and gyms, *vastu* experts, astrologers and the like, in the last few decades, all trying to profit by helping people to stay healthy or regain health lost, due to their present lifestyles which we have largely imitated from western cultures.

Therefore, while more attention is required for choosing meals sensibly and any deviations in weight corrected immediately, before it gets out of hand, we also need to focus on balancing living styles between the traditional and the modern if health is to improve in a holistic manner.

Today's developed societies are sick with money, power and material pursuits, but have no peace of mind. The extroverted mind brings only agitation and chaos because the thoughts gather momentum and lead to anger, sorrow and animal-like or beastly behaviour. The presence of divinity changes the direction of the thoughts and introverts the mind to make thoughts quiet and peaceful. By surrendering regrets, anxieties and fears to any anchor, the mind becomes calm and peaceful.

Western societies are therefore now looking eastwards and to India in search of gurus or teachers and institutions offering meditation techniques and yoga, all in search of peace. In the garb of helping poor nations materially too, they are involving themselves in charities, by helping NGOs involved with the upliftment and empowerment of the less fortunate in each country. From these acts, they draw their peace of mind and fulfilment in life.

Poverty can only be alleviated if the *haves* share with the *have-nots* what they do not require anymore. An apt but anonymous saying comes to mind[39]:

> ***Looking at and sharing with the less better off in society, helps to develop equal mindedness.***
>
> ***Find out how much God has given you and from it take what you need; the remainder is needed by others.***

---

[39] From calender published by Help-Age India, for 2007.

THE WAY TO PEACE

Chapter 12

Peace is a state of internal bliss and everyone is capable of finding it, irrespective of caste, creed or social status. Unfortunately it cannot be bought with material wealth, power or position because it is not a commodity, but can only be acquired with the grace of the Lord, attainable by looking to Him for help, since the *atma* alone is the embodiment of bliss.

By birth, man is endowed with the *panchpranas* or five life breaths, the *panch indriyas* or the five senses and the *panchbhutas* or the five elements. The five elements are present in the form of sound, touch, form, taste and smell, through which all experiences are gained according to the type of path man follows. Therefore, the *shastras* advocated that we all need to be associated with good people to earn a good name in order to lead a good life.

Whether infants are born to a rich family or a poor one the children are pure, innocent and similar in every way both with the same life breath and no name. It is man who gives them name, identity and social status as they grow. They thus, get the idea of being different from each other and the concepts of ***you, me*** and ***I*** get acquired. This is the root of all differences in the world leading to fear, lust, greed, anger, revenge, jealousy, hatred and terror, and a loss of the joy, peace and bliss that God sent us with.

Even the prophets and incarnations were not born with names, their parents called their children Krishna, Rama, Jesus, and so on, but they had the same divine atma in them, the same life breaths and elements. Similarly, there are hundreds of sweets available in the market but they have the same essential ingredient, sugar, in them. It is we who attribute names and forms even to God and develop differences between people on the basis of religion by chanting one name and condemning the other. All the strife in the world today is manmade though some may attribute it to God's discriminating ways.

All religions that exist preach the same message of brotherhood, unity and morality, exhorting people to love God and surrender to Him what is verily His. If only man surrenders all his thoughts, actions and deeds irrespective of their quality, there will only be peace and goodwill among people. It is then that, man will find bliss in this world to enjoy the beautiful creation of which he is only a part and through whom the divine current flows and functions.[40]

People sometimes complain that God is unkind since He gives misery to some and happiness to others, why does this happen, if all are the same in His eyes. According to the Hindu scriptures, it is a blessing to be the recipient of the Lord's anger. If an unmotivated, all loving, all compassionate God shows displeasure towards anyone, it is for his own good. Just as a loving mother disciplines her unruly child by force, it does not mean she is unkind or cruel. At that time, the child may resent his or her mother but later as an adult, he can only be grateful to her.

Love becomes intensified by diversity and crisis, as has been seen in this country whenever disaster has struck. Everybody becomes one at that time without distinctions of caste, creed, region, religion or language. Be it a disaster in one's family, region, country or the world, everyone's heart goes out to those who need help. People even pray more intensely, hold *yagnas* for peace and tranquility, and remember God's grace as never before.

---

40 *Sanathana Sarathi,* Vol. 39, No. 11-12, Nov-Dec. 1995, p.334.

MESSAGE FROM THE SCRIPTURES

The *Ramayana* has a life-giving message for all, especially those who lead artificial lives as of today, and keep repeating the name of Rama without even a thought given to the right or wrong of what they are doing in their daily lives. Such recitations of God's name, whatever be the religion followed, is meaningless unless it sows the seed of love in the heart. What then is the message of the Ramayana for us:

- Know what is right
- Utter the truth
- Be righteous
- Practice unity
- Have the spirit of equanimity
- Be noble citizens
- Love all

Know what is right

This can only be known if one listens to one's conscience, our inner self, that tells us clearly what is right and what is wrong. It is when we are too involved with the noise of the external world, to which we do not listen attentively, and even if we do, we choose to do the wrong thing or go on the wrong path. When we suffer the consequences of our choice we blame God for the ills suffered. In the words of Janina Gomes :[41]

> ***God never gives up on us. He mows, refines, prunes, melts and moulds us into forms that reflect His own true image and glory.***

God chastises those he wants to purify, the misunderstanding of being reviled and forsaken, purifies us of all the ill in our lives, so that we can introspect and reflect more perfectly the image of the divine within us. But, God gives us challenges that He has chosen for us that we can handle. In that sense we are cared for and safe if only we are with Him at all times.

---

[41] Janina Gomes: *Keep fear at bay with love and hope*, http//spirituality-indiatimes.com

Utter the Truth

Truth is what you utter that you think is right. If we are truthful in all our dealings with others, God will always be by our side and shower His grace on us. Telling the truth may put others in difficult situations sometimes, and may cause us to suffer, but stick to it. People who do not stick by the truth and change their statements get caught out sometime or other, and ultimately lose their respect in society. However, our Gurus have always taught, that it is not necessary to speak the truth if it hurts others. They advise that keeping quiet is the best option and praying for them is the right thing to do in life. When *sathya* or truth is given up, chaos results.

Be Righteous

Where there is truth, righteousness follows from it because both of them are the inherent qualities of man. Righteousness or *dharma* is acting according to your spoken words. For the sake of upholding dharma, one needs to use the *buddhi* or enlightened intellect and engage in social activity. The prayer *dharmam saranam gachchaami* advocated by Lord Buddha means *I seek refuge in Dharma.* When Dharma is discarded might becomes right. So, live in society and serve it selflessly thinking that you are serving God. The ultimate message of Buddha was *ahimsa* or non-violence, which Gandhiji also followed and advocated for achievement in life.

According to Sri Jagdish Prasad Jain, the President of the Jain Mission in New Delhi, forgiveness is the first of the ten virtues of righteousness and celebrated during the 10-day festival of *Paryushan parva.* He exhorts everyone to seek each other's forgiveness for any offending action.

In Buddhism, the quality of *karuna* or compassion and kindness includes the ability and willingness to forgive. The Quran enjoins followers by saying — ***Be foremost in seeking forgiveness*** (51:1). Jesus spoke from the cross thus — ***Father forgive them for they know not what they do.*** (Luke 23:34). By forgiving, strained relationships can be healed through:

- Soothing emotional pain
- Developing forbearance and tolerance

- Being positive
- Developing will power
- Overcoming resentment
- Reducing feeling of hurt and resentment
- Accepting the weaknesses of others
- Improving understanding of self and others

Forgiveness is an attribute of a calm and peaceful mind and ushers the beginning of peace, happiness and enlightenment. For those who brood over little things, injuries and wrongs there is only restlessness in the mind, leading to jealousy, hatred and violent behaviour. Hatred and violence multiplied in retaliation creates a spiral of destruction. As Mahatma Gandhi once said — ***An eye for an eye leaves the world blind.***

Remember that ***the worst sinner has a future, even as it's greatest saint had a past. No one is so good or so bad as he imagines.*** These were the words of Dr. S. Radhakrishnan, former President of India, a philosopher and guide, on whose birth anniversary we celebrate Teacher's Day today.

Revenge is like a virus that eats into the mind and poisons the whole body physically and spiritually. Resentment is a mental fever which burns up our mental energies and taking offence is a form of moral sickness which saps the healthy flow of kindliness and goodwill. Elaeanor Roosevelt once said ***learn from the mistakes of others. You can't live long enough to make them all yourself.*** So the person who forgives and forgets the mistakes of others sets up positive energy in the body helping to create a climate of peace.

Practice Unity

Unity of thought, word and action is essential and emanates from the heart. It is therefore important to see that the thoughts are positive, words are truthful and actions that are good for others are undertaken. This will make the heart feel good, peaceful and happy, and its environment will draw the same vibrations. For the practice of these however, a certain amount of detachment or renunciation is essential.

Differences in society are created by man. He alone is respected who has mastered the mind. When actions are motivated only for family and possessions, the result is conflict and differences. But if all are considered the children of God there is no room in the mind for differences or debates over the mundane, like states fighting over sharing water, electricity and the like.

Have the Spirit of Equanimity

Exhibit the spirit of equanimity in facing pleasure, success or profit, as well as the pain of failure or loss. Share what you have with others to get the true enjoyment from your success. Everyone has experienced at some time in their lives, that joy gets doubled and sorrows become halved when shared with others. It is for this reason that people even unknown to each other, tend to visit neighbours in times of bereavement to share their sorrows. For sharing joys, one has the family and friends, who bothers about neighbours in happy times.

Be Noble Citizens

People pay a lot of money today for their children to study in the best schools as against the value education that was imparted at home in the past. Professionals too are more trusted if they charge more. The result is selfishness, self-centredness, possessiveness, and egoistic behaviour. How many such educated students actually spend time to teach the child of the housemaid free of cost, because the latter cannot afford to send her child to school. One does not have to go far to serve others in society if there is a will to do so.

Give and share with others to receive the grace of the Lord, for money cannot buy either His grace or blessings of elders and gurus. What good is it to celebrate one day of the year as Teacher's Day if the rest of the year is spent in ridiculing or criticizing them, instead of emphasizing their qualities and learning from them.

It is the moral duty of every person to be a noble citizen, not only in times of disaster or war but at all times, by unitedly, sharing, preserving and using the resources of the nation to move forward, setting an example to the world as our sages and prophets did in the past. If the nation has to progress, examples of pure devotion need to be set for all those around you, especially children, who learn fast by imitation, in their formative years.

Love All

Love everything and everybody around you, give and share what you have with others and try to make them happy. Love is the only *dharma* or right conduct that exists. Love for all spreads fast and unknowingly thus filling the whole environment with love, happiness and peace. Sai Baba exhorts us to ***help ever, hurt never*** for He is all pervading and omnipresent in all creation.

Divine love is the most powerful magnet in the world. There are so many examples to be taken from our sacred texts, some of which are:

- The power of Krishna's love attracted the *gopis.*
- Festivals and rituals attract because of the love, unity and devotion they generate in the heart.
- Men and women attract each other through vibrations between them.
- An animal responds to love.
- The plants grow well when cared for and loved.
- Birds sing in harmony at dawn.

The chanting of *Om* is the most effective method of cultivating Love, as it represents the origin of creation and is the source of sustenance and strength. It is the *prana* of every being, the root of all sounds in existence.

True culture coexists in the recognition of the unity behind the diversity in mankind and if it is based on love and oneness of spirit, it is worth emulating as it leads to peaceful coexistence.

Share Beauty and Bliss

The Ramayana taught the integral relationship between beauty and bliss. Beauty therefore should not be skin deep only as is the case today, people trying to beautify themselves for the stage or a party by using all kinds of creams and cosmetics. Beauty should come from within and shine forth through the eyes, bringing glow to the skin, sweetness to the tongue and a feeling of bliss in the heart.

Only deeds and not people are remembered, so perform your deeds through life with love and respect to make them memorable enough. All scholarship and religious observances are of no value without the mental transformation that will root out crime, corruption, untruth or *adharma*, all of which subject the common man to trouble and misery.

Education which is not based on ethics, morality and spirituality is worthless. All education, wealth, ritualistic worship or penances are of no value without genuine devotion. It is only devotion that can elevate a person to the highest level, and it is common experience that without faith, even eminent people holding power and position get degraded.

Express Gratitude

There is a dire need to express gratitude for all that we have and get by way of services. Ram was ever grateful to Hanuman for his help during his years of exile. Gratitude gives peace in the heart and sets in positive vibrations between people, whatever may be the situation being dealt with or encountered. Whether it is a patient showing gratitude to a doctor, a child to a mother, employer to an employee and most of all to God for the gifts he has given us.

We need to be grateful to the five basic elements, ether, air, fire, water and earth which are manifestations of the divine. These are the source of the five sensory qualities of sound, touch, sight, taste and smell, which we use constantly for our enjoyment in life.

Unfortunately, everything in nature is taken so much for granted that we forget to be grateful for, and the result is disorder and discontent in the face of plenty. What we need to understand is the 3 'R's that Sri Sathya Sai has repeatedly reminded us of, and they are that:[42]

Every action has a Reaction
Every sound has a Resound
Every thought has a Reflection

In short, we are totally responsible for the state of affairs in the world, because no one can avoid the consequences of their actions, speech and

42 *Sanathana Sarathi,* Vol. 49, No. 5, May 2006, p.132.

thoughts and have to enjoy or suffer them according to the structures made and practiced through life.

It is said that Brahma pervades the entire universe as *Primordial Sound*, and therefore the sanctity of speech needs to be preserved by observing silence and truthfulness. Whenever one speaks, the sounds should be full of auspiciousness, purity, splendour, softness, and sweetness, thus conducting ourselves in befitting the sanctity of the heart with which we are endowed. If the mind is pure the speech will reflect purity.

Present Scenario

The educational system has failed to bring out the spiritual effulgence in man, and so he is oblivious of his own real nature. Students gain some information about great intellectuals through books, but very few remember them today. This is evident from the answers given to quiz and general knowledge questions through competitions. It is only when readings from the lives of great people are learnt, emulated and practiced that knowledge is gained.

On the other hand, the names of almost illiterate persons like Sri Ramakrishna Paramahamsa, Sri Shirdi Sai, Sant Kabir, Nanak, Buddha, Dayanand and others are remembered and cherished because of their spiritual eminence and service to humanity, since they infused society with morality and dharma.

People today lead meaningless lives with no ideals to inspire them, because they forget the basic truths and pursue the material life. Worldly life is inescapable, but needs to be lived with a clear goal in view if anything is to be achieved through action, guided by the body, mind, intellect and the divine otherwise a hero becomes a zero if he forgets his own divinity. Unfortunately there are seven sins plaguing the country today which are:[43]

- Business without morality
- Politics without principles

[43] *Sarahana Sarathi,* Vol. 43, No. 7, July 2000, p. back cover.

- Education without character
- Worship without sacrifice
- Acquisition of wealth without hard work
- Existence without regard for ancient scriptures
- Devotion without austerity.

Prosperity and peace can only be regained if these are removed from society on a war footing. Today people talk of unity but do not practice it. All thoughts and actions need to be related to the role one is required to play if the social fabric of society is to be maintained.

When there is true love in the heart, there is no room for hatred. Man has been endowed with six qualities and six enemies to discriminate between and maintain a balance in life, as indicated through Table 12.1.[44]

Table 12.1: Qualities and enemies of man.

Qualities	Sanskrit	Enemies	Sanskrit
Faith or confidence	Vishwasam	Desire	Kaama
Daring and determination	Saahasam	Anger	Krodha
Courage	Dhairyam	Greed	Lobha
Intelligence	Buddhi	Fascination	Moha
Energy	Shakti	Pride	Mada
Valour	Paraakramam	Envy/hatred	Mathsarya

These qualities are not acquired by education or through inheritance. They can only be attained through self-confidence or *atma-vishwaas*. Both however exist as part of creation with the mind as the master. Anger, hatred and envy, poison the mind thereby all actions get polluted. Anger cannot be destroyed by anger nor cruelty by cruelty or hatred by hatred, they can only be destroyed by love, compassion, forebearance and non-violence. When thoughts, words and deeds, become revengeful and venomous it becomes necessary to infuse them with love.

Ravana who was a great scholar and performed severe penances was destroyed by one evil quality — lust. Again Hiranyakashyap's hatred for

[44] *Sanathana Sarathi,* Vol. 41, No. 1, January 1998, p.7. Also quoted in the Bhagavad Gita by Lord Krishna.

the Lord, made him subject his own son to extreme ordeals. His anger was the cause of his destruction.

Christ too was a victim of envy, but His message of love to devotees was to spread compassion and proclaim their oneness and not diversity. He declared Himself as the *Messenger of God* and again said ***I and my Father are one.*** Similarly Baba gives a message to all saying:[45]

Life is a ***game*** *play it.*
Life is a **dream** *realize it*
Life is **love** *enjoy it*
Life is a **challenge** meet it

The messages of Buddha, Muhammed, Guru Nanak and others have all spread love, brotherhood and oneness from time to time. Unity can only come when people live in harmony, without giving room for conflict, discord or unrest. A life lived with love undoubtedly brings peace and joy.

Today, man resorts to all types of craftiness, lies, tricks, deceit in his day-to-day interactions with people in order to buy peace with them and avoid being scolded or assaulted for wrong doing. Does that bring peace? No, that is why people are perpetually haunted by fear of something or the other. Freedom from fear can only be developed by firm faith in God who then showers His grace on us to make us happy, content and peaceful.

Devotion is not a business, so only offer to God if you want nothing in return. God needs nothing from us as He has given us all, even the divinity which is our very breath of life, just cherish it with full faith.

At present, wherever one turns there is conflict, even in the Middle East which is the birthplace of three religions – Judaism, Christianity and Islam. If we tell people that the only way to resolve conflict is by following the path of love and peace, we would be called foolish. **Do you really believe that love can solve the problems of warring individuals, families, communities, religions and nations?** would be the scoffing question. Yes, love can solve the problems, because violence in word and

---

45 *Sanathana Sarathi,* Vol. 41, No.9, Sept. 98.

action is an animal trait not a human one, the latter has been given a mind and intellect to discriminate between right and wrong and love and peace is a matter of right thinking.

During the Second World War, millions of people were killed, but today there is a greater understanding of love and peace, and therefore more and more warring parties and nations are resolving problems through negotiations and arbitration. Russia and America are no longer enemies, and have considerably reduced their nuclear arsenal, a situation which could not be imagined during the cold war days.

Sai Baba has already indicated that we are entering the golden age by speaking of a:

> ***spiritual revolution more powerful and pervasive than any that man has undergone so far – not political, economic, scientific or technological, but more basic...(that will) sharpen the inner vision of man so that he can see the Atmic reality. Its impact will surely envelop and enrich all human communities and transform mankind into a stream of seekers flowing smoothly into the limitless sea of Divinity.***[46]

He has also said that:

> ***Love transcends everything going beyond caste, colour, creed, race, religion, gender, age and everything.***

One-day, human values will be taught in the Middle East too. While these are not related to any particular religion they are already in the sacred texts of all religions including the Quran. Love has also been discovered in practice through the path of Sufism which resonates equally in other religions too, and can be equated to Bhakti yoga. However, it is of no use if one simply worships the name of God, without any attempt to cultivate love, peace, fortitude, equanimity and bliss in the mind and heart. Narasimha Murthy[47] has put this beautifully, saying:

Look back and ***Thank*** *God*
Look ahead and ***Trust*** *God*
Look within and ***See*** *God.*

---

46 *Sanathana Sarathi,* Vol.49 No.8, Aug. 2006, p. 244-249.

47 *Sanathana Sarathi,* June 2006, p.173.

To which an ardent devotee has added:

*Look around and **Serve** God.*

Thus:

*Living **with** God is education*
*Living **for** Him is devotion*
*Living **in** Him is spirituality.*

Today's youth is seeking a certain clarity in its thought processes, and spirituality provides just that. A number of examples of young professionals and students in metros are spending their weekends doing social service, yoga, meditation, reiki healing, visiting temples and so on, instead of their usual partying.[48]

This change in direction is probably due to the physical, mental and emotional traumas they are being subjected to by events like riots, blasts, tsunamis and earthquakes, in addition to the pressurizing work situations which they find difficult to cope with. The media too, has played an important role in bringing messages, yoga and spiritual discourses to their doorsteps, all in a language they can understand and identify with.

The youth are now gradually turning their minds and thoughts from the *pleasant* or pleasurable to the *good.* Those who choose the pleasant become passionate towards it and gradually get driven to immoral and unethical means to achieve their goals. Whereas, those who choose the good, though not pleasant initially, has the foundations of high morals and ethics. This brings great achievements and contentment, becoming ultimately pleasant. As Swami Chinmayananda puts it:

> ***Every moment man has the freedom to start a new life. For this, first the right goal needs to be chosen and secondly one needs to be heroic and large hearted enough to live up to the chosen goal.***

The past can be reversed only by intelligent, well planned and continuous efforts put into the present for which many sacrifices will be needed. It is the youth of our great country that can plan intelligently in

---

[48] Times News Network, Times Life, August 6, 2006, p. 3.

the knowledge world of today, and put in consistent effort to build a better and not a sadder future than the present.

A community, society and nation can be safe, secure and happy only when its people are mutually helpful and bound together in sincere service. Every generation needs education and training in intelligent cooperation and service, or else the world has to face confusion, chaos and terror.

Way to Peace

The only way to peace is to unite all of humanity through a religion of Love, which is the only one language of the heart of mankind. B.R.Ambedkar once said:

> ***The basic idea underlying religion is to create an atmosphere for the spiritual development of the individual.***

There are basically two paths leading to oneness, one is that of *acceptance* and the other is *recognition*. Albert Einstein expressed similar views by saying that the two ways in which to live life are one, ***as though nothing is a miracle*** and the other, ***as though everything is a miracle.***

Acceptance

This path involves extending goodwill to all in every direction, embracing all as part of the harmonious oneness of nature or creation.

Recognition

This involves recognizing that everything around is an illusion. The two paths stand opposed but ultimately reach one, to the spontaneous awareness of the all-pervading Oneness.

Swami Sukhabodhananda in a lecture, told the story of a rich man who lost his wealth, but when asked questions about it replied:[49]

> ***All the wealth I had was a loan from the Lord. I was only a trustee.... He has the right to take it whenever He wants.***

---

[49] Amit Bhattacharya, Times Nation, Times of India, October 5, 2006.

The same has been reflected in the *Sukhmani Sahib* in different words, where the idea expressed is:

> ***God has given us ten treasures, but if He takes away even one, we begin to lament. What would we do if he took away all of them?***

So, real wealth is love, devotion and purity, because they help us to experience life differently. The problems we face humble us as also when bad things happen they make us better not bitter. God chastises those He wants to purify. The misunderstanding that He forsakes us only helps us to reflect more perfectly the divine image within us. He chooses challenges for us only according to what we can handle.

Right action, true knowledge and genuine love are the only ways to freedom as Gerard K. O'Neill advised :

> ***First guard the freedom of ideas at all costs,(and then) be alert that dictators have always played on the natural human tendency to blame others and over simplify. Don't regard yourself as a guardian of freedom unless you respect and preserve the rights of people you disagree with to free, public, unhampered expression.***

Even Abraham Lincoln a former US president had proclaimed that *those who deny freedom to others deserve it not for themselves.*

Therefore, the virtue to adopt is patience to last out the storms and trials that come our way, through faith and love, even though new controversies may prop up about God from time to time. Today questions like the gender of God is being answered by the highest church on the globe.[51] It is so hilarious, because who can think of divinity as having form first and then stoop to mental levels of even thinking about gender.

Certainly not in India, where everything and everyone is considered as God with or without form. Mothers have always been revered for their virtues, in all the scriptural texts, rituals and folklore. Even with form we have been guided by the Divine Mother, Holy Mother, Anandmayi Ma and others from time to time representing different religious orders. The five pillars of peace as taught by our great sages and avatars are *Sathya, Dharma, Shanti, Prema and Ahimsa.*

The real choice lies with each one of us to decide on a *Way to Peace* that is suitable for us in modern India, learning from our age-old traditions and finding newer ways of achieving the goal by sharing with others their traditions and adopting what best gives us all peace. Here the Sanskrit *shloka* comes to mind ***Loka samastha sukhino bhavantu*** which translates to *may everyone in the world be happy.*

Peace is thus, not only the absence of war, but is a virtue, a mental state, a disposition for confidence and justice.

RECIPES

Recipes carrying nutritional information have been provided for fasting and feasting occasions, along with their nutritional values to guide the user. The recipes are followed by some guidelines for planning balanced meals, so that special days can be enjoyed without detrimental effects on health and well being. This section covers:

- ❒ Recipes for Fasting Feasting
- ❒ Recipes for Feasting
- ❒ Menu Ideas

RECIPES FOR FASTING

13 Chapter

There are a variety of fasts or *vrats* followed in different regions and under different religious rituals which have their own variations and restrictions. *Vrat* basically means a restricted mode of eating, wherein one is permitted to eat only certain number of food items, and that too at restricted times.

There are some fasts like *Santoshi maa ka vrat* where no sour item can be used, like lemon, curds, tamarind, and so on. The fast is followed by consuming only *saboodana khichidi* once through the day, along with tea or coffee. Other restricted items are all grains, cereals, and their products including flours. Spices like red chilli powder, *garam masala*, etc. are also avoided in certain fasts. Then there are those in which salt is not permitted in any item consumed if at all.

Another version is the most restricted fast of the Jains, where they can only drink boiled water, that too after sunrise and before sunset. Nothing else is allowed during the day and night. Extreme followers do not even brush their teeth with toothpaste, or take medicines of any kind.

Navratras is that time of the year when food and beverage managers are quite worried about how to promote sales. For, with the navratras in force and the devout keeping fasts and remaining off non-vegetarian food for 8 or 9 days, there is a dramatic drop in sales. Most hoteliers have now worked their way around this problem and offer food that has no onions and garlic and is pure vegetarian. This works like magic as those businessmen who would normally avoid going out for a meal, can now actually take out a business partner and eat a hearty meal without flouting any religious norm.

In this section, there are various types of recipes which can be prepared and consumed on fast days within the norms of fasting restrictions for each fast. Some of the non-cereal items used are sago, waterchestnut flour, fruit, potato, sweet potato, milk and milk products. Potato wafers, fries, banana chips, jaggery, peanuts and their *chikkis* and other preparations are all allowed. Lemon, or other juices can be consumed during fasts. Recipes of snacks and some meal items only have been given in this chapter. The idea was to include certain substitute foods which could be used in recipes in place of those avoided on fast days. In case of partial fasting some ideas have been given to help the user in planning meals.

The shelf life of the dishes is not given for any recipe, since they are required to be prepared and eaten fresh. Recipes are provided along with the number of servings it prepares and the size of each serving. The essential nutritional information per serving is also provided to guide the user. The abbreviations used in the recipes are : g-gram; t-teaspoon; T-tablespoon; ml-millilitre.

1. KOOTU CAKE

The Navratra meal comprises of strictly vegetarian food with no onion or garlic. Select items of non-cereal foods are permitted also called *Phal-ahaari-khana*. Manufactured salt is not permitted but natural *sendha namak* or rock salt is used in food preparation. The only spices used are red chillies, cumin and turmeric along with fresh herbs like coriander, green chillies and ginger which are moderately used for flavouring. Ideally *ghee* or clarified butter is the cooking medium. The meals eaten during these days are made of special grains, and only certain vegetables and spices are permitted. The breads are made of either *singhara ka atta*, that is, dried waterchestnut flour or of *kootu ka atta* or buckwheat flour.

Ingredients	Amount
Kootu flour	120 g
Butter (without salt)	60 g
Castor sugar	90 g
Milk powder	60 g
Milk	150 ml
Baking powder	5 g (1t)
Sodium bicarbonate (cooking soda)	¼ t
Salt	a pinch
Cardamom powder	½ t

Method

1. Mix salt, soda, baking powder with kootu flour and sieve it.
2. Cream the butter and sugar in a bowl till light and fluffy.
3. Mix milk powder into the above creamed mixture.
4. Add flour and liquid milk in small amounts mixing well with each addition. Add cardamom powder and mix well.
5. Pour the mixture into the prepared cake tin and bake in a moderate oven at 350° F for 30-35 minutes or till done (a tooth pick inserted into it comes out clean).
6. Remove from cake tin. Cool on a wire rack before cutting.

No. of servings : 8

Size of serving : 1/8th slice

Nutrients per serving

Energy (Kcal)	Protein (g)	Iron (mg)	Calcium (mg)	Fibre (g)
207	4.7	2.4	113	1.3

2. KOOTU IDLI

Ingredients	Amount
Kootu	50 g
Curd	75 g
Peanuts	15 g
Mustard seeds	¼ t
Green chilli	½ t chopped
Coriander leaves	a few
Oil	10 g (2t)
Salt	to taste
Sodium-bicarbonate	a pinch

Variation: *Singhara atta* or any other non-cereal flour can be used in place of ***kootu***. The nutrients however will be changed in the variation.

Method

1. Lightly fry kootu in 2.5g (½t) of oil.
2. Heat 5 g of the oil. Add mustard seeds. When they start spluttering, add the peanuts. Fry till golden brown. Add beaten curds, chopped green chillies and coriander leaves, salt and soda to kootu mixture. Mix well. Keep it aside for half an hour.
3. Smear the idli steamer with oil and steam spoonfuls of the above mixture in the idli steamer for 15 minutes.

No. of servings : 1

Size of serving : 3 idlis

Nutrients per serving

Energy (Kcal)	Protein (g)	Iron (mg)	Calcium (mg)	Fibre (g)
127	3.74	2.8	43	1.6

3. TIL LADOOS

Ingredients	Amount
Til seeds	50 g
Jaggery	50 g
Water	10 ml (2 t)

Method

1. Pick and roast *til* without discoloration.
2. Break jaggery into small pieces and add water. Heat on low fire to dissolve the jaggery. Once the jaggery dissolves increase the heat and cook.
3. Cook the syrup to softball stage i.e. when a drop of syrup is dropped in a bowl of cold water it forms a soft ball. It does not dissolve in the water.
4. Add til, remove from fire and shape quickly into smooth balls.

No of servings : 3

Size of serving : 2

Nutrients per serving

Energy (Kcal)	Protein (g)	Iron (mg)	Calcium (mg)	Fibre (g)
158	3.2	2	256	0

4. KOOTU BISCUITS

Ingredients	Amount
Kootu flour	50 g
Butter	30 g
Castor sugar	30 g (2 T)
Coconut powder	30 g
Baking powder	¼ t
Milk	to make the dough(approx 2t)

Variation: Singhara atta or any other non-cereal flour can be used in place of kootu. The nutrients however will be changed in the variation.

Method

1. Sieve the flour, salt and baking powder together.
2. Cream butter and sugar.
3. Add milk a little at a time to the creamed mixture.
4. If the mixture shows signs of curdling, a little flour may be added.

5. Add *ajwain* seeds.
6. Add flour and mix to a soft dough.
7. Roll out on a floured board into 1/4th inch thickness, cut into biscuits with cutter and pick each biscuit with a fork.
8. Place on a greased baking tray and bake in a moderate oven 177° C (350° F) till golden brown in colour.
9. Cool on a wire rack.

No. of servings : 12

Size of serving : 2

Nutrients per serving

Energy (Kcal)	Protein (g)	Iron (mg)	Calcium (mg)	Fibre (g)
353	3.7	5.1	67.5	3.1

5. SWEET POTATO HALWA

Lemon sherbet is had during the fast. This quenches thirst and gives energy too. The permitted foods during these 9 days are potatoes, sweet potatoes (*shakarkandi*), pumpkin, and cucumber, fruits, milk and milk products. All preparations are made strictly without the addition of any garlic or onions.

Ingredients	Amount
Sweet potatoes	125 g
Sugar	10 g
Ghee	15 g
Green cardamom	1
Almonds	2
Raisins	4 - 5

Variation: potatoes and fresh water chestnuts can be used in place of sweet potatoes. The nutrients however will be changed in the variation.

Method

1. Wash and boil potatoes.
2. Peel and mash them properly.

3. Heat ghee, add mashed potatoes and cook with constant stirring till brown.
4. Add sugar and continue stirring till the mixture leaves the sides of the *karahi*.
4. Add sugar and continue stirring till the mixture leaves the sides of the *karahi*.
5. Add raisins and cardamom powder. Mix in half of the chopped nuts.
6. Remove the *halwa* in a plate. Garnish with rest of the chopped nuts and serve.

No. of servings : 1

Size of serving : 1 bowl

Nutrients per serving

Energy (Kcal)	Protein (g)	Iron (mg)	Calcium (mg)	Fibre (g)
344	2.0	0.51	69	1.03

6. SINGHARA ATTA HALWA

Ingredients	Amount
Singhara atta	25 g
Ghee	20 g
Sugar	20 g
Water	90 ml
Blanched almonds	3
Raisins	6
Green cardamom	1

Variation: Kootu atta or any other non cereal flour can be used in place of singhara atta. The nutrients however will be changed in the variation.

Method

1. Add water and sugar in a sauce pan and bring to boil to make syrup of sugar and water.

2. Heat ghee in a *karahi.*
3. Add singhara atta and fry with constant stirring on a slow fire.
4. Add syrup to fried *atta* being cooked on slow fire. Keep cooking with constant stirring till all the syrup is absorbed and *halwa* starts leaving the sides of the *karahi.*
5. Garnish with powdered cardamom and chopped nuts.

No. of servings : 1

Size of serving: 1 bowl

Nutrients per serving

Energy (Kcal)	Protein (g)	Iron (mg)	Calcium (mg)	Fibre (g)
368	4.0	0.9	26	0.04

7. KOOTU PARANTHA

Ingredients	Amount
Kootu flour	80 g
Potato	50 g
Water	enough to make dough (30 ml approx)
Salt/*sendha namak*	to taste
Dry kootu flour for rolling	a little
Ghee	10 g (2 t)

Variation: Singhara atta or any other non-cereal flour can be used in place of kootu. The nutrients however will be changed in the variation.

Method

1. Wash, boil, peel and mash the potatoes.
2. Mix the potatoes, flour and salt together and make a dough using water. This flour is not like the normal flour so do not add too much of water.
3. Keep the dough covered for about half an hour and then knead again.
4. Divide the dough into three balls dusting with atta if it sticks.
5. Roll each ball into small round. You will have to roll by patting

with hand. If you want to roll with a rolling pin, increase the proportion of potatoes.

6. Heat *tawa*. Cook the *parantha* on a hot *tawa*.
7. When one side is lightly cooked, turn it over and cook the entire side lightly.
8. Now apply fat and fry paranthas on both sides till golden brown in colour.

No. of servings : 3

Size of serving : 1

Nutrients per serving

Energy (Kcal)	Protein (g)	Iron (mg)	Calcium (mg)	Fibre (g)
397	9.04	12.6	56	7.2

8. SABU DANA VADA

Ingredients	Amount
Potatoes	75 g
Sago *(Sabu dana)*	30 g
Peanuts	20 g
Green chillies	1
Coriander leaves	few
Salt	to taste
Red chilli powder (optional)	¼ t
Amchur powder (optional)	¼ t
Garam masala	¼ t
Fat	for frying

Method

1. Boil, peel and mash the potatoes.
2. Wash and soak the sago for 5-7 minutes in water.
3. Roast the peanuts, remove skin and grind coarsely.
4. Wash and chop green chillies and coriander leaves.
5. Squeeze out water from soaked sago. Mix soaked sago, roasted

peanuts, green chillis, coriander leaves, salt, red chilli powder, garam masala and amchur with potato mixture.

6. Divide the whole mixture into 2 balls and shape them into *vadas*.
7. Deep fry in hot fat till golden brown.
8. Serve hot with *chutney* or sauce.

No. of servings : 1

Size of serving: 2 vadas

Nutrients per serving

Energy (Kcal)	Protein (g)	Iron (mg)	Calcium (mg)	Fibre (g)
381	6.3	1.3	29	0.9

9. SPECIAL VRAT NAMKEEN

Ingredients	Amount
Sago	50 g
Peanuts	30 g
Makhane	30 g
Ghee	25 g
Sugar	25 g
Chopped coconut	40 g
Mint leaves	a few
Salt	¼ t

Method

1. Pick and clean the makhane and peanuts. Heat ghee in a *kadhai* (wok). Fry sago in ghee till golden brown in colour.
2. Then fry peanuts and *makhane* separately
3. Then fry coconut pieces and mint leaves.
4. Mix fried sago, *makhane*, peanuts and coconut pieces and mint leaves. Add rock salt, and sugar.
5. Serve immediately or cool to room temperature, immediately put in an air tight jar/container, lest they get soggy.

No. of servings : 4-5

Size of serving : 1 small bowl.

Nutrients per serving

Energy (Kcal)	Protein (g)	Iron (mg)	Calcium (mg)	Fibre (g)
260	3.3	1.2	50	0.9

10. KOOTU AALLO TIKKI

Ingredients	Amount
Potatoes	75 g
Kootu flour	50 g
Green chilli	1
Salt	to taste
Red chilli powder (optional)	¼ t
Amchur powder (optional)	¼ t
Garam masala (optional)	a pinch
Fat	for frying

Variation: Singhara atta or any other non-cereal flour can be used in place of kootu. The nutrients however will be changed in the variation.

Method

1. Boil, peel and mash potatoes.
2. Add kootu flour, green chillies, and all the spices. Mix well.
3. Divide the mixture into equal parts and shape into cutlets.
4. Grease griddle with a little oil, heat. Place cutlets, allow to cook on low flame till golden.
5. Flip and cook other side, drizzling more oil if required.
6. Serve hot.

No. of servings : 1

Size of serving : 2 *tikkis*

Nutrients per serving

Energy (Kcal)	Protein (g)	Iron (mg)	Calcium (mg)	Fibre (g)
324	6.3	18.1	40	4.6

11. RAW BANANA TIKKI

Jains are basically vegetarians with further taboos on their food, which bars the intake of some vegetables, especially onions, garlic, potato, and root vegetables. But the degree and strictness to which it is followed, depends on individuals, and their family eating habits. Many convenient substitutes are there to enable one to make similar dishes, and therefore enjoy the goodness of the recipes. For example, raw bananas can be used as potato for all practical purposes, custard in milk could be used in place of egg and so on. If *amchur* is a taboo then lemon juice could be used as a substitute.

Ingredients	Amount
Raw banana	75 g
Kootu flour	50 g
Green chilli	1-2
Salt	2 g
Red chilli powder (optional)	2 g
Amchur powder (optional)	2 g
Garam masala (optional)	1 g
Fat	for frying

Variation: Singhara atta or any other non-cereal flour can be used in place of kootu. The nutrients however will be changed in the variation.

Method

1. Boil, peel and mash raw banana.
2. Add kootu flour, green chillies and all the spices. Mix well.
3. Divide the mixture into two equal parts and shape into cutlets.
4. Fry. Drain on brown paper.

No. of servings : 1

Size of serving : 2

Nutrients per serving

Energy (Kcal)	Protein (g)	Iron (mg)	Calcium (mg)	Fibre (g)
339	6.1	8.0	45	4.6

12. SABU DANA KHEER

Ingredients	Amount
Milk	250 ml
Sago (Sabudana)	10g
Water	½ cup
Sugar	30 g
Green cardamom	1
Almond	2
Raisins	4-5

Variation: *Samak ke chawal* or any other non-cereal can be used in place of sago. The nutrients however will be changed in the variation.

Method

1. Pick, wash and soak the sago in half cup of water for half an hour.
2. Boil the sago in the same water till it is tender.
3. Add milk and simmer on slow fire for 15-20 minutes with frequent stirring.
4. When it is of creamy consistency, add sugar and stir till it is dissolved.
5. Cook so that the mixture becomes creamy again.
6. Remove from fire, add crushed green cardamom seeds.
7. Serve hot or cold garnished with shredded almonds and raisins.

No. of servings : 1

Size of serving : 1 bowl.

Nutrients per serving

Energy (Kcal)	Protein (g)	Iron (mg)	Calcium (mg)	Fibre (g)
462	8.4	0.8	307	0.03

13. SABU DANA KHICHDI

Ingredients	Amount
Potatoes	75 g
Sago	30 g
Peanuts	20 g
Green chilli	1
Coriander leaves	a few
Salt	to taste
Red chilli powder (optional)	a pinch
Amchur powder (optional)	a pinch
Garam masala (optional)	a pinch
Fat	10g (2 t)
Sugar	5 g

Method

1. Boil, peel and mash the potatoes.
2. Pick, wash and soak the sago in half cup of water for half an hour.
3. Boil the sago in the same water till it is tender.
4. Heat ghee in a pan. Add peanuts. Fry them a little.
5. When peanuts turn brownish-red in colour, add cumin seeds and fry for a while.
6. Add the sago and then the mashed potatoes. Add all the spices and sugar. Mix well. Let it cook for about a minute.
7. Serve hot garnished with chopped coriander.

No. of servings : 1

Size of serving : 1 bowl.

Nutrients per serving

Energy (Kcal)	Protein (g)	Iron (mg)	Calcium (mg)	Fibre (g)
401	6.3	1.3	29	0.9

14. SINGHARA ATTA PURI

Ingredients	Amount
Potatoes	30 g
Singhara atta	80 g
Melted fat	10 g (2 t)
Salt	to taste
Water	to knead a dough
Fat	for frying

Variation: Kootu atta or any other non-cereal flour can be used in place of singhara atta. The nutrients however will be changed in the variation.

Method

1. Boil, peel and mash the potatoes.
2. Mix singhara atta with salt.
3. Rub the melted fat in the flour thouroughly.
4. Mix the mashed potatoes to the mixture and add the seasoning.
5. Make firm dough using little water. This flour is not like the normal flour so do not add too much of water.
6. Divide the dough into 5–6 small balls.
7. Pat each ball into a thin round using oil in the palm.
8. Heat fat in a *karahi* till moderately hot and fry each puri on both sides by pressing the sides of the *puri* and the perforated spoon till puffed up and golden brown.
9. Serve hot with curd.

No. of servings : 2

Size of serving : 3 *puris.*

Nutrients per serving

Energy (Kcal)	Protein (g)	Iron (mg)	Calcium (mg)	Fibre (g)
237	5.6	1.0	29.5	0.1

15. SIGHARA ATTA SWEET PURI

Ingredients	Amount
Singhara atta	80 g
Potatoes	30 g
Melted fat	10 g (2 t)
Water	to knead a dough
Fat	for frying
For syrup	
Sugar	200 g
Water	125 ml
Milk	1 t (for cleaning the syrup)

Variation: Kootu atta or any other non-cereal flour can be used in place of Singhara atta. The nutrients however will be changed in the variation.

Method

1. Make the puris as explained in the previous recipe and then proceed.
2. Add sugar to water. Bring to boil. Clean the syrup with milk. Cook the syrup for a few minutes and let it cool.
3. Soak the puris in the sugar syrup. Allow to soak for about 10 minutes. Serve hot.

No. of servings : 2

Size of serving : 3 puris.

Nutrients per serving

Energy (Kcal)	Protein (g)	Iron (mg)	Calcium (mg)	Fibre (g)
637	5.6	1.0	29.5	0.1

16. AALOO CHAT

Ingredients	Amount
Potatoes	100 g
Green chilli	½

Coriander leaves	a few
Salt	to taste
Red chilli powder (optional)	a pinch
Amchur powder (optional)	a pinch
Garam masala (optional)	a pinch
Lemon	1
Fat	for frying

Variation: Colocasia or water chestnuts can be used in place of potatoes. The nutrients however will be changed in the variation.

Method

1. Boil, peel and chop the potatoes into cubes.
2. Fry these until golden brown.
3. Add green chilli, all the seasonings. Mix well.
4. Serve hot garnished with chopped coriander leaves.

No. of servings : 1

Size of serving : 1 plate.

Nutrients per serving

Energy (Kcal)	Protein (g)	Iron (mg)	Calcium (mg)	Fibre (g)
187	1.6	0.5	10	0.4

17. PHIRNI

Ingredients	Amount
Milk	250 g (1 cup)
Samak ke chawal	10 g (2 t)
Sugar	20 g
Almonds	2
Kewra essence or	1 drop or
Green cardamom	1

Method

1. Soak the rice for 1-2 hours.
2. Grind the rice with little cold milk in the liquidiser. Add rest of the milk (cold).

3. Cook the milk and rice mixture with constant stirring till it is of creamy consistency.
4. Add sugar and give one boil. Remove from fire. Add a drop of essence.
5. Put the mixture in small glass bowl and leave in the fridge to set.
6. Serve garnished with shredded almonds.

No. of servings : 1

Size of serving : 1 bowl.

Nutrients per serving

Energy (Kcal)	Protein (g)	Iron (mg)	Calcium (mg)	Fibre (g)
295	9.1	0.7	306	0.1

18. PANEER KHEER

Ingredients	Amount
Milk	250 g
Paneer	25 g
Sugar	15 g
Almond	1
Raisins	4-5
Kewra essence	1 drop or
Green cardamom	1

Method

1. Cut the paneer into very small cubes and cook in milk on slow fire stirring occasionally till the *kheer* thickens.
2. Add sugar and give one boil.
3. Remove from fire and add essence. Serve cold garnished with shredded almond and raisins.

No. of servings : 1

Size of serving : 1 bowl

Nutrients per serving

Energy (Kcal)	Protein (g)	Iron (mg)	Calcium (mg)	Fibre (g)
313	11.6	0.7	426	.02

19. PUMPKIN HALWA

Ingredients	Amount
Pumpkin (yellow)	100 g
Sugar	35 g
Coconut powder	20 g
Ghee	20 g
Almonds	2
Raisins	4-5
Green cardamom	1

Method

1. Wash, peel and grate the pumpkin.
2. Heat ghee and add cardamom seeds. Fry for a while and add grated pumpkin.
3. Cook for two minutes. Then add 2-3 spoons of water and cook till the pumpkin is tender.
4. Add sugar and continue cooking till it thickens. Add coconut powder. Mix well and cook for a while. Remove the *halwa* in a plate and serve garnished with chopped nuts.

No. of servings : 1

Size of serving : 1 bowl

Nutrients per serving

Energy (Kcal)	Protein (g)	Iron (mg)	Calcium (mg)	Fibre (g)
482	3.2	2.3	96.3	2.1

20. PLAIN BURFI

Ingredients	Amount
Khoya	100 g
Castor sugar	35 g
Milk	2 t
Almonds	2
Fat	for greasing

Method

1. Grate or mash the khoya well.
2. Heat *khoya* in a *karahi* with 10 ml of milk and cook for a few minutes on slow fire with continuous stirring.
3. Remove from fire and add castor sugar and mix.
4. Cook it again with continuous stirring on slow fire till the mixture leaves the sides of the pan.
5. Remove from fire and mix in chopped nuts.
6. Spread on a greased *thali* and allow to cool. Cut into *burfi* and serve.

No. of serving : 2

Size of serving : 2 *burfis*.

Nutrients per serving

Energy (Kcal)	Protein (g)	Iron (mg)	Calcium (mg)	Fibre (g)
289	7.8	3.4	350	0.01

21. COCONUT BURFI

Ingredients	Amount
Khoya	100 g
Coconut powder	50 g
Castor sugar	50 g
Kewra essence / Green cardamom	1 drop/1
Colour (optional)	few drops
Fat	for greasing

Method

1. Grate or mash the *khoya* well.
2. Cook it on slow fire for a few minutes with constant stirring.
3. Remove from fire and add castor sugar and mix.
4. Cook it again on slow heat and add desiccated coconut.
5. Continue cooking with constant stirring till the mixture leaves the sides of the pan. Remove from fire.
6. Add essence and colour and mix well.

7. Spread the mixture evenly on greased plate.
8. Cut into pieces when cold and set.

No. of servings : 2

Size of serving : 2

Nutrients per serving

Energy (Kcal)	Protein (g)	Iron (mg)	Calcium (mg)	Fibre (g)
472	9.1	5.5	445	0.4

22. GHIA BURFI

Ingredients	Amount
Khoya	100 g
Ghia	100 g
Sugar	50 g
Ghee	1t
Water	1½ t
Kewra essence	1-2 drops
or	
Green cardamom	1

Method

1. Peel, wash and grate the *ghia*.
2. Heat fat, add grated *ghia* and fry a little. Add water and cook covered till tender.
3. Add sugar and cook with constant stirring till the mixture thickens.
4. Grate *khoya* and add to *ghia* mixture and mix well. Cook till the mixture leaves the sides of the pan.
5. Remove from fire and add essence or cardamom.
6. Spread over greased *thali* and cut into pieces when set.

No. of servings : 2

Size of serving : 2

Nutrients per serving

Energy (Kcal)	Protein (g)	Iron (mg)	Calcium (mg)	Fibre (g)
334	7.4	3.2	338	0.3

23. KOOTU BURFI

Ingredients	Amount
Kootu flour	50 g
Sugar	35 g
Khoya	15 g
Ghee	25 g (+ for greasing)
Green cardamom	1-2
Water	1½ t

Variation: Singhara atta or any other non-cereal flour can be used in place of kootu. The nutrients however will be changed in the variation.

Method

1. Sift the kootu flour.
2. Fry the flour in ghee over slow heat for 3-4 minutes.
3. Make sugar syrup of two-thread consistency using sugar and water.
4. Add the sugar syrup to kootu flour and mix in grated *khoya* and crushed cardamom. Cook the mixture till it leaves the sides of the pan.
5. Spread the mixture on a greased *thali.*
6. Cut it into pieces and serve.

No. of servings : 2

Size of serving : 2

Nutrients per serving

Energy (Kcal)	Protein (g)	Iron (mg)	Calcium (mg)	Fibre (g)
294	4.1	3.9	73	2.2

24. KAJU BURFI

Ingredients	Amount
Kaju (cashewnuts)	50 g
Sugar	50 g
Kewra essence	few drops
Ghee	for greasing
Water	2 T (30 ml)

Method

1. Grind *kaju* to a very fine powder.
2. Add 30 ml water to the sugar and cook till the syrup is of two-thread consistency.
3. Add powdered *kaju* and essence. Mix well and remove from fire.
4. Apply a little fat on the hands and make a ball of the above mixture.
5. Roll it immediately on a greased rolling board to about 1/6th inch thickness.
6. Cut into diamond shape *burfis*.

No. of serving : 2

Size of serving : 3

Nutrients per serving

Energy (Kcal)	Protein (g)	Iron (mg)	Calcium (mg)	Fibre (g)
249	5.3	1.5	16	0.4

25. PEANUT BURFI

Ingredients	Amount
Peanut	50 g
Sugar	50 g
Kewra essence	few drops
Ghee	for greasing

Method

1. Grind peanuts to a very fine powder.
2. Add 30 ml water to the sugar and cook till the syrup is of two-thread consistency.
3. Add powdered peanuts and essence. Mix well and remove from fire.
4. Apply a little fat on the hands and make a ball of the above mixture.
5. Roll it immediately on a greased rolling board to about 1/6th inch thickness.
6. Cut into diamond shape *burfis*.

No. of serving : 2

Size of serving : 3

Nutrients per serving

Energy (Kcal)	Protein (g)	Iron (mg)	Calcium (mg)	Fibre (g)
161	4.2	0.4	15	0.7

26. KOOTU FLOUR PAKORAS

Ingredients	Amount
Kootu Atta	30g
Salt/rock salt	1/2 t
Oil	for frying
Water	enough to make batter
Paneer	50 g
Garam masala (optional)	1/8 t
Carom seeds (optional)	a few grains

Variation: Singhara atta or any other non-cereal flour can be used in place of kootu. Potato, pumpkin or water chestnuts can also be used in place of *paneer*. The nutrients however will be changed in the variation.

Method

1. Mix the flour, salt, garam masala and carom seeds. Then slowly add water to make a smooth paste.
2. Heat oil in a deep pan (*kadai*).
3. Cut the *paneer* into slices.
4. Dip each piece into the batter and deep-fry a few of them at a time on moderate heat.
5. Drain on brown paper. Sprinkle with some *chaat masala* or *amchur* powder and serve immediately.

No. of serving : 1

Size of serving : 6

Nutrients per serving

Energy (Kcal)	Protein (g)	Iron (mg)	Calcium (mg)	Fibre (g)
361	15.1	5.7	397	2.6

27. SPICY SHAKARKANDI (SWEET POTATOES)

Ingredients	Amount
Sweet potatoes	100 g
Ghee	1 t
Jeera	¼ t
Salt	¼ t
Pepper	¼ t
Castor sugar	¼ t
Lemon	1
Coriander leaves	a few
Green chillies	1

Method

1. Boil, peel and cube the sweet potatoes.
2. Heat ghee in a small pan. Add jeera. When jeera turns golden, add green chillies. Fry for 1-2 minutes.
3. Add sweet potato, salt and pepper. Fry for 1-2 minutes. Add lemon juice. Mix well and then add sugar.
4. Garnish with coriander leaves and serve hot.

No. of serving : 1

Size of serving : 1 small bowl

Nutrients per serving

Energy (Kcal)	Protein (g)	Iron (mg)	Calcium (mg)	Fibre (g)
215	1.2	0.2	46	0.8

28. SAMAK KE CHAWAL KHICHDI

Ingredients	Amount
Samak ke chaawal, washed	80 gms
Ghee	10 g (2 t)
Zeera	1 t
Laung	2
Daalchini	tiny piece

(Contd...)

Choti elaichi	1
Potato, diced	75 g
Sendha namak	to taste
Chilli powder (optional)	¼ t
Water	160 ml
Coriander leaves	few

Method

1. Heat ghee, add *zeera*, *laung*, *elaichi* and *daalchini*. When slightly coloured, add potato and rice. Stir-fry till they look a bit fried.
2. Add salt, chilli powder and water, bring to a boil. Lower the flame and simmer, covered, for about 15 minutes or till cooked thorough and the water is absorbed.
3. Serve hot garnished with *hara dhania*.

No. of serving : 1

Size of serving :1 full plate.

Nutrients per serving

Energy (Kcal)	Protein (g)	Iron (mg)	Calcium (mg)	Fibre (g)
435	6.6	1.2	45	0.5

29. KULFI

Ingredients	Amount
Milk	350 ml (1½ cup)
Sugar	20 g / 4 t
Almonds	2
Pistachio	2
Kewra essence / Cardamom	a few drops / 2

Variation: Mango, strawberries or other fruits can be used in the recipe. The nutrients however will be changed in the variation.

Method

1. Clean a *kulfi* mould with soap and boiling water.

2. Boil the milk in a *karahi* till it is less than half the volume. Stir occasionally.
3. Mix the sugar and stir till thoroughly dissolved.
4. Remove from heat and cool.
5. Add the finely chopped nuts and essence.
6. Fill the kulfi mould, screw top carefully and freeze in an upright position (about 3 hrs)
7. When frozen serve.

No. of serving : 1

Size of serving :1 mould.

Nutrients per serving

Energy (Kcal)	Protein (g)	Iron (mg)	Calcium (mg)	Fibre (g)
314	11.2	0.7	420	0

30. CHENNA MURKI

Ingredients	Amount
Paneer	50 g
Sugar	35 g / 2 T
Water	30 ml / 2 T
Milk	5 ml / 1 t
Kewra essence (optional)	2 drops

Method

1. Cut the *paneer* into cubes.
2. In a small *karahi* dissolve the sugar in the water and heat. When the sugar dissolves, bring to a boil and to clean the syrup add diluted milk and boil for 2 minutes. Strain through a muslin cloth on a steel strainer.
3. Add the paneer cubes to the syrup and cook on medium heat. To prevent caramelization of sugar on the sides wipe the sides with a wet cloth. Continue to cook till soft ball stage i.e. when a ball of the syrup is dropped in a bowl of water, it does not dissolve and forms a soft ball.

4. Remove the *karahi* from heat when syrup is of a thick consistency. Continue to stir lightly to uniformly coat the cubes till the mixture cools completely.

No. of serving : 1

Size of serving : 10 pieces

Nutrients per serving

Energy (Kcal)	Protein (g)	Iron (mg)	Calcium (mg)	Fibre (g)
275	9.3	0	110	0

31. THANDAI

Thandai is a very popular drink traditionally prepared as an offering to Lord Shiva during the festival of Mahashivratri.

Ingredients	Amount
Full cream milk	1 litre
Castor sugar	½ cup
Peppercorns	10 - 12
Saffron	a few strands
Blend together:	
Almonds (Soaked and peeled)	¼ cup
Khus khus	30 g/2 T
Saunf	30 g/2 T
Cardamom powder	½ t
White peppercorns	20

Method

1. Boil the milk and allow it to cool completely. Keep aside.
2. Add the ground mixture and refrigerate for 3 to 4 hours.
3. Strain the mixture through a sieve, add the sugar, peppercorns and saffron and mix well
4. Serve chilled.

No. of serving : 6

Size of serving : 1 glass

Nutrients per serving

Energy (Kcal)	Protein (g)	Iron (mg)	Calcium (mg)	Fibre (g)
282	8.1	1.0	231	0.2

Thirty-one fasting recipes have been detailed with ingredients and methods of preparation giving size of serving and number of servings that each recipe produces, to guide the user to adjust with planned menus.

HATHEESING JAIN TEMPLE

SUN TEMPLE AT MODHERA

GREAT STUPA : THE OLDEST STONE STRUCTURE IN INDIA

Plate No. 1(a): Holy Places of India

THE SPECIAL NAVRATRI CELEBRATIONS, GANDHINAGAR

DANDIYA MASTI: DANCING TO THE BEAT

Plate No. 3: Navaratra Celebrations

KRISHNA

RADHA KRISHNA

AT VRINDAVAN: MAKING DRESSES FOR RADHA-KRISHNA IDOLS

Plate No. 4(a): Janamashtmi Celebrations

YASHODA-KRISHNA

DRESSED AS LORD KRISHNA A CHILD TRIES TO KNOCK DOWN AN EARTHEN POT CONTAINING BUTTER

Plate No. 4(b): Janamashtmi Celebrations—Raas Leela

GANESHA IDOLS

A DEVOTEE CARRIES LORD GANESHA

Plate No. 5(a): Ganesha Chaturthi

IMMERSION OF GANESHA IDOL

Plate No. 5(b): End of Ganesha Chaturthi Celebrations

RECIPES FOR FEASTING

14 Chapter

Feasting is an integral part of our culture and no feast is complete without food. This section presents a few mouth-watering delicacies consumed during feasting in India.

Traditionally, feasting has never been advocated by our sages after fasting, but certain disciplines regarding breaking of fasts were laid down after each type of fast, which has been discussed under each occasion in previous chapters. But, this has changed today.

Whatever the reason for feasting it usually starts with light beverages that range from lemonades, juices to wines and other hard drinks which are not within the purview of this book. Some recipes for snacks eaten during festivals and other feasting recipes are presented as samples along with their nutritive values since awareness of health and well being has increased in the knowledge society of today.

1. PEANUT BRITTLE

Brittle is a popular snack eaten during the harvest festival of Lohri.

Ingredients	Amount
Peanuts	40 g
Jaggery	60 g
Water	30 ml/ 2T
Ghee/oil	for greasing

Variation: Roasted *channa dal/ til/ murmura* can be used in place of peanuts. The nutrients however will be changed in the variation.

Method

1. Roast the peanuts, when cool, skin and crush them a little.
2. Grease a plate/marble surface and the rolling pin.
3. Break the jaggery into a *karahi*. Add water and heat on a low fire to dissolve the jaggery. Once the jaggery dissolves, increase the heat and boil the syrup vigorously and stir all the time.
4. Cook the syrup to hardball stage *i.e.* when a drop of syrup is dropped in a bowl of cold water, it forms a hard unmouldable ball. This ball when put in the mouth should be brittle and not stick to the jaws.
5. Immediately remove from heat and quickly stir in the peanuts.
6. Immediately pour on to the greased surface and spread evenly with the greased rolling pin. Mark into pieces and let it cool.
7. Cut into squares when sufficiently cool and hardened.
8. Store in a container lined with butter paper.

No. of servings : 2

Size of serving : 2 pieces

Nutrients per serving

Energy (Kcal)	Protein (g)	Iron (mg)	Calcium (mg)	Fibre (g)
229	5.2	1.3	44	0.9

2. SARKKARAI/SWEET PONGAL

It is a popular recipe cooked during the harvest festival of Pongal.

Ingredients	Amount
Rice	10 g
Condensed milk	½ tin
Jaggery	25 g
Cloves, powdered	1
Cardamom, powdered	1
Cashewnuts, chopped	5 g
Raisins	5 g
Water	50 ml

Method

1. Heat ghee in a pan, fry cashews and raisins till golden brown. Strain and keep aside.
2. In a separate pan, wash rice well and cook in water till soft. Add a little more water while cooking, if necessary.
3. When the rice is done and water almost evaporated, add jaggery and condensed milk and reduce the flame.
4. When almost dry, add cloves and cardamom powder and mix well. Serve hot with nuts and raisins.

No. of servings : 1

Size of serving : 1 bowl

Nutrients per serving

Energy (Kcal)	Protein (g)	Iron (mg)	Calcium (mg)	Fibre (g)
256	7.2	0.7	241	0.4

3. MODAK

Round sweets /dumplings of rice flour stuffed with dry fruits and coconut usually served as prasaad during Ganesh Chaturthi.

Ingredients	Amount
For the rice dough	
Rice flour	100 g
Water	200 ml
Oil	5 ml/1 t
For the stuffing	
Coconut, grated	80 g
Sugar	40 g
Dry fruits	20 g
Milk	20 ml

Method

For the Rice Dough

1. Boil the water and oil and remove from heat. To it add the rice flour, cover and allow it to cool. Later, knead well and keep aside.

For the Stuffing

1. Mix all the ingredients mentioned under stuffing except milk.
2. Put this mixture on a medium heat and cook stirring all the time.
3. Then add the milk, mixing well and remove off the heat once it is totally dry.

To Proceed

1. Make balls of the rice dough, make a small depression in the center and place the stuffing in the middle.
2. Now join the open edges together and give it a shape like a whole garlic.
3. Steam these modaks for 10 minutes, take off, cool and keep in airtight containers.

No. of servings : 2

Size of serving : 5

Nutrients per serving

Energy (Kcal)	Protein (g)	Iron (mg)	Calcium (mg)	Fibre (g)
610	8.3	4.2	200	2.9

PUJA CUISINE - SHASHTI

Durga Puja is the time for celebrations, of which delicious delicacies are always the part of this festive occasion. Shasthi is the first day of the five-day celebration. Some recipies to serve your family are presented.

4. LUCHI

Ingredients	Amount
Flour	80 g
Oil	1t + for frying
Salt	to taste
Warm water	to knead the flour

Method

1. Mix flour, 1t of oil and salt and knead into a soft dough with a warm water.
2. Make small balls. Flatten them into round *chappatis.*
3. Deep fry them.

No. of servings : 2

Size of serving : 2

Nutrients per serving

Energy (Kcal)	Protein (g)	Iron (mg)	Calcium (mg)	Fibre (g)
204	9.7	3.9	38	5.6

5. ALURDAM

Ingredients	Amount
Small-sized potatoes	100g
Mustard	½ t

(Contd...)

Curry leaves	a few
Tamarind	5 g
Green chillies	2
Salt	to taste
Ginger paste	5 g
Sugar	1 t
Oil	2 t

Method

1. Wash, boil and peel the potatoes.
2. Soak tamarind in a cup of hot water for 20 minutes.
3. Squeeze the tamarind and extract the pulp.
4. Heat oil in pan and fry ginger, mustard, curry leaves till brown.
5. Then add the boiled potatoes & fry for a minute or two.
6. Then add chillies, sugar & salt and add tamarind juice.
7. Stir and serve hot with luchi.

No. of servings : 1

Size of serving : 1 bowl

Nutrients per serving

Energy (Kcal)	Protein (g)	Iron (mg)	Calcium (mg)	Fibre (g)
210	1.7	0.7	11	0.5

6. CHOLAR DAL

Ingredients	Amount
Chholar dal	30 g
Oil	5 g
Cumin seeds	½ t
Ginger	5 g
Tejpatta	1
Green chillies	1
Grated coconut	10 g
Turmeric	1/6 t
Sugar	1t
Hing	a pinch

Method

1. Boil chholar dal in 1 cup of water.
2. Heat oil in pan, add *hing*, *jeera*, *tejpatta*, grated ginger, chopped chilles, grated coconut, salt, sugar, termeric and fry for sometime.
3. Pour the boiled dal in the pan.
4. Cook for sometime and serve hot.

No. of servings : 1

Size of serving : 1 bowl

Nutrients per serving

Energy (Kcal)	Protein (g)	Iron (mg)	Calcium (mg)	Fibre (g)
235	7.5	1.8	24	1.2

7. BEGUN BHAJA

Ingredients	Amount
Brinjal	100 g (2 medium)
Salt	to taste
Turmeric	a pinch
Mustard oil	for frying

Steps:

1. Cut brinjal into rounds or lengthwise.
2. Rub in turmeric and salt.
3. Deep fry till tender.
4. Serve hot

No. of servings : 1

Size of serving : 1 bowl

Nutrients per serving

Energy (Kcal)	Protein (g)	Iron (mg)	Calcium (mg)	Fibre (g)
114	1.4	0.4	18	1.3

8. PAYESH

Ingredients	Amount
Milk	250 ml (1 cup)
Sugar	20 g (4 t)
Rice	10 g
Raisins	5-7
Almonds	2-3
Cashewnuts	2

Steps:

1. Pick and wash the rice. Soak it in ½ cup water for half an hour.
2. Heat milk in a large pan. Add the soaked rice.
3. Simmer until the rice is cooked and the milk is reduced to 3 quarters its original volume.
4. Add sugar. Continue cooking until milk is reduced to half and thickens. Add the raisins, chopped almonds and cashew nuts.
5. Remove from heat. Cool and serve.

No. of servings : 1

Size of serving : 1 bowl

Nutrients per serving

Energy (Kcal)	Protein (g)	Iron (mg)	Calcium (mg)	Fibre (g)
256	7.2	0.7	241	0.4

9. GULAB JAMUN

Ingredients	Amount
Milk	50 ml / 1/5 cup
Whey water	15 ml / 1 T
or	
Tartaric acid	a pinch
Dhap/ soft *khoa*	50 g

(Contd...)

Sodium bicarbonate (Cooking soda)	a pinch
Curd	¾ t
Maida	12 g / 2 ½ t
Sugar	150 g/ 2/3 cup
Water	120 ml / ½ cup
Milk	15 ml / 1T
Water	15 ml / 1T
Fat	for frying

Method

1. Mix the sugar with the water in a saucepan and heat. When the sugar dissolves, bring to a boil and to clean the syrup add diluted milk and boil for 2 minutes. Strain through a muslin cloth stretched on a steel strainer.
2. Boil the milk, remove from heat and curdle with some whey water or tartaric acid. When the milk curdles completely add cold water till the liquid is just lukewarm.
3. Strain the liquid through a muslin cloth to get the paneer.
4. Mix the *paneer* with *dhap* till no coarse grains remain. Mix soda with curd and add to the dhap. Add *maida* and mix to the dough.
5. Take a portion of the prepared dough and make it into a big roll. Break off walnut sized pieces for *gulab jamuns*. Shape into very smooth balls or rolls.
6. Heat ghee in a karahi to a low moderate temperature. Remove the karahi from heat and add the gulab jamuns. When the ghee stops bubbling put the karahi back on the fire and cook on slow heat. When evenly browned, drain and put in the hot syrup. Heat the syrup if it has gone cold. Remove the karahi from fire to cool the fat a little and then put the next lot of gulab jamuns and so on. If the syrup gets too thick then dilute it with water.
7. Serve hot.

No. of servings : 2

Size of serving : 2

Nutrients per serving

Energy (Kcal)	Protein (g)	Iron (mg)	Calcium (mg)	Fibre (g)
330	6.7	0.2	279	0.2

10. GUJIA

A popular sweet made of refined wheat flour stuffed with *khoa*, dry fruits and coconut, commonly consumed during the colourful festival of Holi.

Ingredients	Amount
Maida	60 g
Ghee	10 g/2 t
Cold water	15 ml/ 1 T
For the filling	
Khoa	30 g
Semolina	10 g
Desiccated coconut	10 g
Almonds	2 g
Cashewnuts	2 g
Pistachio	2 g
Castor sugar	20 g/ 4 t
Syrup for Gujia	
Sugar	50 g
Water	3 T/ 45 ml

Variation: Gujias can be served without the coating of syrup, if desired. The nutrients however will be changed in the variation.

Method

1. Take the *maida* in a plate. Make a well in the centre. Add the melted ghee and mix lightly with fingertips. Add water, little at a time to ensure uniform hydration. Make a stiff dough.
2. Crumble the *khoa*. Prepare the filling by cooking crumbled *khoa* for some time, remove, cool.

3. Roast the *suji.* Add the roasted *suji,* desiccated coconut and nuts. Mix well, add the sugar.
4. Make six little balls out of the dough and roll into small thin circles.
5. Divide filling into six equal portions.
6. Put one portion of mixture at the center of each circle. Moisten the edges with a little thick maida paste and fold into a semi circle. Press the edges together very firmly. Crimp the edges by hand or use a gujia mould.
7. Deep fry to a golden colour on very slow heat.
8. Make a syrup of sugar and water, to clean it boil it with diluted milk and cook the syrup to a two-thread consistency.
9. Dip the gujias in syrup and drain them.
10. Serve hot/cold.

No. of servings : 3

Size of serving : 2

Nutrients per serving

Energy (Kcal)	Protein (g)	Iron (mg)	Calcium (mg)	Fibre (g)
313	4.8	0.9	114	1.3

11. PINEAPPLE UPSIDE-DOWN PUDDING

An ideal dessert for Christmas, Thanksgiving, birthdays or any other celebration.

Ingredients	Amount
Sugar	30 g
Pineapple rings (canned)	2
Glaced cherries	1
Walnuts	2
For pudding	
Butter	60 g

(Contd...)

Castor sugar	60 g
Egg	1½
Maida	75 g
Baking powder	¾ t
Semolina	15 g
Milk	1-2 T
Pineapple essence	½ t
For glaze	
Arrowroot or cornflour	1t
Pineapple Juice	75 ml/ 5 T

Method

1. Grease a 12 cm × 8 cm long rectangular sandwich tin. Sprinkle the sugar and caramelize it on low heat to a golden brown colour; spread it around sides and base. Let it cool. Set oven at 175° C (35° F) to preheat.
2. Arrange pineapple rings, cherries and walnuts in a pattern over base.
3. Place all the cake ingredients except the milk in a mixing bowl and beat with a spoon until smooth adding enough of the milk and pineapple essence to make it of a soft dropping consistency.
4. Spread carefully into tin on top of pineapple base, smoothening the top to level it.
5. Bake in the oven at 175° C for 30-35 minutes or until the top is firm and the pudding slightly shrinks from the sides of the tin.
6. Remove from the oven; leave for 2-3 minutes; then invert it on to a plate leaving the tin in position. Delay in turning out should be avoided to prevent the caramel from sticking to the tin.
7. In the meantime, mix arrowroot or cornflour and juice in a small pan; stir over gentle heat until boiling and transparent and slightly thick.

8. Remove the pudding carefully from the tin; spoon over a little of the glaze; serve the reminder as a sauce in a small bowl.

No. of servings : 6

Size of serving : 1 piece

Nutrients per serving

Energy (Kcal)	Protein (g)	Iron (mg)	Calcium (mg)	Fibre (g)
206	3.3	0.9	23	0.4

12. STUFFED LICHEE

Ingredients	Amount
Fresh lichees	15
For the Filling :	
Paneer	½ cup
Milk	2 T
Sugar	10 g/ 2 t
Vanilla essence	½ t

Method

1. Carefully deseed the lichees.
2. Stuff each deseeded lichee with a teaspoon of the filling. Refrigerate for 30 minutes.
3. Serve chilled.

No. of servings : 2-3

Size of serving : 4-5

Nutrients per serving

Energy (Kcal)	Protein (g)	Iron (mg)	Calcium (mg)	Fibre (g)
334	19.5	0.2	246	0.07

13. EGGLESS CAKE

Ingredients	Amount
Maida	60 g
Baking powder	¼ t

(Contd...)

Sodium bicarbonate (Cooking soda)	¼ t
Butter	30 g
Condensed milk	200 g
Yellow colour	1-2 drops
Vanilla essence	¼ t
Aerated soda/limca	50ml

Variation: Pineapple or lemon essence can also be used in place of vanilla essence.

Method

1. Preheat oven at 150°C (325°F). grease a 10 cm square tin.
2. Sieve together the flour, baking powder and sodium bicarbonate.
3. Melt the butter and cool. Add the condensed milk and beat well till light and fluffy. Add the colour and essence.
4. To this, add a spoonful of flour and aerated soda and fold in well. Continue to do this till all the flour and soda is used up.
5. Pour into a greased tin and bake for 40 minutes till done.
6. Remove from oven, cool. Serve.

No. of servings : 3

Size of serving : 1

Nutrients per serving

Energy (Kcal)	Protein (g)	Iron (mg)	Calcium (mg)	Fibre (g)
355	7.4	0.7	192	0.6

14. BEANS AND MACARONI

Ingredients	Amount
Macaroni	40 g
Salt	a pinch
Beans	100 g

(Contd...)

Water	1 T/ 15 ml
Tomato	60 g
Butter	1 T/ 15 g
Cheese	25 g
Pepper powder	a pinch

Method

1. Cook the macaroni in plenty of salted water till tender but firm. Drain it in a colander.
2. Skin and chop the tomato.
3. String and dice the beans in a diamond shape, cook it in 1T water. Drain and toss them in half the butter.
4. Fry the tomato in the remaining melted butter for about 4 minutes.
5. Add the drained macaroni, reheat, and then stir in the grated cheese and seasoning.
6. Arrange the beans in the center of a warmed serving dish and place the macaroni mixture on either side or around them.

No. of servings : 1

Size of serving : 1 plate

Nutrients per serving

Energy (Kcal)	Protein (g)	Iron (mg)	Calcium (mg)	Fibre (g)
335	12.1	2.2	243	3.7

15. NAAN

Ingredients	Amount
Maida	100 g
Salt	½ t
Baking powder	½ t
Oil	1t
Water	½ t
Curd	25 g
Milk	50 ml
Poppy seeds	½ t
Fresh yeast	3 g
Sugar	½ t

Method

1. Sieve the refined flour (maida) with the salt and baking powder.
2. Rub in the oil.
3. Dissolve the yeast in warm water and sugar.
4. Add the yeast, curd and milk to flour and make a dough. Cover the dough with a wet cloth for one hour.
5. Divide the dough in two portions
6. Make into balls and roll to 5 cm thickness. Stretch out on one side to make an oblong shape.
7. Bake in an oven till done. A tandoor can also be used for the same.

No. of servings : 2

Size of serving : 1

Nutrients per serving

Energy (Kcal)	Protein (g)	Iron (mg)	Calcium (mg)	Fibre (g)
199	6.7	2.1	60	1.5

16. SPINACH PURIS

Ingredients	Amount
Wheat flour	80 g
Spinach	25 g
Salt	¼ t
Red chilli powder	¼ t
Oil	1t + for frying

Variation: Methi can be used in place of spinach or plain puris can also be made without any greens. The nutrients however will be changed in the variation.

Method

1. Wash and chop the spinach leaves and cook them in a pan covered with a lid for five minutes on slow fire.

2. Uncover the pan and dry any liquid which is left.
3. Grind the cooked leaves to a fine paste.
4. Add seasonings to the wheat flour and rub in the oil.
5. Make a stiff dough of flour using ground paste. If needed some water may also be used.
6. Leave the dough covered for 20-30 minutes.
7. Knead the dough again for few minutes.
8. Divide the dough into 5-6 parts and shape into balls.
9. Roll each ball into a thin round using oil.
10. Heat fat in a *karahi.* Fry in moderately hot oil.

No. of servings : 1

Size of serving : 5 puris

Nutrients per serving

Energy (Kcal)	Protein (g)	Iron (mg)	Calcium (mg)	Fibre (g)
398	10.18	4.21	56.65	1.7

17. PALAK PANEER

Ingredients	Amount
Spinach	150 g
Water	1T/15 ml
Salt	to taste
Oil	2t
Cumin seeds	¼ t
Black cardamom	1
Cinnamon	a small stick
Pepper corns	2-3
Cloves	2-3
Onion	25 g
Ginger	5 g
Garlic	2 cloves
Tomato	50 g
Paneer	40 g

Variation: Sautéed mushrooms or boiled corn or potatoes can be used in place of paneer. The nutrients however will be changed in the variation.

Method

1. Clean and wash the spinach.
2. Pressure-cook the spinach with water for 5 minutes. Blend in a blender or grind to a paste.
3. Take a *karahi* and heat 2t of oil in it. Fry the cumin seeds, cloves, pepper and crushed cardamom. Fry for a minute and then add finely chopped garlic and ginger and fry till golden brown. Now add pureed tomatoes.
4. Cook till the oil separates.
5. Add the spinach paste and allow to cook on low flame for 20 minutes. You can adjust the consistency by adding water.
6. Add pieces of paneer.
7. Serve hot.

No. of servings : 1

Size of serving : 1 bowl

Nutrients per serving

Energy (Kcal)	Protein (g)	Iron (mg)	Calcium (mg)	Fibre (g)
239	11.2	2.1	228	7.7

18. NARGISI KOFTA CURRY

Ingredients	Amount
Potato	150 g
Paneer	60 g
Salt	¼ t + a pinch
Yellow colour	1 drop
Ginger	5 g
Garlic	1 clove
Green chilli	½

(Contd...)

Pepper powder	a pinch
Maida	½ t
Bread crumbs	20 g
Oil	for frying
For batter	
Water	2 T/ 30 ml
Maida	10 g
For curry	
Garlic	2 cloves
Ginger	5 g
Coriander powder	¼ t
Cumin seeds	¼ t
Oil	10 g
Onion	60 g
Red chilli powder	a pinch
Salt	1/6th t
Water	4 t
Turmeric powder	a pinch
Tomato	30 g
Coriander leaves	a few
Garam masala	a pinch

Variation: *Nargisi koftas* can be served without the gravy also as a snack.

Method

1. Boil and mash the potatoes.
2. Crumble the paneer and add the salt. Add the yellow colour to 1/3rd portion. Leave the other portion white.
3. Grind the ginger, garlic and green chilli and add to the mashed potato. Add the salt and pepper.
4. Add the maida to the white paneer and knead till all grains disappear. Flatten it and fill it will yellow paneer ball and shape it into a ball.
5. Divide the potato mixture into two parts. Put the paneer ball on the flattened potato mixture and work up till it fully encloses the paneer ball. Seal the top well.

6. Dip the balls in flour batter and roll it in bread crumbs.
7. Deep fry till golden brown. Cut into halves.
8. Heat the oil in a pan. Add cumin seeds, fry a little and then add chopped garlic, ginger. Fry for some time and then add chopped onion. Fry till golden brown.
9. Then blend this mixture in a blender.
10. Return this mixture to the pan and add pureed tomato and continue to cook till the fat separates. Add the seasonings.
11. Add ½ cup water and simmer for 10 minutes in a closed pan over low heat.
12. Put the koftas in the gravy.
13. Serve hot garnished with coriander leaves and garam masala.

No. of servings : 1

Size of serving : 1 bowl (2 koftas)

Nutrients per serving

Energy (Kcal)	Protein (g)	Iron (mg)	Calcium (mg)	Fibre (g)
609	17.1	2	188	6.7

19. CAULIFLOWER AU GRATIN

Ingredients	Amount
Cauliflower	100 g
Butter	15 g
Maida	15 g/ 1T
Milk	150 ml
Pepper powder	a pinch
Salt	to taste
Mustard powder	a pinch
Nutmeg powder	a pinch
Cheese	25 g
Bread crumbs	25 g

Variation: Sautéed mushrooms or corn or potatoes can be used in place or in combination with cauliflower. The nutrients however will be changed in the variation.

Method

1. Cut the cauliflower into florets and cook in boiling salted water until just tender.
2. Drain well and place in a greased ovenproof dish.
3. For the white sauce, heat 2 t of butter, let it melt and then add the flour. Stir it well and cook. Don't let the flour turn brown. Once it is cooked, turn off the gas and let it cool for 2-3 minutes and then add the milk slowly. Stir constantly with constant stirring and cook till thick and smooth.
4. Season the sauce with the salt, pepper, mustard powder and nutmeg.
5. Pour the sauce over the cauliflower and sprinkle with the grated cheese and breadcrumbs and dot it with remaining butter.
6. Bake until the cheese is brown.
7. Serve hot.

No. of servings : 1

Size of serving : 1 bowl

Nutrients per serving

Energy (Kcal)	Protein (g)	Iron (mg)	Calcium (mg)	Fibre (g)
475	16	2.3	375	3.7

20. MEXICAN RICE

Ingredients	Amount
Rice	80 g
Water	enough to soak rice
Oil	15 ml/1T
Cumin seeds	¼ t
Cinnamon	2 cm piece
Black cardamom	1
Onion	50 g + 20 g
Minced meat	80 g
Tomato	150 g
Salt	½ t
Red chilli powder	a pinch

Variation: Paneer or mushrooms can be used in place of meat. The nutrients however will be changed in the variation.

Method

1. Pick, wash and soak the rice for half an hour.
2. Fry 20 g of thinly sliced onions for the garnishing. Fry cumin seeds, cinnamon, crushed cardamom and sliced onions in the same oil till golden brown. Add the minced meat and fry on a slow fire for 10 minutes. Add about ¼ cup of water and cook till three fourths done.
3. Blanch tomato and blend it in a blender and strain. See that it is double the volume of rice; otherwise add water.
4. Drain the rice, add to the cooked minced meat along with the salt, chilli powder and tomato puree. Cover and simmer on slow fire till done.
5. Steam for 10-15 minutes.
6. Serve hot garnished with fried onions.

No. of servings : 1

Size of serving : 1 dinner plate

Nutrients per serving

Energy (Kcal)	Protein (g)	Iron (mg)	Calcium (mg)	Fibre (g)
562	22.5	5.6	209	5.6

The above twenty feasting recipes presented with their nutritive values, can act as guides for planning balanced menus for meals, keeping in mind the menu ideas given in chapter 14 for effective menu planning.

MENU IDEAS

A lot of people today, do not like to leave their work stations or leisure for taking complete meals, and hence the need to provide some menu ideas. The recipes given in chapter 13–14 are segregated for preparation and use in meals after *Fasting* and for *Feasting*. For the former, the ideas will help to start with light but balanced meals helping the body to return gradually to normal eating without undue strain and within the restrictions of the fast especially if it lasts for a prolonged period.

For the latter the suggestions offered will help to plate balanced meals from the choices offered when invited out, as also plan menus when hosting parties as well.

During feasts and celebrations the variety offered is so vast that over- or under-eating results, and when such occasions are too frequent they can have deleterious effects on health.

FASTING

The post-fasting period requires much greater care and patience in comparison to the pre-fasting period. This is because one feels genuinely hungry, and the taste acuity is sharper with fresh salivary excretions, self-control and patience with food and eating is therefore important at this stage. Benefits of fasting become long lasting only if proper care is taken at the end of the fast, since the digestive system and its various glands have been inactive during the fasting period. Hence, feeding and eating needs to be gradually introduced. Sometimes the benefits of a fast may only be felt a few days after its completion.

While the recipes provide ideas of substitute foods used as ingredients in lieu of restricted ones for certain fasts, whether partial or complete, menus after fasting must be planned taking the following points into consideration :

- Drink light liquids such as *nimbu pani* or luke warm water in small doses, before eating after a fast. Small quantities of citrus fruits or juices may be taken.
- The meal must be light after a fast, the full meal being introduced only gradually.
- Start with liquids and progress to fluid, then soft and finally normal meals.
- Take care to provide a balance of nutrients and fibre at all stages.
- Fatty foods need to be avoided for a few hours or even days depending on the period of the fast.
- Overeating should be strictly avoided to gain maximum benefits from fasting, both for the body and mind.
- Physical exertion too should only be introduced gradually towards normal activity levels.

These rules may not be followed strictly fo: a one- or two-day fasts as the body is able to adapt both ways easily to bring itself quickly to equilibrium and thus to normality. In order to give an idea about the nutrient essentials and fibre content of each dish the recipes given are provided with this information.

Planning Menus

Using the above guidelines some of the recipes provided may be used as substitutes in normal family meals. For example, if it is a non-cereal fast, then other items of the meal remaining the same, substitute flours or seeds may be used instead of the staple wheat or rice flours or grains. Suggestive menus are given in Table 15.1. It may however be noticed that all the food items in the sample menus are not those for which recipes have been given. The ideas given here are to stimulate the preparation of creative menus resembling normal home meals both modern and traditional, restricting the use of items determined by the rules of the fast.

Table 15.1: Menu suggestions for after-fast meals (non-cereal)

Menu	Meal	Substitutions
A	Vegetable *khichdi* Curd or fruit raita Apple juice/ nimbu pani	Substitute rice/*dalia*/*suji* with sago or *samak rice*
B	Chapati Sauteed green vegetable Potato chaat or salad Fruit curd	Substitute wheat flour with kootu or singhara flour
C	Sweet-corn vegetable soup Potato-nut cutlet Green salad with walnuts Fruit cup with cream	Binding may be sago flour/ kootu/ singhara flour.

In case of a fast in which salt is not permitted in addition to staple cereals, milk and milk products, fruits, vegetables, flour substitutes may be used as indicated in Table 15.2.

Table 15.2: Menus for fast with no salt and cereals

Menu	Meal	Substitutions
A	Fruit milk shake Masala dosa Coconut chutney Barfi	Rice substituted with samak rice

(Contd...)

B	Mushroom soup Raw banana cutlet Sautéed green vegetable with *paneer* Vegetable and fruit salad Pumpkin kheer	
C	Kootu Puri Potato curry Spinach raita *Ghia* halwa	Kootu flour instead of wheat

Note: Lemon and herbs may be used with other spices like tamarind, black pepper for taste, only addition of salt in cooking is to be avoided.

There are fasts in which sour ingredients or foods are not permitted such as tomatoes, tamarind, curd, fermented foods, citrus fruits etc. For such fast days the sample menus are given in Table15.3 which may be used as a guide to planning.

Table 15.3: Sample menus without sour and cereal foods

Menu	Meal	Substitutions
A	Thandai *Samak* chawal pulao Ghia paneer vegetable Pudina chutney Peanut chikki	Samak rice for normal rice/ dalia Extra salt and pepper for tamarind
B	Spinach carrot soup Cauliflower au Gratin Whole *Bhindi* Fried chipped potato Kulfi with nuts	Samak rice powder in place of refined flour.
C	Apple juice Puri Chana curry Sweet potato chaat Onion beetroot salad Cottage cheese kheer	*singhara* flour for wheat flour salt pepper for lemon or tamarind

Some fasts prohibit the use of root and all vegetables grown under the soil even though they may not be strictly classified as roots such as potato, onion, ginger, garlic and other food items which are pungent tasting or with strong odours. But cereals and pulses are permitted in the one meal that is consumed before sunset on each fast day. Some menu samples for such fasts are presented in Table 15.4.

Table 15.4: Menus for fasts avoiding roots and other specified foods

Menu	Meal	Substitutions
A	Cauliflower paratha Sauteed paneer pea vegetable Cucumber pomegranate salad Plain curd Cashew barfi	
B	Pumpkin sambar Carrot Idli Mixed vegetables Fruit salad Payasam	Other than those avoided
C	Lentil soup Mushroom and capsicum pizza Sauteed potatoes Beans and corn vegetable Apple pie with custard	

These menu suggestions will prove useful for all kinds of meals and they can be used to break short 1 to 2-day fasts. For prolonged fasting, the guidelines in Chapter 6 should be followed and ideas from these menus can be used for developing more and different menus, according to one's eating habits and home disciplines. A rough guide for balancing menus is to use one food at least from each of the different food groups namely milk group, vegetable and fruit group, fat and oil group, cereals, pulses and beans, and sugars. Organically farmed products are preferable as they are more nutritious, flavourful and enjoyable without danger of chemicals and additives.

Only vegetarian menus have been exhibited because it is traditional to be vegetarian when one resorts to fasting, even if otherwise people are non-vegetarian.

FEASTING

Menus for feasting are of greater variety, and usually vegetarian and non-vegetarian meals are provided. The wide choice presented by the host is meant to provide choices to people according to what they like to eat. Large parties are usually preceded by cocktails being served consisting of both soft and hard or mixed drinks called *mocktails*. Any restrictions in menu planning are due to self-imposed disciplines due to traditional, cultural or regional differences. Such as, Muslims do not eat pork, Hindus do not eat beef and so on.

Restrictions placed on oneself such as avoiding red meat or fish, being totally vegetarian, avoiding milk and its products because of lactose sensitivity, avoiding sweets and desserts or restricting salt are all very personal and may have traditional roots or be imposed by health considerations.

Irrespective of personal restrictions the main feature in selection of foods for a meal is to provide nutritional balance. Such meals promote health by providing adequately for energy, protein, minerals and vitamin requirements of the body. The rule of thumb in food selection is to use at least one food from each food group as indicated in Fig.15.1 or in short have as much variety in meals as possible, limiting quantity so as not to overeat.

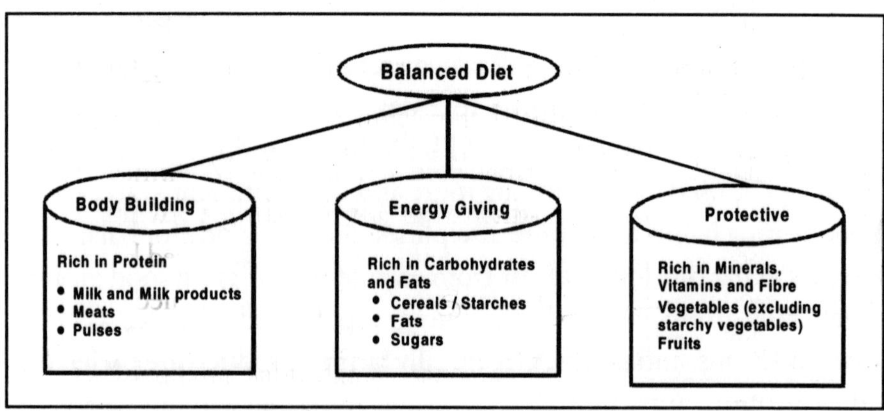

Fig. 15.1 The Food Groups

Fig.15.1 also indicates which nutrient is predominant in each food group to make people aware of what and how much to take from the group according to their specific requirements. Balanced meals while feasting would include, foods chosen from all the food groups including the meat and fish group since the strictly vegetarian rule does not apply to feasting menus, although people can make their own choices from the variety provided.

In addition, balance should also be maintained between drinking and eating maintaining the quality of the meal on the plate as against the quantity that may ultimately be overeaten or wasted, because of inability to consume all of as per the appetite. So while feasting, eat for the stomach and not for the eyes. A few guidelines may prove useful:

- Stop drinking at least 20 minutes before a meal.
- Sit down comfortably to eat and focus on the food to enjoy it without talking.
- Eat slowly in bite size quantities, and masticate food properly.
- Serve only enough on your plate and avoid second helpings.
- Eat to feel comfortable and not full.
- Rest in seated position after a meal for 15-20 minutes.
- Give a gap of at least 30 minutes between eating and lying down.
- Eat at fixed times and avoid feeling too hungry before a meal.
- Take a light starter before the meal such as a crisp salad, soup or juice depending on the weather at the time.

In small family-scale feasting there may be sit down dinners or laid out buffets. In contrast to traditional methods of feasting when family members used to be seated on mats in the kitchens and served hot freshly prepared foods on *thalis*. Today, celebrations are accompanied by drinks and leisurely dining, and parties go on till late at night.

Present Scenario

Buffets are much preferred nowadays because people can choose from a great variety according to their health requirements, diabetics avoiding refined carbohydrates and sweets, people with heart problems choosing to take less salted and fatty foods and so on.

With lifestyle changes, the balance in home meals too, has become skewed. Most people prefer to order foods from restaurants, fast foods outlets and takeaways or arrange parties in hotels and clubs where many guests can be accommodated in the ambience and décor required for the occasion. Others choose their favourite foods for feasting menus, in preference to balanced meals. Today, convenience in arranging meals is given greater preference to other factors that may contribute to health and well being.

Some feasting recipes have been included in Chapter 14 along with nutritional information for each recipe, to guide the user. Sample menus are not being presented for feasting, as the number of recipes that can be prepared, bought and served is almost as limitless as the people in the different regions of the country. To add to this, the global influence on food choices has further increased the variety of foods available to the common person, in terms of specialty restaurants offering Chinese, Japanese, Korean, Mexican, Italian, Greek and other country specific foods.

India is a place of leisure and feasting and every event reflects the joy in people's hearts as is experienced by visitors in the form of the Indian hospitality which has come to be universally recognized and appreciated. The foods and cooking practices too vary from region to region and are a cause of fascination in terms of the variety that can be offered to the tourist or visitor.

REFERENCES

1. Ahmed, Firoz Bhakht. *Calling Muslim Clerics.* Innervoice@hindustantimes.com
2. Ataur-Rahim, Muhammad. *Jesus — Prophet of Islam.* Tahrike Tarsile Quran Inc., New York. 1991.
3. Anonymous. Navdurga. Geeta Press, Gorakhpur.
4. Bhargava Dinesh, Dina Nath. *Sri Hari Gita.* Manav Dharm Karyalaya, New Delhi. (n.d.)
5. Bharill, Hukum Chand. *Dharam ke Das lakshan* (Hindi). 6th Edn., Pandit Todarmal Samarak Trust, Jaipur. 1988.
6. Bisen, Malini. Bawarchi: *Indian Festivals: Pongal* on Google
7. Chaitanya Keerti Swami. Innervoice@hindustantimes.com
8. Champion, Selwyn Gurney. *The eleven religions and their proverbial lore.* George Routledge and Sons Ltd., London. 1945. p. 204-10.
9. Chaudhary, Abhishek. In *Children's World.* CBT Publication. October, 2006.
10. Chetanananda Swami. *They Lived With God.* 1st Indian Edn., Advaita Ashram, Mayavati. 1991.

11. Chinmayananda Swami. *Meditation and Life.* Chinmaya Publications Trust, Madras. 1948.
12. Chopra, Deepak. *Ageless Body, Timeless Mind.* Harmony Books, 1993. p. 216.
13. Dhokalia, R.P. *Eternal Human Values and World Religions.* NCERT, New Delhi. 2001.
14. Gala Dhiren. *Efficacy of Fasting,* Navneet Publications (India) Limited, 2003.
15. Ganesan, Parur S. *Invocation to Goddesses of might, wealth & knowledge.* spiritualityindiatimes.com
16. Gopalan C., Ramasastri B.V., Balasubramanian S.C., 2004. *Nutritive Value of Indian Foods.* National Institute of Nutrition, ICMR, Hyderabad.
17. Henri de Lubac, S.J. *Aspects of Buddhism,* Sheed and Ward, London. 1953.
18. Hosseini, Khaled. *The Kite Runner,* Bloomsbury Publishing plc. London. 2004.
19. Jain, Veersagar. (Edn), *Purudev-Pratishtha* (Souvenir), Jain Milan Pub., New Delhi. 2004. pp. 116-22 and 123-24.
20. Khanna Kumud et al. *The Art and Science of Cooking. A Students' Manual.* Phoenix Publishing House Pvt. Ltd., New Delhi. 1998.
21. Khullar, Pranav. The Speaking Tree. http://spirituality.indiatimes.com.
22. Khullar, Pranav, *Ramadaan Diary from Fatehpur Sikri.* http://spirituality indiatimes.com
23. Lippincot, Kristen. *Astronomy: The Ladybird Discovery Encyclopedia of the Natural World,* Ladybird Books Ltd., U.K. 1994. pp. 264-65.
24. Lidell, Lucy; Narayani and Rabinovitch, Giris. *The Book of Yoga.* Shivananda Yoga Centre, Ebury Press, Delhi. (n.d.)
25. Maheshwari, Jagdish C. *It's All in Timing.* Noble House, 1997.

26. Misra, Anoop, Gulati, Seema, Dutta, Rupali. Asian Indian Diets : Nutrient composition and relationship to diabetes and coronary heart disease. *Nutrion and Disease Management,* Update series, CRNNS, Media workshop India Private Limited, 2006.
27. Muhammad Ali, Maulvi, *The Holy Quran,* 2nd Edn., Ahmaddiya Anjuman-i-ishat-i-Islam, Lahore, India. 1920.
28. Mukundcharandas Sadhu. *Hindu Festivals : Origins, Sentiments and Rituals,* Swaminarayan Aksharpith Amdavad, India. 2005.
29. Mukundcharandas, Sadhu. *Vachanamrut Handbook,* Swaminarayan Aksharpith, 2004. pp. 244-5.
30. Nanavatty, Piloo. *The Gathas of Zarathushtra,* Mapin Publishing Private Ltd., Ahmedabad. 1999.
31. Om, Meena. http://spirituality.indiatimes.com
32. Purnananda, Maa. *The Good and the Pleasant.* Inner voice @ Hindustan times.com
33. Radhakrishnan, S. *The Bhagvad Gita,* Blackie and Son (India) Ltd. Mumbai, 19, pp.55.
34. Raina Usha, Kashyap Sushma, et al. *Basic Food Preparation. A complete manual,* Orient Longman Limited, New Delhi. 2001.
35. Robinson, C.H., Lawler, M.R Chenoweth, W.L. Garwick. A.E. *Normal and Therapeutic Nutrition,* Edn., 17, MacMillan Publishing Company, New York. p. 470.
36. Roy, A.K. *A history of the Jainas,* Gitanjali Publishing House, New Delhi, 1984.
37. Sarma K. Lakshman. *The Fasting cure,* 2nd. Edn., The Nature Cure Publishing House, Pudukkottai, S.I.R.Y., 1948.
38. Sri Sathya Sai Baba. Avtar Vani: Ramnaumi Discourse. *Sanathana Sarathi Vol. 49, No.5,* May 2006, p. 139.
39. Sri Sathya Sai. Avatar Vani: Gokulashtami Sandesh. *Sanathana Sarathi.* Vol.37, No. 10, October, 1994. p. 259.

40. Ibid. Onam: the message of sacrifice. *Sanathana Sarathi*, Vol.37, No.10, Oct. 1994. p. 268.
41. Ibid. Avtar Vani: Spiritual Significance of Shivratri. *Sanathana Sarathi,* Vol.39, No.3, March 1996. p. 63-67.
42. Ibid. Three Pillars of Peace. *Sanathana Sarathi.* Vol.41, No. 8, August 1998. p. 235.
43. Ibid. Man is the Embodiment of Trinity. *Sanathana Sarathi.* Vol. 43, No. 8, August 2000. p. 249.
44. Ibid. Women are the Embodiments of Nobility and Virtue. *Sanathana Sarathi* Vol. 43, No. 9, Sept. 2000. p. 280.
45. Ibid. Spiritual Revolution. *Sanathana Sarathi.* Vol. 49, No. 8, August 2006. p. back cover.
46. Sharma, Robin. *Discover Your Destiny.* p. 59.
47. Singh, Binay. Times News Network. 12 July, Varanasi. 2006.
48. Sri Sushil Kumar Shastri (Muni).*Jain Dharam Jeevan Dharam.* Sri Akhil Bhartiya Swetambar Sthanakwasi Jain Press, New Delhi. p. 38-46.
49. Suri, Megha. *Delhi's only synagogue to turn 50,* Times of India. September 23, 2006.
50. Verma, C.D. Love your Lohri. innervoice@hindustantimes.com
51. Vettam Mani. *Puranic Encyclopaedia,* English Edn, Motilal Banarasidas, New Delhi, 1975.
52. Vishwanath Shastri (Pandit). *Ekadashi Mahatmaya (*Hindi*).* Vimal Press, Mathura, 1985.
53. Wajid Ali, Syed. *Enjoy the soothing effect of Sufiana.* http://spirituality.indiatimes.com

Websites

1. http://www.dishq.org/religious/shivratri.htm
2. ——————.download/hindufest.htm
3. ——————.religious/religions.htm
4. ——————.gitapress.org

5. ——————.festivalsofindia.in/urs
6. —————— .webindia123.com
7. ——————.kalbadevisarvajanin.com/sashti.php
8. ——————.mjain.net/cookbooks/jain_book.pdf
9. ——————.jainworld.com
10. ——————.jainsamaj.com
11. ——————.jainstudy.org
12. ——————.jainheritagecentres.com
13. ——————.bengalinet.com
14. ——————.friendshipday.org
15. ——————.indianchild.com/teachers_day_india.htm
16. ——————.new-year-gifts.indiangiftsportal.com
17. ——————.topics-mag.com
18. ——————.indianchild.com

....

GLOSSARY

A

- Aarati - a practice of performing an ignited camphor offering at the culmination of a puja as a formal act of conclusion and connection.
- Abhisheka - a ritual involving the bathing of the Lord in form with fruit juices, milk and honey, with sacred chanting and devotion, usually prior to installation of the deity in a home or temple.
- Abeer - red powder used in the swing festival of Dol Yatra.
- Adharma - evil or untruthful.
- Adhikmas - refers to the extra or residual month in approximately three lunar years.
- Adi - wealth
- Agni - fire
- Ahamkara - egoism
- Ahimsa - nonviolence, which according to teachings of the Buddha excludes violence in thoughts, words and deeds.
- Akashvani - All India Radio
- Akal Bodhon - another name of Durga Puja
- Akbar - One of Moghul emperors who ruled India.
- Akhrot - walnut

- Akinchan - refers to self imposed limits on worldly possessions.
- Algoza - a folk instrument
- Allah - a muslim name for God.
- Aloo - potato
- Alpana - another name of Rangoli, also called arpana in some regions.
- Amar Jawan Jyoti - a monument that carries the names of soldiers who sacrificed themselves for the country.
- Amavasya - moonless night
- Amchur - dry mango powder
- Amrita - nectar
- Amrud - guava
- Ananta Chaturdasi - last day of the ten day festival of Das Lakshan Parva, as celebrated by Digambaras.
- Anares - a fried preparation of rice flour topped with sesame seeds.
- Angithi - a traditional mobile stove lighted by coal, dung and firewood or dung cakes made from coal dust and cowdung.
- Anshan - complete fasting
- Anupreksha s - matters of deep thinking according to the Jain scriptures.
- Arbi - colocasia
- Arihantas - conquerors of the self.
- Arjava - honesty and righteousness
- Arya Samaj - a reformed sect of Hindus devoted to the Vedas for spiritual guidance, who rejected the concept of idol worship.
- Ashtami - the 8th day of the dark or the bright half of a lunar month.
- Ashtasheel - one of the ritual arranged on Buddha Purnima.
- Ashwin shukla paksha - the bright half of the lunar month of Ashwin.

- Aso Vad - the dark fortnight of the lunar month of Aso or Ashwin.
- Aswayuja - lunar month corresponding to the months of September-October in the solar calendar.
- Athai - is the period of eight days when the Shwetambaras celebrate Paryushan Parva.
- Athapoovu - elaborate circular floral decoration used to decorate homes during the Onam festival. See also rangoli.
- Atithi - guest
- Atma - soul
- Atta - flour
- Avani Avittam - South Indian name of Rakshabandhan.
- Ayambil - is a fast during which only simple bland food is taken, and even eating green vegetables, milk and spices is abstained from.
- Ayudha Puja - Navami is observed as Ayudha Puja in Kerala, Tamil Nadu and Mysore.
- Ayurvedic - herbal products of ancient India, designed to maintain health and wellness. Ayurveda is an ancient medical science and is being revived again as an alternate to allopathic remedies.
- Azaan - call for *namaaz* or prayer from the mosque.

B

- Baaina - the women give a *baaina* consisting of fruits, sweets, nuts, gifts and money to their mothers-in-law as a mark of respect on Karva Chauth.
- Bael - a plant whose trifoliate leaves are offered in the worship of Lord Shiva. The fruit when ripe is eaten or preserved for future use.

- Baisakh - a lunar month falling between April-May according to the solar calendar.
- Baisakhi - a harvest festival of North India.
- Bakrid - see Eid-ul-Zuha
- Balev - Rakshabandhan is called Balev by Brahmins and it marks the thread changing ceremony, when young Brahmin boys discard their old sacred threads and change new ones ritualistically.
- Banslochan - nodes of the bamboo shoot
- Bael leaves - the trifoliate leaves represent the working and surrender of the Ida, Puigala and Sushumana Nadi to the higher self, and therefore considered sacred.
- Bal Krishna - child Krishna
- Baraatis - wedding guests
- Barah Wafat - see Eid-e-Milad
- Basant Panchmi - a spring festival
- Batashas - a sweet made of pure sugar as in fondant.
- Besan - Bengal gram flour
- Bhadrapada - also referred to as Bhadarwa or Bhado and is a month of Hindu lunar calendar falling between August-September.
- Bhagya - destiny
- Bhai - brother
- Bhai-Bij - also referred to as Bhai or Bhaiya Dooj, Bhai Pota, Bhai Tika in the different regions, and is a festival celebrating brother-sister love that binds them.
- Bhai Phota - Bhai Dooj is celebrated by the name of Bhai Phota in Bengal.
- Bhai Tika - Bhai Dooj is celebrated by the name of Bhai Tika in Nepal.
- Bhagawad Gita - holy text book of Hindus.
- Bhakta - devotee

- Bhakti - devotion
- Bhajans - devotional songs
- Bhang - a traditional drink prepared by crushing the dried leaves and buds of the cannabis plant.
- Bhangra - folk dance of Punjab.
- Bhiksha - receiving alms
- Bhindi - ladies finger
- Bhogi - harvest festival of Andhra Pradesh.
- Bhogi Kottus - drums made from the hides of buffaloes, used as musical instruments during the Pongal festivities.
- Bhogi Pongal - first day of Pongal celebration.
- Bhutas - elements
- Bidi - a local cigarette
- Bihu - harvest festival of Assam.
- Bindi - the vermillion dot on the forehead of Indian women.
- Bismillah - means *in the name of God* usually spoken before anything is commenced.
- Bodhi tree - the tree under which Gautam Buddha attained enlightenment.
- Bodhidham Mela - a popular fair that is held in the village Bidyapara in Chittagong on Buddha Purnima.
- Bodhon - the face of Goddess Durga is unveiled through a ritual called Bodhonon Shasthi.
- Bommai Kolu - dolls arranged in Karnataka, Tamil Nadu and Andhra homes on artificially constructed steps on the first day of Navratri.
- Brahmacharya - celibacy
- Buddhi - intelligence
- Budhwar - Wednesday
- Burfee - an Indian sweet much like fudge.

C

- Chaat - a savoury concoction of root vegetables, pulses, cereals and spices.
- Chacha - uncle
- Chadar - sheet offered by devotees in a dargah.
- Chaitra - a lunar month which falls between March-April according to the solar calendar.
- Chakra - wheel
- Chalisa - sacred text of prayer.
- Chalkumro - a type of pumpkin
- Chana - chickpea.
- Channa dal - Bengal gram pulse
- Chapati - flat, hard, unleavened bread.
- Chaturmas - four months of the rainy season in which Jains observe fast.
- Chaulai - a green leafy vegetable.
- Chauth or Chaturthi/Chaturdasi - the 4th day of every month.
- Chawal - rice
- Chhoti - small
- Chikki - a jaggery preparation made with peanuts or sesame seeds.
- Choona - lime
- Chowkpurana - another name of rangoli.
- Chunari - a veil.

D

- Daalchini - cinnamon
- Daas - servant
- Dahi - a traditional way of fermenting milk by Lactobacillus casei to make a set product called curd in India.

- Dahi-handi - This involves an earthenware pot suspended from a height of about 20 to 40 feet filled with milk, curds, butter, honey and fruits.
- Dal - pulse
- Dakshinayan - a period when the Gods rest.
- Dalia - broken wheat
- Dandi - A place where to Gandhiji walked 100 km to make salt illegally.
- Dandiya - a group dance using small sticks (Dandies).
- Darshan - devotional meeting.
- Dashmi - the tenth day
- Das Lakshana Parva - also called Paryushan, which is the ten-day fasting festival of Jains.
- Das Lakshana - ten commandments
- Dastarkhaan - a large white sheet spread on a carpet
- Degs - cauldrons
- Deraavaasi - A group of temple goers called Shwetambers who indulge in idol worship.
- Devaki - mother of Lord Krishna.
- Devi - Goddess
- Devo - God
- Dhairya - courage
- Dhakis - dances to welcome the Goddess during Durga Puja.
- Dhammapada - the sacred book containing teachings of Lord Buddha.
- Dhan - material
- Dhania - coriander
- Dhanya - health
- Dhap - see khoa

- Dharma - duty, law, religion.
- Dhatura - a seed
- Dholak - a musical instrument the shape of an elongated drum, played using the fingers and palms of the hands, from both hands.
- Dhoop - incense
- Dhoti - unstitched cloth of 2-3 metres which men wrap round at the hip, during prayer or given to a priest after puja. The term is also used for a cotton saree with a border that women wear.
- Digambar - a Jain sect whose monks give up all material possessions including clothes.
- Diya - earthen lamp
- Dol Yatra - or swing festival is the another name of holi in Bengal.
- Dooj - two
- Dosa - a south Indian preparation made with rice and pulse batter.
- Dua - prayer
- Dusshera - the tenth day
- Dvesha/Dwesh - aversion
- Dwadashi - the second day after Ekadashi.
- Dwaraka - the birth place of Lord Krishna.
- Dwitiya - see Dwadashi.

E

- Easwara - God
- Eediyeh - gifts and money distributed by elders to children on Eid.
- Eid/Id - celebrations after the holy month of Ramadan.
- Eid Mubarak - greetings exchanged on Eid.

- Eid-ul-Fitr/Id-ul-Fitr - festival of *the breaking of the fast,* celebrated on sighting the new moon, which marks the end of the long fasting period of Ramadan.
- Eid-ul-Milad/Id-e-Milad - also called *Barah Wafat,* is the day when the prophet Mohammad was born and died also.
- Eid-ul-Zuha/Id-ul-Zuha - also called *Bakrid,* a celebration during which Muslims all over the world offer a sacrifice by slaughtering a sheep, cow or goat following traditional Islamic customs.
- Ekadashi - a sacred day which falls on the 11th day of every fortnight after a full moon or a no moon day.
- Ekasana - a fast in which food is eaten only once in the day.
- Elaichi - cardamom. Two varieties are commonly used, black and green.

F

- Farari - a term for fresh, seasonal vegetarian foods such as, roots and tubers like potato, sweet potato, cassava, carrot, beet, suran, fruits, nuts, seeds (sabudana), green bananas and some vegetables like cabbage, cauliflower, ghia (gourd), parval, pumpkin, tomato and some grains. Such foods are considered fit to be offered in temples to deities and used during periods of fasting.
- Fatiha - group recitations.
- Furmety - wheat grains cooked in milk with sugar and spice.

G

- Gajak - sesame seed and jaggery sweet preparation.
- Ganas - celestial beings
- Ganga jal - water from Ganga
- Garam masala - a mixture of spice consisting of roasted and ground peppercorns, black cardamom, cloves, cumin seeds and cinnamon.

- Garba - folk dance popular during navratri festival, originated in Gujarat and Rajasthan. See also Dandiya.
- Gathas - scriptures of Zoroastrians.
- Gautama - name of Lord Buddha.
- Ghee - clarified butter.
- Ghevar - a sweet preparation
- Ghia - bottle gourd
- Gidda - folk dance of Punjab performed by women.
- Ghilaph - offered in a dargah
- Gita - sacred text of the Hindus.
- Gokulashtami - first day celebration of the birth anniversary of Lord Krishna.
- Guru Gobind Singh - 10th Guru of Sikhs.
- Gopal - name by which Lord Krishna is often called because of his love for cows and their caregivers.
- Gopis - women devotees of Krishna.
- Gosht/Goshtaba - meat preparation.
- Graha - home as in grahalakshmi. It also refers to a planetary position.
- Granth Sahib - the sacred book treated as the Guru of all Sikhs, and placed in all gurudwaras and in homes of the devout who follow the messages of Guru Nanak Dev.
- Grishm - Summer season
- Gujia - a sweet preparation made at Holi, with flour, coconut, nuts and jaggery or sugar.
- Gulabjamuns - an Indian fried sweet made of milk products and steeped in sugar syrup.
- Gulal - color powders used for playing Holi.
- Gunas - the three attributes of human beings, referred to as satvik, rajasik and tamasik in our sacred texts.

- Gur - jaggery
- Guru - teachers
- Gurudwaras - temple of Sikhs
- Guruwar - Thursday.

H

- Haaq - a dish prepared and served at a wazwan feast.
- Haj - the pilgrimage of Muslims to Mecca and Medina.
- Haldi - turmeric
- Halkhata - books of accounts.
- Halwa - an Indian dessert made in many varieties using different ingredients, like wheat flour, semolina or pulses soaked and ground. Each one is roasted in ghee and then sugar syrup added till of desired consistency. The Halwa gets the name of the ingredient from which it is made such as wheat halwa, dal halwa and so on.
- Handi - an earthenware pot
- Hans - swan
- Hara - green
- Harijans - name given by Gandhiji for people who were considered untouchables by the upper caste Brahmins.
- Hemant - Winter season
- Hey Ram - Gandhiji's last words.
- Himachalis - people of Himachal Pradesh.
- Hindus - followers of Hinduism
- Hing - asafetida
- Holi - a spring festival of colors.
- Hriday - heart

I

- Idgah - where the prayers are led by the Imam.
- Idli - a rice and dal steamed preparation.
- Iftar - an Eid party
- Indriyas - senses
- Irsha - jealousy or hatred.

J

- Jainas/Jains - followers of Jainism.
- Jallikattu - a bull fight in which money bags are tied to the horns of the animals, and unarmed young men are asked to wrest them from the bull's horns. This is generally arranged during Pongal celebrations.
- Jalotsavams - water festivals
- Janamashtami - birth anniversary of Lord Krishna.
- Janyeyu
- Japa/japam - repetition of God's name.
- Jataka - tales based on legends intended to inculcate value education in people.
- Jatra - Folk theatre performed during Durga Puja.
- Jau - a minor cereal, no more used as a staple.
- Jawan - soldier
- Jayanti - birth anniversary
- Jeera/Zeera - cumin seeds
- Jhol - curry
- Jhula - swing
- Jiva - living being.
- Jyoti - light
- Jyotirlings - lighted replicas of the Shivling.

K

- Kababs - snacks made of mince meat and spices and deep fried or grilled.
- Kachalu - a root vegetable, used as food.
- Kachcha - underwear
- Kada - bangle
- Kada Prasaad - halwa made of wheat flour served as prasaad in gurudwaras.
- Kaikottikali - a group dance of Kerala.
- Kailash - abode of Lord Shiva and Parvati.
- Kaivalya - attainment of transcendental state of the body, mind and soul in an individual, who then gets endowed with cosmic consciousness and complete emancipation.
- Kajal - a black powder or paste used traditionally as an eyeliner, prepared by burning camphor in ancient India.
- Kaju - cashew nuts
- Kalashtami - second day celebration of the birth of Krishna.
- Kaleva - red sacred threads
- Kama - desire or lust
- Kamalasana - the one who is seated on a thousand petalled lotus, each petal representing a particular quality.
- Karma - action.
- Kandal - a flower which is white in colour.
- Kanga - comb
- Kans - brother of Devaki.
- Karahi - wok
- Kartika - a lunar month covering the period October-November i.e., autumn-winter.
- Kar Seva - offering help in the daily chores of the gurudwaras.

- Karuna - compassion
- Karvas - spherical clay pots with a spout.
- Kashmiris - people from Kashmir
- Kashiphal - pumpkin.
- Katori - small bowl
- Kathas - narrations from the sacred texts.
- Kattha - a reddish paste used in preparing paan.
- Kauravas - brothers of the Pandavas in the epic Mahabharata.
- Kawad - Shiva Ratri occurs twice a year namely Kawad which fulls in rainy season and Shiva vivaha which falls in Spring.
- Kaya - a flower
- Keralites - people of Kerala
- Kesar - saffron.
- Kesh - hair
- Kewra - a flavouring used for desserts
- Khadims - service staff
- Khalsa - a religious sect of the Sikhs.
- Khajoor - dates
- Khana - food
- Khandaan - the extended family
- Khandavi - is a savoury snack made from pulse flour and is now available in all sweet shops everywhere. Typically it is a Gujarati dish.
- Kheer - Rice pudding
- Khichri - a soft rice-pulse salty preparation.
- Khoya - milk that has been reduced to a solid, generally used in preparation of Indian sweets.
- Khus khus - poppy seeds
- Kirpan - sword
- Kirtans - devotional music

- Kirtanists - singers of devotional music
- Kofta - ingredients mixed with pulse flour and fried into balls. These are then cooked in gravy and served with meals as a curry.
- Kolakuli - customary tradition observed by embracing each other on the tenth day of Durga Puja.
- Kolam - another name of Rangoli
- Konrai - a flower with golden pollen
- Kootu - buckwheat (a cereal eaten during Navratra fasts)
- Krishna paksh - period of the waning moon
- Krishnashtami - first day celebration of the birth anniversary of Lord Krishna
- Krodha - anger
- Kshama - forgiveness
- Kshamapna/Kshamabhavo divas - it is the day following the last day of the celebration of Paryushan. Everyone asks for forgiveness from relatives, friends and neighbours for any offence which may have been intentionally or unintentionally committed.
- Kshatriyas - the warrior caste
- Kulfi - a frozen dessert made with milk and nuts.
- Kum Kum - red vermillion powder put on the forehead by women.
- Kumbh Mela - holy festival occurs once in 12 years and celebrated by congregating on the banks of holy rivers, for an auspicious dip.

L

- Ladoo - a typical Indian sweet made into the shape of a ball, of various sizes. The ingredients can vary widely.
- Lakshmana - younger brother of Lord Rama

- Lambodara - another name of Lord Ganesha
- Langars - meals prepared and served to devotees and consumed as prasaad by congregations in gurudwaras.
- Lassi - a beverage made from curd, that could be sweet, salty or spiced.
- Lauki - bottle gourd
- Laundh - extra or residual month in the lunar calendar
- Laung - clove
- Leela - play depicting life story of Lord Krishna.
- Lichees - a fruit
- Linga - the object of worship installed in temples for the puja of Lord Shiva.
- Lobha - greed
- Loh - a thick iron sheet skillet used for making chappaties for community feasts.
- Lohri - harvest festival of North India.
- Loi - a belief that the festival of Lohri got its name from the name of Loi, the wife of Sant Kabir. It is a Punjabi name for the festival.
- Luchi - a fried Bengali preparation made of refined wheat flour.

M

- Ma - mother
- Maada - pride
- Magha - another name of Rangoli
- Magha - a lunar month covering November-December.
- Mahabodhi tree - the tree under which Gautam Buddha attained enlightenment.
- Mahalaya - the period before Durga Puja starts.

- Mahavir - the founder of Jainism.
- Mahavisnu - the philosophy of Mahavir.
- Mahotsava - festival
- Maida - refined wheat flour.
- Maidan - field
- Makara - sign of the zodiac-capricorn.
- Makhana - lotus stem seeds
- Makki-ki-roti - flat hard un-leavened bread made of maize flour.
- Mala - rosary
- Mandap - see pandal.
- Mangala graha - auspicious period, according to astrological signs.
- Mangalsutra - a necklace made with blank beads worn by married women.
- Mangalwar - Tuesday
- Manji Virattu - a game in which young men chase the running bulls with their bells tingling. Generally arranged on Pongal.
- Mantra - a sacred word or verse.
- Mardawa - means gentleness of nature or humility or giving up of pride.
- Marsiyas - effigies.
- Marteswagan Korma - prepared and eaten during Wazwan feast
- Masala - spices
- Mathri - a spiced savoury snack made from cereal flour.
- Matka - an earthenware pot.
- Matru Bhakti - reverence of mother.
- Mathsarya - envy, hatred.

- Mattu Pongal - third day celebration of Pongal.
- Maun/Maunam - observing silence.
- Mehfil - congregation
- Mehfilkhana - a large hall meant for mehfils.
- Mehndi - henna
- Mela - fair
- Methi - fenugreek
- Misri - large sugar crystals.
- Mithai - sweets
- Modakas - rice flour and jaggery dumplings offered on Ganesh Chaturthi.
- Moghul - name of the tribe of Muslim rulers who ruled India for a long time.
- Moha - attachment, fascination.
- Mohalla - locality
- Moharram - is a day of mourning observed with solemnity and fasting, commemorating the martyrdom of Hussain, the younger grandson of Prophet Mohammad.
- Moksha - salvation, liberation from the cycle of birth and death.
- Mooshika - mouse
- Muezzin - a muslim priest
- Muggu - another name of rangoli
- Murmura - puffed rice
- Murti - statue of a person of eminence or a deity.
- Mushaira - gatherings in which poetic compositions are recited.

N

- Naam - name
- Narial Poornima - another name for the festival of Rakshabandhan.

- Namaaz - a muslim prayer, usually conducted five times a day.
- Namaskar - see Pranaam
- Namokar Mantra - a Jain prayer
- Navami/Naumi - ninth day
- Navami Bhog - is a traditional ritual on navami during Durga Puja celebrations in which Goddess Durga is offered food which is later distributed among the devotees as *prasaad.*
- Navapatrika - nine plants
- Navratri - festival of nine nights, usually a period of fasting dedicated to Goddess Durga in her many forms. The fasts precede the Durga puja.
- Neema - offering in a dargah
- Neerkshir vivek - water-milk wisdom
- Nimbu - lemon
- Nirjal - a fast without food and water.
- Nirvana - utter extinction of egoism or self; a state of eternal bliss.
- Nishkam Karm - work that is performed sincerely and without expectations.

O

- Om - an auspicious sign
- Onam - harvest festival celebrated in the state of Kerala in South India.
- Onjalattam - swings

P

- Paap - sins
- Paksh - the fortnight during which the moon is waxing and it is above the horizon.

- Panch - five
- Panchami - fifth day
- Panchasheel – one of the ritual arranged on Buddha Purnima.
- Pandal - a temporary structure put up for installation of deities during festivals and celebrations.
- Pandits - priests
- Paneer - cottage cheese
- Pani - water
- Panj Piaras - five volunteers of different castes who were chosen by Guru Gobind Singh to lead the rest while forming the Khalsa Panth. These came from Punjab, U.P., Andhra Pradesh and Bihar. The Panj Piaras in turn baptized Guru Gobind Singh into the Khalsa brotherhood.
- Panjiri - also called Panchjiri. It is so named because it has five basic ingredients, which are powdered ginger, dill, coriander, sugar, ghee or butter. People sometimes enrich it with other ingredients like poppy seeds, cardamom, desiccated coconut, resins and other dried fruits.
- Papad - a dehydrated pancake made from pulses and other carbohydrate pastes.
- Pakori - savoury fried snack.
- Paramhansas - People who have achieved enlightenment, and are born to help others recognize their divinity and serve others.
- Paratha - a chapatti which is griddle fried.
- Parikrama - the act of going around the temple three times.
- Parsi - followers of the religion of Zoroastrianism
- Parva - festival
- Paryushan - ten day fasting festival of Jains. It is also called Das Lakshana Parva.

- Paush - a lunar month covering the solar months of December-January.
- Payasam - a sweet dish made of rice and milk.
- Pedas - an Indian sweet made of khoa or concentrated milk.
- Petha - white pumpkin used for making special sweets famous in Agra, but made all over North India.
- Phagun - a lunar month covering February-March.
- Phal-ahar - fruits and vegetable diet or meal usually taken during partial fasts.
- Pheni - very fine ingredient resembling sphaghetti, made of wheat flour, roasted and used for making kheer during Karvachouth.
- Phirni - a dessert made with rice flour, milk and sugar.
- Phota - to apply a mark on the forehead with sandalwood paste.
- Phuliya - puffed rice
- Pinda - balls of rice and flour.
- Pitri-paksha - time for special puja to express reverence and gratitude to deceased elders.
- Poila Baisakh - Bengali new year's day. It is the most significant day for traders to open new books of accounts.
- Pongal - harvest festival of Tamil Nadu.
- Ponga - boil
- Pongapani - a new mud pot on which artistic designs are drawn. This pot is used on Pongal to cook their traditional dish.
- Pooja/Puja - worship
- Prabhu - Hindi name of Lord
- Pradayak - to bestow
- Prana - life breaths
- Pranaam - to greet a person by bowing one's head and with

folded hands both signs of humility and respect. The Hindi word is Namaskar, which means I bow to the divine who is within you.

- Prasaad - food offered to God and distributed to all present as His grace.
- Prathama - first
- Pratikraman - introspection
- Prayaag - the confluence of three holy rivers. The point where they meet is known as Prayaag, considered auspicious for devotees bathing there on Makar Sankranti. Prayaag is in Allahabad.
- Prema - love
- Pucca Food - food cooked in ghee or milk for the purpose of sanctification. Also called satvik food indicating freedom from infection.
- Pudina - mint
- Pujan - prayer
- Pulao - fried rice
- Punjabis - people from Punjab in North India.
- Punya - good deeds
- Puranas - sacred ancient texts.
- Puranic - ancient
- Puri - a place in Orissa which houses the famous Jagannath temple.
- Purnima - full moon night.
- Pushpanjali - offering flowers to deities.
- Puttaparthi - a village which is the abode of Sri Sathya Sai Baba in Anantpur district of Andhra Pradesh. It is now the centre for free value education and medical treatment. It has an airport too.

Q

- Qawaalis - devotional sufi compositions set in classical Indian music, rendered by groups in mosques or during cultural events.
- Qawwals - professional singers of sufi music.
- Quran - the holy book of Muslims.

R

- Raag - classical song
- Raas - celebration pertaining to Lord Krishna
- Rabi - winter crops in India
- Rabi-ul-Awwal - the third month of the Muslim year.
- Radha - Sri Krishna's favourite gopi and devotee worshipped along with Krishna in temples, for her flawless devotion.
- Raita - a beaten curd preparation.
- Raghupati Raghava Raja Ram - Gandhiji's favourite prayer song in congregation.
- Rajasik - person who is attached to worldly pleasures and comforts of life.
- Rakhi - sacred thread tied by sisters on their brother's wrist.
- Raksha - protection
- Rakshabandhan - brother-sister festival signifying their bond of mutual protection and love.
- Ramnaumi/Ram Navmi - birth anniversary celebration of Lord Rama.
- Rama-lila - play depicting the life and heroic deeds of Rama.
- Ramadaan or Ramzan
- Rangbhari - full with colors
- Rangbhari ekadashi - another name for holi called so because it falls on Ekadashi in March every year.

- Rangoli - motifs drawn on the floor with different coloured powders, flowers or dried grains to welcome guests on auspicious occasions.
- Rasa - sensory
- Rasam - a spiced soup typically served in the south.
- Rasa-parityaga - a form of restraint observed in Jain fasts which is based on taste-selection.
- Rath - chariot
- Ratri - a sanskrit word which signifies, that which relives with the ethereal, mental and material. In Hindi it means the night.
- Ravana - the ancient learned king of Lanka, whom Rama destroyed because he abducted Sita.
- Raviwar - Sunday
- Reiki - an art of healing
- Rewari - sesame seed and jaggery preparation popularly consumed at Lohri and through the winter months. Also made with sugar.
- Rishis - holy wise men, saints, hermits and priests.
- Rig Veda - a vedic text.
- Rohri - jaggery
- Roli - vermilion
- Roganjosh - meat curry
- Roti - chappati or unleavened Indian bread.
- Rozas - Muslims fasts which are observed for 29 or 30 days or till the sighting of the new moon.

S

- Sabudana/Sabutdana - sago
- Sadhna - practice

- Sadhus - monks
- Sagar - ocean
- Sakhyam - friendship
- Samadhi - A meditative posture intended to take the mind inwards toward a state of super consciousness or awareness where the consciousness of one's surroundings is temporarily obliterated.
- Samak rice - a cereal permitted in no cereals fasts.
- Salamti - an act of bowing or greeting in respect also refered to as *salaam.*
- Salat - Muslim prayers
- Salat-ur-Asr - Late afternoon prayer of Muslims. The time extends till just before sunset.
- Salat-ul-duha - a Muslim prayer which is held at about breakfast time. This is the time at which the two Id prayers are said.
- Salat-ul-Fajr - Early morning prayer of Muslims conducted after dawn and before sunrise.
- Salat-ul-Isha - a prayer of Muslims, which is held in early night when the red glow of sunset, disappears in the West. The time extends till midnight.
- Salat-ul-lail - a Muslim prayer which is offered late in the night after refreshed from sleep and before dawn. This prayer is specially recommended after dawn.
- Salat-ul-Maghrib - a Muslim prayer held immediately after the sun sets.
- Salat-ur-Zuhr - This is the normal Friday congregational prayer in mosques. It is held in early afternoon when the sun begins to decline. Its time extends to the next prayer.
- Samak ke chawal - a cereal permitted during a fast in which cereals are restricted.
- Sambhar - an arhar or other pulse preparation in which vegetables, tamarind and spices are used.

- Samsara - world
- Samvatsari Parva - last day of the eight day festival of Paryushan, as celebrated by Shvetambaras.
- Sankranti - means the entry of the sun from one rashi or zodiac sign to another. The daylight hours increase from this day. When it enters the Capricorn it is called Makar Sankranti and is associated with the harvest festival in Karnataka, Bihar and Uttar Pradesh.
- Sanatana Dharma - a religious order set up to propagate worship with form.
- Sanmati - another name of Lord Mahavir, meaning wisdom.
- Sanskriti - culture
- Santaan - progeny
- Sanyama - means discipline, practicing moderation and abstinence in everyday life.
- Saradotsav - another name of Durga Puja celebrations
- Sarangi - a musical instrument
- Saraswati - Goddess of knowledge, music and culture.
- Sargi - is given by the mother-in-law to her daughter-in-law a day before Karva Chauth.
- Sarkkarai Pongal - a special sweet made with rice and jaggery to celebrate the harvest at Pongal in South India.
- Sarposh - lid
- Sarson-ka-saag - a mustard leaves preparation typical of Punjab, and eaten generally with maize flour roti in winter.
- Sathya/Satya - truth.
- Satsang - congregational prayers or devotional singing.
- Satvik - pure, refers to good behaviour guided by truth. Also refers to foods made in a clean environment and prepared with love and devotion.

- Satya - truth
- Satyug - the golden age as described by the ancient texts.
- Saunf - fennel seeds
- Sendha Namak - rock salt
- Seva - service
- Shadrastyag - a feature of the fasts of paramhansas in which monks have to avoid food with the six tastes - salty, sweet, chilly hot, sour, bitter and oily.
- Shakkar - jaggery or unrefined sugar.
- Shakti - power or strength
- Shanti - peace
- Shauch - means cleanliness or freedom from defilement
- Shishir - Dewy season
- Shishya - student or disciple
- Shivling - the form in which Lord Shiva is worshipped.
- Shiv Puran - the sacred text dealing with anecdotes, rituals, meaning and worship of Shiva.
- Shiv Ratri - Shiva ratri falls on the eve of the new moon day (chaturdasi) in the middle of the months of Magh and Phalgun (Feb.-March). Shiv ratri occurs twice a year namely Kawad which falls in the monsoon season.
- Shiva Vivaha - this ratri is celebrated as the wedding night of Lord Shiva to Parvati and falls in spring.
- Shloka - a religious verse
- Shringar - self decoration or the art of getting cosmetically dressed.
- Shukla - bright
- Simha - the zodiac sign corresponding to Leo.
- Sindoor - a mark made by the Hindu women with vermilion on the forehead as a mark of being married.

- Sindur Khela - the vermilion game played by married women during Durga Puja.
- Singhara - water chestnut
- Sita - wife of Lord Rama
- Sitaphal - Yellow ripe pumpkin.
- Shakarkandi - sweet potato
- Shaniwar - Saturday
- Sharad - Autumn season
- Shasthi - sixth day after Mahalaya when Goddess Durga is welcomed.
- Shastras - sacred texts.
- Sramanic - holy
- Shrawan - a lunar month
- Shukla paksh - the bright fortnight of the waxing moon.
- Shukrawar - Friday
- Shvetambar - a Jain sect whose monks give up all material possessions but they are clad in white.
- Siddhi - spiritual potency
- Somwar - Monday
- Sri Satya Sai - the Kaliyug avatar of the 21st century.
- Sthaanak vaasi - a group among Shwetambers who do not worship idols.
- Strotam - verse
- Subji - vegetable
- Sudarshan Chakra - disc held by Lord Krishna in His hand.
- Suhaagan - a woman whose husband is alive.
- Suji - semolina
- Surya - sun
- Surya Pongal - second day celebration of Pongal.

- Sutrapath - one of the rituals arranged on Buddha Purnima.
- Sutrasraban - one of the rituals arranged on Buddha Purnima.
- Swaras - notes of music
- Swastik - an auspicious sign.

T

- Tabarruk - blessed food
- Tamas - an attribute of laziness, lethargy or impurity, described in the sacred texts.
- Tamasic - see Tamas.
- Tandoor - an Indian traditional mud oven
- Tapa - devotional penance or leading the life of a recluse or hermit while keeping oneself engaged in meditation and study of religion.
- Tarpan - the final day of *Pitru paksha.*
- Tattwa - means essence in you or the ultimate reality.
- Tawa - skillet used for making chappatis.
- Tazia - a mausoleum-like artifact, taken in procession on the day of Moharram.
- Tejpatta - bay leaf
- Teraapanthi - A group among Shwetambers who do not worship idols and emphasize thirteen virtues.
- Tesu - a flower used to extract orange color on Holi.
- Thal/Thali - plate
- Thandai - a drink made with cannabis, almonds, and milk. It is drunk by the devout during Shivaratri.
- Thiruvathirakali - a group dance of Kerala
- Thrikkakkara - another name of Lord Vishnu.
- Thumbithullal - a group dance of Kerala

- Tika - applying a mark on the forehead with vermilion mixed with 2-3 grains of rice, sugar and water.
- Tikki - cutlet
- Til - sesame seeds
- Tilak - see Tika.
- Tilgul - ladoos made of jaggery and sesame seeds.
- Tilohri - traditional name of Lohri which was derived from the tradition of eating til and rohri (jaggery) on this day.
- Tirthankar - is a spiritual guide who helps one to cross the ocean of worldly existence. The 24th and last Tirthankar was Lord Mahavira.
- Tithi - time occupied by the moon in increasing its distance from the sun by 12 degrees. Thus, it is the exact point of time when the moon moves eastwards from the sun after amas.
- Torans - decorations made with mango leaves and marigolds are hung on doorways on auspicious days like Diwali or inauguration functions, etc.
- Trayodasi - 13th day
- Trident - an auspicious sign
- Trikarana shuddhi - means triple purity. According to Lord Buddha, non-violence is not merely refraining from inflicting injury on others with limbs and weapons, it has to be practiced with purity of mind, tongue and the body.
- Tritiya - third
- Tulsi - a sacred plant worshipped by Hindus.
- Tyaga - renunciation or sacrifice.

U

- Upakaram - good deed
- Upwaas - fast

- Unodari - a form of restraint observed in Jain fasts, which means eating less.
- Urs - also called Ziarats, is a typical Kashmiri festival held annually at the shrines of Muslim saints on their death anniversaries.
- Utsav/Utsavam - festival
- Uttarayan - Uttar means north and ayan means to move. The day on which the sun moves from the south towards the north is known as Uttarayan.

V

- Vadas - fried preparations of pulse or sago
- Vahan - vehicle
- Vairagya - detachment
- Vaisakh vakats - decorations made of bamboo and arranged in the houses on Buddha Purnima.
- Valmiki - author of the Ramayana.
- Vande Matram - National song composed by Bankim Chandra Chattopadhyay
- Vanjli - folk instruments
- Vardhaman - means ever advancing so Lord Mahavir was known as Vardhaman.
- Varsha - monsoon season
- Varuna - sea God.
- Vasant - spring season
- Vaastu - science of natural forces affecting the living environment.
- Vasudev - father of Lord Krishna.
- Veena - a musical instrument
- Veena vadini - another name of Goddess Saraswati.

- Vidya Aramban Day - another name of Dusshera when children and adults are initiated into learning.
- Viharas - living places especially for Buddhist monks.
- Vijaya - victory.
- Vijay Dashmi - another name of Dusshera.
- Vinayaka - another name of Lord Ganesha.
- Visarjan - immersion in a flowing water body such as a lake, river or ocean.
- Vishwaas - faith
- Vrat - fasting or exercising controls ordained by the vedic samhitas, and associated with penance or tapas.
- Vrindavan - a place in U.P. where Lord Krishna spent his childhood.
- Vritti-sankshepa - a form of restraint observed in Jain fasts which means selective restraint.

W

- Wazwan - a traditional feast of Kashmir.

Y

- Yadava - a dynasty
- Yajnas - havans through which the God of Fire or Agni is worshipped by reciting Sanskrit shlokas or verses invoking the Lord's grace for putting an end to all evil or wrong doing.
- Yakhni - prepared and eaten during Wazwan.
- Yama Dwiteeya - another name for Bhai Dooj.
- Yamuna - a tributary of the holy Ganges river.
- Yatra - journey
- Yug - period.

Z

- Zakat-al-Fitr - an obligatory charitable gift from every Muslim given to the poor and needy during Eid-ul-Fitr.
- Zari - a thread of gold used in embroidery and saree weaving. Pure gold thread was used for temple sarees in which deities were dressed.
- Ziarats - see Urs.
- Zuhar namaaz - the afternoon prayers of Muslims.